Everything Was Forever, Until It Was No More

IN/FORMATION *Series*

Series Editor
Paul Rabinow

A list of titles in the series appears at the back of the book

Everything Was Forever, Until It Was No More

The Last Soviet Generation

Alexei Yurchak

PRINCETON UNIVERSITY PRESS
PRINCETON AND OXFORD

Copyright © 2005 by Princeton University Press
Published by Princeton University Press,
41 William Street, Princeton, New Jersey 08540

In the United Kingdom: Princeton University Press, 3 Market Place,
Woodstock, Oxfordshire OX20 1SY

All Rights Reserved

Library of Congress Cataloging-in-Publication Data

Yurchak, Alexei, 1960–
    Everything was forever, until it was no more : the last Soviet generation / Alexei
Yurchak.
        p. cm.
    Includes bibliographical references and index.
    ISBN 0-691-12116-8 (cl : alk. paper)—ISBN 0-691-12117-6 (pb : alk. paper)
        1. Soviet Union—Civilization. 2. Soviet Union—Intellectual life.
    3. Socialism and culture—Soviet Union. I. Title.

    DK266.4.Y87 2005
    947.085—dc22   2004042384

British Library Cataloging-in-Publication Data is available

This book has been composed in Sabon

pup.princeton.edu

10 9 8 7 6 5 4 3 2 1

To my parents,

Vladimir and Natalia

Contents

CONTENTS

Acknowledgments

Many friends of Russian, foreign, mixed, and confused identities have shared their friendship and intellectual curiosity over the years. Many of them have helped me obtain materials, and reflected on the meanings of Soviet life. I am grateful in particular to Andrei Andreyev, Thomas Campbell, George Faraday, David Fisher, Jessica Gorter, Alexandr Kan, Lena Khaetskaia, Andrei Krivolapov, Victor Mazin, Alla Mitrofanova, Margaret Paxson, Andrei Postnikov, Igor Rozov, Vitaly Savchuk, Oleg Timofeyev, Olesya Turkina, and Evgenii Yufit. Over the past twenty years, inspiring conversations with my friend Svetlana Kozlova have helped to shape my interests and ideas. I am continually grateful to the musicians and actors of the rock band and theater AVIA for their intelligence, camaraderie, and cheerful experimentation with communist ideologies; and especially to Nikolai Gusev and Anton Adassinksy—the two masters of the absurd, whose art and everyday aesthetics refined my views of Soviet history.

I would like to thank my professors at Duke University: Claudia Strauss, Ann Allison, Barbara Hernstein-Smith, Thomas Lahusen, William O'Barr, and Naomi Quinn. Colleagues and friends, at the University of California at Berkeley's anthropology department and at other universities, have exposed me to intellectual ideas that have deepened my understanding of the subjects of my research. I am particularly grateful for the critical comments and suggestions on various versions and parts of this text that were provided by Ivan Arenas, Diana Blank, Victoria Bonnell, David Brandenburger, George Breslauer, Michael Burawoy, Terence Deacon, Dace Dzenovska, Gil Eyal, Sergei Oushakine, Irina Paperno, Tobias Rees, Annelise Riles, Stas Savitsky, Kim Scheppele, Maria Stoilkova; and also to the students in my Berkeley graduate seminars on post-socialism (fall 2004) and on discourse and performativity (fall 2003). Steven Collier, Zeynep Gursel, and Nancy Ries read various versions of the whole manuscript with great care, providing countless helpful comments and suggestions. Special thanks to Yuri Slezkine for his support, unparalleled Soviet-Texan wit, and for detecting hidden conundrums in the text; and also to Eduardo Cohn, for being a true friend and supportive colleague, who read the whole text at the crucial final stage, and for forcing me to clarify many points.

Several centers and institutes provided their support at different stages of the project: The Harriman Institute at Columbia University; the Centre for Research in Arts, Social Sciences and Humanities at Cambridge University; and the Townsend Center for the Humanities at the University of California, Berkeley. My gratitude extends to Hildegard Diemberger, for her belief in this project, and for organizing, with Robbie Barnett, two seminars around comparative studies of late-socialist elites at Cambridge and Columbia. I am especially grateful to Caroline Humphrey for her warmth and encouragement over the years, and to all the friends and colleagues at Cambridge University who shared intellectual excitement, warm beer, and punting trips on the Cam (with odd Londoners falling in).

At Princeton University Press I want to thank Mary Murrell, my original editor and scrupulous copyeditor, who saw the project through from the very beginning, as well as her successor, the editor Fred Appel, and production editor Debbie Tegarden, for their patience, intelligence, and support. Thanks to Sylvia Benson and Jenna Rice, my student assistants at Berkeley, for meticulous formatting, indexing, and bibliographic research.

My parents have insisted on hearing many parts of the text in the Russian translation—a challenging exercise that forced me to refine many arguments. My deepest gratitude goes to Melanie Feakins for her critical involvement with the text, for her love, and for her British vowels.

Everything Was Forever, Until It Was No More

Chapter 1
Late Socialism:
An Eternal State

Mimicry is a very bad concept, since it relies on binary logic to describe phenomena of an entirely different nature. The crocodile does not reproduce a tree trunk, any more than the chameleon reproduces the colors of its surroundings. The Pink Panther imitates nothing, it reproduces nothing, it paints the world its color, pink on pink.
—Gilles Deleuze and Felix Guattari, *A Thousand Plateaus: Capitalism and Schizophrenia*[1]

An Eternal State

"It had never even occurred to me that in the Soviet Union anything could ever change. Let alone that it could disappear. No one expected it. Neither children, nor adults. There was a complete impression that everything was forever." So spoke Andrei Makarevich, the famous songwriter and musician,[2] in a televised interview (1994). In his published memoirs, Makarevich later remembered that he, like millions of Soviet citizens, had always felt that he lived in an eternal state (*vechnoe gosudarstvo*) (2002, 14). It was not until around 1986 and 1987, when reforms of *perestroika* (reconstruction) were already afoot, that the possibility of the socialist system not lasting forever even entered his mind. Many others have described a similar experience of the profound feeling of the Soviet system's permanence and immutability, and the complete unexpectedness of its collapse. And yet, Makarevich and many Soviet people also quickly discovered another peculiar fact: despite the seeming abruptness of the collapse, they found themselves prepared for it. A peculiar paradox became apparent in those years: although the system's collapse had been unimaginable before it began, it appeared unsurprising when it happened.

---

[1] Deleuze and Guattari (2002, 11).
[2] The lead singer of *Mashina Vremeni* (Time Machine), a Russian rock band.

When the policies of perestroika and *glasnost'* (openness, public discussion) were introduced in 1985, most people did not anticipate that any radical changes would follow. These campaigns were thought to be no different from the endless state-orchestrated campaigns before them: campaigns that came and went, while life went on as usual. However, within a year or two the realization that something unimaginable was taking place began to dawn on the Soviet people. Many speak of having experienced a sudden "break of consciousness" (*perelom soznania*) and "stunning shock" (*sil'neishii shok*) quickly followed by excitement and readiness to participate in the transformation. Although different people experienced that moment differently, the type of experience they describe is similar, and many remember it vividly.

Tonya, a school teacher born in Leningrad in 1966, describes the moment she first realized, around 1987, that "something impossible" (*chto-to nevozmozhnoe*) was taking place: "I was reading on the metro and suddenly experienced an utter shock. I remember that moment very well. . . . I was reading Lev Razgon's story 'Uninvented' (*Nepridumannoe*),[3] just published in *Iunost'* [the literary journal *Youth*]. I could never have imagined that anything even remotely comparable would be published. After that the stream of publications became overwhelming." Inna (born in Leningrad in 1958)[4] remembers her own "first moment of surprise" (*pervyi moment udivleniia*), which also occurred around 1987 and 1988: "For me perestroika began with the first publication in *Ogonek*[5] of a few poems by [Nikolai] Gumilev," a poet of the *Akmeist* circle whose poetry had not been published in the Soviet Union since the 1920s.[6] Inna had already read the poetry in handwritten copies but had never expected it to appear in state publications. It was not the poems that surprised her but their appearance in the press.

The stream of new publications began to rise exponentially, and the practice of reading everything, exchanging texts with friends, and discussing what one had read soon became a national obsession. Between 1987 and 1988, the circulation of most newspapers and literary journals jumped astronomically, as much as tenfold and more in the course of

---

[3] In his memoirs, Razgon recounts the seventeen years he spent in Stalinist camps, from 1938 to 1955. In 1987 and 1988, several stories from it were published in the *Ogonek* weekly and the *Iunost'* literary journal. Soon after the book was published in its entirety.

[4] See more about Inna in chapter 4.

[5] The weekly magazine *Ogonek* was the most popular voice of perestroika.

[6] The poet Nikolai Gumilev, Anna Akhmatova's first husband, had not been published since his arrest in 1921 for his alleged participation in an anti-Bolshevik conspiracy that, it would be revealed sixty years later during perestroika, was a fabrication of the ChK (the precursor of the KGB) (Volkov 1995, 537). See chapter 4 on the symbolic importance of Gumilev in the 1970s and 1980s.

one year.[7] Often it was impossible to find many of the more popular publications at newsstands because of the speed at which they sold out. In letters to the weekly magazine *Ogonek*, readers complained of having to stand in line at a local kiosk at 5 A.M., two hours before it opened, to have any chance of buying the magazine. Like everyone else, Tonya tried to read as much as possible: "My friend Katia and I started subscribing to monthly literary journals (*tosltye zhurnaly*): *Oktiabr'*, *Nash Sovremennik, Novyi Mir, Znamia, Iunost'*. Everyone tried to subscribe to different journals so they could exchange them with friends and have access to more materials. Everyone around us was doing this. I spent the whole year incessantly reading these publications."

Reading journals, watching live television broadcasts, and talking to friends who were doing the same quickly produced new language, topics, comparisons, metaphors, and ideas, ultimately leading to a profound change of discourse and consciousness. As a result of this process, in the late 1980s, there was a widespread realization that the state socialism which had seemed so eternal might in fact be coming to an end. Italian literary scholar Vittorio Strada, who spent much time in the Soviet Union before the transformation began, summarized the experience of the fast-forwarded history that he encountered among the Soviet people in the late 1980s: "[N]o one, or almost no one, could imagine that the collapse . . . would happen so soon and so fast. . . . The timing of the end and the way in which it occurred were simply startling" (Strada 1998, 13).

The abrupt change was also quite exciting. Tonya, who had always felt proud of being a Soviet person and never identified with the dissidents, unexpectedly found herself quickly engrossed in the new critical discourse and, in her words, "felt elated" that most people were doing it—"this was all so sudden and unexpected and it completely overtook me." Tonya remembers reading

Evgeniia Ginzburg's *Steep Route* (*Krutoi marshrut*),[8] then Solzhenitsyn, then Vasilii Grossman.[9] Grossman was the first to imply that

[7] Daily newspapers were the first to rise in circulation, during the Nineteenth Party Conference in 1986. The circulation of *Argumenty i fakty*, for example, rose from a few hundred thousand to several million around 1986 and 1987. By the end of 1987 the same had also happened to many weeklies (e.g., *Ogonek* and *Moskovskie novosti*) and monthly "thick" journals (*Novyi mir, Druzhba narodov*, and others).

[8] *Krutoi marshrut*, by Evgeniia Semenovna Ginzburg, had the subtitle *Khronika vremen kul'ta lichnosti* (A chronicle from the times of the cult of personality). The book is a memoir of the eighteen years the author spent in Stalin's camps. It was written in the late 1960s (first part) and 1970s (second part), and for many years existed in samizdat. The book's first official Soviet publication, to which Tonya refers, occurred in 1988, eleven years after Ginzburg's death. Evgeniia Ginzburg was the mother of the famous writer Vassily Aksyonov.

[9] Vasilii Semenovich Grossman's novel *Life and Fate* (*Zhizn' i sud'ba*), about his experiences of World War II and Stalin's camps, was written in the late 1950s and early 1960s,

3

Communism could be a form of fascism. This had never occurred to me before. He did not say this openly but simply compared the tortures in the two systems. I remember reading it lying on the sofa in my room and experiencing an intense feeling of a revolution happening all around me. It was stunning. I had a break of consciousness (*perelom soznania*). Then came the books of Vladimir Voinovich. I shared everything with my uncle Slava.

As these and endless other stories about the late 1980s suggest, the system's collapse had been profoundly unexpected and unimaginable to many Soviet people until it happened, and yet, it quickly appeared perfectly logical and exciting when it began. Many discovered that, unbeknownst to themselves, they had always been ready for it, that they had always known that life in socialism was shaped through a curious paradox, that the system was always felt to be both stagnating and immutable, fragile and vigorous, bleak and full of promise. These experiences suggest an important set of questions about Soviet socialism: What was the nature of the late Soviet system and way of life that had this paradox at its core? On what kind of internal systemic shifts at the level of discourse, ideology, social relations, and time was this paradox predicated? Furthermore, what was the nature of the production and communication of knowledge in this system, and of the forms in which it was coded, circulated, received, and interpreted? These questions are not about the causes for the collapse but about the conditions that made the collapse possible without making it anticipated. With these questions in mind, this book sets out to explore late socialism—the period that spanned approximately thirty years, between the mid-1950s and the mid-1980s, before the changes of perestroika began, when the system was still being experienced as eternal. This book will investigate this period through the eyes of its last generation, focusing on these people's relations with ideology, discourse, and ritual, and on the multiple unanticipated meanings, communities, relations, identities, interests, and pursuits that these relations allowed to emerge.

Binary Socialism

One of the motivations for writing this book is to question certain problematic assumptions about Soviet socialism, which are implicitly and

---

and was confiscated by the KGB because it represented a picture of the war that was strikingly different from the official representation. A copy of the manuscript was secretly brought to the West, where it was published in 1980. The first Soviet publication of the novel was by the literary journal *Oktiabr'* in 1989, twenty-five years after the writer's death.

explicitly reproduced in much academic and journalistic writing today. These common assumptions include the following: socialism was "bad" and "immoral" or had been experienced as such by Soviet people before the changes of perestroika, and, further, the collapse of Soviet socialism was predicated on this badness and immorality. These assumptions are manifest today in the terminology used to describe that system—for example, in the widespread use of phrases such as "the Soviet regime," with the myriad assumptions often packed into it—and in the use of binary categories to describe Soviet reality such as oppression and resistance, repression and freedom, the state and the people, official economy and second economy, official culture and counterculture, totalitarian language and counterlanguage, public self and private self, truth and lie, reality and dissimulation, morality and corruption, and so on.[10] These terminologies have occupied a dominant position in the accounts of Soviet socialism produced in the West and, since the end of socialism, in the former Soviet Union as well.

In the most extreme examples of this discourse, Soviet citizens are portrayed as having no agency: in this portrayal, they allegedly subscribed to "communist values" either because they were coerced to do so or because they had no means of reflecting upon them critically. In the late 1980s, Françoise Thom argued that, in the context of ubiquitous ideological language, linguistic "symbols cease[d] to work properly," making the Soviet Union "a world without meaning, without events and without humanity" (Thom 1989, 156). In the late 1990s, Frank Ellis went further:

"When reason, common sense, and decency are assaulted often enough, then personality is crippled, and human intelligence disintegrates or is warped. The barrier between truth and lies is effectively destroyed. . . . Schooled in such a climate, fearful and deprived of any intellectual initiative, Homo Sovieticus could never be more than a mouthpiece for the party's ideas and slogans, not so much a human being then, as a receptacle to be emptied and filled as party policy dictated." (Ellis 1998, 208)

Even when granted some agency in accounts of this type, the voices of these subjects are often still unheard due to oppression and fear. For example, John Young describes Soviet citizens as "non-conforming" dissidents, who "counter the deceptions of government by setting forth 'the facts' in contrast to official falsehood" in "conversations with frustrated friends behind closed doors, in sign language devised by family members

[10] See dichotomies reproduced in Kupina (1999); Shlapentokh (1989); Wierzbicka (1990); Zaslavsky and Fabris (1983); Zemskaia (1996); Zemstov (1984). For a discussion of the assumptions behind modern binaries in general, see Mitchell (1990).

who suspect the secret police have bugged their apartment, in a manu-script or on a tape recording passed around from person to person" (Young 1991, 226). These are extreme examples; however, they repre-sent a definite trend in conceptualizing Soviet life.[11]

Binary metaphors are also widespread in retrospective analyses of social-ism written inside the former Soviet Union since the "collapse." In such ac-counts, Soviet culture is divided into the "official" and the "unofficial"—a division that, according to sociologists Uvarova and Rogov, can be traced back to a particular dissident ideology of the 1970s which held that "nothing good could appear in an [official] Soviet journal in principle; and a real text could only be published in an unofficial publication (*samizdat*) or a foreign publication (*tamizdat*)" (1998). Critiquing this division, Uvarova and Rogov propose instead to divide Soviet culture into censored (*podtsenzurnaia*) and uncensored (*nepodtsenzurnaia*). This change of terms helps to highlight the ambivalence of cultural pro-duction in the Soviet Union; however, it still reduces Soviet reality to a binary division between the state (censored) and the society beyond it (uncensored), failing to account for the fact that many of the common cultural phenomena in socialism that were allowed, tolerated, or even promoted within the realm of the officially censored were nevertheless quite distinct from the ideological texts of the Party.

One reason for the persistence of these binary models is the particular "situatedness" (Haraway 1991) of much critical knowledge about Soviet socialism: it has been produced either outside of, or in retrospect to, socialism, in contexts dominated by antisocialist, nonsocialist, or post-socialist political, moral, and cultural agendas and truths. As Rogov demonstrates in his research, diaries from Brezhnev's period, produced during the 1970s, and memoirs produced retrospectively in the 1990s are not only written in two distinct voices and languages; they also eval-uate the everyday realities of Soviet socialism, both implicitly and explic-itly, in two different ways. The memoirs not only tend to be much more critical of the socialist system than the diaries, but also to conceive of it and of the author's place within it in terms that emerged only in ret-rospect (Rogov 1998).[12] Patrick Seriot has also shown that by the end of perestroika in the late 1980s, it had become politically important, especially for members of the intelligentsia, to emphasize that during socialism there was no "mixing [of] the language of power with their own language" and that their own language was "a free space to be

---

[11] One significant element of this genre is a reliance on what Mitchell diagnoses as a dominant "master metaphor" in the social sciences that conceives of power and resistance through the "distinction between persuading and coercing" (Mitchell 1990, 545).

[12] For a discussion of the memoirs about the Soviet past published in the 1980s and 90s see Paperno (2002).

extended through struggle" (Seriot 1992, 205–6). But this story of divided languages was, to a large extent, a retrospective late- and post-perestroika construction.

Furthermore, the term stagnation (*zastoi*), which figures prominently as a tag for the period of Brezhnev's rule, also emerged only in retrospect, during the time of Gorbachev's reforms, after Brezhnev's period had ended and the socialist system was undergoing its rapid transformation.[13] In fact, the very conceptualization of the late 1960s and 1970s, when Brezhnev was the party's general secretary, as a certain "period" with concrete historical features, also emerged retrospectively during perestroika. According to Rogov, "The [Soviet] person in the 1970s had a rather vague understanding about the historical coordinates of his epoch, considerably vaguer than became apparent to the same person from the perspective of the late 1980s and 1990s" (1998, 7). The perestroika critical discourse which exposed many unknown facts about the Soviet past and critically articulated many realities that had been implicitly known but unarticulated until then, also contributed to the creation of certain myths about it that were colored by the newly emergent revolutionary ideas and political agendas of the late 1980s. Many binary categories in the accounts of the vanishing system gained their prominence within that revolutionary context.

At the same time, some of the roots of these binary categories go much deeper, originating in the broad "regimes of knowledge" formed under the conditions of the Cold War, when the entity of "the Soviet bloc" had been articulated in opposition to "the West" and as distinct from "the third world." The act of critiquing isolated binaries does not necessarily deconstruct these deeper underlying assumptions behind them. For example, Susan Gal and Gail Kligman provided a crucial critique of many binary divisions that dominate the studies of state socialism, arguing that in these societies "[r]ather than any clear-cut 'us' versus 'them' or 'private' versus 'public,' there was a ubiquitous self-embedding or interweaving of these categories."[14] And yet, they connected this critique with another claim that "[e]veryone was to some extent complicit in the system of patronage, lying, theft, hedging, and duplicity through which the system operated," and that often even "intimates, family members and friends informed on each other" (Gal and Kligman 2000, 51). The emphasis on such categories as duplicity, lying, and informing on others—which suggest moral quandaries at the core of the people's relations with the system

---

[13] The term was used at that time in relation to two other terms, thaw and perestroika, which had entered public discourse earlier, the former in the 1950s, the latter in 1985 (Rogov 1998, 7).

[14] For a critique of binaries in the descriptions of socialism see also Lampland (1995, 273–75, 304).

and with each other—implicitly reproduces an underlying assumption that socialism was based on a complex web of immoralities.

Everyday Realities

The Soviet system produced tremendous suffering, repression, fear, and lack of freedom, all of which are well documented. But focusing only on that side of the system will not take us very far if we want to answer the question posed by this book about the internal paradoxes of life under socialism. What tends to get lost in the binary accounts is the crucial and seemingly paradoxical fact that, for great numbers of Soviet citizens, many of the fundamental values, ideals, and realities of socialist life (such as equality, community, selflessness, altruism, friendship, ethical relations, safety, education, work, creativity, and concern for the future) were of genuine importance, despite the fact that many of their everyday practices routinely transgressed, reinterpreted, or refused certain norms and rules represented in the official ideology of the socialist state. For many, "socialism" as a system of human values and as an everyday reality of "normal life" (*normal'naia zhizn'*)[15] was not necessarily equivalent to "the state" or "ideology"; indeed, living socialism to them often meant something quite different from the official interpretations provided by state rhetoric.

An undeniable constitutive part of today's phenomenon of "post-Soviet nostalgia," which is a complex post-Soviet construct,[16] is the longing for the very real humane values, ethics, friendships, and creative possibilities that the reality of socialism afforded—often in spite of the state's proclaimed goals—and that were as irreducibly part of the everyday life of socialism as were the feelings of dullness and alienation. A Russian philosopher wrote in 1995 that, from the vantage point of the first post-Soviet years, he had come to recognize that the grayness and fear of Soviet reality had been indivisibly linked with a very real optimism and warmth, with accompanying forms of "human happiness," "comforts and well-being," and "cordiality, successes and order" in a "well-furnished common space of living" (Savchuk 1995). A Russian photographer, echoing the same realization, made a "banal confession" that for him personally the "crash of Communism" was also, in retrospect, the crash of something very personal, innocent, and full of hope,

[15] See chapters 3 and 4 for more on "normal life."

[16] For a comprehensive discussion of the phenomenon of "nostalgia" in the postsocialist world and for a critique of this concept's sociological usefulness, see Nadkarni and Shevchenko (2004). On postsocialist nostalgia see Boym (2001), Berdahl (1999), and Bach (2002).

8

of the "passionate sincerity and genuineness" that marked childhood and youth (Vilenskii 1995). A critical examination of such retrospections is essential to an understanding of Soviet socialism. Without understanding the ethical and aesthetic paradoxes that "really existing socialism" acquired in the lives of many of its citizens, and without understanding the creative and positive meanings with which they endowed their socialist lives—sometimes in line with the announced goals of the state, sometimes in spite of them, and sometimes relating to them in ways that did not fit either-or dichotomies—we would fail to understand what kind of social system socialism was and why its sudden transformation was so unimaginable and yet unsurprising to the people living within it.

For the analysis of this seemingly paradoxical mix of the negative and positive values, of alienations and attachments, we need a language that does not reduce the description of socialist reality to dichotomies of the official and the unofficial, the state and the people, and to moral judgments shaped within cold war ideologies. Recent critical discussion of language from postcolonial studies provides some insight relevant to the socialist context.[17] Dipesh Chakrabarty criticizes some postcolonial historiography for the use of a kind of language that implicitly produces "Europe" as "the sovereign, theoretical subject of all histories, including the ones we call 'Indian,' 'Chinese,' 'Kenyan,' and so on," reducing these other histories to "variations on a master narrative that could be called 'the history of Europe'" (2000, 27). Chakrabarty's call for a language that would decenter and "provincialize" the "master narrative" of Europe in postcolonial historiography is relevant to the writings on socialism; however, in the case of socialism, especially in Russia, the object of "provincializing" would not just be "Europe" but, more specifically, "Western Europe"[18]—a post-Soviet "master narrative" in the history of socialism that implicitly and explicitly reproduces binary categories of the Cold War and of the opposition between "first world" and "second world."

This book is also an attempt to look for such a language and thereby to reconstruct some ethical and aesthetic complexities of socialist life, as well as the creative, imaginative, and often paradoxical cultural forms that it took. The challenge of such a task is to avoid a priori negative accounts of

---

[17] At the same time drawing any parallels between socialism and colonialism, which is a growing trend, must be done with extreme caution to avoid equating one with the other at the expense of the profound political, ethical, and aesthetic differences between these projects. As Timothy Brennan points out, the differences between colonialism and socialism concern not simply methods of dividing "imperial" spoils or organizing "administration, hierarchy, and sovereignty over land," but, more importantly, "aesthetic taste and social value" and "intellectual excitement and moral intention" (Brennan 2001, 39). See also Beissinger and Young (2002).

[18] See Yurchak (2003b) and Moore (2002), and Lampland's discussion of socialist history (1995, 336).

socialism without falling into the opposite extreme of romanticizing it. By showing the realities of actually existing socialism—where control, coercion, alienation, fear, and moral quandaries were irreducibly mixed with ideals, communal ethics, dignity, creativity, and care for the future—this book attempts to contemplate and rehumanize Soviet socialist life.[19]

Lefort's Paradox

Like Western democracy, Soviet socialism was part of modernity. Foucault stressed that even such "pathological forms" of power as Stalinism and fascism, "in spite of their historical uniqueness . . . are not quite original. They used and extended mechanisms already present in most other societies . . . [and] used to a large extent the ideas and the devices of our political rationality" (Foucault 1983, 209). As a modern project, Soviet socialism shared the key contradictions of modernity.

One of the central contradictions of socialism is a version of what Claude Lefort called a general paradox within the ideology of modernity: the split between *ideological enunciation* (which reflects the theoretical ideals of the Enlightenment) and *ideological rule* (manifest in the practical concerns of the modern state's political authority). The paradox, that we will call "Lefort's paradox," lies in the fact that ideological rule must be "abstracted from any question concerning its origins," thus remaining outside of ideological enunciation and, as a result, rendering that enunciation deficient. In other words, to fulfill its political function of reproducing power, the ideological discourse must claim to represent an "objective truth" that exists outside of it; however, the external nature of this "objective truth" renders the ideological discourse inherently lacking in the means to describe it in total, which can ultimately undermine this discourse's legitimacy and the power that it supports. This inherent contradiction of any version of modern ideology, argues Lefort, can be concealed only by the figure of the "master," who, by being presented as standing *outside* ideological discourse and possessing *external* knowledge of the objective truth, temporarily conceals the contradiction by allowing it "to appear through himself" (1986, 211–12).[20] In other words, modern ideological discourse, based on the utopian ideals of the Enlightenment, gains its legitimacy from an imaginary position that is external

---

[19] Going beyond preexisting binaries in our understanding of socialism will also contribute to developing a critical perspective on the contemporary rise of a global neoliberal hegemony—itself a distinctly postcommunist phenomenon—and to question what Wendy Brown (2003) calls "*homo œconomicus* as the norm of the human" and the "formations of economy, society, state and (non)morality" that accompany this norm.

[20] See also Bhabha (1990, 298); and Žižek (1991a, 145–47).

10

to it and will experience a crisis of legitimacy if that imaginary external position is questioned or destroyed.

In the society built on communist ideals, this paradox appeared through the announced objective of achieving the full liberation of the society and individual (building of communism, creation of the New Man) by means of subsuming that society and individual under full party control. The Soviet citizen was called upon to submit completely to party leadership, to cultivate a collectivist ethic, and repress individualism, while at the same time becoming an enlightened and independent-minded individual who pursues knowledge and is inquisitive and creative.[21] This Soviet version of Lefort's paradox was not a chance development; it grew out of the very revolutionary project itself. In 1825, Saint-Simon, an early theorist of the political, intellectual, and artistic avant-garde, whose ideas influenced Marx, Lenin, and Russian revolutionaries, wrote that the project of liberating the society required establishing a political and aesthetic avant-garde that would exercise "over society a positive power, a true priestly function . . . marching forcefully in the van of all the intellectual faculties." This avant-garde, wrote Saint-Simon, should address itself "to the imagination and to the sentiments of mankind [and] should therefore always exercise the liveliest and most decisive action." For this purpose the arts and politics should unite under "a common drive and a general idea" (quoted in Egbert 1967, 343).

The conception of a political and artistic avant-garde as a creative force united by one idea for the purposes of leading and perfecting society put this tandem before an enduring paradox: the process of leading and perfecting had to be subsumed under the control of a political program and, at the same time, to be free from control in order to focus on the creative, experimental, and innovating process for the production of a better future (Egbert 1967, 343–46).

In the Russian revolutionary context, this paradox of modern ideology became institutionalized by the Bolshevik Revolution of 1917. The new process of cultural production was supposed to advance radical social ideas and revolutionize consciousness by achieving two relatively incommensurable goals: to practice an experimental, innovative aesthetics that was constantly ready to defy old canons and, at the same time, to subsume these creative experimentations and innovations under the strict

---

[21] This version of Lefort's paradox can be compared with how it plays itself out in late capitalism. For example, Susan Bordo argues that enunciations and practices of capitalist ideology put the Western subject in a "double bind" between, on the one hand, a workaholic ethic and repression of consumer desire and, on the other, the capitulation to desire and achievement of immediate satisfaction. Bordo attributes the unprecedented epidemia of anorexia and bulimia in the West, in the 1980s and 90s partly to the intensification of this double bind (1990).

11

control of the vanguard party. Immediately after the revolution, Lenin wrote in a letter to Klara Tzetkin that Communists could not sit in idleness allowing the "cultural process" to develop chaotically: they "must strive with clear consciousness to control that entire process in order to form and define its results" (Arnol'dov et al. 1984, 176). Lenin accused members of the Second International of separatism because some of them argued that, having come to power, the proletariat should stop interfering with creative cultural production and experimentation. On the contrary, argued Lenin, the only means of achieving the goal of the ultimate liberation of culture and consciousness in communism was to intensify the party's management of all spheres of cultural life. A person could not become truly liberated spontaneously; that person had to be educated and cultivated. On Lenin's insistence, the Bolshevik Party adopted a resolution stressing that all organizations of the *Proletkul't* (People's Commissariat of Proletarian Culture) had "an unconditional obligation to regard themselves as strictly subsidiary organs" to the organizations of the *Narkompros* (People's Commissariat of Enlightenment) (Arnol'dov et al. 1984, 171). In other words, cultural organizations (all forms of intellectual, scientific, and artistic practice) were subsidiary to educational and political organizations, and all forms of cultural production were to be fully supervised by the party. It was that subsidiary position, went the argument, that would allow these organizations to exercise their full creative potential for the building of the new society.

The Soviet state's constant anxiety about publicly justifying state control of cultural production while simultaneously attempting to promote its independence and experimentation reflected this paradox. As late as 1984, a book entitled *Marxist-Leninist Theory of Culture* (*Marksistsko-leninskaia teoriia kul'tury*), authored by a collective of theoreticians of culture from Moscow's Institute of Marxism-Leninism (Arnol'dov et al.), was still defending this point. Some may say—their book begins—that to be truly creative, the work of cultural production in intellectual, scientific and artistic fields cannot be controlled and directed. The book goes on to argue that although this view is not altogether erroneous, it tells only one side of the story, ignoring the irreducible duality of all cultural production. In fact, the book argues, creative work is always both "a strictly private affair" of a creative individual and a "labor of social utility" that creates "spiritual values" and "socio-moral norms" in society. In the socialist society, both aspects of cultural production are recognized as equally important, since in this society "the formation of the new person goes not spontaneously, but consciously, as a result of a purposeful educational work." Therefore, in the socialist context, the independence of creativity and the control of creative work by the party are not mutually contradictory but must be pursued simultaneously (Arnol'dov et al.

1984, 162, 163). What is remarkable about the discourse in this book is not the argument itself but that this imaginary dispute needed to be revisited throughout Soviet history, suggesting the enduring tension at socialism's core.

This tension was not limited to scientific and artistic spheres but concerned all discourses and forms of knowledge that were produced and circulated in Soviet society. In the earlier periods of Soviet history, as the following chapters will show, the loud voices of the political, scientific, and artistic avant-garde concealed this paradox. They located themselves "outside" the field of ideological discourse and from that external position made public comments about and adjustments to that discourse. An explosion of creativity and experimentation marked the early postrevolutionary years but ultimately gave way to the suppression of the intellectual avant-garde and all experimental culture and science and to the introduction of a strict and unified party control.[22] This shift was enabled and made to appear logical by the paradox inherent in the very ideology of the revolutionary project.

It was Stalin who now played the role of Lefort's "master" who stood outside of ideological discourse, making editorial comments about it from that external position and in this way concealing the paradox through himself. This external position enabled the production and wide circulation of a public metadiscourse about all forms of political, artistic, and scientific expression that evaluated them for precision and accuracy against an external canon—the Marxist-Leninist dogma. Stalin's "external" editorial position vis-à-vis all forms of discourse and knowledge, which provided him with unique access to the external canon against which to evaluate them, was crucial in the emergence of those phenomena that became the trademarks of his regime: his immense political power; the cult of his personality; his personal involvement in editing political speeches, scientific papers, films, and musical compositions; the campaign of purges in party organizations; and the ultimate Great Terror in which millions perished. In the last years of Stalin's rule, and especially after his death in 1953 and the subsequent denunciation of his cult of personality, that external position vis-à-vis discourse and knowledge vanished. The main result of this development was not the denunciation of a concrete leader, but a major reorganization of the entire discursive regime of state socialism: a position external to ideological (political, scientific, artistic) discourse, from which a metadiscourse about it could be launched, ceased to exist, and therefore the metadiscourse on ideology

[22] Groys marks the beginning of the "Stalinist phase" of Soviet history at April 23, 1932, when the Central Committee of the party adopted a decree that "disbanded all artistic groups and declared that all Soviet 'creative workers' would be organized according to profession in unitary 'creative unions' of artists, architects, and so on" (Groys 1992, 33).

disappeared from public circulation (see discussion of this process in chapter 2).

Since there was no longer an external voice that could conceal the Lefort's paradox of Soviet ideology, the incongruence of goals and means that constituted that paradox became unleashed. This change ultimately led to a profound transformation of the structure of all types of Soviet ideological discourse (from the language of ideology to the nature of ideological rituals, practices, and organizations) during late socialism. As a result of that transformation, it became less important to read ideological representations for "literal" (referential) meanings than to reproduce their precise structural forms. This transformation of the discursive regime eventually led to a profound shift within Soviet culture during the late period, opening up spaces of indeterminacy, creativity, and unanticipated meanings in the context of strictly formulaic ideological forms, rituals, and organizations. In this way Lefort's paradox returned to haunt the Soviet system. It enabled a profound internal reinterpretation and displacement of the socialist system, creating a set of contradictory conditions that made the system's implosion seem so unexpected when it began, and at the same time so unsurprising and fast once it had occurred.

Acts and Rituals

During the late Soviet period, the form of ideological representations—documents, speeches, ritualized practices, slogans, posters, monuments, and urban visual propaganda—became increasingly normalized, ubiquitous, and predictable. This standardization of the form of discourse developed gradually, as a result of the disappearance, in the 1950s, of the external editorial voice that commented on that discourse. With that shift, the form of the ideological representations became fixed and replicated—unchanged from one context to the next. These representations no longer had to be read literally, at least in most contexts, to work perfectly well as elements of the hegemonic representation. This fixed and normalized discursive system was akin to the kind of discourse that Bakhtin terms "authoritative discourse" (*avtoritetnoe slovo*). For Bakhtin, authoritative discourse coheres around a strict external idea or dogma (whether religious, political, or otherwise) and occupies a particular position within the discursive regime of a period. It has two main features. First, because of a special "script" in which it is coded, authoritative discourse is sharply demarcated from all other types of discourse that coexist with it, which means that it does not depend on them, it precedes them, and it cannot be changed by them. Second, all these other types of discourse are organized around it. Their existence depends on being positioned in relation to it, having to refer to it, quote it, praise it, interpret it, apply it, and so forth, but they cannot, for example, interfere with its code and change it. Regardless of whether this demarcated and fixed authoritative discourse is successful in persuading its authors and audiences, they experience it as immutable and therefore unquestionable (Bakhtin 1994, 342–43).[23] To stress that during late socialism the newly normalized Soviet ideological discourse no longer functioned at the level of meaning as a kind of ideology in the usual sense of the word, I will refer to it henceforth as "authoritative discourse."

The change in the functioning of Soviet ideology during late socialism was reflected in how Soviet citizens participated in ideological rituals and events, as described in many ethnographic accounts. For example, it is well known that during the period from the 1960s to the 1980s, the overwhelming majority of Soviet people participated in May Day and Revolution Day parades in Soviet cities. The apotheosis of such parades in the cities was the walk across the central square in front of the city's party leaders, who stood on a high platform and waved to the marching masses. People cheered as official slogans blared from the loudspeakers, and the thundering roar of these hundreds of thousands of voices sounded impressive and unanimous. According to Soviet newspapers at the time, these massive events "convincingly demonstrate[d] the unbreakable union of the party and the people. . . ." (*Pravda* May 2, 1981). In practice, however, most people in the parades paid little attention to the slogans, and many were not aware who exactly was depicted on the Politburo portraits they carried.

Most Soviet citizens also regularly participated in various state elections for city or district government positions. These elections usually had a single official candidate and invariably produced a massive vote of support, though in practice the voters were relatively uninterested and/or ignorant as to who they were voting for. Sergei (born in 1962) remembers: "Usually I was not quite sure what type of elections these were, or who the candidate was. I would just go to the local election center, take the ballot with the candidate's name, and put it in the voting box. This was the whole procedure for me. I would forget the name of the candidate a few minutes later. I don't remember ever worrying that I was not more interested or that the elections were 'fake.'" Most young people also regularly attended Komsomol (Communist Union of Youth) meetings at schools, colleges, factories, and other locations. At such meetings, it was not uncommon for people to participate in certain procedures without

---

[23] Michael Holquist explains that authoritative discourse is "privileged language that approaches us from without; it is distanced, taboo, and permits no play with its framing context (sacred writ, for example). We receive it. It has great power over us, but only while in power; if ever dethroned it immediately becomes a dead thing, a relic" (Bakhtin 1994, 424).

15

paying close attention to their literal meanings, such as voting in favor of resolutions without knowing what they said. This was not always the case, but it was certainly a dominant paradigm. Among small groups, the required Komsomol meetings were often reported without actually being held. Anna (born in 1961) remembers regular Komsomol meetings in her student group (twenty to twenty-five people) in college in the early 1980s, where "the *komsorg* (the meeting's convener) would often suggest: 'Maybe we should just write down that we had a discussion and voted in favor of the resolution, without actually having the discussion? I understand that everyone has things to attend to at home.'"

What should we make of these acts of mass participation and support in which people regularly paid little attention to the literal meanings of the ritualized acts and pronouncements in which they participated? Can these acts be described as pure masquerade and dissimulation, practiced in public for the gaze of the state and collective surveillance? This book argues that these acts cannot be reduced in this way, and instead offers a different interpretation. An examination of how these ritualized events and texts operated and what they meant to those enacting them is crucial to an understanding of the inherent paradoxes of late socialism. In most contexts these unanimous acts, gestures, and utterances of support did not refer to the literal meaning of ideological statements, resolutions, and figures, but rather performed a different role. For this analysis, we need first to understand the discursive conditions under which authoritative discourse was produced, circulated, and received in late socialism.

Actors in Masks

One common attempt to explain how ideological texts and rituals function in contexts dominated by unchallengeable authoritative discourse whose meanings are not necessarily read literally is to assert that citizens act "as if" they support these slogans and rituals in public, while privately believing something different. Underlying this model are theories of mimicry and dissimulation. A recently influential approach to these theories can be found in the work of Peter Sloterdijk. In *Critique of Cynical Reason* Sloterdijk argues that in the contemporary West the success of ideology is based not on Marx's classic formula of "false consciousness" ("they do not know it, but they are doing it"), but on what he calls "enlightened false consciousness" ("they know very well what they are doing, but still, they are doing it"). According to Sloterdijk, many Western subjects are postmodern cynics who insist on wearing a mask of misrecognition because they know that the ideology of the consumer society is unavoidable, even though they also know perfectly well that this ideology misrepresents social reality (Sloterdijk 1993; Žižek 1991a, 29). This model of acting "as if" echoes James Scott's (1990) discussion of the discourse of subaltern subjects that proceeds in two distinct transcripts, "official" and "hidden"—one representing a mask, the other the truth behind it. Lisa Wedeen, in a recent analysis of the "authoritarian" rule of President Asad in Syria, draws on Sloterdijk and Scott to argue that the art of publicly acting "as if" they subscribed to ideological claims, without really believing them, allowed common citizens "to keep their actual thought private," sustaining a "gap . . . between performance and belief" (Wedeen 1999, 82). Slavoj Žižek (1991a) draws on a similar model of acting "as if" to theorize the basis of power in Eastern European state socialism.

In 1978, in the famous essay "The Power of the Powerless," Václav Havel (1986) constructs a similar model of state socialism in the Eastern Europe of the 1970s. According to Havel, the citizens of socialist Czechoslovakia lived "in lies": they acted in public as if they supported ideological slogans and messages even though privately they believed them to be false. This mode of conformism, argues Havel, allowed them to be left alone by the regime and to avoid personal problems—a reasoning Havel found morally reprehensible (1986, 49–51). In the Soviet Russian context, a related model has been developed by Oleg Kharkhordin. Kharkhordin argues that the subject of late Soviet society was a dissimulator who acted differently in two different spheres, the "official public" and the "hidden intimate." According to that model the dissimulating subject was split: its hidden intimate self was only "available to the gaze of the closest friends or family members but sometimes kept secret even from them" (1999, 357), making it possible to spot these dissimulators only when they "suddenly let their strict self-control go and [broke] their utmost secrecy" (275).

All these models share a crucial problem: although they provide an alternative to the binary division between the recognition and misrecognition of ideology, they do so by producing another problematic binary between "truth" and "falsity," "reality" and "mask," "revealing" and "dissimulating." According to this binary model, such public political acts as voting in favor of an official resolution or displaying a pro-government slogan at a rally should be interpreted "literally"—as declarations of one's support for the state that are either true ("real" support) or false ("dissimulation" of support).[24] Several problematic assumptions about language, knowledge, meaning, and personhood lie at the basis of this understanding. In this view, the only function of language is to refer to

[24] See the discussions of such acts in Kharkhordin (1999) and Wedeen (1999).

17

the world and to state facts about it. That is why models based on such an understanding divide language into "codes," such as official, or public, transcript and hidden, or intimate, transcript.[25] Knowledge in this view exists before discourse. Discourse reflects knowledge and does not produce it. Meaning, accordingly, is a psychological state that is fully formed in the mind of the speaker before the act of speaking.[26] The speaking person, in these models, is a unified, bounded, sovereign individual who possesses a "unique self-constituted" consciousness (Mitchell 1990, 545) and a "unitary speaking ego" (Hanks 2000, 182), and whose authentic voice can be hidden or revealed.[27]

The Performative

In hopes of articulating a more nuanced understanding of late socialism and its paradoxes, we need to go beyond these problematic assumptions to examine how people living within that system engaged with, interpreted, and created their reality. The analysis in this book will consider discourse and forms of knowledge that circulated in everyday Soviet life not as divided into spheres or codes that are fixed and bounded, but as processes that are never completely known in advance and that are actively produced and reinterpreted (Haraway 1991, 190–91; Fabian 2001, 24).

Many theories of language focus on its active and processual aspects. For example, Voloshinov stressed that the use of language involves a situated process in which meaning is produced, not simply reflected or communicated (Voloshinov 1986, 86).[28] In his critique of the models of language that posit isolated bounded consciousness Bakhtin also pointed out that they ignore the ongoing and agentive processes constitutive of the event. Such models, he argued, can only transcribe an event as an accomplished static fact "at the cost of losing those actual creative forces which generated the event at the moment it was still being accomplished

[25] See Susan Gal's thorough critique of Scott's model of language (1995). For other critiques, see also Mitchell (1990), Humphrey (1994), and Oushakine (2001).

[26] See similar critiques in Rosaldo (1982, 212); Hill and Mannheim (1992); Duranti (1993, 25); Yurchak (2003b).

[27] Ironically, even accounts of the "split" person in these models are in fact based on a unitary model of personhood: the "split" is a constitutive element of the dissimulating act, which is employed or acted out by a preexisting (pre-split) "intimate hidden self" to conceal oneself from public view or to reveal oneself to intimate friends. Thus, Kharkhordin's model of the subject contains a peculiar tension between the subject who possesses an authentic "intimate self" that can be hidden and revealed, and the subject who exists as the result of hiding and revealing. See critique of split subject models in Strauss (1997).

[28] See also Hanks (2000, 143); Hanks (1993, 153n2); Duranti (1997; 1993); Gal (1994).

(when it was still open), i.e., at the cost of losing the living and in principle nonmerging participants in the event" (1990, 87). Instead, the productive and dialogic view of language developed by Bakhtin and his colleagues understands the speaking self as "voice" that is never bounded or static but always "dialogized," because speaking implies inhabiting multiple voices that are not "self-enclosed or deaf to one another" but that "hear each other constantly, call back and forth to each other, and are reflected in one another" (1984, 75).[29]

The productive nature of language is also central to John Austin's analysis of "performatives" and the traditions in the study of language that are related to this approach (1999). Introducing speech act theory, Austin argues that in addition to "constative" utterances that state something (present facts or describe reality, such as "it is cold," "my name is Joe"), language includes a whole class of utterances that *do* something. Such utterances as "Guilty!" (uttered by a judge in a courtroom), "I name this ship the Queen Elizabeth" (at an official launching ceremony), or "I bet you sixpence it will rain tomorrow" perform an action that changes things in social reality instead of describing that reality. Austin calls this class of utterances "performative utterances" or "performatives." Constative utterances convey meaning and can be true or false; performative utterances deliver force and cannot be true or false—instead they can be felicitous or infelicitous.

Austin points out that what makes an utterance a performative is not the intention of the speaker, but rather the accepted conventions surrounding the utterance, which involve the appropriate person uttering the appropriate words in the appropriate circumstances in order to obtain conventional results. If the conventions are not in place, the performative will not succeed regardless of the intention of the speaker (1999, 12–18). Conversely, if the conventions are in place, the performative will succeed regardless of intention. The issue of intention is central here, in light of our critical assessment of the abovementioned models that posit meaning in discourse as a psychological state that preexists the act of speaking. For example, speech acts such as oaths do not have to be intended, as a psychological state, to be performed. If a person makes an oath in court to tell the truth, though internally planning to conceal the truth, this does not make the execution of the oath any less real or efficacious, nor does it exonerate the person from legal repercussions if the lie is discovered. In other words, the very binding of this speech act within the system of laws, rules, or conventions (making it a recognized

[29] See also Bakhtin (1994, 304–5; 1990, 137); Todorov (1998); Clark and Holquist (1984); Holquist (1990, 175); Gardiner (1992, 73); Hirschkop (1997, 59–60); Kristeva (1986).

19

oath with consequences) does not depend on whether the speaker intended the words uttered during the oath "for real" or "as if."[30]

In a critical reading of speech act theory Derrida pushed further Austin's point that it is the conventions of a speech act, and not the intention of the speaker, that make a performative successful. The conventionality of a speech act implies that it must be formulated according to a recognized "coded" or "iterable" model—that is, it must function as a citation that is repeatable in an endless number of contexts (Derrida 1977, 191–92). However, the exhaustive knowledge of context cannot be achieved because any context is open to broader description and because contexts in which new citations of the same speech act can appear are potentially infinite (Derrida 1977, 185–86). Because of the citationality of a speech act and the indeterminacy of context, the meaning of any given speech act is never completely determined in advance. Each speech act can break with context in unpredictable ways and achieve effects and mean things that were not intended in advance. This ability of the speech act to break with context, argues Derrida, is a constitutive element of its performative force.[31] By stressing the structural ability of a conventional formula to be used in unanticipated ways, Derrida's argument recognizes the possibility for change and unpredictability even within strictly controlled and reproduced norms and conventions. At the same time, by limiting the discussion to the semiotic level of discourse, Derrida downplays the role that external social conventions, institutions, and power relations also play in constituting the performative force of a conventional utterance.

In a different critical reading of performative acts, Pierre Bourdieu (1991) focused precisely on that external dimension, adding a sociological analysis of Austin's "conventions" that are necessary for a successful performance of speech acts. Bourdieu argues that the source of power of conventional speech acts "resides in the institutional conditions of their production and reception" (111) and that their power is "nothing other than the *delegated power* of the spokesperson" (107). Although Bourdieu's focus provides a necessary external perspective on the social and institutional nature of power and the process of its delegation, it still privileges just one side of the performative: it downplays the role of the semiotic nature of discourse in constituting the performative force and consequently downplays the possibility for change in discourse that institutions cannot determine or anticipate in advance.

---

[30] Austin does not bracket out intention altogether, but he stresses that it is not necessarily a constitutive part of the performative force. For example, if an oath is made in the appropriate circumstances but without the intention to follow it, performative force is "abused" but successfully carried out (Austin 1999, 16).

[31] See an elaboration of this point in Culler (1981, 24–25) and a critical assessment of Derrida's critique of Austin in Cavell (1995) and in Searle (1977; 1983).

A synthesis of Derrida's and Bourdieu's critical readings of Austin's theory would allow one to consider both constitutive elements of the performative force of a speech act—the delegated power of external social contexts and institutions and the semiotic power of discourse to produce unpredictable meanings and effects in new contexts. It is precisely because the two elements of the performative force—sociological and semiotic—operate simultaneously that speech acts even in strictly controlled institutionalized contexts can take on meanings and produce effects for which they were not intended. This possibility of an unanticipated outcome constitutes, Judith Butler argues, "the political promise of the performative, one that positions the performative at the center of a political hegemony" (Butler 1997b, 161). This point is crucial for the following discussion of ideological rituals and utterances and the effects they produce.

Speech Acts and Ritualized Acts

Austin's and later work on performatives in speech has been influential in a number of fields. It has affected the analysis of various forms of ritualized practice that are not necessarily linguistic and the analysis of how aspects of subjectivity may be produced in such practice. For example, Judith Butler focuses on the ritualized repetition of embodied norms as performative acts—acts that do not simply refer to an a priori existing "pure body" but shape that body as sexed, raced, classed, and so forth (1990, 1993).[32] Drawing on Derrida's and Bourdieu's critical readings of performativity, Butler argues against theories of the subject and meaning according to which the subject is fully given in advance, only to perform the discourse later on. Rather, she asserts, the subject is enabled through discourse, without being completely determined by it:

> [A] regularized and constrained repetition of norms is not performed *by* a subject; this repetition is what enables a subject and constitutes the temporal conditions for the subject. This iterability implies that "performance" is not a singular "act" or event, but a ritualized production, and ritual reiteration under and through constraint, under and through force of prohibition and taboo, with the threat of ostracism and even death controlling and compelling the shape of the production, but not, I will insist, determining it fully in advance. (Butler, quoted in Hollywood 2002, 98)

Drawing on Butler's work and theories of the ritual in anthropology and religious studies, Amy Hollywood proposes to broaden the discus-

[32] See also Morris (1995).

21

sion of the performative to various "ritualized acts" that are repeated in different contexts and whose meanings are neither completely known in advance nor determined by the participants' intentions (Hollywood 2002, 113).[33] Catherine Bell further points out that through the repetition of ritualized actions in different contexts, persons are produced and produce themselves as "ritualized agents . . . who have an intrinsic knowledge of these schemes embedded in their bodies, in their sense of reality, and in their understanding of how to act in ways that both maintain and qualify the complex microrelations of power" (Bell 1992, 221).

This view of ritualized acts and speech acts as constitutive of the person is different from the view of these acts as divided between mask (acting "as if ") and reality, truth and lie. In the mask/truth models the person is first posited and then is involved in the act of wearing masks or revealing truths. By contrast, most performative theories do not posit the person completely in advance, before the acts—the person is enabled performatively in the repetition of the act.[34] As philosopher Aldo Tassi points out, there is no performative person that preexists the person wearing a mask: "There is no role that stands 'behind' all our other roles and defines what we 'really' are, no more than there is an act of knowing (a knowing that) that stands 'behind' the acts of knowing and defines the possession of knowledge (knowing how)" (Tassi 1993, 207).

Constative and Performative Dimensions

At the end of his book Austin pointed out that any strict division into constative and performative acts is an abstraction, and "every genuine speech act is both" (1999, 147). Speech acts should not be seen as either just constative or just performative; rather, concludes Austin, depending on the circumstances, they are more or less constative and more or less performative. Developing this insight I will speak of performative and constative "dimensions" of speech and discourse in general. The relative importance of these dimensions in discourse may change historically.[35] The same is true of ritualized acts in a broader sense.

The kind of act that is constituted by the uttering of a conventional formula in a given context cannot be understood by attending merely to the

[33] Schechner (1985; 1993; 2003) also provides a view of aesthetic performance as emerging and productive, in which the actor undergoes temporary or permanent changes; see in particular his concepts of "transformation" and "transportation" (1985). On the intentionality in ritual, see Humphrey and Laidlaw (1994).

[34] This view of the person can be traced back to Aristotle.

[35] Austin writes: "[P]erhaps we have here not really two poles, but rather an historical development" (1999, 145–6).

structure of the utterance or to generic elements of the context known in advance. One must attend to the context-in-emergence, the context in which the utterance is being repeated. One must attend to the "actual creative forces that generated the event at the moment it was still being accomplished (when it was still open)" (Bakhtin 1990, 87). In this book, when analyzing speech acts such as slogans, party speeches, and addresses, and ritualized acts such as votes and meetings, we will speak of their coexisting constative and performative dimensions. From the perspective of this coexistence, the act of voting in the conventional context of a meeting does two things at once: it states one's opinion (the constative dimension) and binds the vote within the system of rules and norms where it is recognized as a legitimate vote (the performative dimension). The unity of the constative and performative dimensions makes the vote what it is: a statement of opinion that is recognized as having consequences in legal, administrative, institutional, and cultural terms.

These two dimensions of discourse do not constitute a new binary. They are not in a binary either-or relationship; rather they are indivisible and mutually productive (as the discussion below shows). For example, the opinion one states when voting may be affected by whether the vote is legally binding with actual consequences: a recorded vote at a faculty meeting is different from an informal vote among friends (and this difference may affect how one votes). Since the relative importance of the constative and performative dimensions of a ritualized act and speech act in any given new instance can never be completely known in advance, the constative and performative dimensions may "drift" historically. For example, the importance of the constative dimension may diminish, while the performative may grow in importance. Suppose that during elections in certain institutional circumstances, it is no longer crucial for people to state their opinions about the candidate, but it is still very important to participate in the act of voting. A person may be aware that in the elections there will always be only one candidate (or one resolution), although still conscious that a successful execution of the ritual of voting will enable other important practices and events to happen, such as the reproduction of the institution itself and of one's position as its member (as its student, employee, citizen) with all the possibilities that follow from that position. In such a context, it may be less important for whom one votes than that one votes. In other words, the person may not have to pay much attention to the constative dimension of the vote (the literal meaning of a resolution or a candidate), but will still have to attend closely to the vote's performative dimension. This would include paying attention to the pragmatic markers of the ritual, such as the question, "Who is in favor?", and the appropriate response of raising one's hand in an affirmative gesture. The performative dimension continues to be central in this ritualized act,

23

but the constative dimension has moved from its original meaning. The successful achievement of the result (such as reproducing the institution and one's position in it) does not necessarily depend on what one's opinion about the candidate is or even whether one has an opinion at all.

Performative Shift

A general shift at the level of concrete ritualized forms of discourse, in which the performative dimension's importance grows, while the constative dimension opens up to new meanings, can and does occur in different historical and cultural contexts. Consider an example from the contemporary United States. Today a number of private universities, colleges, and schools in several states require teachers and professors to take a "loyalty oath" to ensure that they do not "hold or foster undesirable political beliefs. . . . While the statutes vary, [these institutions] generally deny the right to teach to those who cannot or will not take the loyalty oath" (Chin and Rao 2003, 431–32). Recently, a sociologist of law took such a loyalty oath at a midwestern university when her appointment as a professor began. From a political standpoint she disagreed with the practice of taking loyalty oaths, and later, in her role as professor of the sociology of law, she voiced political positions counter to those mentioned in the oath and challenged the oath-taking practice itself. However, before she could do this, she first had to take the oath, understanding that without this act she would not be employed or recognized by the institution as a legitimate member with a voice authorized to participate in teaching, research, and the institution's politics (committees, meetings, elections, and so forth), including even the possibility to question publicly the practice of taking oaths. Here, the constative dimension of the ritualized act experiences a shift, while the performative dimension remains fixed and important: taking the oath opens a world of possibilities where new constative meanings become possible, including a professorial position with a recognized political voice within the institution. In the sociologist's words, "The oath did not mean much if you took it, but it meant a lot if you didn't."[36]

This example illustrates the general principle of how some discursive acts or whole types of discourse can drift historically in the direction of an increasingly expanding performative dimension and increasingly open or even irrelevant constative dimension. During Soviet late socialism, the performative dimension of authoritative speech acts and rituals became particularly important in most contexts and during most events. One person who participated in large Komsomol meetings in the 1970s

---

[36] Interview with author.

and 1980s described how he often spent the meetings reading a book. However, "when a vote had to be taken, everyone roused—a certain sensor clicked in the head: 'Who is in favor?'—and you raised your hand automatically" (see a discussion of such ritualized practices within the Komsomol in chapter 3). Here the emphasis on the performative dimension of authoritative discourse was unique both in scale and substance. Most ritualized acts of authoritative discourse during this time underwent such a transformation. Participating in these acts reproduced oneself as a "normal" Soviet person within the system of relations, collectivities, and subject positions, with all the constraints and possibilities that position entailed, even including the possibility, after the meetings, to engage in interests, pursuits, and meanings that ran against those that were stated in the resolutions one had voted for. It would obviously be wrong to see these acts of voting simply as constative statements about supporting the resolution that are either true (real support) or false (dissimulation of support). These acts are not about stating facts and describing opinions but about doing things and opening new possibilities.

The uniqueness of the late-socialist context lay in the fact that those who ran the Komsomol and party meetings and procedures themselves understood perfectly well that the constative dimension of most ritualized acts and texts had become reinterpreted from its original meaning. They therefore emphasized the centrality of the performative dimension of this discourse in the reproduction of social norms, positions, relations, and institutions. This emphasis on the performative dimension took place in most contexts where authoritative discourse was reproduced or circulated: in votes, speeches, reports, slogans, meetings, parades, elections, various institutional practices, and so on. It became increasingly more important to participate in the reproduction of the *form* of these ritualized acts of authoritative discourse than to engage with their constative meanings. It is crucial to point out, however, that this does not mean either that these ritualized acts become meaningless and empty or that other meanings in public life were diminishing or becoming totally constrained. On the contrary, the performative reproduction of the form of rituals and speech acts actually *enabled* the emergence of diverse, multiple, and unpredictable meanings in everyday life, including those that did not correspond to the constative meanings of authoritative discourse.

The reopening of Lefort's paradox of Soviet ideology in the 1950s brought about the shift that resulted in the rise of the performative dimension of authoritative discourse during late socialism. This also made the constative dimension of discourse increasingly unanchored, indeterminate, and often irrelevant. The next chapter discusses how this shift happened and how it affected the structure of authoritative discourse and ritualized practice; the chapters that follow discuss what new meanings

25

became possible as a result of this shift. For now, it is important to note that this transformation toward the performative was not planned; it was a byproduct of the changes—beginning in the 1950s—in the conditions under which Soviet authoritative discourse was produced, circulated, and received. A model of authoritative discourse in which the literal precision of statements and representations was evaluated against an external canon (described in the opinion of an external editor) was gradually displaced by a model in which the external canon was no longer available. As a result of this shift of conditions, the authoritative discourse underwent a major internal normalization at the structural level. The normalized and fixed structures of this discourse became increasingly frozen and were replicated from one context to the next practically intact. This process of replication took place at the level of texts,[37] the visual discourse of ideology (posters, films, monuments, architecture), ritualistic discourse (meetings, reports, institutional practice, celebrations), and in many centralized "formal structures" of everyday practice (De Certeau 1988, xv) (such as school curriculum, prices of goods, and the general organization of urban time and space). Eventually, the replication of the fixed and normalized forms of discourse became an end in itself, and the constative meanings of these discursive forms became increasingly unimportant. This book will refer to this process—in which the performative dimension of ritualized and speech acts rises in importance (it is important to participate in the reproduction of these acts at the level of form), while the constative dimension of these acts become open-ended, indeterminate, or simply irrelevant—as *performative shift*.[38] Performative shift was a central principle through which authoritative discourse in late socialism operated and through which practice was represented and organized.[39]

[37] See Urban on "transduction" (the replication of textual forms) (1996, 30).

[38] Elsewhere I theorized this shift of discourse as *heteronymous shift* (Yurchak 2001a; 2003b), from "heteronym"—meaning a word of the same written form as another word but different in meaning (e.g., *bass*, a string instrument and the fish; *tear*, to rip and a teardrop). The term *heteronymous shift* emphasized that the meanings for which reproduced forms of authoritative discourse stood could slide in unpredictable directions. The term *performative shift* employed in this book is related to that idea. However, it also emphasizes another point: that shift of meaning is possible because of a mutually constitutive relationship between the performative and the constative dimensions of discourse. The rise of the performative dimension of discourse to dominance (the fact that a ritualized form is fixed and performing it is unavoidable) enables a shift at the level of the constative dimension.

[39] Many practices in the socialist "economy of shortage" were organized according to the performative shift. Consider a central symbol of industrial production in late socialism—the fulfillment of the "plan." To industrial managers involved in Soviet industry it was crucial that the plan was successfully fulfilled at the level of form (in numbers, figures, statistics, reports, etc.). These managers needed, among other things, to design various methods (resource bargaining, padding, barter, etc.) in order to avoid the obstacles imposed by the

Creative Productions

A complex system of institutional and power relations made possible the ubiquitous replication of ritualized acts and utterances of authoritative discourse. For example, if party and Komsomol activists did not reproduce these forms of authoritative language, or if they publicly engaged in a critical rewriting of that language, they would risk receiving an official reprimand, losing their job, or more serious repercussions. The common perception that authoritative discourse was simply unavoidable and unchangeable further shaped the reproduction of ritualized forms of this discourse. This perception was predicated on the particular conditions of production and circulation of authoritative discourse, with the state having hegemonic power to impose a widely circulating representation of reality formulated in that discourse, thus guaranteeing that any alternative representation or counter-representation would not acquire the same widely circulating status as a shared "public" discourse.[40]

However, the ritualized acts and speech acts of authoritative discourse were not replicated simply because of these institutional power relations, control, or the threat of punishment. They were replicated because of the importance of the performative dimension. Reproducing the forms of authoritative discourse acquired a strong performative role: it enabled people to engage in new, unanticipated meanings, aspects of everyday life, interests, and activities, which sprang up everywhere in late socialism and were not necessarily determined by the ideological constative meanings of authoritative discourse.

The new, unanticipated meanings did not coincide with those explicitly described by or envisioned in authoritative discourse. However, this process should not necessarily be seen as "resistance" to the norms and meanings articulated in that discourse. As Derrida argued, the ability of a sign to break with context in itself is politically and ethically neutral, until invested with new meaning (Hollywood 2002, 107). In a critical reading of

---

functioning of the socialist economy itself. As a result, the plan was often fulfilled with the help of the practices that violated the literal meanings for which the plan was supposedly designed (e.g., the satisfaction of a social need for which it was designed). See Nove (1977); Kornai (1980); Verdery (1996); Ledeneva (1998). The "plan" as a symbol of the socialist economy experienced performative shift. It was meticulously reproduced in representation (in reports, statistics, figures), but the meaning associated with it became open and somewhat unpredictable, allowing for the introduction of new meanings. See also Lampland's brilliant discussion of the "fetish of plan" (1995).

[40] For example, when in August 1968, seven people at Moscow's Red Square unveiled slogans protesting the Soviet invasion of Czechoslovakia, the group was arrested within a couple of minutes and the event was ignored by the Soviet press, remaining unknown to most of the Soviet population until twenty years later, when it was publicly discussed during perestroika.

Butler's discussion of performativity, Saba Mahmood draws on Butler's Foucauldian point that "the possibility of resistance to norms [is located] within the structure of power itself rather than in the consciousness of an autonomous individual," but argues against the tendency to equate agency with resistance: "[I]f the ability to effect change in the world and in oneself is historically and culturally specific (both in terms of what constitutes 'change' and the capacity by which it is effected), then its meaning and sense cannot be fixed a priori. . . . [Indeed] agentival capacity is entailed not only in those acts that result in (progressive) change but also those that aim toward continuity, stasis, and stability" (Mahmood 2001, 212).[41]

We should add to this critical reading that agentival capacity can also be entailed in acts that are neither about change nor about continuity, but about introducing minute internal displacements and mutations into the discursive regime in which they are articulated. Such acts may appear inconsequential to most participants and remain invisible to most observers. They do not have to contradict the political and ethical parameters of the system and, importantly, may even allow one to preserve the possibilities, promises, positive ideals, and ethical values of the system while avoiding the negative and oppressive constraints within which these are articulated. This view of how new meanings are produced through the repetition of authoritative speech acts and rituals refuses a binary division between form and meaning or between real meaning and pretense of meaning.[42] In the late Soviet case, the performative repetition of the rituals and texts of authoritative discourse, and the engagement in different new meanings that were not described by the constative dimension of these rituals and texts, still did not preclude a person from feeling an affinity for many of the meanings, possibilities, values, and promises of socialism. It even allowed one to recapture these meanings, values, and promises from the inflexible interpretations provided by the party rhetoric.[43]

The following chapters argue that the performative shift of authoritative discourse that occurred in the 1950s and 1960s allowed Soviet people to develop a complexly differentiating relationship to ideological meanings, norms, and values. Depending on the context, they might reject a certain meaning, norm, or value, be apathetic about another, continue

[41] See also Hollywood (2002, 107n57); Morris (1995, 15); Fraser (1995).

[42] See, for example, Deleuze and Guattari's concept of "deterritorialization" (2002)—a strategy of decentering binary oppositions (which Guattari calls "territorialized couplings" [1995]) without constructing alternative dichotomies. See also my chapter 4 for a discussion of this concept.

[43] Barnett points out that in the context of state socialism in China the unchangeable and unavoidable ideological discourse of the state nevertheless "offers room for maneuver within the terms of its own rhetoric," allowing its citizens to assume "that they were entitled to illustrate and act out imaginatively the promise within socialist discourse" (Barnett 2002, 284).

28

actively subscribing to a third, creatively reinterpret a fourth, and so on. These dispositions were emergent, not static. The unanimous participation of Soviet citizens in the performative reproduction of speech acts and rituals of authoritative discourse contributed to the general perception of that system's monolithic immutability, while at the same time enabling diverse and unpredictable meanings and styles of living to spring up everywhere within it. In a seemingly paradoxical twist, the immutable and predictable aspects of state socialism, and its creative and unpredictable possibilities, became mutually constitutive.

Materials and Methods

Because of the immense social change that came with perestroika, when socialism began imploding, and the shift in the voice and tone of the retrospective post-Soviet discourse that emerged in the 1990s, it is important in the investigation of the period before perestroika to draw on two types of materials: *contemporaneous* and *retrospective*. The contemporaneous materials used here consist of accounts of late socialism produced during that period. These include personal accounts (diaries, letters, written notes, drawings, pictures, jokes, slang, other examples of oral genres, music recordings, and amateur films) and official Soviet publications (texts of speeches and documents, newspaper articles, fiction, films, photos, and cartoons). The retrospective materials consist of the accounts of that period that were produced later, during perestroika and the first post-Soviet decade. These include interviews and conversations conducted by the author (around fifty semistructured interviews with former party and Komsomol leaders, speechwriters, propaganda artists, rank-and-file Komsomol members, students, workers, engineers, members of "amateur" cultural communities, among others), as well as dozens of published interviews, memoirs, essays, films, and fiction. These materials appear in the author's translation unless stated otherwise; where it is necessary to the analysis, the original Russian is given in Latin transliteration.

I collected the bulk of these materials during fifteen-month fieldwork research in St. Petersburg in 1994 and 1995. To broaden the scope of this research, in the summers of 1996, 1997, and 1998, I collected more interviews, diaries, and personal correspondences from a larger field: St. Petersburg and several other Russian cities including Moscow, Kaliningrad, Smolensk, Sovetsk, Novosibirsk, Yakutsk, and Penza.[44] The

[44] In most cases, I provide only the first names of informants to protect their identity. In a few sensitive cases, the first names are also changed, as well as revealing details of their situation, such as names of schools and institutions. A few well-known people among the informants are referred to by their real names with their consent.

29

original research began with the following notice that ran for two months in the summer of 1994 in several St. Petersburg weeklies:

How well do we remember our lives before 1985, before the changes of perestroika? Our feelings and experiences of the Soviet years are documented in personal writings, diaries, and correspondences that date to that time. These are important historical documents that should not be allowed to vanish. I am conducting a sociological[45] study of the period between the 1960s and the beginning of perestroika and am looking for personal written accounts of daily life at that time.

The advertisement provided a contact number. The response was quite enthusiastic. Dozens of people of all ages and occupations wanted to share their written materials from that period or simply to talk about the problem, which seemed to interest them all: what was it about their life before 1985 that made its change so unexpected and yet so profound and fast? Although many materials came from people of older generations, the majority came from people in their thirties and forties—those who came of age during the last two decades before perestroika. Members of these younger cohorts may have been more likely to read newspaper advertisements and respond to them, to keep diaries, or save correspondences. However, from conversations with different people something else also became apparent. Although the sudden transformation of socialism was equally unexpected by and equally unsurprising to different generations and social groups, it was the younger people, those who had graduated from secondary schools in the 1970s and early 1980s, who seemed particularly struck by the suddenness of the event and yet surprisingly to themselves turned out to be particularly prepared for it. These people most wanted to make sense of this event and their experience of it.

Generations are not natural, they are produced through common experience and through discourse about it. Under appropriate conditions, age may provide what Karl Mannheim called a common "location in the historical dimension of the social process," creating a shared perspective on that process (Mannheim 1952, 290). And the shared experience of coming of age during a particular period may also contribute to sharing understandings and meanings, and the processes through which they are reproduced (Rofel 1999, 22). DeMartini (1985) stresses two different understandings of a generation: as a *cohort* and as a *lineage*. The cohort emphasizes the difference in age, assuming that age peers have certain things in common with each other as well as characteristics that distinguish

---

[45] In the Russian context, as in many continental European contexts, the term "sociologist" represents this type of research more accurately than the term "anthropologist."

them from other cohorts. The lineage emphasizes the relations between generations, assuming that there is a strong bond between parents and children, and a continuity of social and political consciousness. These two understandings of a generation do not have to be contradictory. They may coexist, and this is how the generation is understood in this book. In Russia, the discourse about the importance of the generational experience is widespread and powerful. Many people who appear in this book think and talk about the importance of their growing up during the late Soviet period. It is common in Russia to compare the experiences of different generations, to use specific names to identify them, to mention events and cultural phenomena that are seen as important for the formation of a common generational experience, to describe the continuities between generations, and so on. These discourses not only reflect generations but also contribute to their production.

This book maintains that because of the performative shift of authoritative discourse and the subsequent normalization of that discourse, the post-Stalinist period between the mid-1950s and mid-1980s became thought of as a particular period with shared characteristics, which is here called late socialism. In some of the literature addressing this period, the thirty years are divided into two shorter periods that have been mentioned above: the thaw (*ottepel'*), the period of Khrushchev's reforms, and the stagnation (*zastoi*), Brezhnev's period. The Soviet intervention in Czechoslovakia in the summer of 1968 is often considered the symbolic divide between the two (Strada 1998, 11). These two periods roughly correspond to two generations—the older generation that is sometimes called the "sixties" (*shestidesiatniki*, identified by the name of their formative decade) and the younger group, here called the "last Soviet generation."

This study focuses on this younger generation—people who were born between the 1950s and early 1970s and came of age between the 1970s and the mid-1980s (see also Boym 1994; Lur'e 1997 and 1998). In the mid-1980s approximately 90 million people, almost one-third of the Soviet population, were between the ages of 15 and 34—therefore belonging to what I am calling the last Soviet generation.[46] Although differences in social class, gender, education, ethnicity, profession, geographic area, and language provided for differences in the experiences of socialism by these people, they nevertheless shared particular understandings, meanings, and processes of that period, having come of age during the 1970s and mid-1980s. As Russian philologist Marina Kniazeva has pointed out, that

[46] The total population at that time was approximately 281 million people (Itogi Vsesoiuznoi perepisi naseleniia 1989 goda [Results of the All-Union 1989 Census]. 1992. Moscow: Goskomstat SSSR).

31

generation of people, whom she calls "the children of stagnation" (*deti za-stoia*), unlike previous and subsequent generations, had no "inaugural event" around which to coalesce as a cohort (1990). The identity of the older generations was formed around events such as the revolution, the war, the denunciation of Stalin; the identity of the younger generations has been formed around the collapse of the Soviet Union. Unlike these older and younger groups, the common identity of the last Soviet generation was formed by a shared experience of the normalized, ubiquitous, and immutable authoritative discourse of the Brezhnev's years.

Most people of that generation were also members of the Komsomol during the 1970s and 1980s. This membership made them one of the largest groups to collectively participate in the reproduction and reception of authoritative texts and rituals in the local contexts of schools, institutes, factories, and so forth, where Komsomol organizations operated. Having grown up entirely during Brezhnev's period, they had not experienced any major transformations of the Soviet system and way of life until perestroika and became particularly skilled, from early years in school, in the performative reproduction of the forms of authoritative discourse. At the same time, they also became actively engaged in creating various new pursuits, identities, and forms of living that were enabled by authoritative discourse, but not necessarily defined by it. This complex relationship, as argued earlier, allowed them to maintain an affinity for the many aesthetic possibilities and ethical values of socialism, while at the same time interpreting them in new terms that were not necessarily anticipated by the state—thus avoiding many of the system's limitations and forms of controls.

This discussion of the last Soviet generation is linked to broader considerations of method employed in the book. This book is not about a representative norm of Soviet life or an average Soviet experience. Rather, it investigates internal shifts that were emerging within the Soviet system during late socialism at the level of discourse, ideology, and knowledge but that became apparent for what they were only much later, when the system collapsed. This is why this analysis does not consider many important historical events, political developments, economic conditions, social classes, ethnic groups, or gender differences. It focuses instead on members of younger generations of educated urbanites from different Russian cities and towns who were involved in ideological institutions, rituals, and discourses of the Soviet state and who practiced various cultural pursuits, from science to literature and music. Although the discourses, activities, relations, and values of this cohort are not necessarily representative of an average social experience of the period, they serve as a powerful lens through which emerging internal shifts in that system become visible.

A closely related methodological issue is how the author of this text figures in it. I rarely refer to myself in the text as the "I" of the events, observations, and analysis. This is a conscious decision that I have considered seriously. Being self-reflective about the position of the observer and writer is a crucial ingredient of any analysis, and anthropology has a long-standing tradition of doing this. But this self-reflective position should not be confused with constructing an authorial self that is linguistically present in the text as sovereign and unitary. The authorial voice is always deeply decentered and multivoiced, the point that Bakhtin, one of the inspirations of this book, argued forcefully. This book could only become possible because of the multiple temporal, spatial, and cultural decenterings of my authorial self. The book is written partly through the voice of someone who had a personal experience of living in the Soviet Union during the late socialist period and witnessed the Soviet Union's disintegration, but equally so through the voice of someone who has lived for the last fifteen years in the United States, who studied in an American graduate school, who become a professional anthropologist in the United States, and who learned to occupy a retrospective position and different cultural and linguistic locations to reconsider and analyze the meanings and origins of past events. Furthermore, this book is provoked by experiencing not only Soviet life, but also post-Soviet transformations and Western and postsocialist social science writings about both. The realization that the following text became possible only because of these multiple decentered positions and temporalities of my authorial voice makes me reluctant to write from the first person perspective and uncomfortable with the label "native anthropologist."

Survey of Chapters

Chapter 2 proceeds with a two-level analysis of Soviet authoritative discourse. First is a historical analysis that reconstructs the genealogy of a major discursive shift that, in the 1950s and 1960s, brought about the progressive normalization and hardening of the form of authoritative discourse. Second is an analysis of the principles and rules according to which the new strictly formalized authoritative discourse and especially its language part became organized. The chapter draws on materials such as the published texts of party leaders, futurist poets, and linguists; newspaper editorials; ideological speeches; and the author's interviews with speechwriters and consultants at the party's Central Committee, and with artists and designers of visual propaganda. Chapter 2 makes another methodological point demonstrating how a combination of discourse analysis, linguistic analysis, and genealogical analysis may create

33

a tool for investigating shifts in discursive formations. This method is also employed in the following chapters.

Chapter 3 analyzes how members of the last Soviet generation were involved in the reproduction of the norm of authoritative discourse in the context of the Komsomol organization to which most of them belonged in the 1970s and early 1980s. This chapter also begins the analysis, which is pursued in full in the following chapters, of how the performative reproduction of the authoritative forms in texts and rituals allowed these young people to invent multiple new meanings, pursuits, relations, socialities, and lifestyles that were neither necessarily determined by constative meanings of authoritative discourse nor opposed to them. This chapter focuses in particular on the practices and contexts of "ideological production" (the writing of speeches, texts, and reports; the conducting of rituals) and on the people who ran these practices and contexts: the local "ideological producers" (Komsomol organizers, secretaries, and rank-and-file members).

Chapter 4 shifts the analysis from the practices and contexts of ideological production to the contexts of cultural milieus[47] based on networks of friends, common intellectual pursuits, and practices of *obshchenie* (endless conversations, interactions, and forms of "being with others"). This chapter focuses on urban cultural milieus of the 1960s and 1970s, whose members thought of themselves as living in a reality "different" from the "ordinary" Soviet world. These communities of archeologists, theoretical physicists, literature lovers, mountain climbers, rock musicians, and so on, created a kind of "deterritorialized" reality that did not fit the binary categories of either support of or opposition to the state. The chapter argues that these cultural milieus should be analyzed not as exceptions to the "norm" of late Soviet life, but as paradigmatic examples of how that norm became everywhere decentered and reinterpreted. Although the existence of these cultural milieus was not necessarily thought of by their participants as a form of resistance to the socialist state, the cultural work that went on within them contributed to a dramatic reinterpretation of the socialist system, ultimately and "invisibly" undermining many of the announced Soviet principles and goals.

Chapter 5 analyzes the "imaginary" worlds that emerged within late-socialist life, especially in the life of the younger generations. It focuses in particular on the cultural and discursive phenomenon that it calls the "Imaginary West:" a local cultural construct and imaginary that was based

---

[47] The term "milieu" is used here in the cultural studies sense. For example, Grossberg (2000) argues that the metaphor of "social space" encompasses two elements: a "territory" (a dynamic site for carrying out actions) and a "milieu" (the social relations and possibilities for actions and events within that site). For a genealogy of the term "milieu," see Rabinow (1989, 31–34).

on the forms of knowledge and aesthetics associated with the "West," but not necessarily referring to any "real" West, and that also contributed to "deterritorializing" the world of everyday socialism from within. The production of this cultural construct within Soviet life was enabled by the performative shift of Soviet authoritative discourse described earlier, and the paradoxes of the cultural politics of the Soviet state that became exacerbated by this shift. This chapter conducts a genealogy of the Imaginary West, starting with the 1950s and 1960s, and analyzes the principles and dynamics of that imaginary world when it came to dominance in the lives of young people in the 1970s and 1980s.

Chapter 6 draws on diaries, memoirs, newspaper articles, and, in particular, on a personal correspondence between two young men in the late 1970s. In this chapter I argue that for some young people during that period, the meanings and ideals of communism and the influences, imaginations, and desires of the Imaginary West did not necessarily contradict each other; on the contrary, they could become rearticulated together in one discourse about a future society.

Chapter 7 focuses on the aesthetics of irony, the humor of the absurd, *anekdoty*, and absurdist pranks that emerged in the 1970s and 1980s as ubiquitous elements of everyday life. This chapter argues against the traditional analyses of these forms of humor as examples of resistance to the system or subversion of its announced goals. Rather, I argue that this aesthetic was one of the cultural principles through which the deterritorialized late Soviet culture was produced and reinterpreted.

The conclusion revisits the book's central set of questions: What paradoxes at the core of the late Soviet system made the collapse of that system appear to its citizens as both completely sudden and unexpected and yet completely unsurprising? On what kind of internal displacements at the level of discourse, knowledge, ideology, meaning, space and time were these paradoxes predicated? And how was knowledge produced, coded, circulated, received, and interpreted under these conditions?

Chapter 2
Hegemony of Form:
Stalin's Uncanny Paradigm Shift

Quests for my own word are in fact quests for a word that is not my
own, a word that is more than myself. . . . I myself can only be a character and not the primary author.
—Mikhail Bakhtin[1]

The only real people are the people who never existed, and if a novelist
is base enough to go to life for his personages he should at least pre-
tend that they are creations, and not boast of them as copies. The justifi-
cation of a character in a novel is not that other persons are what they
are, but that the author is what he is. Otherwise the novel is not a work
of art.
—Oscar Wilde[2]

Authoritative Discourse

The protagonist of a popular Soviet television comedy released in 1975,
The Irony of Fate (Ironiia sud'by), gets drunk with his buddies in a
Moscow sauna on New Year's Eve and by accident ends up on a plane to
Leningrad. Upon arriving in Leningrad, the drunk hero, still thinking he
is in Moscow, gives a taxi driver his Moscow address. A street of the
same name, Second Street of Builders (*Vtoraia ulitsa stroitelei*), exists in
Leningrad; as in Moscow, the street is located in a new district built in
the 1970s on the outskirts of the city. The big apartment blocks in the
district look identical to those in Moscow, as do the shops and bus stops.
Even the stairs, apartment numbers, and doors keys are the same. The
hero arrives at "his" address and lets himself into a Leningrad apartment,
confident that he has arrived at his Moscow home. The layout of the
apartment, the furniture, and the household appliances are all sufficiently
identical for the still-tipsy hero to confuse them for his possessions. He

[1] Bakhtin (1999, 149).
[2] Wilde (1930, 14).

lies down on the sofa to take a nap and wait for the New Year. A comedy of errors ensues, and after many amusing incidents and romantic songs, the protagonist falls in love with the woman who lives in the Leningrad apartment, and she with him.

This comedy makes apparent the standardization and predictability of Soviet life in the 1970s, when street names, architectural styles, door keys, and household possessions seemed completely interchangeable. These standardizations of everyday tools, references, and scenes were part of a larger standardization of discourse during the Soviet period, epitomized in the ubiquitous ideological slogans and posters that covered urban space. These signs were so common, identical, and predictable that they had become transparent to pedestrians—and were simply a "huge backdrop to daily life" (Havel 1986): even when traveling to an unfamiliar city one would see the same familiar and predictable slogans with only occasional regional variations. Party organizations controlled this Soviet authoritative discourse, and its circulation throughout everyday life in newspaper articles, speeches, propaganda billboards, school textbooks, urban monuments, street names, film newsreels, meetings, parades, elections, and so on.

This chapter places the period of Soviet late socialism in its historical context, providing a detailed analysis of how in the early 1950s the Soviet discursive regime experienced a major transformation that ultimately led to authoritative representation becoming highly normalized, fixed, and citational at all levels of structural organization. The analysis in this chapter focuses on language; however, the same normalization also occurred in non-linguistic registers of authoritative discourse. In authoritative language, this normalization took place at syntactic, morphological, semantic, narrative, stylistic, temporal, and other levels. The same shift toward increased standardization and citationality occurred in the authoritative discourse of visual propaganda and rituals: often it became more important to reproduce the precise form of ideological representations than to adhere to their constative meanings (that is, how they stated facts and described the world and whether these statements and descriptions were true). In other words, the performative dimension of authoritative discourse started to play a much greater role than its constative dimension. Eventually this precise reproduction of authoritative form enabled the creation of new, unanticipated meanings in everyday Soviet life and contributed to making the system at the same time monolithic and internally vulnerable to a sudden implosion. To understand how this normalized discourse came about and what forms it ultimately took, we need to start with its historical development.

Revolutionary Language

As in revolutionary France,[3] the revolutionary years in Russia (from around 1910 into the 1920s) were marked by dynamic experiments with language. A new telegraphic language of acronyms was created to name cultural movements, state institutions, and political concepts.[4] Many of the invented words, along with words borrowed from other languages, were so unusual and "not adapted to the sound and formal system of the Russian language" that, a linguist at the time observed, they were "appropriated with great difficulty by the people not accustomed to foreign phonetics" (Selishchev 1928, 166).[5]

That remarkably innovative language was not a chance development. Its unfamiliar sound was meant to serve as a powerful tool for revolutionizing consciousness. Various actors enthusiastically performed the linguistic experiments—from official institutions of the Bolshevik state, to political associations, to artistic, literary, and scholarly groups over whom the state had limited control. This revolutionary atmosphere of euphoria and experimentation influenced early Soviet linguistics (1917–1940s). The "New Theory of language," developed by archaeologist and ethnographer Nikolai Marr, shared the artistic and political avant-garde belief that old science had to be thrown away and replaced with new communist science and aesthetics that required a new way of seeing the world. Marr wrote in the 1920s:

> The New Theory of Language [requires] most of all and first of all a new linguistic thinking. One needs to unlearn the very basis of our relationship to language and its phenomena, and to learn how to think in a new way. Those who had the misfortune of being language specialists in the past and working in the old traditions of language science must move on to a whole new way of reasoning. . . . The New Theory of language requires one to cast away not only the old scientific [thinking], but also the old social thinking. (quoted in Alpatov 1991, 67)

According to the New Theory, language was a social phenomenon that needed to be analyzed in purely Marxist terms. Marr argued that all languages developed toward unification by means of revolutionary explosions and mixing, that languages change together with societies, from class to

[3] See, for example, Guilhaumou (1989); de Certeau (1975); Frey (1925).

[4] Typical examples included: *Narkompros* (for *Narodnyi kommissariat prosveshcheniia*, People's Commissariat of Enlightenment), *Proletkul't* (for *Proletarskaia kul'tura*, Department of Proletarian Culture), *Agitprop* (for *Agitatsiia i propaganda*, Department of Agitation and Propaganda).

[5] On the poor comprehension of the new language among newspaper readers, see also Gorham (2000, 138–39) and Ryazanova-Clarke and Wade (1999, 15–18).

classless, and that in the communist society all spoken languages would finally merge into one communist language (Marr 1977, 31).

Members of the poetic movement OBERIU (Society of Real Art), following politicians and scientists, wrote in their manifesto: "We are not only creators of new poetic language, but also creators of a new feeling of life" (Grigor'ev 1986, 243). Meanwhile, the Russian Futurist poets were working on a whole new "transrational language" (*zaumnyi iazyk*), creating new words, neologisms, and grammatical structures that broke with the conventions of common languages.[6] Linguist Roman Jakobson, who at that time was close to the Futurists, noted that the meaning of the poetry written in transrational language lay "both in its disruptive gesture . . . and in its formal reorganization of language" (Rudy 1997, xiii). The task the Russian Futurists had set for themselves was to create one new language of humanity that would replace all other human languages in the society of the future.[7] A central figure among the Russian Futurists, Velimir Khlebnikov, whom friends called the President of Planet Earth (*predsedatel' zemnogo shara*), wrote in the 1919 manifesto "Artists of the World!":

> The goal is to create a common written language shared by all the peoples of this third satellite of the Sun, to invent written symbols that can be understood and accepted by our entire star, populated as it is with human beings and lost here in the universe. You can see that such a task is worthy of the time we live in. . . . Let us hope that one single written language may henceforth accompany the longterm destinies of mankind and prove to be the new vortex that unites us, the new integrator of the human race (Khlebnikov 1987, 364–65).

Stalin the External "Master"

By the end of the 1920s, the cacophony of avant-garde experimentations in politics, science, and poetry, well suited to the spirit of revolution, increasingly became a problem for the Bolshevik leadership and its pressing tasks of managing culture and state-building (Gorham 2000, 140, 142; Smith 1998). These tasks required a centralized and rational management of all spheres of social and cultural life, including political discourse and specifically language. This is why in the late 1920s revolutionary discourse

---

[6] See Clark (1995, 40); Rudy (1997, xii); Jameson (1972); Lemon and Reis (1965). Clark translates *zaumnyi iazyk* as "trans-sense language."

[7] See Kruchenykh (1998a and 1998b). Similar linguistic experimentation went on among the Italian Futurists. See F. T. Marinetti's (1913) "Destruction of Syntax–Imagination without Strings–Words-in-Freedom" (Apollonio 1973, 95–106).

was put under increasingly strict and unifying party control and independent verbal experimentation came to a halt. The project was one of two revolutionary tasks that reflected the central paradox of Soviet ideology, to which I referred in chapter 1 as Lefort's paradox. This was the paradox between incommensurable goals and means—achieving complete liberation of social, cultural, and personal life by means of complete party control over social, cultural, and personal life. This paradox was inherent in the political, intellectual, and artistic avant-garde that embraced a contradictory ethos of experimentation and creativity, and at the same time of professional revolutionaries who gave themselves up to the vanguard party based on strict centralized discipline. The transition toward stricter and more unifying control in the late 1920s was in fact made easier by this inherent paradox. Although in the course of this transition the control by the party leadership over all forms of social and cultural life became stricter and more centralized, the party leadership itself retained the identity of the avant-garde political body and concomitant understanding of culture in general and of language in particular as "a tool of development and struggle" whose ultimate product would be a communist consciousness. According to this model of language, there existed a position outside of language from which one could verify how adequately that language represented reality and how it should be adjusted accordingly (Seriot 1985).

It was argued that "language, as any tool, need[ed] to be perfected, polished, and carefully protected from whatever kind of contamination and the slightest decay" (Kondakov 1941, 14). This is why the influence of the key premise of Marr's New Theory—according to which language as a class phenomenon could develop and improve toward communist language—continued to dominate Soviet linguistics for many years after Marr's death in the 1930s. The party authors continued arguing, not unlike avant-garde politicians and artists, that the language used in Bolshevik writing was superior to the language used by "bourgeois and opportunist authors" in its precision, the degree of its "scientific truthfulness" (*nauchnost'*), and its orientation to the future, and that the party's task was "to inoculate" (*privit'*) the readers with concrete vocabulary, phraseology, and slogans written in this superior language (Kondakov 1941, 117, 123).

According to Lefort, as discussed in chapter 1, the paradox of modern ideology can be concealed only by the figure of an external "master" who, being "presented as possessor of the knowledge of the rule allows the contradiction to appear through himself" (1986, 212–14).[8] The "master" legitimates ideological discourse from a position external to it,

---

[8] See also Bhabha (1990, 298).

publicly commenting on the correctness or incorrectness of ideological statements and evaluating them for precision against an external canon to which he has exclusive access. After the suppression of political factions and debates in the party, as well as of the artistic avant-garde, in the late 1920s and early 1930s, the position of the "master" external to ideological discourse came to focus in one point occupied by Stalin. Although this shift was not inevitable, it was not illogical either: as mentioned above, the very ethos of the avant-garde, both political and aesthetic, itself paved the way for this change.[9]

From this position external to discourse, Stalin in the 1930s and 1940s led the production of a widely circulating metadiscourse on ideological representations, in which linguistic formulations, literary texts, artistic products, and scientific theories were publicly evaluated as correct or incorrect from the point of view of the scientific Marxist-Leninist analysis of the world, and suggestions were made as to how to improve them accordingly.

For example, when the multivolume *History of the Civil War* was being prepared,[10] the editorial board headed by Stalin carefully reviewed the text, introducing as many as seven hundred corrections in the first volume alone, and providing extensive comments about these corrections that were widely published in the press. In their comments, the editorial board explained what was wrong with the descriptions of reality that needed to be corrected, and how their new formulations improved those descriptions. The stated goal of these corrections and comments was to achieve "conceptual clarity, theoretical precision, and political vigilance" of the discourse. The board made sure this metadiscourse was widely distributed: the corrections and comments were reprinted in Soviet newspapers, in reference and self-education books such as *Language of the Newspaper* (*Iazyk gazety*), which was published in 1941 for newspaper

[9] As Boris Groys remarks: "The avant-garde's dream of placing all art under direct party control to implement its program of life-building (that is, 'socialism in one country' as the true and consummate work of collective art) had now come true. The author of this program, however, was not Rodchenko or Maiakovsky, but Stalin, whose political power made him the heir to their artistic project" (Groys 1992, 34). Groys places the beginning of the "Stalinist phase" of Soviet history on April 23, 1932, when the Central Committee of the party adopted a decree that "disbanded all artistic groups and declared that all Soviet 'creative workers' would be organized according to profession in unitary 'creative unions' of artists, architects, and so on" (33). Although this argument privileges the artistic avant-garde over the political one, which is a problematic point, it captures the general discursive shift and its approximate date. Further, it would be wrong to suggest that Stalinism was an inevitable product of the Russian revolution, as Groys sometimes seems to suggest. Rather, Lefort's paradox of Soviet modernity allowed for the phenomenon of Stalinism.

[10] By Maxim Gorky. In fact, only volume 1 of the planned collection was published (Gorky et al. 1937).

employees and wider audiences with a printing of twenty-five thousand (Kondakov 1941, 122).

The initial draft of *History of the Civil War* described Alexandr Kerenskii (the former prime minister of the provisional government overthrown by the Bolshevik Revolution in 1917) as a "conciliator [*so-glashatel'*] and reconciler [*primiritel'*] of the bourgeoisie and the toilers." To this definition Stalin and the editorial board added one phrase—"in the interests of the bourgeoisie"—and accompanied this correction with the explanation that the new formula should help "all readers to realize the true role of this reconciler." Another passage in the *History* explained: "Lenin's slogan 'All Power to the Soviets!' called for a complete destruction [*razgrom*] of the bourgeois apparatus and the creation of a new, Soviet apparatus of power." Critiquing this formulation, the editorial board pointed out that Marx spoke not about the "destruction" but about the "breaking up" (*slom*) of the bourgeois machine. Therefore, Lenin's slogan should also be understood not in terms of complete destruction but in terms of breaking up the old system and recycling it into the construction of the new one (Kondakov 1941, 122–23).

During the preparation of the draft of the new Soviet constitution in the 1930s, the Soviet press similarly published a "nationwide discussion" (*vse-narodnoe obsuzhdenie*) of the proposed text, which, even if not a "real" discussion, nevertheless constituted a widely circulating metadiscourse on ideological language. In the name of Stalin, the Soviet press published responses to Soviet readers' suggestions about concrete formulations in the constitution, evaluating these suggestions and explaining why some of the suggested formulations could be accepted and others could not.[11] Again, in these evaluations, the final criterion was how precisely the linguistic forms described reality in accordance with external Marxist-Leninist canon. For example, in a number of letters published in *Pravda*, readers argued that Soviet society had changed: individual peasants had been transformed into Soviet collective farmers, and a whole new class of Soviet intelligentsia had emerged. For this reason, the letters suggested replacing an old formulation, which referred to the Soviet Union as "the socialist state of workers and peasants" (*sotsialisticheskoe gosudarstvo rabochikh i krest'ian*), with a new formulation that referred to it as "the state of toilers" (*gosudarstvo trudiashchikhsia*). Stalin publicly responded to these letters in a speech that was reprinted in the newspapers. Rejecting the suggested formulation, he explained that it ignored the Marxist-Leninist class analysis of reality: "It is well known that the Soviet

---

[11] Whether these suggestions were from real or imaginary readers matters less for the point we are discussing than that they constituted a metadiscourse circulating in newspapers and brochures that commented about and evaluated these suggestions.

society consists of two classes, the workers and the peasants. This is precisely what the first paragraph of the Constitution states. . . . One may ask, and what about the working intelligentsia? The intelligentsia has never been and cannot be a class; it is just a social group (*sotsial'naia prosloika*)."[12]

Stalin similarly edited the proposed text of the new Soviet national anthem, which had been written by the poet Sergei Mikhalkov and was chosen from among more than sixty entries.[13] Stalin's remarks on the occasion again showed concern for the ideological precision with which the song described reality. He suggested that Mikhalkov's phrase "noble union" (*soyuz blagorodnyi*), which referred to the Soviet Union, was unfortunate because the word "noble" implied not only "good" but also "the nobility class." This phrase was replaced with the word "unbreakable" (*nerushimyi*). Stalin also suggested that another formulation, which referred to the Soviet Union as created by the "people's will" (*volei narodnoi*), was problematic since it was reminiscent of "People's Will" (*Narodnaia volia*), the name of a late nineteenth-century terrorist revolutionary organization. The phrase was replaced with "the will of the peoples" (*volei narodov*).[14]

This metadiscourse originated from a position external to authoritative language. From this position, the metadiscourse evaluated and calibrated authoritative language against an independent external "canon" of Marxist-Leninist dogma, knowledge (or interpretation) of which was possessed by the "master" (Stalin), who stood outside discourse.[15] In 1935, reflecting Stalin's exclusive external position vis-à-vis language, the chairman of the Central Executive Committee of the USSR, Mikhail Kalinin announced in a speech published in the newspaper *Komsomol'skaia pravda*: "If you asked me who knows the Russian language better than anyone else, I would answer, "Stalin." We must learn from him the economy, lucidity, and crystal purity of language."[16] Writer

[12] Stalin's speech at the Extraordinary VIII All-Union Congress of Soviets, (November 25, 1936, quoted in Kondakov 1941, 126).

[13] The music for the anthem was composed by Alexandr Alexandrov.

[14] From a televised interview with Sergei Mikhalkov on the Russian television channel NTV, June 30, 1998.

[15] Stalin also occupied the same position of external "master" vis-à-vis various other genres of Soviet ideological, scientific, and artistic discourse, from agriculture and genetics to physics and chemistry, and to music and cinema. For example, Stalin provided critical comments on how the second part of Sergei Eisenstein's film *Ivan the Terrible* should be changed so that it would interpret history in more precise ideological terms. (Eisenstein describes Stalin's instructions in his diary; see Bergan (1997).

[16] "Safeguard and learn the great Russian language" [*Beregite i izuchaite velikii russkii iazyk*], *Komsomolskaia pravda*, July 2, 1946, p. 1. See also Kalinin (1935) and Blinov (1948, 15).

Maxim Gorky in a private letter to Stalin suggested that his writing represented "a model of proper writing" and requested a piece for the journal *Literary Training* (*Literaturnaia ucheba*) (Gorham 2000, 149).

Stalin's Paradigm Shift

In 1950, it was from this position of "master" external to authoritative discourse that Stalin launched a major paradigm shift in how authoritative discourse was to be evaluated for precision. Ironically, that shift eventually undermined the very possibility of having this external position and the public metadiscourse originating from it.

Stalin launched this intervention in many spheres of intellectual, scientific, political, and aesthetic discourse. One of the important examples was Stalin's intervention in linguistics. It began with a June 1950 *Pravda* article, where he critiqued Marr's New Theory of language as idealist and vulgar Marxism: "Marr got himself into a muddle and put linguistics into a muddle. Soviet linguistics cannot be advanced on the basis of an incorrect formula" (Stalin 1950a).[17] He also attacked all other vulgar Marxist models of language that posited it as either a tool of production or a superstructure. Following this initial article, Stalin provided further public clarifications of his position in response to readers' letters. Soon all these texts came out in book form (Stalin 1950d). Among the texts published in this book was an exchange between Stalin and a reader on the question of why and how language is distinct both from the "superstructure" and the "base." Stalin argued that despite the recent changes in the superstructure in Russian society after the revolution, the Russian language had remained the same: "In the course of the past thirty years, the old, capitalist base has been eliminated in Russia and a new, socialist base built. Correspondingly, the superstructure on the capitalist base has been eliminated and a new superstructure created corresponding to the socialist base. The old political, legal, and other institutions, consequently, have been supplanted by new, socialist institutions. But in spite of this the Russian language has remained basically what it was before the October Revolution" (Stalin 1950b). Arguing that language was also different from the base, Stalin had also written: "[T]here is a profound difference between language and tools of production [base]" because "tools of production create material goods, while language creates nothing or 'creates' only words. . . . If language could create material goods then chatterers would be the richest people in the world" (Stalin 1950b).

---

[17] See also Gray (1993, 27); Gorham (2000, 140, 142); Slezkine (1996, 842); Clark (1995, 201–23); Medvedev (1997).

Following these comments was a letter from a *Pravda* reader, saying: "Your [June 1950] article convincingly shows that language is neither the base nor the superstructure. Would it be right to regard language as a phenomenon characteristic of both the base and the superstructure, or would it be more correct to regard language as an intermediate phenomenon?" To this Stalin publicly replied that although language exists socially and therefore necessarily becomes reflected in the base and the superstructure, it is nevertheless an independent objective phenomenon that "cannot be included either in the category of bases or in the category of superstructures. Nor can it be included in the category of 'intermediate' phenomena between the base and the superstructure, for such 'intermediate' phenomena do not exist" (Stalin 1950b). Language, Stalin went on to say, was outside the whole dialectic of base and superstructure and possessed unique "specific features" unaccounted for by this dialectic. These specific features enabled language to serve "society as a means of intercourse between people, as a means for exchanging thoughts in society, as a means enabling people to understand one another and to coordinate joint work in all spheres of human activity" (Stalin 1950b).

In his original article on June 20, Stalin argued that the "specific features" of language reflected facts of objective reality akin to biology and geometry, which is why the grammar of language did not simply change with every transformation of the base and the superstructure, but was "the outcome of a process of abstraction performed by the human mind over a long period of time" (Stalin 1950a). Stalin expanded this idea further on August 2: "I insist that thought can appear only on the basis of language material, that for people who know a language there can be no naked thought that is disconnected from language material." It was precisely because of the objective nature of language that language could be investigated scientifically; if language did not reflect objective reality, the science of "linguistics would lose its right to independent existence" (Stalin 1950c). Two implications followed from Stalin's intervention into the science of language. Since language was not part of the superstructure, language could not automatically change in the revolutionary leaps promised by Marr. And, since language was not a tool of production, its straightforward political manipulation was not the way to produce a communist consciousness. Instead, Stalin insisted, Soviet linguistics needed to study the "objective scientific laws" that governed a much deeper relationship between the structure of language, evolution, cognition, psychology, and biology.

Stalin's intervention was the logical conclusion of a broader campaign to eradicate the remnants of idealist avant-garde thinking in science and aesthetics and to replace them with the "realism" of objective scientific laws. The shift in methodological perspective resulting from this campaign was reflected in a new mode of determining the *nauchnost'* (scientific truthfulness) of all scientific investigations. Earlier, in the 1930s, the *nauchnost'* of a theory was closely associated with the *partiinost'* (consistency of one's thinking with the party worldview) of a scientist; but now *nauchnost'* was associated with "objective scientific laws."

This shift took place in all scientific and aesthetic fields freeing them "from an excessive economic determinism" (Clark 1995, 221). For example, in 1948, commenting on a draft of Lyssenko's speech that argued for a class-based nature of all science, including genetics, Stalin, who had previously supported Lyssenko, wrote in the margins: "Ha-ha-ha!!! And what about mathematics? And what about Darwinism?" (Rossianov 1993, 443; Joravsky 1970). In 1948, Stalin's Minister of Culture Andrei Zhdanov attacked the Soviet composers Prokofiev and Shostakovich for writing music that was too experimental, "unharmonious," and "unmelodious" and that violated "the fundamental physiology of normal human hearing," disturbing "the balance of mental and physiological functions." It was necessary, argued Zhdanov, to develop music based on objective scientific laws of human nature (Zhdanov 1950, 74). In 1952, appropriating Stalin's critique of language as a new program for investigation, the newly founded journal *Voprosy iazykoznaniia* (*Issues of Linguistics*) appealed in its first issue for a thorough "renovation and reconstruction" of Soviet linguistics on the basis of objective scientific laws: "Soviet linguists have not yet closely approached some crucial problems in the study of language, have not yet begun its concrete and profound Marxist investigation. These issues concern the research on the connection between language and thought . . . the connection between the development of thought and the perfection of the grammatical order of language."

These critical campaigns marked a shift from the model of discourse based on the publicly circulating subjective knowledge of a "master" who was located outside discourse and calibrated it against an independent "canon" toward a model based on "objective scientific laws" that were not known in advance, not controlled by anyone exclusively, and therefore did not form any external canon. This shift meant that there was no longer any external discursive location from which a metadiscourse on ideological precision could originate. This metadiscourse therefore could no longer exist.

Stalin's intervention, ironically, had undermined the very position external to discourse from which he had launched this intervention. In 1956, three years after Stalin's death, Khrushchev pushed this transformation even further by publicly denouncing Stalin's cult of personality, which finalized the destruction of any location external to authoritative discourse. Lefort's "master," located outside authoritative discourse ceased

46

to exist. No one could any longer have an exclusive access to the external canon of the dogma. This shift reopened Lefort's paradox at the core of Soviet ideology, leading to a major transformation of the Soviet discursive and cultural regime. With this shift the epoch of late socialism began.

The Normalization of Language

The disappearance of the metadiscourse on ideology affected all spheres of cultural production in the Soviet Union. It had a particularly important impact on the nature of ideological language and ritual. The processes of composing, editing, and discussing party documents and texts became increasingly hidden from public view, remaining within the confines of the Central Committee (hereafter CC) and local Party committees. "Specialists in ideological linguistics," the Soviet linguist Igor Kliamkin later wrote, began in the late 1950s to "discuss their professional problems behind closed doors" (quoted in Han-Pira 1991, 21). The only publicly visible positions remained those of the enunciators of authoritative language, such as local secretaries of the party or Komsomol, who tried to repeat the central model of this language but did not engage in a discussion or evaluation of it in front of their audiences or readers.

Since there was no longer any unambiguous and uniquely explained external canon against which to calibrate one's own texts for ideological precision, what constituted the "norm" of that language became increasingly unknowable, and any new text could potentially be read as a "deviation." The party secretaries and CC speechwriters could only look to one another's texts to normalize their own. As a result, in the late 1950s and early 1960s, this discourse experienced progressive normalization, with the different texts written in it sounding increasingly like excerpts from one text. Party speeches and documents written in the CC were increasingly subjected to endless editing, behind closed doors, to produce texts that minimized the subjective stamp of the author and were preferably identical in style and structure to texts previously written by others; this led to a progressive uniformity, anonymity, and predictability of authoritative language. These conditions of production brought about a shift in the nature of discourse enunciated by the party leadership, local party secretaries, newspaper editors, and others involved in the production of authoritative texts. This discourse became based on an implicit understanding that the meaning of authoritative texts depended on the objective scientific laws of language and was independent of anyone's subjective opinion.

47

This understanding was close to the so-called "semantic model" of language, according to which the literal meaning of texts is considered to be directly linked to linguistic form and independent of context. In various institutional contexts where this model of language is dominant (e.g., in literary education in many school systems throughout the world), "literacy" is treated as the technical skill of uncovering literal meanings contained within texts—a skill that can be measured "in context-independent, quantifiable fashion" (Mertz 1996, 232). When this implicit understanding came to dominance in Soviet authoritative language, what we may call "ideological literacy" came to be treated in the party and Komsomol institutions as the technical skill of reproducing the precise passages and structures of that language in one's texts and speeches, paying particular attention to the linguistic form, and, unlike in the past, not engaging in any public discussions of how these texts might be interpreted by different audiences and in different contexts.

According to Fyodor Burlatskii, a consultant and speechwriter in the CC of Khrushchev and later Brezhnev, in the late 1950s and early 1960s "the main problem for the new leaders, such as Andropov, Ponamaryov, and other CC secretaries, was not to commit a political mistake by writing something irregular," something that did not fit the existing model. The dominant objective was to produce texts in which "one was unable to question any phrase" or to notice "a single step sideways from the norm" (*nikakogo otstupleniia ot normy*).[18] In order to not transgress the norm, one needed to repeat the forms of language that had already been in wide use in authoritative texts. This shift was progressive throughout the 1960s:

> When Khrushchev made a speech he always read it from the written text. Only occasionally would he say: "And now allow me to diverge from the text" [*a teper' pozvol'te mne otoiti ot teksta*]. He would start speaking in the working class language that he learned during the party discussions of the early 1930s. . . . However, he realized well that this was a divergence from the norm and tried not to overuse it. . . . As for Brezhnev, he never diverged [from the text]. He was anxious not to step outside the limits of the accepted norm, not to repeat the precise party language.[19]

Producers of party texts were increasingly preoccupied with minimizing one's authorial voice and making them sound like texts produced earlier. A joke from that era reflects this shift. General Secretary Brezhnev, along with other CC members, is at a Soviet art exhibition. After

[18] Author interview.
[19] Ibid.

the tour, the CC members gather around Brezhnev to hear what he thinks. Brezhnev waits for a minute and then declares: "Very interesting. But let us hear what they think at the top."

Most texts at the CC were now written and edited collectively, in the hermetically sealed spaces of the CC departments. One of the fiercest editors was Mikhail Suslov, the secretary of ideology. In the phrase "Marxism-Leninism and proletariat internationalism," Suslov insisted on replacing the conjunction "and" with a dash because, he said, "Marxism-Leninism already is proletariat internationalism" and "opposing one to the other" by the use of "and" would be incorrect (Burlatskii 1988, 188). Such editing remarks were not made public. The phrase with the dash was fixed, and was repeated in various texts without further discussion. Similar editing went on behind the doors of key publications of the CC. In an attempt to avoid anything that could be seen as not following the norm the editors of the journal *Kommunist* "replaced unusual words with the usual ones, squeezed out any literariness [*literaturshchina*], and combined several sentences into one paragraph-long sentence by adding commas and obliterating verbs."[20] Another CC secretary, Yurii Andropov, made his consultants rewrite speeches an endless number of times, and at the final stage of editing:

> would himself sit at the head of the table with all the consultants, four or six of us, around him. He liked to have many consultants together. We would edit the final version. He would read a phrase aloud and say: "Something is wrong here. We need to find a different formulation." Someone would suggest a word. He would write it down. Then another person would suggest another word. Then another person. We rewrote the speech collectively. Then the text was returned to the typist. Then Andropov read it to us again, then again. We kept changing the formulations until they sounded right.[21]

Through the process of collective writing, mutual imitation, and regularized editing, individual styles were evened out and personal accountability for texts minimized. On the structural level, different instances of authoritative language were becoming more alike and more predictable. The CC speechwriters used a slang term for the new style of composition, calling it "block-writing" (*blochnoe pis'mo*) because relatively fixed "blocks" of discourse reproduced from text to text now "consisted not only of single phrases but also of whole paragraphs." The narrative structure of the texts was becoming circular, to the point that many formulaic speeches and addresses could be read "top to bottom and bottom to top with similar

---

[20] Ibid.
[21] Ibid.

results."[22] Attempts among the leadership to avoid any ambiguity in their texts led not only to an increasing normalization of linguistic structure but also pushed this new norm toward increasing unwieldiness. Sentences became longer, the number of verbs diminished, nouns were increasingly strung into chains to form long noun phrases, modifiers became multiple and employed superlative degrees, and so on (see below). This shift away from verbs and toward more cumbersome formalized constructions was crucial, as we will explore shortly. Soviet authoritative language was becoming increasingly citational and circular at all levels of structure (syntax, morphology, narrative, etc.) and in all contexts. Every new text in this genre functioned as a citation of prior ones at all these structural levels, adding to the accumulated authority and immutability of this discourse as a whole.

Although any authoritative language, political or religious, contains many formulaic structures, clichéd "sound bites," and ritualized features—and is therefore highly citational—the new authoritative language of late socialism had acquired certain unique characteristics. This language had become what I term *hypernormalized*—that is, the process of its normalization did not simply affect all levels of linguistic, textual, and narrative structure but also became an end in itself, resulting in fixed and cumbersome forms of language that were often neither interpreted nor easily interpretable at the level of constative meaning. This shift to the hypernormalized language in which the constative dimension was increasingly being unanchored is key for our understanding of late socialism.

Monosemic Language

Linguistic studies tried to provide a scientific basis for the primacy of this new hypernormalized form of language throughout the period between the 1960s and the early 1980s. In 1982, the journal *Issues of Linguistics* published an article that compared "lexical meaning" in Russian and bourgeois political discourses. In line with the semantic model of language, the author, a professional linguist, argued that "in the consciousness of the native speakers of Russian" political terms had lost their polysemic (multiple) meanings and had become monosemic—that is, they conveyed meanings that were "ideologically bound" (*ideologicheski sviazanny*) to the single Marxist-Leninist reality in all contexts of Soviet life. Because of this link to one predetermined context, Russian political language was ostensibly freed from ambiguity and indeterminacy and was instead furnished with clear literal meanings. Conversely, bourgeois political languages were polysemic: political terms in English, French, and

[22] Ibid.

German conveyed multiple and unfixed meanings that were not ideologically bound to any single form of reality, because bourgeois life was divided between multiple contexts inhabited by antagonistic class ideologies (Kriuchkova 1982, 30–31). This disparity in the structure of meaning between Soviet Russian and foreign languages, argued the author, challenged Soviet interpreters from foreign languages with "a dual task: not only to translate terms . . . but also to reflect adequately their ideological substance" (32). For this reason, interpreters were advised to use special indexical markers—such as quotation marks, the term "so-called," and so forth—that would signal to Soviet readers that the foreign phrases were not used in the proper monosemic sense "accepted in our literature" (32).

A reference book entitled *A Short Dictionary of Political, Economic, and Technical Terms*, addressing "the young reader, Komsomol propagandist, agitator, journalist, and all those who are engaged in political self-education," offered a list of five hundred monosemic phrases from "political, economic, and technical" spheres of life, describing in minute detail their fixed ideologically bound meanings. This monosemic phraseology varied from single words to long phrases, all furnished with strikingly precise meanings. Entries starting with the letter (in Russian) "A" included: *absenteeism* (*absenteizm*), described as "mass evasion of the voters of bourgeois countries from taking part in parliamentary and other elections"; *aggression* (*agressiia*), the "attack of one or several imperialist states on another country or countries"; *anticommunism* (*antikommunizm*), "the main politico-ideological weapon of imperialism in the contemporary epoch"; and even such complex blocks as *"absolute impoverishment* (*absoliutnoe obnishchanie*) of proletariat,*"* described as the plight of the working class in capitalist countries (Borodin 1962, 5, 12).[23] These scientific and educational materials contributed to hypernormalizing the linguistic form and to the growing understanding that, as long as one reproduced the precise forms of language, the correctness of the meanings conveyed was guaranteed.

The Pragmatic Model

Under these conditions, the form of authoritative texts became increasingly more important than concerns about the meanings corresponding to that form.

[23] Published instructions on monosemic language were also common in China. As late as 1992, the Central Propaganda Department of the Chinese Communist Party was publishing a weekly bulletin, *Propaganda Vocabulary Must Be Accurate*, and the New China News Agency published brochures for Party propagandists entitled *Instructions on Terminology* (Schoenhals 1992, 8–9).

A story told by Soviet linguist Eric Han-Pira illustrates how the shift to fixed form and uncoupled meaning of authoritative language manifested itself in the CC's management of discourse. For many years the Soviet media, when announcing the funeral ceremonies of the most important figures of the party and the state, used a cliché formulation: "buried on Red Square by the Kremlin wall" (*pokhoronen na Krasnoi ploshchadi u kremlëvskoi steny*). Since this cliché was frequently repeated, Soviet citizens knew it by heart. In the 1960s, however, because of a lack of space, fewer and fewer dignitaries were still actually buried by the Kremlin wall; most were cremated, and urns with their ashes were placed in niches inside the wall itself. By that time, the ritual was being televised and millions of Soviet viewers could see that the linguistic formulation no longer provided a literal description of the ritual. This incongruity eventually compelled fifteen professors of linguistics from the Russian Language Institute of the Soviet Academy of Sciences to write a letter to the CC suggesting that the phrase be modified to better represent the current reality: the new phrase would say: "The urn with ashes was placed in the Kremlin wall" (*urna s prakhom byla ustanovlena v kremlëvskoi stene*). Several weeks later, a representative of the CC phoned the Russian Language Institute and explained that the CC leadership had discussed the linguists' suggestion and decided to decline it, keeping the original formulation. No reason was given (Han-Pira 1991, 21). It seemed that to the CC it was more important that the form of authoritative representation remain stable and immutable rather than that it represent reality literally.

Innumerable brochures for party propagandists, newspaper editors, and common citizens continued to stress, as in the past, the importance of composing texts and speaking the language that conveyed precise "party-spirited" [*partiinye*] meanings (Lukashanets 1988, 171). However, what constituted party-spirited meanings of linguistic formulations was no longer publicly discussed; instead it was now claimed that precise meanings were guaranteed by the exact replication of the *form* from already existing party texts. The 1969 *Reference Book for the Secretary of a Primary Party Organization* (*Spravochnik sekretaria pervichnoi partiinoi organizatsii*) criticized those secretaries and propagandists who still allowed themselves to speculate on ideological issues *in their own terms*, an act that invariably led them to slip into "superficial pseudo-scientific language" (Kravchenko 1969, 55). A 1979 booklet for local political lecturers (*politinformatory*) emphasized that these lecturers must mediate "to the masses the truthful word of the party," avoiding their own reformulations or speculations (Erastov 1979). A 1975 book urged lecturers to be creative but explained that creativity in one's discourse amounted to the technical aspects of delivery, such as loudness of voice, eye contact, gesticulation, and occasional humor (Leont'ev et al. 1975).

A book published before the hypernormalization of authoritative language—the aforementioned *Language of the Newspaper* (Kondakov 1941)—critiqued concrete ideological formulations made by local party committees, explaining what was right or wrong about them and how they could be improved. By contrast, a comparable book published after the change with a printing of twenty thousand—*How the Newspaper Is Made* (Grebnev 1967)—did not question any of the local party formulations and, in fact, explicitly stressed that a newspaper's task was to avoid any public critique of the local party secretary's discourse. The book gave an example of a "grave mistake" committed by the editor of a local newspaper in a northern region, *Za novyi sever* (*For the New North*), who published a polemical exchange on an ideological topic between the newspaper's editorial board and the region's party *obkom* (regional committee). The editor's mistake was not that he disagreed with the opinion of the local party committee, but that he made the discussion public. If the editor disagreed with a party committee's view, the book explained, it was "the editor's duty" to provide his critique "at the meeting of the party committee, and, if needed, [to] address a higher party body, all the way up to the Central Committee of the Communist Party of the Soviet Union [CPSU]," always keeping this critique within the spaces of the party committees, away from public venues such as newspapers (Grebnev 1967, 29).

With increasing emphasis on the replication of form, what meanings or functions concrete texts and slogans had in what contexts was becoming increasingly unpredictable; meaning was sliding in unanticipated directions. In other words, this discourse was experiencing the performative shift I described in chapter 1: its performative dimension (reproduction of conventionalized and ritualized forms) was becoming more important than the constative dimension (constative meanings which might be associated with these forms). The implicit model of language that underlay this production of texts now shifted further toward the so-called "pragmatic model" of language, according to which the same text may have multiple meanings depending on how one chooses to link it to different contexts and other texts; under this model, the same formulation can mean different things in different readings. A version of the pragmatic model of language is practiced, for example, in Anglo-American legal discourse, where in the context of a hearing, legal adversaries often argue for different interpretations of the same text or document, by linking it to different previous cases, precedents, pieces of evidence, and so on (Mertz 1996, 234–35). What distinguished this model in the Soviet context, however, was the fact that language was not simply fixed in concrete texts, as in the example of legal practice, but was normalized across the whole authoritative genre of Soviet discourse. With the increasing normalization of authoritative discourse, and the decoupling of form from meaning, even shifts in party policy could be represented by the same formulations. For example, Mikhail Suslov, Secretary of Ideology at the politburo, often used identical quotations from Lenin's texts to support different ideological decisions, including ideological decisions that might otherwise seem to contradict one another. For this purpose, Suslov had a personal collection of thousands of quotations from Lenin for all occasions, written on index cards and located in file cabinets in his office. Choosing a quotation that looked appropriate for a given argument, Suslov would insert it into the text, thereby presenting the argument for a given ideological decision in terms of continuity with the past rather than in terms of change (Burlatskii 1988, 189).

Under the new conditions, local producers of ideological texts also preferred to replicate ideological formulations word for word, even when some formulations appeared erroneous. Occasionally, this relationship between form and meaning could lead to paradoxical and comical situations. Several former propaganda artists recalled that in the early 1980s, KZhOI (The Leningrad Workshop of Visual Art and Design), which produced visual propaganda material for the decoration of urban spaces, received a party circular with the text of a slogan that had to be painted and mounted on a facade in the city center for the occasion of the November 7 (Revolution Day) celebrations. The text contained a mistake—a comma was in the wrong place, rendering the slogan nonsensical. Although the workshop artists noticed the mistake, they were not prepared to edit the text unless the change was authorized by higher party organizations. When the chief artist of the workshop went to the local party *raikom* (district committee) to ask for authorization to make the change, none of the secretaries wanted to authorize the change—although in person they agreed it was a mistake—because the formulation had originated in the *gorkom* (city committee). The importance of replicating existing language forms was at these local levels of the hierarchy more compelling than the concerns about the literal meaning being conveyed.[24]

The Discourse of Visual Propaganda and Rituals

The normalization of form also progressed in nonlinguistic genres of authoritative discourse such as visual propaganda and political rituals. The discourse of visual propaganda on the streets included portraits

---

[24] Author's interview with former KZhOI artists. Several artists recalled this story. It may in fact be apocryphal; however, it captures well the doubts and concerns they had to face reproducing slogans and following instructions.

and monuments of Lenin and Marx, photographs of politburo members, installations and constructions with hammers and sickles, billboards with pictures of the district's best workers, banners with slogans, posters, appeals, pledges, and more. In the early postrevolutionary years, artistic groups and political organizations experimented with visual propaganda as they did with language (Bonnell 1997; Stites 1989). Beginning in the late 1920s, visual propaganda came under increasingly strict party control, accompanied by a public metadiscourse discussing and evaluating the work of artists, sculptors, architects, filmmakers, and so on.

As with authoritative language, from the 1950s on the form and style of visual propaganda became increasingly standardized and centralized. An example of this development was the image of Lenin. In the late 1960s, during the campaign for the preparation for Lenin's one hundredth birthday in 1970, the artists of KZhOI were informed of a circular sent from the CC in Moscow saying that very few people still remembered Lenin personally and therefore he had to be depicted "more as a heroic symbol than a common man."[25] Lenin was subsequently portrayed as a younger, taller, and more muscular figure, in a more fixed and repeatable style, in fewer contexts and poses, with fewer painting and sculpting techniques, materials, colors, and textures, and with fixed elements of visual structure from one representation to the next.

The new style became normalized, the number of possible visual representations of Lenin diminished, and the newly formalized images were assigned an official name in the artistic discourse: "Our Il'ich" (*Nash Il'ich*)—Lenin as a common person; "Squinting Lenin" (*Lenin s prishchurom*)—a witty Lenin; "Lenin with children" (*Lenin i deti*)—a domestic, kind Lenin; "Lenin the Leader" (*Lenin vozhd'*)—a superhuman Lenin; and "Lenin in the underground" (*Lenin v podpol'e*)—a revolutionary Lenin. Because of the limited number and the formulaic style of these images, artists also referred to them among themselves in professional jargon, using the numbers these clichés were assigned: "One could hear: 'I just finished a fiver [*piaterochku*].' There were also two images of Lenin writing: 'Lenin in his office,' known as a sixer [*shestërka*], and 'Lenin in a green office,'[26] known as a sevener [*semërka*]. In the sixer he is sitting on a chair and in the sevener on a tree stump."[27]

Artists stocked normalized images of Lenin in their studios to have enough material to "quote" from. This guaranteed that the norm was

[25] Author interviews with artists.
[26] *V zelenom kabinete*—hiding from the tsarist police in a forest near Razliv.
[27] Author interviews with KZhOI and district artists.

reproduced, minimizing the stamp of the artist's personal style, but it speeded up the process of painting and that translated into higher pay. Artists developed painting techniques that can be called "block-painting," by analogy with the "block-writing" developed by speech-writers, that included exact replication of visual elements, forms, designs, colors, styles, and textures across different contexts. According to Misha, a KZhOI artist: "The objects that were most in demand among artists were the death mask of Lenin and a cast of his head. Every respectable artist who had anything to do with ideology tried to obtain them through personal contacts at the factory of monuments [skul'pturnyi kombinat]. They were endlessly replicated." Lenin's death mask and head cast were not ordinary ideological images, but semiotic "indexes" that pointed to one of the key organizing concepts of Soviet ideology, its master signifier "Lenin." They pointed to his actual physical body that could be observed in the mausoleum at the center of the state in Red Square. Such ideological images constituted an important indexical trace of Lenin's physical body throughout the Soviet symbolic order; the importance of this trace will become evident gradually in this and the following chapters.

Propaganda painting, like speechwriting, became more collective and anonymous, and was increasingly organized like an assembly line. Yurii, a district artist, explains: "There was a great demand for the portraits of Lenin for different institutes, plants, schools, and so forth. So, it was common for artists to draw five or six Lenin portraits simultaneously. First, canvases were mounted on frames and identical pencil sketches were made on all of them, the next day the general outline drawing [ob-shchaia propiska] was made on each canvas, the day after Lenin's faces were worked on, then his suits, then his ties, and so on." Such techniques further narrowed the specialization of artists not only to certain types of Lenin portraits but also to concrete details of his image: one artist specialized in painting the general outlines of Lenin's face, another one was a master of Lenin's nose and ears, the third painted his suit and tie, and so on.

Mikhail described the brigade of artists working in the studios of Leningrad Chief Artist Lastochkin: they "were all the best professionals, and could draw or sculpt any image of Lenin with their eyes closed. To entertain themselves, they sometimes made bets to see who could draw better from memory a certain version of Lenin's head, nose, or left ear from any angle." The same assembly-line method was used to paint large portraits of politburo members. The fixed styles and techniques used for these portraits remained practically identical over the years, with only slight quantitative, but not qualitative, changes—for example, the number of medals on Brezhnev's suit, or a slight aging of his face every few years. Marta, an instructor on ideology for a Leningrad raikom, explains: "Every time Brezhnev was awarded a new order I had to make sure that my district artists, working overnight, added that order on all his portraits in the district." The style of Brezhnev's portraits, however, remained the same. Any changes to his images were done at night, making the process of change practically invisible to most people. Even though the presence of an additional medal on Brezhnev's suit was publicly known, this fact was symbolically represented in terms of immutability rather than change, which was an example of the hypernormalization of this authoritative symbol. Visual normalization also affected the depiction of more generic figures: the features, expressions, and poses of Soviet people on propaganda posters, and the colors and techniques in which they were depicted, became increasingly normalized, simplified (with fewer colors, shadows, facial expressions, angles, and details), and citational between images and contexts.

These normalized linguistic and visual registers of authoritative discourse in cities were organized into a unified interdiscursive system, a "hegemony of representation" (Yurchak 1997a), with slogans falling into three categories in relation to the urban space they inhabited. Slogans in all three categories were linked structurally and thematically, with differences only in the scale of the references they made. The first category included the most general and context-independent slogans, such as: "The People and Party Are United!" (*Narod i partiia ediny!*), "Glory to the CPSU!" (*Slava KPSS!*), "Forward to the Victory of Communism!" (*Vperëd k pobede kommunizma!*), and so on. The second category included more time- and context-specific slogans, such as: "Bring the decisions of the XXVIIth Congress of the CPSU to Life!" (*Pretvorim resheniia XXVII-go s"ezda KPSS v zhizn'!*), "Long Live May First!" (*Da zdravstvuet pervomai!*), or "Let's Commemorate the One Hundredth Anniversary of V. I. Lenin with New Labor Victories!" (*Otmetim stoletnii iubilei V. I. Lenina novymi trudovymi pobedami!*). The third category included the more localized and contextualized slogans that hung in factories, stadiums, and schools; for example, "Workers of the Kirov plant, strengthen the friendship between peoples!" (*Trudiashchiesia Kirovskogo zavoda, krepite druzhbu mezhdu narodami!*) or "Sportsmen of Leningrad, hold higher the banner of Soviet sport!" (*Sportsmeny Leningrada, vyshe znamia sovetskogo sporta!*).

According to artist Misha, the first category of slogans hung on the facades of buildings and were the most public, addressing everyone; their number in a district depended on the "quotient of ideological density" (*koeffitsient ideologicheskoi plotnosti*)—approximate number of slogans, posters, portraits per unit of space (e.g., a hundred meters of the street)—assigned to the district. In city centers it was highest and taken as 1.0;

other areas were assigned quotients in relation to this maximum. Near the seat of Soviet government, on Moscow's Red Square, it was 1.1. In Leningrad, the most important ideological space was Palace Square—the site of the May Day and Revolution Day parades.

Other major ideological sites in every city included central squares and thoroughfares (*magistrali*) used by government cars;[28] these were also assigned individual ideological quotients with each thoroughfare looking similar to the others in terms of the density and the type of posters and slogans hung along it. Which portraits, slogans, and billboards decorated these sites was determined by the Department of Ideology at the party gorkom; but the CC provided the list of possible types of visuals and precise texts of slogans. The rest of the district around these special sites the propaganda artists decorated themselves, using the district "propaganda map" (*karta nagliadnoi agitatsii*) and again the list of precise slogans circulated by the CC. According to Marta, the instructor on ideology mentioned earlier, all raikom instructors in the city knew the list of possible slogans and also which slogans were already hanging in the bordering district. They tried to coordinate their choice of slogans accordingly, to avoid blunt overlaps between messages, and to ensure continuity. If the slogan "Glory to Soviet Science!" was already hanging near the border between two districts, the artist of the other district would choose to hang another slogan from the list on his side of the border, for example, "Glory to Labor!"

The normalization and standardization of the visual form was also reflected in propaganda photographs and films. For decades, regional documentary film studios produced regular newsreels (*Kinokhronika*) about current events in the region. From the late 1960s, under the supervision of the local party committees, the visual style of the newsreels became more formulaic, and many "unusual" images were edited or cut out altogether. Increasingly, the same footage was used repeatedly in different newsreels to represent different events. These "blocks" of footage consisted of formulaic scenes—an audience clapping or voting in a large hall, crowds marching during May Day parades, agricultural work on collective farms, and so on. According to documentary filmmaker Yurii Zanin, of the St. Petersburg Documentary Film Studios, throughout the 1970s all winter newsreels from Leningrad incorporated identical footage filmed during the 1970 New Year celebration.[29]

Like visual and linguistic discourse, the discourse of public rituals also became increasingly standardized, following a unified and centrally

---

[28] In Leningrad these thoroughfares included Kirovskii Avenue, Nevsky Avenue, Moskovskii Avenue, and Moskovskoe Highway.

[29] Author interview.

orchestrated scheme. Until the late 1950s, public rituals for different occasions and in different places did not follow one centralized scheme and "had never been part of a sustained and general campaign" (Lane 1981, 3). But around that time, the Soviet state began standardizing and simplifying rituals all over the country. Civic rituals that had previously been designed and conducted by local social, cultural, and educational institutions became united into one centralized "system of rituals" run by the party. Rituals for different occasions were increasingly organized according to standardized scripts designed in the CC. Their structures became more formulaic, with whole "blocks" of ritualized practice replicated from one context and type of anniversary to the next (Lane 1981, 46–47; Aliev 1968, 5; Glebkin 1998, 130, 137). The newly standardized system of rituals included meetings, Lenin examinations, celebrations, May Day and Revolution Day parades, and so on.

The parades were meticulously planned and approved in a centralized and standardized fashion. The design of parades became more formalized and was prepared well in advance. As chief district artist Yurii explains: "Palace Square decorations were designed in minute detail. For each November 7 and May 1 parade the city artistic council prepared a detailed model of the square with tiny copies of each moving truck with mounted billboards and each marching column with slogans. . . . Each year the design for the square had to be approved in advance, at first by the Leningrad party gorkom and then by the ideology department of the Central Committee in Moscow."

With the simultaneous standardization and normalization of authoritative language, visual propaganda, and ritualized practice, the structure of large party and Komsomol meetings also became increasingly formulaic and predictable on all levels. Such meetings were meticulously planned in advance, minimizing any spontaneity. The organizers carefully planned the order of speakers at the meetings, texts that they would read, any "spontaneous" comments members of the audience were going to make, responses to these comments from the presidium, motions initiated by participants, votes and their results, and so on.

The Shift of Voice and Temporality

As noted above, with the increasing normalization of all forms of authoritative discourse, the performative dimension of that discourse began to play a greater role than its constative dimension. It became more important to participate in the execution of the ritualized acts and

59

reproduction of ritualized texts of this discourse than to attend to their constative meanings. There were two reasons for this: not participating in these acts at all could cause problems, and participating in them provided conditions for being engaged in many other actions and pursuits, not all of which had to follow the constative meanings of these rituals of ideology. *How* the discourse represented became more important than *what* it represented. This does not mean that meanings simply had become unimportant, or that everyday life became a series of automatic actions devoid of meaning. Quite the contrary, the performative replication of the precise forms of authoritative representation rendered the constative meanings associated with this representation unanchored, increasingly unpredictable, and open to new interpretations, enabling the emergence of new and unanticipated meanings, relations, and lifestyles in various contexts of everyday life.

Detailed exposition and analysis of the specific meanings that were being produced within Soviet life will be provided in subsequent chapters. But for now, to begin to understand how the form of authoritative language became fixed and replicated across contexts, we must first analyze the discursive principles according to which this hyper-normalized structure of authoritative language became organized. These principles can be grouped into two types: the transformation of the author's voice into the voice of a mediator of knowledge, rather than a creator of knowledge; and the shift of the temporality of discourse into the past. This meant that ultimately the discourse as a whole mediated knowledge as always already known rather than as new assertions. This made the authorial voices in this discourse less present in the texture of discourse and less exposed to potential scrutiny. To put it differently, the normalized principles of discourse contributed to the growing anonymity of the authorial voice and to ever greater normalization of texts.[30] These two central shifts were mapped onto all structural levels of discourse and language, including syntax, semantics, narrative structure, rhetorical organization, intertextuality, interdiscursivity, and so on. It is important to repeat that the ideological effects of these language forms cannot be inferred from the texts themselves; these effects will only become clear through the specific contexts of Soviet life in which they were produced and circulated.

---

[30] This process of increasing anonymity and citationality of discourse, under particular conditions of reproduction, can be described in the general terms formulated by Greg Urban: "The more discourse is overtly coded as nonpersonal, that is, not as something generated by the originator but as transmitted by him or her, and the less it is linked to a present context and circumstances, the more likely will the copier be to replicate it; hence, the more shareable it is" (1996, 40).

Citational Temporality

Authoritative language became citational during late socialism not only because it cited concrete previous texts and structures but, more generally, because it was built on a deep foundation of prior temporalities: all types of information, new and old, were presented as knowledge previously asserted and commonly known. The temporal organization anchored the rhetorical structure of this language, making it possible to convey new ideas and facts only by coding them in terms of prior ones. Through this anchoring the authorial voices of the producers of texts were transformed into the voices of mediators of preestablished knowledge. And conversely, by privileging the voice of the mediator of knowledge, those who reproduced instances of this discourse contributed to shifting its temporality into the past. The prior temporality was encoded into all structural levels of this hypernormalized language.

This model of language was based on a restricted repertoire of principles on the levels of syntax, semantics, morphology, lexicon, narrative structure, style, and so on. We will call these the generative principles of authoritative language to suggest that most ideological formulations and texts were generated according to these principles (by analogy with the concept of "generative process" used by the Russian formalists[31]). Any number of texts in the authoritative genre could be written by applying this set of discursive principles, making all instances of this language operate at the structural level as citations of one text. As with Bakhtin's authoritative discourse, every utterance in that genre of language was a "transmitted" version of another utterance, which existed before it in some prior, usually unnamed text (Bakhtin 1994, 342). The hypernormalized form of this language was not only predictable and citational but also increasingly cumbersome, leading to a notoriously "wooden" sound that gave it its popular slang name, "oak language" (*dubovyi iazyk*). Growing up during that period, members of the last Soviet generation became especially fluent in composing formulaic texts according to these generative principles, reproducing them in ritualized contexts, and reacting to them in ritualized ways—but without necessarily reverting to reading them "literally," in their constative dimension. These highly ritualized texts and discursive structures operated primarily in a performative dimension, as acts that enabled the participants to create meanings and engage in practices that went beyond the meanings and practices this discourse represented in its constative statements.

[31] See Bakhtin and Medvedev (1991). This concept is different from Noam Chomsky's use of the term "generative," which implies the innateness of certain rules.

Examples of this genre of texts were provided daily by Soviet central and regional papers, which had a total circulation of nearly 200 million in 1984.[32] A pivotal role in presenting examples of this discourse was played by the newspaper *Pravda*, an institution of the party's central committee, whose editor-in-chief attended weekly meetings of the CC secretariat and some politburo meetings (Roxburgh 1987, 60). *Pravda's* front page presented party resolutions, comments, and news written almost exclusively in the authoritative genre. Among the front-page texts, a daily leading article, a *peredovitsa*, occupied a special role. Collectively written by professional CC writers, never signed by any name, it provided a daily comment on a broad, abstract ideological theme, with titles ranging from "Under the Banner of May First" (*Pod znamenem pervomaia*) to "The Solidarity of the People of Labor" (*Solidarnost' liudei truda*) to "The Ideological Conviction of the Soviet Person" (*Ideinost' sovetskogo cheloveka*). The topics of the *peredovitsa* were decided in batches, at least two weeks in advance, in the CC (Roxburgh 1987, 80)—an arrangement which illustrates that the main task of these texts was to represent the permanence of authoritative representation of the world, rather than the unpredictability of current events.

In general, at the level of narrative structure, this discourse privileged references to past and future events, avoiding new assertions about the present and avoiding the voice of eyewitness accounts—that is, avoiding the voice of "authors."[33] Thus, even contemporary events were described as confirmations of previously established facts. This contributed to the shift toward prior temporality, and forms of knowledge that had been always-already established, again converting the voice of the author into one of mediator.

Let us consider, as an example, the leading article published in *Pravda* on July 1, 1977: "The Ideological Conviction of the Soviet Person" (see figure 2.1).[34] This article refers to the public "reactions to" (instead of "discussion of") a new Soviet constitution during the Brezhnev period. Earlier in this chapter we looked at a similar public discussion that took place on the pages of Soviet newspapers in 1938, when the text of the previous constitution, Stalin's, was being prepared. The differences between these two discursive events reveal the differences between the models of authoritative language in the two historical periods. The discussions in 1938 included published suggestions and formulations by individual readers and collectives (whether composed by readers or editors)

[32] In 1984, the Soviet Union published 8,327 daily and weekly newspapers, with a total circulation of 185,275,000, and 1,500 magazines and journals (Roxburgh 1987, 55).

[33] See Pocheptsov (1997, 53–54) on the absence of the eyewitness voice in Soviet political language.

[34] *Ideinost' sovetskogo cheloveka.*

and a published metadiscourse that evaluated these suggestions and commented on them in a voice external to this discourse. The 1977 article, by contrast, simply stated that the Soviet people unanimously supported the text of the new constitution, not referring to any public metadiscursive critiques or evaluations.

Manifest Intertextuality

One of the central principles of Soviet authoritative language was manifest intertextuality,[35] which amounted to a precise or near-precise citation of various language "blocks" from one text to the next. It is easy to provide endless examples of such intertextual citation. Compare excerpts from two random texts written by different people, in different years, for different publications, but on the same topic: the antagonism between socialism and capitalism. A 1980 book about the Komsomol reads:

> In the struggle between the two world outlooks there is no room for neutrality and compromises. With imperialist propaganda becoming more sophisticated, the political education of Soviet young people grows in importance. . . . [T]he central task of the Komsomol . . . [is] the education of young people in the spirit of communist ideology, Soviet patriotism, internationalism . . . the active propaganda of the achievements and advantages of the socialist system (Andreyev 1980, 100).[36]

Practically identical "blocks" are contained in three excerpts from the 1977 *Pravda* article (figure 2.1):

> "In the struggle between two world outlooks there can be no room for neutrality or compromise," said the General Secretary of the CC of the CPSU comrade L. I. Brezhnev at the XXVth Party congress. [*paragraph 8*]

> [I]mperialist propaganda is becoming more sophisticated. This imposes a high responsibility on the Soviet people. [*paragraph 7*]

> The central task . . . of the party organizations should be . . . the further growth of the inner maturity and ideological conviction of toilers and . . . the propaganda of the Soviet way of life and advantages of the socialist system. [*paragraph 10*]

[35] The term was proposed by Fairclough (1992).

[36] A group of professional political writers of the CC of the Komsomol wrote the book collectively.

Pravda, July 1, 1977 [abridged with paragraph numbers added]

1. The high level of social consciousness of the toilers of our country, their richest collective experience, and political reason [*politicheskii razum*] manifest themselves [*proiavliaiutsia*] with an exceptional completeness in the days of the all-people [*vsenarodnogo*] discussion of the draft [*proekta*] of the constitution of the USSR.

2. In all its greatness [*velichii*] and beauty, the spiritual image of the fighter and creator, of the citizen of the developed socialist society, reveals itself [*raskryvaetsia*] to the world both in the chiseled [*chekannykh*] lines of the outstanding document of the contemporary times, and in the living existence, in the everyday reality of the communist construction.

3. The new Soviet person, brought up by the Leninist Party, is our historic achievement, the most important result of the sixty-year-long road walked under the banner of the Great October. This is a person who harmoniously unites [*garmonicheski soediniaet*] in himself the communist conviction and an interminable energy of life, a high level of culture and knowledge, and the skills to apply [*umenie primeniat'*] them in practice.

4. Selfless devotion to the ideas of communism and confidence in the triumph of these ideas, to which the future of the socialist Motherland is inseparably linked, make up [*sostavliaiut*] the basis of the politico-ideological [*ideino-politicheskogo*] and moral image [*oblik*] and character of the Soviet people. This deep confidence is clearly expressed in the words of the National Anthem of the Soviet Union, "In the victory of the immortal ideas of communism we see the destiny of our country." . . .

5. The interests of the communist construction and of the formation of a new person require [*trebuiut*] further perfection of the ideological practice. This concerns [*rech' idet*] firstly the growth of the scale and level of political enlightenment of the toilers, of the Marxist-Leninist education of the cadres and of all Soviet people, both communists and non-party members. While inciting [*priobshchaia*] the masses to the study of the revolutionary theory, the party organizations simultaneously are called [*prizvany*] to explicate [*raz"iasniat'*] to them convincingly the home and foreign policy of the CPSU, the contemporary political situation, and the concrete tasks ensuing from it. . . .

7. Life has fully confirmed the conclusion of the XXVth Congress of the CPSU that positive changes in world politics and the international relaxation of tension create [*sozdaiut*] favorable conditions for a wide expansion of the ideas of socialism, but that, on the other hand, the ideological antagonism of the two systems is becoming more active, while imperialist propaganda is becoming more sophisticated. This imposes a high responsibility [*ko mnogomu obiazyvaet*] on the Soviet people.

8. "In the struggle between two world outlooks there can be no room for neutrality or compromise," said the general secretary of the CC of the CPSU, comrade L. I. Brezhnev, at the XXVth Party Congress. "A high political vigilance, an active, expeditious, and convincing propagandist work, and a timely rebuff to hostile ideological sabotage are needed here."

9. A nonconconciliatory attitude toward any manifestations of the bourgeois ideology, political carelessness, and complacency, an honest evaluation of these phenomena, and an active struggle with them are the central obligations of all communists and a duty of every collective and of every Soviet person.

10. The central tasks at which the efforts of the party organizations should be targeted [*dolzhny byt' natseleny*] are the further growth of the inner maturity and ideological conviction [*ideinosti*] of toilers and the development and strengthening in them of the qualities of political fighters. The affirmation of these qualities is allowed [*sposobstvuet*] by the martial [*boevoi*], assaulting character of our ideological work and a swift and sharp unmasking of the tricks and means of bourgeois propaganda. Because of the discussion of the draft of the constitution of the USSR and the approach of the sixtieth anniversary of the October Revolution, the propaganda of the Soviet way of life and advantages of the socialist system over the capitalist one acquires [*priobretaet*] an even greater significance.

11. Turning our eyes [*obrashchaias'*] to the draft of the main law of the country, we see ever more clearly [*my vse iasnee vidim*] the real historical advantages of our social order, of our society of developed socialism—the society of high level of organization, ideological conviction [*ideinosti*], and conscientiousness of toilers, the society of patriots and internationalists. Ideological conviction [*ideinaia ubezhdennost'*] is the source of the spiritual energy of the Soviet people, of their social optimism and mighty power in the struggle for the triumph of the communist ideals.

FIGURE 2.1. The Ideological Conviction of the Soviet Person. Author's translation.

Manifest intertextuality was also at work in the production of the visual and ritualistic registers of authoritative discourse, as seen above. Furthermore, visual, linguistic, ritualistic, and other registers of this discourse were connected to each other through manifest interdiscursivity. For example, the master signifier Lenin served in texts as the uniting name for all citations and pronouncements, and in visual representation as the uniting image for most flyers, posters, flags, billboards, and monuments.

65

Complex Modifiers

Another generative principle of this language included the use of a limited repertoire of modifiers for particular concepts: certain nouns and verbs tended to be accompanied by concrete adjectives. For example, as Caroline Humphrey observes, local papers in small Siberian towns during the late Soviet period tended to describe "success" (*uspekh*) and "labor" (*trud*) as "creative" (*tvorcheskii*), "help" (*pomoshch'*) as "brotherly" (*bratskaia*), and "participation" (*uchastie*) as "active" (*aktivnoe*) (Humphrey 1989, 159). We must add that many modifiers used in this genre were complex modifiers that consisted of a fixed string of adjectives, often in comparative form. The following passage from paragraph 1 of figure 2.1 illustrates this principle (complex modifiers are underlined):

> The <u>high level</u> of social consciousness of the toilers of our country, their <u>richest collective</u> experience, and political reason manifest themselves with an <u>exceptional completeness</u> in the days of the all-people discussion of the draft of the constitution of the USSR.
>
> [*<u>Vysokii uroven'</u> obshchestvennogo soznania trudiashchikhsia nashei strany, ikh <u>bogateishii kollektivnyi</u> opyt i politicheskii razum s <u>iskliuchitel'noi polnotoi</u> proiavliaiutsia v dni vsenarodnogo obsuzhdeniia proekta konstitutsii SSSR.*]

Each of the three underlined phrases is a complex modifier for a noun: here, "social consciousness" is of a *high level*, "experience" is the *richest collective*, and "manifestation" is of an *exceptional completeness*. From the first glance these modifiers construct presuppositions (implicit assumptions)—ideas that are treated as obvious, taken-for-granted facts, without necessarily being such (Levinson 1983; Fairclough 1992, 120; 1989, 152–54; Austin 1999, 48). In the first phrase, the double modifier "high level" contains two presuppositions of the existence of the Soviet toilers' unified consciousness; both modifiers treat that consciousness as a known fact rather than as a contested claim: To be *high*, social consciousness must exist, and to be measured comparatively, by levels (high level, low level), it must exist. To illustrate this point, compare these two phrases: "deep-sea fishing" and "the sea is deep." In the first phrase, the fact that the sea is deep (in certain places) is presupposed, treated as a known and incontestable fact. In the second phrase, the fact of depth is treated as new and contestable information. The same goes for the second underlined phrase in our excerpt. It presupposes the existence of a shared toilers' "experience": to be *rich*, to be measured by comparative or superlative degree (the *richest*), and to be *collective*, this experience must exist. Complex modifiers of this type were not only frequent in this discourse, but they tended to constitute fixed phraseological blocks that were cited almost intact in different contexts and texts. Similar complex modifiers can be found throughout the *Pravda* text and in all other authoritative texts of the period.

Ultimately, the presuppositions used in these texts should not be interpreted at face value. The result of using them was not that ideological claims necessarily appeared natural to their audiences, or were impossible to question, but rather, as I have said before, that the voices of the authors and enunciators of this discourse were transformed into those of mediators of prior knowledge rather than creators of new knowledge.

In general, with the performative shift of authoritative discourse its generative principles (such as complex modifiers and other principles discussed below) had progressively ceased working as presuppositions. Understanding how original presuppositions had become something else is crucial for this analysis. In earlier periods, the goal behind many generative principles of ideological discourse was to control its constative dimension by controlling the meanings that were implicitly communicated through presuppositions (recall Stalin's meticulous editing of history books and the national anthem). However, when authoritative discourse experienced the performative shift during late socialism that original goal was lost because, as argued earlier, the constative dimension of discourse became unanchored and open to new, unpredictable interpretations. The forms of language that were originally devised to construct presuppositions (i.e., to control the constative dimension of discourse) had now become hypernormalized and acquired a very different function: they were no longer about implicitly stating facts but rather about conveying the idea that authoritative discourse was immutable, citational, anonymous, and removed into the past in terms of temporarily. These were not presuppositions in the sense this term has in pragmatics (Levinson 1983).

This conclusion has implications not only for the analysis of Soviet political discourse but for broader theories and methods of discourse analysis. The analysis of presuppositions in discourse that goes on at the level of the constative dimension must consider the possibility that a performative shift of discourse may unanchor its constative dimension, opening the constative aspects of meaning, including presuppositions, to unpredictable interpretations.

Complex Nominalizations

As we saw earlier, one of the editing strategies in the authoritative genre of language was to convert several shorter phrases into one long phrase by adding commas and omitting verbs. This technique resulted in the production of long and unwieldy noun phrases. Patrick Seriot found that during the late socialist period noun phrases in general appeared with much greater frequency in the Russian texts written in the ideological genre than in other genres of Russian language (Seriot 1986, 34). The proliferation of noun phrases, like the proliferation of complex modifiers, was an effect of the general move toward minimizing the authorial specificity of the enunciator's voice, shifting its temporality into the past, and eradicating any potential newness, indeterminacy, or ambiguity. Noun phrases, like modifiers, can be used as powerful techniques for creating presuppositions and presenting information as something that has been earlier preestablished and as simply being mediated. In paragraph 2 of figure 2.1, the underlined passage before the verb ("reveals itself") is a long noun phrase of this type[37]:

In all its greatness and beauty, the spiritual image of the fighter and creator, of the citizen of the developed socialist society, reveals itself to the world both in the chiseled lines of the outstanding document of the contemporary times, and in the living existence, in the everyday reality of the communist construction.

[I v chekannykh strokakh vydaiushchegosia dokumenta sovremennosti, i v zhivoi deistvitel'nosti, v povsednevnykh budniakh kommunisticheskogo stroitel'stva raskryvaetsia pered mirom vo vsem velichii i krasote dukhovnyi obraz bortsa i sozidatelia, grazhdanina razvitogo sotsialisticheskogo obshchestva.]

This noun phrase is packed with several presuppositions that can be exposed by rephrasing it in corresponding verbal phrases (Seriot 1986):

the citizen of the developed socialist society *is* a fighter and creator;
the fighter and creator *possesses* a spiritual image;
the spiritual image *is* great and beautiful; (and so on).

Each of these verbal phrases formulates an assertion that is presented as new or contestable information that can be questioned by posing a direct question: "*Is* the citizen a fighter and creator?"; "*Does* he/she possess a spiritual image?"; "*Is* the image great and beautiful?" However, when verbal phrases are converted into noun phrases (nominalized), these assertions are presupposed as preestablished, known "facts."[38] The corresponding

---

[37] In the Russian original, the underlined phrase follows the verb, but the change in order of phrases in the translation does not affect the ultimate result.

[38] Consider again the comparison above between the phrases "deep-sea fishing" (noun phrase, the depth is asserted as a known fact) and "the sea is deep" (verbal phrase, the depth is claimed as new information).

verbal phrases and noun phrases represent the same forms of knowledge but with different temporalities: the knowledge represented in noun phrases is "removed" into the past in logical time in relation to the knowledge represented in the verbal phrases. In other words, these noun phrases present knowledge in terms of "facts" established *before* the act of speaking, while the verbal phrases present it as new claims made *in* the act of speaking. This is a central point that will be important in the following chapters.

In fact, the temporality of this nominalized discourse was not simply shifted into an abstract past; it was shifted back by multiple historical stages. Because such sentences tended to contain a string of several noun phrases, as in figure 2.1 from *Pravda*, multiple presuppositions "piled up" one on top of the other, with each presupposition removed to a deeper level of prior temporality than the one "to the left" of it. In other words, each presupposition could work only if the prior presupposition ("on the right") had been made first. In the above example from paragraph 2 of figure 2.1, the presupposition that "the spiritual image *is* great and beautiful" is predicated on a prior presupposition that "the fighter and creator *possesses* a spiritual image," which is in turn predicated on the prior presupposition that "the citizen of the developed socialist society *is* a fighter and creator." The construction of such long chains of presuppositions, coded in long noun phrases, shifted the temporality of authoritative discourse into multiple pasts in relation to verbal phrases. This difference between noun phrases and verbal phrases may render the claims made in noun phrases more assertive than those made in verbal phrases. Seriot calls this difference between corresponding verbal and noun phrases "assertion lag" (1986, 46).[39]

However, while Seriot argues that the greater assertiveness of noun phrases produces the effect of making the claims they make appear more natural, I argue that this is not necessarily the case. Indeed, as with complex modifiers discussed above, the function of complex noun chains in Soviet authoritative discourse was no longer to make the discourse appear natural to its audiences (as would be the case with pure presuppositions) but rather to communicate something about the nature of that discourse itself. By removing the temporality of the constative representations into the past, these long noun chains, like many other generative principles of this discourse, conveyed the idea that authoritative discourse was perfectly citational and immutable, that the constative assertions made in it were circular and therefore of secondary importance, and that the voice of every author and enunciator of this discourse became

[39] These nominals may be potentially more "assertive" because they present knowledge as a fact that is commonly known.

transformed into the voice of the mediator of multiply preestablished forms of knowledge.

Displaced Agency

Another type of long noun phrase transformed the authorial voice into the voice of mediator in a different way. Consider the following sentence from paragraph 5 in figure 2.1, which, unlike the previous example, does not simply describe a state of affairs but appears to provide new information, about what is "required":

> The interests of the communist construction and of the formation of a new person require further perfection of the ideological practice (emphasis added).
>
> [Interesy kommunisticheskogo stroitel'stva i formirovaniia novogo cheloveka trebuiut dal'neishego sovershenstvovaniia ideologicheskoi deiatel'nosti.]

In the long noun phrase (underlined), the agent who asserts what is required is displaced in relation to the author of the text. This effect can be demonstrated by comparing this noun phrase with a few corresponding verbal phrases that explicitly state the presupposed assertions contained in the original text (the agent of each assertion is underlined):

1. The author requires that the ideological activity be perfected
2. Communist construction requires that the ideological activity be perfected
3. The interests of the communist construction require that the ideological activity be perfected

In the first sentence, the agent of "requiring" is explicitly stated: it is the author of the text (for example, the party, the CC, or the Komsomol). In the second sentence, the author is removed: the "communist construction" functions as the agent of requiring. However, the author might be still inferred by posing the indirect question—"*Whose* communist construction?"—with the answer being "that of the author." In the third sentence, the author is removed more deeply: it is "*the interests* of the communist construction" that are the agents of requiring. The indirect question, "Whose interests?" can only be answered with, "Those of the communist construction," leaving the author of the assertion unnamed. The more noun phrases are piled up in this manner the more the *agent* of the assertion can be displaced from the *author* of the text. This displacement of agency is equivalent to the shift in the temporalities of all enunciations into the past (where the agent presents prior and shared knowledge). Clearly, this shift also contributes to constructing the authorial voice as that of mediator rather than creator of knowledge contributing to the general circularity of the constative dimension of discourse.

Rhetorical Circularity

Michael Urban demonstrates that in the 1970s and 1980s the speeches by the general secretaries of the party were usually organized, on the rhetorical level, around a "lack"—that is, around a claim that a certain practical problem had to be overcome, such as the "lack" of productivity, food resources, discipline, party control, etc. (1986, 140).[40] Having named the lack, this discourse prescribed, paradoxically, that it should be solved using a means that the discourse had already deemed earlier inadequate or inappropriate for the task. In other words, argues Urban, the rhetorical structure of this discourse was circular. Urban provides the following example: in his speech, General Secretary Chernenko, in the early 1980s, called on the "deputies of soviets (local councils) to 'stimulate and direct the creative initiative' of soviets in order to attract 'the broad masses into an interested participation in the administration of production, government and society.'" At the same time, earlier in the same speech, Chernenko had explicitly prohibited any spontaneity and creative initiative by the Soviets, arguing that all their administrative work should be subsumed under strict and centralized party management (Urban 1986, 141).

Similarly, Chernenko's speeches appealed to Soviet citizens to "organize" and "monitor" industrial production more efficiently than ever before, while simultaneously arguing that these measures ("organizing" and "monitoring") had failed to achieve results in the past. The speeches also appealed for the need to increase the "inventiveness" and "consciousness" of the masses, while at the same time arguing, paradoxically, for the need to contain inventiveness and consciousness within "the confines of the present order" (143). All these appeals—to "monitor" and "organize," to stimulate creative initiative, to increase inventiveness, and so forth—were presented simultaneously as "agents for overcoming the lack" (popular needs satisfaction) and as "mediators of this lack itself" (141). The ultimate circular injunctions of this discourse were that Soviet citizens should develop new approaches and methods of work by using old approaches and methods, and should continue doing the things that had proved futile in the past (140). Such rhetorical circularity

[40] In the previous example, this would be the lack in perfection of the ideological practice.

was a direct effect of Lefort's paradox of modern ideology, which, as I have argued in chapter 1 and above, was expressed in the Soviet context in the attempts to achieve liberation by means of constraint.

The argument of this book is that rhetorical circularity of this type developed, to a large extent, as a result of the spontaneous normalization of authoritative discourse not as conscious political manipulation from the center. This circularity was the effect of a general move toward the eradication of authorial voice, after the "external" voice of the master of discourse and his metadiscourse had been destroyed. This argument differs from Urban's suggestion that the circularity of the party texts was a result of conscious manipulation through which the party leadership represented and reproduced itself as the sole controller and originator of political discourse.

Examples of rhetorical circularity are easily found in the 1977 *Pravda* article (figure 2.1). A sentence in paragraph 10 reads: "The central task . . . of the party organizations . . . is the further growth of the inner maturity and ideological conviction of toilers." Here "inner maturity" and "ideological conviction" are presented as lacking in level and needing growth, and the central task of the party is to overcome this lack. However, earlier in the text (paragraphs 3 and 4), the Soviet toilers are described as people who already possess "communist conviction," "selfless devotion to the ideas of communism" and "confidence in the triumph of these ideas." The text posits a future task after first stating that the goals of the task had already been achieved.

In contrast, the rhetorical structure of authoritative texts in earlier periods of Soviet history, before the hypernormalization of discourse, was not circular precisely because there also existed a public metadiscourse on authoritative language. Compare the above example with a passage from the leading article in *Pravda* on September 21, 1935, which spoke on a similar topic, and was entitled "The Qualities of the Soviet Citizen":

> [T]he high conscientiousness of the revolutionary working class, its irrepressible will for victory, its irreconcilability and decisiveness, which found their best expression in the Communist Party, *must become* the basic characteristics of every toiler of the Soviet country (emphasis added).

The 1935 text lists the characteristics of the working class and then introduces new knowledge, stating that these characteristics must become the property of every Soviet person, including the nonworking class. This rhetorical structure is not circular. This difference in rhetorical structures corresponds to the different discursive regimes: in the earlier period, the external voice of the "master" allowed for this discourse to remain "open-ended," positing an explicitly known objective canon outside that discourse, and therefore providing space for its critical evaluation and improvement against that canon. With the disappearance of that external position, the formal structure of this genre of language closed up and became circular—all new claims and forms of knowledge became limited to knowledge already stated in prior articulations.

Narrative Circularity

One of the organizing principles of any ideological discourse is the use of a limited number of master signifiers that serve as "quilting points"—points at which "heterogeneous symbolic material" is stitched together "into a unified ideological field" (Žižek 1991b, 8; Lacan 1988). For example, a master signifier of the discourse of value is money. In the context of a precapitalist exchange, when one commodity defined the value of another commodity, commodities functioned as signifiers for one another: each signifier could represent the value of any other signifier. However, when one signifier (money) was endowed with the role of representing the value of all other signifiers (commodities), they fell into a meaningful chain of relations vis-à-vis that one signifier, organizing a totalized and unified network. It was through that inversion—from one-for-one to one-for-all—that money was produced as the master signifier of value. In a capitalist economy, this inversion remains invisible (money is a naturalized value), leading to Marx's principle of commodity fetishism (Žižek 1991a, 16–26).

Soviet authoritative discourse was "quilted" into a unified field of knowledge around three master signifiers—Lenin, the Party, and Communism.[41] In fact, these three master signifiers were indivisible and mutually constitutive: the method for describing and improving reality was Marxism-Leninism (Lenin); the agent who used this scientific method to describe and improve reality was the Party; and the goal toward which this improvement was directed was Communism.

These three master signifiers could be seen therefore as one tripartite master signifier, Lenin-Party-Communism. To say that authoritative discourse was quilted into one ideological field of knowledge by this master signifier is to say that this master signifier represented the objective scientific *canon* that was external to authoritative discourse (as described earlier) and where this discourse was anchored. The very ability to enunciate authoritative discourse was predicated on having always to anchor

[41] Each of these master signifiers marked a broad space of meaning and could be replaced with various synonyms: "Communism" was also *socialism, bright future, progress,* and *classless society*; "Lenin" was also *Marxism-Leninism, scientific teaching,* and *scientific method*; "the Party" was also *the leading force of the Soviet society* and *the Soviet government* (See Seriot 1985, 96, 120 and Lefort 1986, 297), Stump (1998, 12, 92).

73

it in that external canon, which in practice meant having always to index with a high degree of precision the external objective reality represented by this canon. This is why it was crucial to establish a link to precise Lenin quotations and portraits (recall the use of Lenin's quotations by the politburo secretary of ideology Suslov and Lenin's death masks by artists in the examples above). There will be more examples of quoting, drawing, and invoking Lenin in the following chapters. Any leader, including Stalin, could be legitimated only through a connection to Lenin (as "Lenin's pupil," "Lenin's choice of successor," "a faithful Marxist-Leninist," etc.). In order to acquire this legitimating link, Stalin presented himself as Lenin's choice of successor (suppressing Lenin's "Letter to the Congress" in which, shortly before his death in 1924, Lenin warned the party against electing Stalin as its general secretary). Khrushchev denounced Stalin's cult of personality in the name of "returning" to the real word of Lenin, which in practice meant that the signifier "Stalin" was disconnected from the master signifier "Lenin." Cities, streets, and institutions carrying Stalin's name were renamed, Stalin monuments were taken away, and Stalin's body was removed from the mausoleum where Lenin's body was displayed, and buried in the ground. Stalin the character disappeared from most books, plays, and films.[42] Despite Stalin's cult of personality and enormous personal power, he could only be a leader as defined through Lenin and the party, not the other way around.[43] For this reason, the ultimate disappearance of the position of the external editor of authoritative discourse did not undermine the Soviet ideological narrative altogether; instead it pushed this narrative structure toward complete circularity. It was only when Lenin was undermined as a master signifier, in the late 1980s, that the Soviet socialist system quickly collapsed.

Performative Dimension

This chapter started by discussing the historical conditions under which the authoritative discourse of late socialism developed. It focused in particular on authoritative language (in party texts, speeches, newspaper

[42] In Mikhail Romm's films about the period of the Bolshevik revolution, *Lenin in October* (1937) and *Lenin in 1918* (1939), the scenes where Stalin had been portrayed as Lenin's closest associate were cut out or reshot with new characters (Bulgakova 1994).

[43] See also Ken Jowitt on the Soviet Communist Party's principle of "charismatic impersonalism," which transcended the role of any living leader (1993, 3–10). The position of the party leader in the regime of ideology also distinguished the Soviet Communist system from the German Nazi system. The latter ideology was based on *Führerprinzip*, according to which the führer played the role of the master signifier of Nazi discourse, making the Nazi system potentially shorter-lived than the Soviet system (Žižek 1982; Nyomarkey 1965, 45).

articles, etc.) and also mentioned similar developments in other forms of authoritative discourse—in particular, in visuals and rituals. After the 1950s, with the disappearance of the "external" voice that provided metadiscussions and evaluations of that language, the language structures became increasingly normalized, cumbersome, citational, and circular. That language became what I termed *hypernormalized*. This development was an unintended result of the attempts by great numbers of people who were engaged in producing texts in authoritative language to minimize the presence of their own authorial voice. By doing so, they converted their voices from that of the producer of new knowledge to that of the mediator of preexisting knowledge.

Linguistic, narrative, and rhetorical structures were not read by most Soviet people at face value, as constative descriptions of the world (either true or false). In fact, the constative dimension of this language became open and unpredictable, and authoritative language acquired a powerful performative function. Replicating its textual forms, linguistic constructions, making speeches and compiling reports in it, participating in acts of voting, and so on had the important effect of enabling new meanings and descriptions of reality and forms of life that were neither limited to nor completely determined by those provided by the constative descriptions in authoritative language.

Binary accounts of socialism that describe it in terms of truth and falsity or official knowledge and unofficial knowledge fail to recognize precisely this performative dimension of authoritative language, reducing it instead to the constative dimension. Since authoritative discourse did not provide an accurate constative description of reality and since no competing description of reality was widely available, one could conclude that the late Soviet world became a kind of "postmodern" universe where grounding in the real world was no longer possible, and where reality became reduced to discursive simulacra (Baudrillard 1988). Thus, Mikhail Epstein argues:

> [N]o one knows . . . whether the harvests reported in Stalin's or Brezhnev's Russia were ever actually reaped, but the fact that the number of tilled hectares or tons of milled grain was always reported down to the tenth of a percent gave these simulacra the character of hyperreality. . . . any reality that differed from the ideology simply ceased to exist—it was replaced by hyperreality, more tangible and reliable than anything else. In the Soviet land, "fairy tale became fact,"[44] as in that American paragon of hyperreality, Disneyland, where reality itself is designed as a "land of imagination" (2000, 5–6; 1995; 1991).

[44] Words from a popular Soviet song: *"my rozhdeny, chtob skazku sdelat' byl'iu"* (we are born to turn fairy tale into fact).

According to Epstein, the Soviet Union became a perfect postmodern society.

His argument is based on three premises: that Soviet authoritative language was hegemonic and constituted the only representation of reality that was shared by all Soviet people; that from the audience's perspective language had only one function: to describe reality and state facts about the world (i.e., it operated only at the constative level); that how adequately language described reality could not be challenged or verified. From these three premises Epstein argues that since Soviet people read authoritative discourse for constative representations of their world, and these representations were hegemonic and could not be verified or challenged, Soviet people could never be certain what was real and what was simulated. Since nothing about the representations of the world was verifiably true or false, the whole of reality became ungrounded, transformed into simulacra.

Although Epstein's point about the hegemonic and unitary nature of authoritative discourse is correct, his assumption that the Soviet people read authoritative language exclusively as a set of constative statements is not. In fact, precisely because authoritative language was hegemonic, unavoidable, and hypernormalized, it was no longer read by its audiences literally, at the level of constative meanings. Therefore, which statements represented "facts" and which did not was relatively unimportant. Instead, Soviet people engaged with authoritative language at the level of the performative dimension, which Epstein ignores. Recall the act of voting in favor of a resolution at a party or Komsomol meeting, which had two dimensions of meaning—constative (description of one's opinion about the resolution) and performative (carrying out an act of "voting" that has binding effects). The performative dimension of this act did not *describe* reality and could not be analyzed as true or false; instead it produced effects and created facts in that reality.

Such acts as repeating precise language forms, participating in rituals, voting in favor, and so forth were meaningful and important because they produced important effects. They enabled Soviet people to engage in the production of new forms and meanings of reality that were tangible, multiple, and grounded in the "real world." These multiple forms of reality were performatively enabled by authoritative discourse, but they were not limited to or constrained by its constative descriptions. Contrary to Epstein's claim that "reality that differed from the ideology simply ceased to exist," that different reality, in fact, exploded into the Soviet world in powerful, multiple, and unanticipated forms. It is to these unexpected effects of ideological discourse that we turn in the following chapters.

Chapter 3
Ideology Inside Out:
Ethics and Poetics

All art is subject to political manipulation,
Except for that which speaks the language of this manipulation
—"Laibach"[1]

Ideological Poetics

A fascinating mixture of sarcasm and nostalgia—for both the recently ended socialism and the new post-Soviet capitalism—animates Victor Pelevin's book *Generation P* (1999), which takes place in Russia in the first post-Soviet decade. The book's title refers to the last Soviet generation, to which Pelevin, born in 1962, himself belongs. In one scene the protagonist, Tatarsky, a member of this generation, is drinking with his former party boss, telling him how impressed he used to be, during the Soviet period, with the boss's skills in writing ideological texts of a powerful rhetorical form and no obvious meaning:

> "You gave such a speech," continued Tatarsky. "At that time I was preparing for the entrance exams to *Litinstitut* [Institute of Literature] and you made me very unhappy. I envied you, because I realized that I would never learn to manipulate words like this. They have no sense at all, but affect [*probiraet*] you so much that you instantly understand everything. That is, you understand not what the person is trying to say, because in fact he is not trying to say anything, but you understand everything about life. I think it was for that reason that such meetings of the *aktiv* [local Komsomol leadership] were conducted. That evening I sat down to write a sonnet but instead I got drunk."

---

[1] Item Three in "Ten Items of the Covenant" (Laibach 1983). Laibach is a Slovenian theatrical rock group that has been experimenting with the notions of ideology and art for over twenty years. For more on Laibach see chapter 7; Žižek (1993b); Gržinić (2000); Erjavec (2003); Djurić and Šuvaković (2003); NSK (1991).

"Do you remember what I was speaking about?" asked Hanin. It was obvious that he was pleased to hear these recollections.

"Uh, something about the Twenty-Seventh Party Congress and its importance."

Hanin coughed and said in a loud and well-trained voice [*khorosho postavlennym golosom*]: "I think there is no need to explain to you, Komsomol activists, why the decisions of the Twenty-Seventh Congress of our Party are considered not only meaningful [*znachimye*] but also momentous [*etapnye*]. And yet the methodological difference between these two concepts often causes some misunderstanding [*nedoponimanie*] even among propagandists and agitators. But the propagandists and agitators are the architects of tomorrow; they must not have any misconceptions about the plan according to which they are going to build the future. . . ."

After a loud hiccup he lost his train of thought.

"This is it," said Tatarsky, "now I recognize it well. The most impressive thing is that you were explaining for the whole hour the methodological differences between meaningfulness [*znachimost'*] and momentousness [*etapnost'*], and I understood perfectly well every individual sentence. But when you try to understand any two sentences together they seem to be divided by some wall. . . . It is impossible. And you can't recount them in your own words either."[2]

Pelevin's satirical account captures the shift in Soviet authoritative language during late socialism. Much of that language's force, as in a foreign language, came through rhythm, sound, and phraseology that looked and sounded impressive. That language influenced its audiences even when not quite understood. It operated on the level of what Roman Jakobson called the *poetic function* of language: the function that is focused on the aesthetic form of language, on the message "for its own sake"; on how it says, not necessarily what it says. Jakobson demonstrates this point with an example:

"Why do you always say *Joan and Margery*, yet never *Margery and Joan*? Do you prefer Joan to her twin sister?" "Not at all, it just sounds smoother." In a sequence of two coordinate names, as far as no rank problems interfere, the precedence of the shorter name suits the speaker, unaccountably for him, as a well-ordered shape of the message. (Jakobson 1960, 357)

---

[2] Translation by author from the Russian (Pelevin 1999, 140–41). I use this translation instead of the available English translation (Pelevin 2000, 106–7) to stress the distinction between the original Russian terms *znachimost'* and *etapnost'*.

The poetic function of language differs from its referential function: even though "Joan and Margery" and "Margery and Joan" may be identical referentially (refer to identical facts), they are different poetically. In the poetic function, the primary role is played by the signifier of the linguistic sign—sound, rhythmic structure, stress, pause, syntactic shape, word and phrase boundaries, and so forth. On this level, units of language can be equivalent or not. For example, two words rhyme if their sound forms are equivalent. By selecting particular equivalences one may compose a poem, witty pun, or political slogan. Jakobson illustrates this process with a political election slogan for Dwight Eisenhower: "I like Ike." The sound equivalences in this phrase—three monosyllables, three diphthongs *ay*, the symmetry of consonants *l, k, k,* the rhyme of *ayk* and *layk*—are the devices of the poetic function. They draw a poetic picture of affect, in which "the loving subject [is] enveloped by the beloved object," accounting for the slogan's "impressiveness and efficiency," which works quite independently of the referential function of the message: it affects the audience even if they have never heard of Ike (Jakobson 1960, 357).

In certain contexts the poetic function may take precedence over other functions of language. In the language of advertising, for example, such slogans as "Just do it" and "Just be" may be cases in point. Another example, as discussed in the previous chapter, is the early revolutionary language in Russia. During late socialism, the poetic function again took center stage in authoritative language. However, instead of breaking with the established conventions of language, as was the case during the revolutionary period, the poetic function during late socialism performed the opposite gesture—multiplying and fixing these forms and making them unavoidable. The texts written in this genre conveyed one unmistakable message: language form can be profoundly meaningful in itself, regardless of whether any other meaning is obvious. The same shift occurred in other genres of authoritative signification—in the structure of rituals, visuals representations, public events, spatial designs, and so on.

Two features of authoritative discourse made that shift possible. First, the hypernormalization of this discourse after the 1950s made it increasingly fixed and citational at all levels of structure and in all contexts (see chapter 2). This discourse experienced the performative shift, with the performative dimension of meaning taking precedence and the constative dimension becoming unanchored and open. Second, the top-down hierarchy of the state institutions (the party, the Komsomol, etc.); the centralized system of decisions, assignments, and reports through which this discourse was controlled, reproduced, and distributed; and the ubiquitous presence of these institutions and their rituals and texts in the lives of most people—all enabled the processes that Bourdieu calls the "delegation" of power to every actor who correctly reproduced in form the acts and utterances of ideology.[3] This shift resulted in a growing importance of the performative dimension of ideological texts, rituals, and visuals and an increasing unanchoring of their constative dimension, at least in most cases where ideology circulated. In other words, repeating ritualized acts and utterances became meaningful because, first, this repetition was seen as unavoidable and, second, it allowed a person to become engaged in other creative and unanticipated meanings and forms of everyday life that these ritualized acts and utterances enabled but did not determine in full.

Chapter 2 analyzed the historical conditions and effects of what I called the hypernormalization of authoritative discourse. This chapter analyzes how the performative reproduction of various levels of this hypernormalized discourse enabled the conditions, spaces, and temporalities for the production of new unanticipated meanings, relations, identities, and forms of sociality.

The chapter focuses ethnographically on the contexts in which common Soviet people, especially the younger generation, routinely encountered, reproduced, and reinterpreted the normalized forms of authoritative texts and rituals as both their audiences and authors, specifically in the local contexts of the Komsomol organization to which most young people at that time belonged. At first I analyze how and what techniques were learned, passed on, invented anew, and routinely practiced by common Komsomol members to reproduce the authoritative form; then I discuss what unanticipated meanings became enabled by that performative reproduction of form. Chapters 4 through 6 will discuss what kind of new meanings and forms of life emerged in other contexts, and what repercussions this emergence had for the socialist system.

Local Komsomol Cadres

From the 1970s through the mid-1980s, most young people interacted with authoritative discourse in secondary schools,[4] universities,[5] factories,

---

[3] See discussion of this process in chapter 1.

[4] I refer to "secondary schools" (*sredniaia shkola*) using the Soviet terminology for the school system in the Russian Federation. School classes past age twelve (ending with graduation at seventeen) were part of secondary school, the equivalent of U.S. junior high and high school combined.

[5] I refer not only to Soviet "universities" (*universitet*) but also institutes (*institut*) (both schools of higher learning), using one label "university" to avoid confusion with "research institutes" (*issledovatel'skii institut*), which were not educational establishments.

and other locations through youth organizations, especially the Komsomol. The Komsomol organization was responsible for organizing much of the youth activities of that generation, from strictly ideological activities—those linked to reading party texts, performing various political assignments, participating in meetings, parades, and elections—to various cultural, social, musical, and sporting events and other activities. The majority of school students became members of the Komsomol by virtue of their age, when they turned fourteen or fifteen (membership in the Komsomol was limited to persons between the ages of fourteen and twenty-eight). Although membership in the Komsomol was not obligatory, it was expected and encouraged, and for certain activities (such as applying to university) it was tacitly understood as a requirement.

During the first half of the 1980s, 90 percent of all secondary school graduates were Komsomol members, and the total membership grew to more than forty million (Riordan 1989, 22). This chapter focuses on the context of local Komsomol organizations and, in particular, on the work of local Komsomol leaders—those hundreds of thousands of *secretaries* and *komsorgs* (Komsomol organizers) who occupied leading positions at the lower levels of the organization's hierarchy and orchestrated the involvement of most younger people in the Komsomol work. The simplified chart of the Komsomol hierarchy in figure 3.1 will help clarify discussions in this chapter. The Komsomol organization in each box of the chart oversees the one below and answers to the one above.[6]

The people described in this chapter came from different professional backgrounds and cities, but all occupied different hierarchical positions within the Komsomol organization, from rank-and-file members in cells, to komsorgs leading the cells, to members and secretaries of Komsomol committees, to raikom secretaries.

Most rank-and-file members were involved in Komsomol work at the level of primary Komsomol organizations and cells, through a system of "assignments" (*porucheniia*). Assignments were designed, orchestrated, distributed, and checked in a centralized and hierarchical fashion: higher Komsomol bodies sent assignments to lower ones and ensured their fulfillment. Assignments included political lectures, ideological examinations, speeches at Komsomol meetings, work on collective farms, preparations for national holidays, participation in parades, helping war veterans, participation in various commissions to check on the work of others, and so on. According to the interpretation provided in the Komsomol literature, these assignments were always well organized and transparent; their fulfillment was encouraged through a system of incentives and

[6] See also Hough (1979); Riordan (1989); Solnick (1998); Brovkin (1998).

```
┌─────────────────────────────────────────────────┐
│         Central Committee of Soviet Komsomol       │
│                      (CC)                          │
│                                                    │
│               Head: First Secretary               │
└─────────────────────────────────────────────────┘
                         ↓
┌─────────────────────────────────────────────────┐
│  Central Committee of Republics, Regions, Provinces,│
│                      etc.                          │
│                                                    │
│               Head: First Secretary               │
└─────────────────────────────────────────────────┘
                         ↓
┌─────────────────────────────────────────────────┐
│                     Obkom                          │
│              (Provincial Committee)                │
│                                                    │
│               Head: First Secretary               │
└─────────────────────────────────────────────────┘
                         ↓
┌─────────────────────────────────────────────────┐
│                    Gorkom                          │
│                (City Committee)                    │
│                                                    │
│               Head: First Secretary               │
└─────────────────────────────────────────────────┘
                         ↓
┌─────────────────────────────────────────────────┐
│                    Raikom                          │
│              (District Committee)                  │
│                                                    │
│               Head: First Secretary               │
└─────────────────────────────────────────────────┘
                         ↓
┌─────────────────────────────────────────────────┐
│    Komsomol Committee of a Primary Komsomol        │
│                 Organization                       │
│  (at a factory, university, secondary school, etc.)│
│                                                    │
│           Head: Committee Secretary                │
│      Comprises: five to ten Committee members      │
└─────────────────────────────────────────────────┘
                         ↓
┌─────────────────────────────────────────────────┐
│                 Komsomol cell                      │
│           (of the Primary Organization)            │
│                                                    │
│        Head: Komsorg (Komsomol organizer)          │
│     Comprises: rank-and-file Komsomol members      │
└─────────────────────────────────────────────────┘
```

FIGURE 3.1. Hierarchy of Komsomol.

demonstrated initiative and active engagement at the grass-roots level (Andreyev 1980, 46, 48). However, as we will see, this description misrepresents the real results of this work—the elaborate and often unintended types of relations that developed between the local Komsomol leadership and rank-and-file members, the techniques through which the Komsomol assignments were carried out, and, ultimately, the complex, multiple, and unanticipated meanings that emerged through the Komsomol work.[7]

The analysis in the following section focuses on the techniques that the Komsomol members at the middle and lower levels of the organization's hierarchy—the overwhelming majority of the Komsomol members—employed in reproducing authoritative texts, speeches, reports, and so forth. This analysis draws some parallels to the analysis of generative principles of authoritative language discussed in the previous chapter in order to demonstrate how the meticulous replication of authoritative forms afforded a profound displacement of their constative meanings.

A Professional Secretary

Komsomol leaders of different levels in the hierarchy received different amounts of training in the techniques of ideological production; the higher the position, the more nuanced the training. The same was the case in the Communist Party. This difference in training meant that the majority of those who occupied lower levels in the organizational hierarchy were not explicitly taught how to compose ideological texts.[8] Among the leading cadres, however, special training was necessary to acquire the skill of reproducing texts and conducting ritualized events and assignments.

Sasha (born in the early 1950s) worked as a chemical engineer in a research institute and for several years served as the secretary of the institute's Komsomol committee. In 1981, he left the institute for a post at the Komsomol raikom of his district in Leningrad. This meant that he abandoned his career in industry and switched to the career of a "professional ideological worker" who would work in the leading institutions of the Komsomol and later the party. When Sasha moved to the raikom he was sent to study for a year at the Higher Party School,[9] an educational graduate-level facility for professional ideological workers of different

[7] On forms of cynicism among Komsomol members in the 1920s and the various ways in which Komsomol work was rearticulated in that early period, see Brovkin (1998).

[8] See chapter 2 on the disappearance of the metadiscourse on ideology.

[9] *Vysshaia partiinaia shkola* or VPSh.

levels who already had university degrees (the students in Sasha's class were raikom employees from all over northwestern Russia). One of the courses in the Higher Party School, entitled "The basics of Marxist-Leninist rhetoric" (*Osnovy marksistsko-leninskoi retoriki*), taught the skills of writing and speaking in the genre of authoritative language. Sasha explains:

> They gave us concrete key words [*kliuchevye slova*] to use in speeches to connect any random theme, for example, a film or a political event, with the current political situation in the country. We were given twenty minutes to think and then the professor asked who wanted to try. She pointed out our mistakes, suggested how to improve our arguments, how to construct better phrases with the given words, and so on.... There were also key phrases that we needed to use: the clichéd phrases [*izbitye frazy*] that everyone had heard an endless number of times. They came to mind easily and were not difficult to reproduce.

During this training process new raikom employees learned which formulations were correct and which were incorrect and why. Sasha learned, for example, the narrative structure of a typical authoritative address at a large Komsomol meeting in a primary organization. Each address had to start with a "political part" (*politicheskaia chast'*). This part had to quote phrases and figures given by the party leaders at the latest plenum, contain a list of generic achievements and successes of the Soviet people, and be composed out of special formulaic phraseology. Sasha explains: "Let's say that Brezhnev mentioned in his speech that the productivity of labor during the past period had increased by half a percent and something else by one percent. We had to insert these figures into our speeches. Whatever you were saying, you had to use them. So, we copied these phrases directly from the press." Such explicit discussions on ideology were conducted only inside the Higher Party School and were not visible to most people. The students were not allowed to carry any of the specialized textbooks and printed materials out of the school. When, after graduating from the Higher Party School, Sasha started working at the raikom, he received lists of figures, facts, quotes, and keywords that needed to be incorporated into texts. Most of these lists came from the gorkom; some came straight from the Central Committee in Moscow. Sasha explains: "These phrases and passages referred to the general activity of the Soviet Union under the leadership of the party ... [and] were usually so well written, with such well-rounded phrases, that we could simply copy whole excerpts and insert them into our own texts, even when speaking about something local."

An Unprofessional Secretary

The lower levels of primary organizations were occupied by hundreds of thousands of "unprofessional" secretaries and komsorgs—those who were regular students or had regular professional occupations in factories and institutes but who also occupied elected positions in the Komsomol. Unlike Sasha, they were not professionally trained to compose authoritative texts and conduct rituals. However, they learned through practice that precise replication of authoritative forms provided them with time to pursue various other activities within the context of the Komsomol—activities that were not necessarily formulaic, that they found meaningful and useful, and that often were not necessarily congruous with the announced tasks of the organization. It was through the Komsomol texts, rituals, and assignments orchestrated by these people that millions of the rank-and-file Komsomol members and non-members encountered ideological activities most frequently.

Andrei (born in 1954) was an engineer at the institute where Sasha used to work, and a member of Sasha's Komsomol committee. When Sasha moved up to the raikom in 1981, Andrei was elected to replace him as the new Komsomol committee secretary. The more experienced Sasha, who now supervised the institute from the raikom, occasionally gave Andrei advice on how to compile reports and write speeches. Andrei explains:

> When you asked Sasha for help with writing something ideological he would joke for a couple of minutes and play hard to get. But then he would sit down and say in a well-trained voice [khorosho-postavlennym golosom], "OK, let's start," and would start dictating these hackneyed phrases [kazënnye frazy]. Don't think it was Leo Tolstoy or something. It was the Komsomol-Party language [komsomol'sko-partiinyi iazyk] that he knew well.

In November 1982, Andrei had to deliver his first major speech as the institute's Komsomol secretary at a large annual meeting in front of four hundred rank-and-file members. The speech had to mention the recent party decisions, the achievements and shortcomings of the institute's Komsomol organization, and its plans for the next year. It also had to make general statements about socialism, the role of the party, and the duties of the Komsomol members. Having no experience in writing such long formulaic texts, Andrei called Sasha for advice and received a simple answer: "Listen, don't break your neck over it, take my old speech in the committee files and use it as a prototype. You may simply copy most

85

of it." According to Andrei, "This was how I wrote all my future texts, and how everyone wrote theirs before and after me."

Andrei could use Sasha's old speech as a prototype without it appearing unusual because of the profound "manifest intertextuality" of this discourse (as discussed in chapter 2), but he could not simply copy it verbatim. He also needed to add some formulations, passages, and longer new parts that dealt with new facts (for example, new party plenums, campaigns, and events in his institute). However, since the text had to be true to the authoritative form, the parts Andrei composed himself had to function as recognizable citations of that form. How Andrei achieved this task illustrates the multiplicity of techniques that circulated among common secretaries and komsorgs, guaranteeing that the form of this discourse remained fixed. For reasons of space let us consider just one typical excerpt from Andrei's speech, comparing it with a corresponding excerpt from Sasha's (identical parts underlined):

Sasha's 1978 speech[10]
<u>One of the main</u> tasks <u>of the Komsomol—[is] political-ideological education of young people. The principal means for</u> its <u>fulfillment is the all-Union [*nationwide*] Lenin examination and the system of Komsomol polit-enlightenment.</u>

Andrei's 1982 speech[11]
<u>One of the main</u> directions in the work <u>of the Komsomol is the political-ideological education of young people.</u> The formation of the Marxist-Leninist worldview, a nonconciliatory attitude toward the bourgeois ideology and morality, the education of young men and women in the spirit of Soviet patriotism and socialist internationalism—these are the primary tasks facing the ideological leadership of our Komsomol organization. <u>The principal means for the fulfillment of</u> the tasks of political-ideological education of young people are <u>the all-Union Lenin examination and the system of Komsomol political enlightenment.</u>

In this typical excerpt, as elsewhere in his speech, Andrei copied some of Sasha's sentences and inserted a few new ones. He copied the

[10] *<u>Odna iz glavnykh</u> zadach <u>komsomola—ideino-politicheskoe vospitanie molodezhi. Osnovnym sredstvom</u> ee <u>resheniia iavliaetsia vsesoiuznyi Leninskii zachet i sistema komsomol'skogo</u> politprosveshcheniia.*

[11] *<u>Odnim iz vazhneishikh</u> napravlenii raboty <u>komsomola iavliaetsia ideino-politicheskoe vospitanie molodëzhi.</u> Formirovanie marksistsko-leninskogo mirovozreniia, neprimirimogo otnosheniia k burzhuaznoi ideologii i morali, vospitanie iunoshei i devushek v dukhe sovetskogo patriotizma i sotsialisticheskogo internatsionalizma—vot perveishie zadachi stoiashchie pered ideologicheskim aktivom nashei komsomol'skoi organizatsii. <u>Osnovnymi sredstvami resheniia</u> zadach ideino-politicheskogo vospitaniia molodezhi iavliaiutsia <u>vsesoiuznyi Leninskii zachet i sistema komsomol'skogo politicheskogo prosveshcheniia.</u>*

two sentences from the excerpt of Sasha's speech but introduced minimal changes in them in order, Andrei explains, "to avoid feeling like a mindless copier." He replaced Sasha's "tasks" (*zadach'*) with "direction" (*napravlenii*) and changed the grammatical case of the noun[12] without affecting the meaning. He replaced Sasha's compound noun "politenlightenment" (*politprosveshcheniia*) with its unpacked synonym, "political enlightenment" (*politicheskogo prosveshcheniia*). He also inserted a new phrase—"the tasks of political-ideological education of young people" (*zadach ideino-politicheskogo vospitaniia molodëzhi*)—to remind his audience what "tasks" had been mentioned above. He needed to do this because he had inserted a new sentence between the two.

Andrei introduced many new sentences like this one into his speech, adding his own flavor to Sasha's text. How did he compose them? In fact, all of his new sentences can be found in the endless texts of the period, suggesting that Andrei copied them from published sources. Some of them he probably composed himself, by applying what chapter 2 called the "generative principles" of authoritative language that he had learned from experience. For example, one phrase in Andrei's new sentence in the example above—"a nonconciliatory attitude toward the bourgeois ideology and morality"—is practically identical to a phrase in 1977 *Pravda* editorial shown in figure 2.1 of the previous chapter: "a nonconciliatory attitude toward any manifestations of the bourgeois ideology, political carelessness, and complacency." (paragraph 9). A close version of another phrase—"the education of young men and women in the spirit of Soviet patriotism and socialist internationalism"—is contained in the book on the Komsomol (Andreyev 1980) also quoted in the previous chapter: "the education of young people in the spirit of communist ideology, Soviet patriotism, internationalism." In writing his speech Andrei replicated some parts of old Sasha's text, added parts from newspapers and party publications, and composed his own parts, always remaining faithful to the authoritative form.

Secondary School Komsorgs and Secretaries

Komsorgs and committee secretaries of small organizations (such as secondary schools) occupied the lowest two levels among Komsomol leaders. Usually people became komsorgs at schools not necessarily because they displayed some extraordinary ideological activism and loyalty but because they enjoyed organizing people and orchestrating social activities,

---

[12] From *odna* (nominal, feminine, singular) to *odnim* (instrumental, masculine, singular).

they were seen by teachers and peers as responsible people, or they simply were unlikely to turn down requests. The same people tended to be reelected to these positions year after year. Marina (born in 1968) started out with leading positions in the organizations for younger children (the "Oktobrist" organization, for children ages seven to ten, and the "pioneer" organization for children ages ten to fourteen).[13] At age fifteen, when most of her classmates became Komsomol members, she was elected to the position of komsorg for her grade. Although the position had its rewards,[14] it also came with unpleasant responsibilities and tedious work, which most students tried to avoid. Marina describes the qualities that she thought made her appropriate for the job: "In my character, I am a social being [*sushchestvo obshchestvennoe*]"; "I don't enjoy being alone"; and "I think I gave the impression of being the type of person who should be elected to these positions, someone who was reliable [*nadëzhnaia*] and obviously liked conducting social activities [*zanimat'sia obshchestvennoi zhizn'iu*]." Those who were komsorgs in secondary school were likely to continue in this role after school. The transition was often automatic, although not inevitable. Lyuba (born in 1958), a komsorg in her secondary school class, also became one in college. She explains: "A former komsorg was branded [*u tebia kleimo*] as a person who was brought up in a certain way, had insider knowledge about procedures [*vkhozh vo vse dela*], understood how things were done [*ponimaet chto k chemu*]." When Lyuba started college, the supervisor of her group (one of her professors), who knew of her Komsomol experience from her file, "told me that he hoped I would participate in the Komsomol work. At the first meeting of our student group he nominated me to the post of the komsorg, and of course I was instantly elected."

A member of a secondary school Komsomol committee, Masha (born in 1970) from the city of Kaliningrad, learned early on about the importance of reproducing precise forms of authoritative discourse. For example, when Masha and most of her classmates were admitted to the pioneer organization, they had to prepare a pioneer notebook (*pionerskaia knizhka*), copy into it the pioneer oath (*pionerskaia kliatva*), and decorate it with appropriate pictures (red flags, red stars, hammers and sickles, and other Soviet symbols). The mother of one of Masha's classmates was a professional artist and drew in her son's pioneer book a beautiful profile of Lenin in a golden circle, surrounded by golden hearts of wheat and red banners. Masha recalls:

---

[13] See Riordan (1989).

[14] She enjoyed closer relations with, and greater respect from, some teachers than most students.

> I liked the picture so much that I asked him to let me copy it. I took it home and spent the whole day drawing. The hardest part was copying Lenin's face. I drew, erased, and redrew it several times. . . . Finally I colored the picture and thought that it turned out very beautifully. The next day everyone brought their booklets to school for the ceremony. When our teacher looked at my drawing, she said in front of everyone: "Masha, if you are not sure that you can draw faces, you should not touch Lenin. You may experiment with others' portraits, but not with Lenin's." I felt very embarrassed.

Lyuba (mentioned above), who was twelve years older than Masha and lived in a different city, learned a remarkably similar lesson from the art teacher at her secondary school in Leningrad:

> In school I drew pretty well and always received good grades in art class. Once for the drawing exhibition devoted to the anniversary of the pioneer organization, I drew a portrait of Lenin in a red pioneer scarf. I wanted to display my picture, but to my surprise our art teacher told me: "I am going to give you a good grade, but you shouldn't display this picture at the exhibition. And don't show it to anyone. Only the best artists can draw Lenin; he should be drawn well."

To Masha and Lyuba these experiences came as a surprise and they remembered them well. They had thought that their portraits demonstrated their pioneer devotion; however, the obvious distortions in the representation of Lenin made both teachers uneasy about publicly displaying them. Their comments made it clear that the problem was not the unsophisticated technique of childish drawings, but that it was applied specifically to Lenin. The teachers were also nervous that such pictures by their students might suggest their own ideological carelessness. What students learned in such experiences was that "Lenin" was not just one among endless Soviet symbols, but a central organizing principle of authoritative discourse, its master signifier and external canon through which all other symbols and concepts were legitimized. That signifier grounded the whole authoritative discourse and was directly linked to the "original." This is why only specially designated propaganda artists depicted Lenin and to guarantee the trace of the original used in their work Lenin's death mask and the cast of his head, linking their images to the actual physical body.[15]

In later grades in secondary school (ages 14–17), Masha became a komsorg and eventually a member of the school's Komsomol committee. Having to write speeches for Komsomol meetings, she learned more

---

[15] See chapter 2 for a discussion of this process of reproduction and of Lenin's role as master signifier.

about the importance of the citational form in the authoritative genre. Masha made a comment that reveals the primacy of the poetic function and the increasing irrelevance of the referential function of this language: "Often I would be unable to explain what I wrote in my own words. Everyone, sort of, had a general feeling that the text sounded precise [chëtko] and impressive [vpechatliaiushche]. Even as a child I was always impressed by such serious and unclear phraseology." After such experiences as her imprecise drawing of Lenin, Masha gradually learned that for her speeches it was necessary to copy precise passages from texts published elsewhere: "Sometimes I . . . copied sentences from an appropriate newspaper editorial. . . . At first, I copied the key phrases that would be useful, and then wrote my own text around them." She had learned the importance of manifest intertextuality, as well as the limits of this principle.

Eventually Masha memorized a lot of phraseology and figured out elaborate principles of composition. In her words, she learned how to create special (osobye) constructions instead of the ordinary (obychnye) ones used in everyday language. The analysis of these language forms demonstrates that Masha learned not only certain phrases and terminologies, but actually figured out rather complex linguistic and stylistic principles of authoritative language for representing voice, authorship, knowledge, temporality—principles discussed in the previous chapter. Masha did not contemplate explicitly what the principles she applied achieved; however, she intuitively used them with great precision. For example, she explains how she would always use a special construction, *revolution that-has-carried-itself-out* [svershivshaiasia revoliutsiia], preferring it to the ordinary one, *revolution that-has-been-carried-out* [sovershënnaia revoliutsiia]. The second phrase, she says, "just sounded better." In fact, this phrase shifted the temporality and authorial voice: the reflexive form *that-has-carried-itself-out* [svershivshaiasia], unlike *that-has-been-carried-out* [sovershënnaia], represented the revolution as an event that happened itself, following objective laws of history, instead of being designed and carried out by concrete actors. Here the actors who led the revolution are implicitly represented as mediators of unavoidable historic necessity, not as creators of an arbitrary historic situation. And because Masha was describing events in terms of these objective laws of history, her own authorial voice was presented as that of a mediator of objective, preexisting, and commonly held knowledge, not as a creator of new knowledge.

Masha also shifted the temporality of discourse by employing complex modifiers with comparative degree. For example, among the special constructions she learned to use were *deeply profound meaning* (glubinnyi smysl) instead of the ordinary *profound meaning* (glubokii smysl) and *unebbing* or *interminable significance* (*neprekhodiashchee znachenie*) instead of just (*bol'shoe znachenie*) *great significance*. The modifier *glubinnyi* (deeply profound), unlike *glubokii* (profound), emphasizes not simply the fact of depth but also its comparative degree: *glubinnyi* usually refers to the deepest depths of something (as the floor of the ocean).[16] Similarly, the modifier "unebbing," unlike "great," emphasizes not just significance but its comparative temporal dimension (unebbing as opposed to finite). Both these double moves contribute to the construction of presuppositions that the "profundity" and "significance" are commonly known prior forms of knowledge. Masha also turned verbal phrases into nominal ones and combined them into long nominal strings, which again produced a number of presuppositions and contributed to shifting her discourse toward prior temporality and a mediator voice. For example, she wrote such phrases as:

> The unebbing significance of the victory of the working class in the Great October Socialist Revolution [is] impossible to overestimate.

> [*Neprekhodiashchee znachenie pobedy rabochego klassa v Velikoi Oktiabr'skoi sotsialisticheskoi revoliutsii nevozmozhno pereotsenit'.*]

The part of the sentence before *is* is a string of noun phrases that conveys several presuppositions, each corresponding to a distinct verbal phrase: the working class won a victory; the victory is significant; the significance is unebbing; and so on. As we saw in chapter 2, arranging these presuppositions into a string, and therefore predicating them on each other, is not about making claims but about shifting the temporality of discourse into multiple levels of the past and conveying knowledge as if it is already known and shared. It is also about converting the authorial voice into one of mediator of prior knowledge, not creator of new knowledge.

Masha also learned that in order to write speeches for the meetings devoted to national holidays, she had to start with lists of long standardized achievements with which the country "greeted" them. She learned not to use "and" before the last word in these lists, because, in her words, this "created an impression that the list had no end, increasing the magnitude of achievements" (which is remarkably similar to how Sasha was trained to refer to national holidays, above). Masha would write:

> The Soviet people in one united outburst of labor greet the anniversary of the Great October [or other event] with new achievements in industrial and agricultural labor, science, culture, education.

---

[16] See the "Complex Modifiers" section of chapter 2 for a similar analysis of comparative modifiers.

[*Sovetskie liudi v edinom trudovom poryve vstrechaiut godovsh-chinu Velikogo Oktiabria novymi dostizheniiami v promyshlennom i sel'skokhoziaistvennom trude, v nauke, kul'ture, obrazovanii.*]

By meticulously citing these multiple levels of authoritative form, from concrete phrases and words, to structural principles, temporal modalities, and voices, Masha gained access to Bourdieu's "delegated power of the spokesperson." The more faithful the language of her speeches and reports was to the authoritative form, the more she inhabited the position of "authorized spokesperson" of the ideological institution (the Komsomol) and therefore the more she was endowed with its "delegated" power (Bourdieu 1991, 107). In this way, the form contributed to the degree of independence that Masha had from the teachers' control. In Masha's words: "I tried to use as many formulaic phrases [*izbitye frazy*] as possible—[when I did so] the teachers were less likely to criticize me for my other work."

Masha reproduced the hypernormalized form of authoritative language with great competence. The particularly acute ability of this hypernormalized language to "break" with context in unpredictable ways opened up spaces for new meanings, and therefore for creativity and imagination, allowing Masha to engage with her Komsomol work in ways that had been neither completely constrained nor anticipated by the claimed constative meanings of formulaic statements or Komsomol rules. At the same time, being creative and imaginative and engaging in unexpected pursuits did not necessarily mean contradicting communist values either. Masha's responsibility in the Komsomol committee was to keep track of the statistics regarding students' grades (*uspevaemost'*) and to identify problems in the educational process. Masha initiated a system to support students who struggled in certain subjects with help from students who were more successful in those subjects. She also compiled schoolwide statistics of grades, according to classes and subjects, and eventually accumulated an archive going back several terms that provided a meaningful comparison between classes, subjects, and teachers.

At the end of every quarter, I sat down with each "class journal" [a journal containing the grades of one class[17]], calculated average grades, figured out percentages, and then wrote a huge report analyzing the dynamic of student performance in the school as a whole. I really enjoyed doing that, and my work became known and respected. A copy of my report went to the school director. . . . I developed good relations with teachers and they would ask me to look up this or that

---

[17] A Soviet "class" refers to a group of thirty to forty students who studied together during all ten years of school.

result in my archive. . . . This helped to make some improvements in the educational process.

She found this work important and meaningful, and enjoyed in it a certain degree of independence from the teachers, whose work her report indirectly evaluated.

"Work with Meaning" by Means of "Pure Pro Forma"

Andrei, the Komsomol secretary above, came to believe that many basic socialist values that he thought were important—education, professional work, social welfare, a collectivist ethic—were enabled by bureaucratic rules and that some forms of the Komsomol work had to be repeated just at the level of the ritual although others had to be performed with a particular focus on meaning. He distinguished between two types of Komsomol activities. Some, which he called "pure pro forma" (*chistaia proforma*, literally, a matter of form) or "ideological shell" (*ideologicheskaia shelukha*), he engaged at the level of the performative dimension, with constative meaning reinterpreted or irrelevant (e.g. sometimes reporting these activities on paper without conducting them in practice). Other activities, which he called "work with meaning" (*rabota so smyslom*)—that is, with the original constative meaning still relevant—he found important, enjoyable, and often initiated himself. The two types were neither in opposition nor easily divided. Rather, Andrei, like Masha, learned that in order to conduct work with meaning, one needed to perform the pro forma rituals and activities—making formulaic speeches, compiling formulaic reports, conducting formulaic rituals, and so on. In other words, performing the pro forma enabled Andrei to engage with other types of work and meanings, including those that coincided with ideological plans of the Komsomol organization and those that did not. Andrei also learned how to minimize the pro forma so that it enabled meaningful work by not taking too much time or energy.

This meant that he reinterpreted for himself much of what the Komsomol stood for in everyday life. However, such active displacement of "ideological" work did not mean that Andrei was acting in opposition to broader ideological goals or resisted broader communist ideals. On the contrary, for him, ignoring the constative meanings of the Komsomal pro forma while engaging wholeheartedly in the Komsomol work with meaning were all part and parcel of how he understood communist identity, goals, and ethics.

93

Work with meaning, in Andrei's case, involved conducting various professional and social activities—for example, the institute's "system of apprenticeship" (*sistema nastavnichestva*) that his committee organized: "When a new young employee was hired, we assigned him a mentor [*nastavnik*] among people with greater experience who could share their professional knowledge and skills . . . [so as] not to leave newcomers lost and completely on their own. That system was very popular." Work with meaning also included regular contests for the best professional skills (*konkurs profmasterstva*) among different categories of young employees (designers, technological engineers, researchers, workers); these contests "generated a lot of interest . . . and were useful and to the point [*po delu*]."

A task that Andrei found particularly meaningful was creating a museum about the role the institute played during World War II, which involved managing a group of young employees who gathered materials for the museum, inviting the institute's veterans to talk about their experiences on the front, among other things. Andrei also enjoyed solving social issues and organizing what he calls "normal life" (*normal'naia zhizn'*): helping young families to arrange kindergartens for their children; organizing a *subbotnik*[18] to clean the institute's premises; gathering Komsomol members to travel to the institute's Pioneer Camp[19] for a weekend of construction work; finding people to work in the collective farm sponsored by the institute;[20] organizing sports competitions; celebrations of anniversaries and professional holidays; concerts of amateur rock bands; poetry readings; dances; the annual New Year's party; and so on.

For organizing these diverse social and cultural activities among young employees, Andrei won several honorary diplomas (*gramota*) from his supervising raikom, "for success in Komsomol-youth work" (*Za uspekhi v komsomol'sko-molodëzhnoi rabote*) and "for the active work in the communist education of youth" (*Za aktivnuiu raboty po kommunisticheskomu vospitaniiu molodëzhi*). Despite the formulaic nature of these awards, Andrei was proud to receive them and kept them on the wall in his office and later at home. For him they were not just empty symbols but signs of recognition of his organizing talents, creativity, and genuine concern for the common good.

Andrei's ability to differentiate between work with meaning and work that was pure formality went deeper. In general, he "believed in the

[18] Voluntary work on a Saturday, for example, devoted to Lenin's birthday in April. In practice, these days were chosen and announced centrally by the state.

[19] Summer camp for kids ages ten to fourteen.

[20] To help ailing Soviet agriculture, most Soviet enterprises were assigned to sponsor certain collective farms in their region by sending employees from the enterprise to help with the harvest and other types of work.

actual [communist] idea" (*veril v samu ideiu*) but felt alienated from the "senseless" (*bessmyslennyi*) formalism in which it tended to be framed:

> We grew up with an idea that Lenin was sacred. Lenin was a symbol of purity, order, wisdom. Absolutely. I assumed that all problems were caused by the later distortions of Lenin's original policies, by Stalin's perverse and bloody rule, and by that moronic [*umalishënnyi*] Brezhnev. I thought that we should return to Lenin's original ideas[21] and then everything would be fine. At that time [the 1970s], it was common to think that if only Lenin had still been alive he would have averted all the bad things [*vsë to plokhoe*] that were taking place.

This is another reference to "Lenin" as a master signifier of authoritative discourse, through which this discourse was grounded externally and all other symbols and concepts were legitimized, as discussed in chapter 2.

Andrei, who eventually joined the Communist Party, differentiated between two meanings of "the party," just as he differentiated between work with meaning and pure pro forma work at the Komsomol: "Although I agreed that the party was the only institution that knew what really needed to be done, I distinguished between the party as the common people [*prostye liudi*] and the party apparatus [*apparat*]." The former was a large community of people who "worked hard and were good, intelligent, and compassionate [*khoroshie, umnye i dushevnye*]"; the latter had inside itself a stagnant bureaucratic group of the "*apparatchiki* [members of the party *apparat*] at the level of the raikoms and gorkoms," who were "rotten inside [*prognivshie*] and distorted [*iskazhali*] good ideas and policies." Andrei believed that "if we got rid of these *apparatchiki* or somehow minimized their influence, then, naturally, the party would be able to work much better." Andrei's example shows that being alienated from boring activities, senseless rhetoric, and corrupt bureaucracy was not necessarily in contradiction with being ethically invested in the communist ideals and being involved in activities designed to achieve communist goals. For him, these two types of sentiments were not in opposition but rather mutually constitutive. And he was clearly not the only one who felt this way.

Igor, who was born in 1960 and a secondary school komsorg in the late 1970s in the town of Sovetsk,[22] also distinguished between the meaningful and the tedious aspects of his Komsomol duties. He had a profoundly ambivalent relationship to the Komsomol practice, despising its tedious formalism yet feeling personally invested in what he saw as its

---

[21] Gorbachev thought this too when he introduced the reforms of perestroika, as did most Soviet people at that time.

[22] In the Kaliningrad region.

collective ethos and concern for the common good. Referring to large collegewide Komsomol meetings at which he sat in the audience along with hundreds of others, Igor says: "How I hated those Komsomol meetings for constant formalism and boredom!" [*kak ia nenavidel eti komsomol'skie sobraniia za beskonechnyi formalizm i skukatu*] Like most of his peers in the audience he usually tried to pay minimal attention to what was going on and to involve himself in other activities:

> If this was a meeting of more than a hundred people . . . I certainly took some book with me—a textbook or something like that. I sat there reading and studying. It was completely irrelevant to me what decisions would be made because I understood perfectly well, and I think everyone did, that the decisions had been made in advance [*zagotovleny zaranee*].[23] The meeting had to be sat through [*otsidet'*]. . . . You could not really talk much, so reading was optimal. Everyone read books. Everyone. And what's interesting, as soon as the meeting began, all heads bowed down and everyone started to read. Some fell asleep. But when a vote had to be taken, everyone roused—a certain sensor clicked in the head; "Who is in favor?"—and you raised your hand automatically.

And yet the formalism of these large meetings, speeches, and votes that alienated Igor from the routine rituals of the Komsomol failed to alienate him from the basic ethical ideals and promises of socialism that the Komsomol still represented for him. Like Andrei, Igor knew that the pure formality of these rituals had to be performed in order for the creative and good aspects of socialist life also to be possible. But, like Andrei, he also believed that it was important to try to minimize the senseless formalities and eventually to get rid of them altogether, preserving the good aspects of socialism. For Igor, the "work with meaning" involved organizing lectures about political events in the world, meetings with war veterans, programs for helping the elderly, disputes about literature, and so on. He even volunteered for the post of the komsorg several years in a row in secondary school and later at the university. He explains his beliefs and ideals, linking them with what he and his family felt were the good and humane aspects of the socialist state:

> I wanted to be in the Komsomol because I wanted to be among the young avant-garde who would work to improve life. . . . I felt that if you lived according to the right scheme—school, institute, work—everything in your life would be fine. . . . Basically, as far as I was concerned, the government's policy was correct. It consisted simply of

[23] The system of prearranged meetings was repeated top to bottom in the Komsomol hierarchy, including the CC plenums (see the discussion of the latter in Solnick 1998, 85).

caring for people, free hospitals, good education. My father was an example of this policy. He was our region's chief doctor and worked hard to improve the medical services for the people. And my mother worked hard as a doctor. We had a fine apartment from the state.

Mikhail (born in 1958) was also an active participant in Komsomol work, and occupied the post of komsorg during his last two years in secondary school and then for four years at the university. In retrospect, speaking from the post-Soviet 1990s, Mikhail contemplates the ambivalent nature of his relationship to Soviet reality:

[As a result of perestroika] I came to an incredible realization about myself. It suddenly became clear to me that in principle I had always known that some of the party leadership was rotten. I had not been too keen on the Komsomol in school, even though I was a komsorg. Like most others, I had often felt nauseated hearing Brezhnev's speeches on television. And like most others I had told political *anekdoty*.[24] I had also understood that Stalin was bad. And yet, despite all this, I had always had a strong conviction, perhaps since I was kindergarten age, that socialism and communism were good and right [*khorosho i pravil'no*]. . . . I had always thought that the actual idea was profoundly correct [*sama ideia gluboko verna*] and that this was how things should be. . . . Of course, I had realized that there were distortions and revisions [*iskazheniia i nasloeniia*] [of the idea]. But I thought that if we managed to get rid of them everything would be great. . . . At some point [before 1985] I was confident that I understood everything about life and that my opinion could not change any more.

Tonya (born in 1966),[25] a rank-and-file Komsomol member, also used to distinguish, before perestroika, between the ethical values of everyday life in socialism, which were important to her, and the many formulaic aspects of that reality from which she felt alienated. Despite this alienation, Tonya always had "a deep feeling that we lived in the best country in the world." Like everyone else, she told political jokes, and yet she also made a point of distinguishing between the right way to tell a joke and the wrong way. There was a proper time and place to tell a joke, and jokes about certain political figures were appropriate but jokes about others were not. Still, her telling jokes did not imply that she completely rejected communist ethical principles. For example, "When I was finishing

[24] Very popular jokes that were repeated by different people in different contexts on a daily basis, often dealing with political and social topics (see chapter 7 for more on *anekdoty*).

[25] This is the same Tonya as mentioned in chapter 1.

[secondary] school [at age 17] and my little brother was still young and did not yet understand a lot of things, he once told me a joke about Lenin. I remember telling him: "You may joke about Brezhnev, but let's not make jokes about Lenin."

The final remark is strikingly reminiscent of the comment (above) that Masha's drawing teacher made about her picture of Lenin: "You may experiment with others' portraits, but not with Lenin's." Although, "political" *anekdoty* about Lenin did circulate in the Soviet discourse, they were not as common as *anekdoty* about other political figures. This relationship to Lenin did not preclude Tonya's sentiments, which she had developed in school, that the ideas formulated in party rhetoric contained "a certain falsity" [*nekuiu lzhivost'*]. For example, she deeply disliked her history teacher for her overly zealous attitude toward the norms of "communist morality" and her earnest repetition of party slogans.

The distinctions that engaged, lower-level Komsomol members made between the ethical values of socialism, on the one hand, and the distortions of these ethical values, on the other hand, reflect the complexities and contradictions with which many young people related to Soviet socialism. This relationship was characterized not by binary oppositions of "us" (common people) versus "them" (the party, the state), but by a seemingly paradoxical coexistence of affinities and alienations, belonging and estrangement, meaningful work and pure formality—the values, attitudes, and identities that were indivisible and constitutive of the forms of life that were "normal," creative, ethical, engaged, and worth being involved in.

"Little Tricks"

This complex dynamic between different dimensions of discourse turned the orchestration of Komsomol work into a very specific challenge. To fulfill assignments at the level of pure formality and still be able to conduct work with meaning, the komsorgs and secretaries needed to secure a very particular kind of participation among the rank-and-file members. This dynamic put them in constant practical and moral dilemmas.

Consider again Masha, whose responsibility, as a member of her secondary school's Komsomol committee, was to keep track of the students' educational progress. The formulaic structure of the speeches that Masha delivered at the Komsomol meetings required her to mention the names of "bad students" who received low grades. Like other Komsomol organizers, Masha faced a dilemma: she wanted to continue doing the work she found socially meaningful and personally fulfilling, yet she also wanted to avoid causing negative consequences for the students she named or being seen as someone who furthered her career at the expense of others. It was important, explains Masha, "to avoid spoiling relations with students, especially for such a [pro forma] reason [*na takoi pochve*]." To deal with this dilemma, she made sure that the students saw the naming of concrete persons as pro forma and perceived her voice as that of the mediator of the required authoritative form and not the originator of the blame. Her strategy is similar to the discursive technique examined in the previous chapter of eschewing authorial responsibility in authoritative texts.

Masha mentioned the names of bad students as was required, but tried to limit this list to students who had been considered "traditionally bad" for years and had been previously criticized by others. However, for her work to be taken seriously, she also needed to mention a few new names that "had not been worn out yet" (*nezataskannye*). To minimize the damage, she rotated the new names as much as possible, and tried to make sure that the people she mentioned did not interpret it as a personal attack: "I spoke with these students beforehand: 'Listen, don't be upset with me, but in my throne speech [*tronnaia rech'*—slang for the secretary's annual speech] I will have to mention you not in a very good light. I have nothing against you. I like you as a person. You understand this, right?' Usually they agreed. That way I always gathered [*nabirala*] the needed number of names." These personal conversations, friendly remarks, and an ironic reference to "my throne speech" communicated to the students that these parts of Masha's upcoming speech should be read not "literally," but as a performative ritual. This enabled Masha to be involved in several meaningful pursuits: to conduct socially important and meaningful work, maintain friendly relations with the rank and file, and pursue her personal aspirations of graduating from school with high honors and going to the university in Leningrad, to which her leadership work in the Komsomol contributed.

Like Masha, Andrei (above) also faced a dilemma: he did not want to lose the respect of his peers by having to force them to do senseless, tedious work, nor did he want to receive an official reprimand from his superiors for failing in his duties. He also did not want to trivialize his Komsomol work altogether, reducing it only to formulaic procedures and losing the meaningful and ethical potential it had. To solve this predicament, Andrei invented what he called "little tricks" (*malen'kie khitrosti*)—techniques that, like Masha's, helped him manage his relations with both the higher and lower levels of the Komsomol hierarchy, completing the assignments that were pure formality, while continuing to do work that had meaning for him. For example, Andrei employed a technique for distributing unpopular routine assignments among the rank and file:

I noticed that if I approached someone saying, "Listen, you should say a few words [*vystupit'*] at the next Komsomol meeting," that person would start inventing millions of reasons why he could not possibly do it and would start begging me to let him off. . . . I would continue to insist very firmly for a while, but then would suddenly give up and say: "Oh, all right. I'll find someone else, if you instead agree to do this little work." I'd offer him [the option] to compile a protocol or draft a report, which was not difficult but was tedious and time-consuming—he had to speak with different people, collect information, write it up. . . . People happily agreed in exchange for not having to make speeches.

Andrei also developed a complex system that allowed him to fulfill, at the level of form only, the unrealistic assignments imposed on his organization by the raikom. Once, the raikom assigned him to organize a "lecture group" (*lektorskaia gruppa*) at his institute. The task was to gather ten rank-and-file Komsomol members, who would make regular "political information lectures" (*politinformatsiia*) throughout the year to their colleagues. Such lectures were conducted in the style of "political education," which meant that a usual topic could be "something like the decisions of the recent party plenum or the Komsomol movements in Hungary." As with making speeches, the prospect of giving regular lectures proved unpopular and people found excuses to avoid it. To solve the problem, explains Andrei:

[O]ur Committee made a decision to create a lecture group on paper. . . . We even had five or six people in it. . . . I said to my friend, a rank-and-file Komsomol member: "You will be the leader." He had to keep a system of reports [*otchëtnost'*] about lectures and, if a report was reviewed by the raikom, to discuss it with a competent look [*s gramotnym vidom*]. And also, when possible, once or twice a year, to arrange real lectures so that there was something to refer to just in case. All other lectures existed purely on paper.

Andrei briefed rank-and-file members, the would-be "lecturers," on how to respond in the unlikely case of a checkup by some commission from a higher level in the hierarchy. Such arrangements were so commonplace that they surprised neither his committee nor the rank-and-file members in his Komsomol group. In fact, his contacts in the raikom were also aware that some arrangement must have taken place. Andrei said to them "in a friendly manner" (*po-druzheski*):

"Guys, you yourselves should understand that we cannot possibly achieve what is being asked of us. This number of lectures is simply physically unrealistic." And they said: "Yes, we can see this, but we are under pressure from above." So we told them that we would make the minimum number of required lectures, and did not explain exactly how we would do it.

The raikom representatives were not likely to question the rank-and-file members directly whether or which lectures had taken place: "Everything was based precisely on this. We knew that no one would ask them. The raikom hardly ever spoke with any real people. Preparing reports was our main task," said Andrei. Several levels of the Komsomol hierarchy participated in this assignment purely at the level of form, making the reports about the lectures, and maintaining a complex system of agreements and unspoken understandings, which were more important than the lectures themselves. Having reviewed reports in different organizations of the district, the raikom inspectors produced their own "review certificate" that went to the gorkom. The lecturing group of Andrei's institute was recognized as "exemplary" for conducting "monthly lectures on international political and social problems." The certificate in particular mentioned "the lectures of an institute employee, Comrade N., about demographic issues and the development of agriculture in the region of Leningrad, [which] enjoyed great success."[26]

Andrei also learned to identify which assignments the higher organizations needed purely for reporting purposes and how to avoid or minimize such assignments:

When gorkom bosses were preparing their reports they always needed to describe Komsomol work in primary organizations around the city. So they called up various enterprises and over the phone assigned their Komsomol secretaries to collect some "examples from real life" [*primery iz zhizni*]. These had to be written stories with real names, figures, and facts. It took them three minutes to impose this task on you, and then you spent the next three days running around to fulfill it. Naturally, I tried to avoid that. If the phone rang in my Komsomol committee I usually answered it cautiously, without giving my name: "Yes?"

If the voice sounded unfamiliar and formal I was instantly on alert. And if it said, "Good day. This is Instructor So-and-So from the gorkom. May I speak with the committee secretary?", I would reply, "He is not in."

If they asked, "Who's this speaking?", I always had a prepared response: "This is Komsomol member Semënov [invented name], I just

[26] This certificate was entitled, "Spravka po proverke komsomol'skoi organizatsii Vsesoiuznogo nauchno-issledovatel'skogo i proektnogo instituta [Name] (Review Certificate of the Komsomol Organization of the All-Union Scientific Research and Design Institute of [Name]"). From Andrei's personal archive.

stopped by the committee to return my Komsomol card, when the phone rang."

"When will the secretary return?"

"Oh, you know, probably in two or three days. He's on a business trip."

"Tell him that the gorkom is preparing a report on something or other, and we need examples from your organization. Urgently! He must call me as soon as he returns."

"Certainly!"

Andrei knew that the gorkom secretary needed examples "urgently" in order to compile his own report to the higher-level institutions about his supervision of the Komsomol activities in the city and that therefore he would rather call other organizations, leaving Andrei alone. He also knew that these examples were seen in the higher-level institutions as pure formality as well.

Since the higher bodies needed to fulfill assignments and compile reports, they also developed strategies that were similar to Andrei's "little tricks" when interacting with the komsorgs and secretaries who were trying to avoid them. For example, the raikoms organized regular conferences devoted to the exchange of experience between representatives of the Komsomol organizations in the district about how they conducted the Komsomol work. At these conferences various local secretaries had to deliver speeches describing their work. The raikom needed to guarantee high attendance at these conferences. Secondary school komsorg Lyuba, mentioned earlier, was regularly delegated by her school to attend these events. For a while she signed her name on the list of attendees upon entering the meeting hall, waited until the first intermission, and left. But others did that too, and by the end of the day the audience had often lost the required quorum for voting. The raikom organizers, who needed to report the vote, changed the system of control. Lyuba explains that they started producing "the list of attendees at the end of the meeting, and you could only sign your name when leaving the auditorium. This meant that I had to sit through [otsidet'] all three or four hours." In response to new measures Lyuba always sat at the very back of the hall and spent the time doing her homework for school.

Activists, Dissidents, and Svoi

In earlier sections of this chapter, we considered some techniques that were used to produce authoritative texts, rituals, and other forms in various Komsomol contexts and the conditions under which this production went on. Let us consider now how these techniques, conditions, texts, and rituals were predicated upon, and contributed to, the unanticipated cultural production of a particular common sociality of young Soviet people, to which these people referred in daily speech as *svoi*.[27] The term *svoi*, which can mean "us," "ours," or "those who belong to our circle," has no exact equivalent in English. To understand the concept it represents, let us investigate it ethnographically. *Svoi* was a kind of sociality that differed from those represented in authoritative discourse as the "Soviet people," "Soviet toilers," and so forth.

The meaning of this sociality of *svoi* should not be reduced to a binary scheme of "us" versus "them" or "common people" versus "the state," which has been a rather common differentiation in many analyses of Soviet society—such as Wanner's description of a common Soviet identity of "us" (*svoi, nashi*) produced by "shared experience with an oppressive state apparatus," in which " '[w]e' bond together against 'them,' the enemy, the state and its institutions" (1998, 9).[28] Although this description makes an important point that the meaning of "us/ours" as a form of solidarity was not determined by state institutions, the binary scheme of this description produces the unfortunate effect of reducing this common identity to the logic of opposition to the state, failing to grasp the mutually embedded and shifting limits of "us/ours," those who are not "us/ours" (*nenashi*), "the state," "the state representatives," and "the people." In a critique of such binary divisions, Caroline Humphrey (1994) points out that the state and state institutions in socialism were not defined vis-à-vis the people or public sphere, but incorporated everyone, top to bottom, through complex, multiple, and shifting "nesting" hierarchies (consecutively embedded like Russian dolls).[29] To understand what was the common identity to which *svoi* referred, let us consider how this term was used in the Komsomol contexts where the production of ideological texts and rituals occurred.

In the contexts of Komsomol realities, the two common terms mentioned above played a central role: *svoi* (us/ours) and *normal'nye liudi* (normal people) or *normal'nyi chelovek* (normal person). These categories were used by most rank-and-file members and secretaries to refer to themselves and their peers, especially when distinguishing themselves from two other types of persons, whom they referred to as *aktivisty* (the activists) and *dissidenty* (the dissidents). These two types, despite having opposing attitudes to authoritative discourse, shared a general approach

[27] Pronounced *svah-EE*.

[28] In her discussion Wanner speaks about the concept of *nashi* (ours) which, in that context, is closely synonymous with *svoi*.

[29] See also Dunham (1976); Kotkin (1995); Humphrey (1983 and 2001); Ledeneva (1998); Kharkhordin (1999); Nafus (2003a).

to it: they privileged the constative dimension of that discourse, reading it as a description of reality and evaluating that description for truth. For the activists, this description was "true"; for the dissidents, it was "false."[30] In reality, the terms dissidents and activists referred to "ideal types": one's relationship vis-à-vis authoritative discourse could be more or less like that of an activist or a dissident. However, these ideal types are useful analytically because most people regularly referred to them as points against which to differentiate a "normal" person.

The activists appealed to people to be more conscientious, tried to raise their enthusiasm and zeal for work, wanted to expose party secretaries who took bribes, wrote letters to the administration and to the press about local officials who were breaking the law, and so on. Among the younger generations, there were so few zealous activists that, when encountered, they often left their peers puzzled: Were these sincere principled people, stupid automatons, or cynical careerists who said the right things to attain status and privilege?[31] Inna (born in 1958), a secondary school teacher who in the late 1970s and early 1980s studied in the history department at Leningrad University, encountered an activist among the students there. He was an idealistic young man who had tried to reform the primary Komsomol organization of their history department, arguing that it was not practicing the Leninist principle of "democratic centralism," on which all party and Komsomol organizations were supposed to be based.[32] For his unsolicited initiatives he received several official reprimands and was eventually expelled from the university. Most students thought he was naïve or foolish. They did not expect the mechanics of local Komsomol practice to follow written principles, and thought that it made more sense to direct one's creative energies elsewhere.

Irina and Natalia (both born in 1958), who were the komsorgs of two departments at a research library, encountered a more puzzling activist, Leonid (born in 1960), who was the secretary of the library's Komsomol committee and their superior. At the Komsomol meetings, according to

[30] See Yurchak (1997a).

[31] For a discussion of the latter type, see Humphrey (2001, 5).

[32] "Democratic centralism" was the organizational principle of the Leninist revolutionary party, originating in Lenin's 1902 article, "*What Is to Be Done?*" (although the term itself was not invented by Lenin). According to this principle, decisions were made collectively and democratically (the minority was subordinated to the majority), but their implementation was ensured through strict discipline and centralized vertical mechanisms of party control. Lenin maintained that this principle guaranteed the highest form of democracy, which promoted individual initiative, critical engagement, and collective discipline. In practice, the centralized control and vertical subordination cancelled out any criticism of already existing policies, eventually eliminating all democratic discussion (see Jowitt 1993).

Natalia, Leonid sounded "like a newspaper editorial [*kak gazetnaia peredovitsa*]," which in itself would not be so unusual had he read his speeches from written notes and in a monotonous voice, like everyone else. Instead, he spoke spontaneously, using no notes, and could go on like this for quite a while. Speaking in the most formulaic language, Leonid passionately denounced Western bourgeois culture, criticized shortcomings in their Komsomol organization, appealed to the young, and made pledges to the old. With a chuckle Irina imitated his voice: "We, the young generation of Komsomol members, pledge to our senior comrades that we will not discredit the honor of something or other."[33]

The most striking thing was that Leonid spoke in this formulaic manner not only at the meetings, but often outside of them too, in daily contexts among his library colleagues. This extreme degree of identification with authoritative language by someone of their age was so unusual that, according to Irina, "when he spoke . . . I had a strange feeling that he could not possibly be serious, that he was simply mocking [*izdevalsia*] everyone."[34] Others thought that perhaps Leonid simply manipulated this image in front of older activists and party leaders for the purposes of his career. After all, his career did progress very well, explains Natalia: "The result was not so bad. He received a degree from the [prestigious] history department [of Leningrad University], became the Komsomol committee secretary at the library, then moved to the raikom, joined the Communist Party, and finally returned to the library as its deputy director. He achieved an impressive career at a young age." A colleague who knew Leonid during his time in the raikom described him as "a careerist [*kar'erist*] in the good and the bad senses of the word who certainly knew what he wanted and pursued that goal quite consciously." And yet Leonid did not fail to surprise them all again. After the fall of the Soviet state in 1992, when membership in the Communist Party not only drew zero prestige but, in most cases, became a liability to one's moral image and professional career, Leonid refused to leave the party, unlike most people, persisting in his communist activism.

Most komsorgs and secretaries at the lower level of the hierarchy were closer to "normal people" than to real activists. Lyuba (mentioned earlier) had worked as a komsorg for a few years, in secondary school and at the university, before she encountered her first "real activist" (*nastoiashchii aktivist*). This young woman, a student from Lyuba's college, was a member of the Komsomol committee and Lyuba's superior. Unlike most committee

---

[33] *My, molodoe pokolenie komsomol'tsev, zaveriaem nashikh starshikh tovarishchei, chto my ne uronem chesti chego-to tam.*

[34] See chapter 7 for a discussion of a particular late-Soviet genre of irony, *stiob*, that was in fact based on an "overidentification" with authoritative discourse.

members, the woman was excessively zealous about Komsomol assignments and demanded that Lyuba perform them all precisely, according to
Komsomol protocol. This made Lyuba's work unbearable: "She forced me
to convene meetings every time there was an important political event or
party plenum, to organize constant political lectures [*politinformatsii*], to
distribute assignments to the rank-and-file Komsomol members. She kept
track of my work closely. It was insane. Because of her I eventually requested to be relieved of my komsorg duties."

Dissidents, like activists, also seemed to take authoritative discourse at
face value. The most outspoken among them, the famous dissident writers,
called upon fellow citizens to refuse official falsities. Alexandr Solzhenitsyn
wrote about how important it was "to live not by lie" (1974), and Václav
Havel, in socialist Czechoslovakia, called upon his compatriots to "live
in truth" (1986). Most people, however, considered dissidents to be irrelevant. Describing a common attitude toward dissident discourse before
perestroika, Nancy Ries quotes a woman who in 1985 (before perestroika) declared with sincerity and passion that Sakharov[35] simply
"doesn't exist for us" (1997, 182). Even though this woman, like the majority, most likely did not read Sakharov's writings until perestroika,
she still insisted on his irrelevance. Her comment was not about Sakharov
per se but rather reflected the attitude toward an imaginary ideal dissident position. Just a couple of years later, during perestroika, when the
discursive regime dramatically changed, Sakharov's moral position suddenly became meaningful and widely respected, and Sakharov's image
flipped from one of cultural irrelevance to one of immense cultural significance.[36]

Thinking back to the pre-perestroika period, when dissidents were still
commonly seen as irrelevant or potentially dangerous, the poet Joseph
Brodsky repudiated Václav Havel's claim that most people avoided dissidents because of fear or the embarrassment of feeling fear. In Brodsky's
opinion, the main reasons for this avoidance were different: "Given the
seeming stability of the system," a dissident was simply "written off" by
most people, regarded by them as "a convenient example of the wrong
deportment" and therefore "a source of considerable moral comfort,"
the way "the healthy majority" sees "the sick" (Brodsky and Havel
1994).[37] Although Brodsky, like Havel, was practically unpublished during the Soviet period, was persecuted by the Soviet state, and was later
forced out of the country, he still distanced himself from the dissident

[35] Andrei Sakharov was a physicist, academician, and outspoken dissident who during
the Soviet period was exiled to the city of Gorky, which was closed to foreigners.

[36] When Sakharov died in December 1989, tens of thousands gathered for his funeral in
Moscow. See Ries (1997, 182).

[37] See also Havel (1993).

position.[38] Brodsky's "healthy majority" is a reference to "normal people" who are avoiding a psychotic moral disposition of exposing lies, to which the "sick" refer.

Among the younger generation, knowing openly dissident persons was as uncommon as knowing real activists. However, occasionally one encountered the so-called *dissidentstvuiushchie*—"dissident-like" people— who held sharply critical views of the Soviet system and often made remarks to that effect, but who did not actively practice dissent. From the perspective of the majority, these "dissident-likes" were not only strange but also potentially dangerous, threatening the stability of normal life.

Alexei (born in 1958), who in the early 1980s worked in a publishing house, describes a dissident-like colleague of Komsomol age who worked in his department: "He refused to pay the Komsomol dues, in his words, 'out of moral principle' [*iz moral'nogo printsipa*]. He was quiet but dissident-like [*tikhii, no dissidentstvuiushchii*]. Most of us disliked him. What he was doing was not just silly and useless but could actually cause problems for others." These problems could range from an official reprimand to the komsorg of his department to time-consuming discussions to which his peers and colleagues would be subjected at meetings. Particularly persistent people of this type were suspected of being in some way "abnormal" (*nenormal'nye*), as in Brodsky's statement above. Eduard (born in 1960) remembers the attitudes of his coworkers toward a young engineer in a radio factory who, in the 1980s, was discovered to have a copy of a dissident article protesting the war in Afghanistan: "Many people said in private conversations that the guy had a screw loose [*byl togo*]. There was also a rumor that he distributed pornography, which I think was untrue."[39] In this story political protest and moral indecency were seen as comparably unhealthy. Olesya (born in 1961) encountered a dissident-like person among the students at the university she attended in the early 1980s:

He always said skeptical things about the party, socialism, and so on. At that time, of course, all of us told *anekdoty* about Brezhnev, which was completely normal [*normal'no*].[40] But that person did not simply tell *anekdoty*—he constantly drew deep conclusions [*glubokie vyvody*]

[38] For more on Brodsky and the reasons for this distancing, see chapter 4.

[39] Since the 1960s, the Soviet state had also treated dissidents as psychiatric patients. When Vladimir Danchev, an announcer on the World Service of Radio Moscow, denounced the Soviet war in Afghanistan on the air, he was put in a psychiatric hospital. A Soviet official replied to questions of Western journalists asking about Danchev's persecution: "He was not punished, because sick people cannot be punished" (quoted in Chomsky 1986, 276). See also chapter 7.

[40] For a discussion of *anekdoty*, see chapter 7. See also Yurchak (1997a).

and wanted to share them with you. . . . We all thought he was a fool. You know the phrase, "Make a fool pray to God and he will smash his forehead" [*zastav' duraka bogu molit'sia, on i lob rasshibet*]? He prayed to his truth [*molilsia svoei pravde*]. . . . Listening to him was an intense experience—it caused not fright, but repulsion [*ne strakh, a otvrashchenie*]. It's one thing to read Dostoyevsky and quite another to interact with his heroes. You may enjoy reading about them but wouldn't enjoy meeting them. When a real person is standing in front of you constantly saying skeptical things, it is unpleasant. That person is expecting some response from you, but you have nothing to say to him. Not because you are unable to analyze like him, but because you don't want to.

Olesya's reference to Dostoyevsky's heroes—the troubled, pariahs, truth-seekers—is reminiscent of the references to the psychotic and the sick above.

Performing *Svoi*

The sociality of the so-called "normal people" or *svoi* (us/ours) differed from the ideal-type activists and dissidents in their reading of authoritative texts and acts, and in their relationship to one another. Let us consider the techniques and conditions that enabled the unanticipated production of this sociality. Among the Komsomol rituals the library komsorg Irina had to coordinate was the collection of Komsomol dues among the rank-and-file members of her cell.[41] She submitted the dues to the library committee, which in turn submitted them to the raikom. If the dues were not paid in time or in full, Irina could receive an official reprimand from the library committee. Such reprimands were not harmless and could impede a person's professional promotion, financial bonus, permission to travel abroad, and so forth. However, it was not uncommon for rank-and-file members to drag their feet paying the dues. The dues were generally considered an unpleasant formality and a waste of money. When Irina collected the dues, people sometimes responded with mild annoyance and jokingly addressed her as "levy collector" (*sborshchik podati*)—a term that pointed to the involuntary yet unavoidable nature of these payments, a certain resentment toward this unavoidable practice, and the common recognition that Irina, as komsorg, was simply fulfilling an assignment imposed on her from above. Most people paid the dues because, explains Irina, "We were all *svoi*. . . . [Most komsorgs] never made anyone pay the dues by force [*ne zastavliali siloi*]. . . .

---

[41] Komsomol dues amounted to about 1 percent of one's monthly salary or stipend.

I would approach people and simply explain in a friendly manner [*po-druzheski*]: 'Listen, you know that we are required by the raikom to collect these dues. Please, don't get us into trouble.'"

Paying and collecting the dues under these conditions was not about ideological statements of allegiance. Like other ritualized authoritative acts, this practice contributed to the production of something this ritual had not been designed to produce: not the collective of conscientious Komsomol members, but a sociality of *svoi* (us/ours), with a particular ethic of responsibility to others, which it implied. The dissident-like person in the earlier example, who refused to pay his dues "out of principle," caused much greater irritation among his colleagues than Irina who collected the dues. Irina belonged to *svoi*; he did not.

Other rituals also contributed to this unanticipated cultural production. Among them were the regular Komsomol meetings. According to Irina, who was responsible for convening these meetings in her department, the raikom supplied local komsorgs with lists of topics for the meetings that they were supposed to hold in the near future. These hierarchical relations and the importance of reproducing the form of authoritative discourse meant that, in Irina's words, while "no one was particularly interested in the meetings . . . everyone understood that they needed to be conducted not because of my silly whim. Why it was needed, no one contemplated." For Nikolai, a computer programmer born in 1959, attendance at the Komsomol meetings was predicated on the experience of belonging to *svoi* and the connected moral responsibility not to cause problems to one of *svoi* who, as komsorg, was responsible for guaranteeing attendance: "It's hard to tell what made me go to these meetings. Perhaps herd instinct [*stadnyi instinkt*]. Because most people with whom I interacted also went. . . . [This also] depended on how our group related to the person who was responsible for the meetings. . . . If he was a *normal* person [*normal'nyi chelovek*], of course you would attend the meetings not to cause him problems." Olesya (introduced earlier) describes a similar dynamic:

> You knew that you had to go to the Komsomol meetings, that you could not simply ignore them. . . . There was a system of "circle binding" [*krugovaia poruka*],[42] of a certain moral responsibility [*moral'noe obiazatel'stvo*]. If you did not pay the Komsomol dues or did not

[42] "Circle binding" refers to the principle of "the collective responsibility to the state," on which the local system of self-government in the Soviet Union was based (see Ssorin-Chaikov 2003, 53). Alena Ledeneva translates this term, in a different context, as "collective guarantee," pointing out that it "derives from *krug* (a peasant community) which provides collective responsibility or guarantee, that is, mutual support and control within a circle of people, in which everybody is dependent upon the other" (Ledeneva 1998, 81n2).

attend the meetings someone else would be reprimanded. Our komsorg was a very nice girl [*ochen' priiatnaia devushka*]. If you did not
come to the meeting, and as a result it did not have the required quorum [for a vote], some idiot from the raikom would chew that girl out
[*dast ei po golove*[43]]. That nice girl, with whom you were friends
[*s kotoroi ty druzhil*], with whom you had coffee every day.

That girl was a normal person (*normal'nyi chelovek*), one of *svoi*. In
these contexts the meaning of *svoi* was broader than in others. For example, Dale Pesmen observes that the name *svoi chelovek* (*svoi* person)
implied that "one could speak openly without fearing that what one said
would be used against one" (2000, 165). In the context of the Komsomol assignments, the terms *svoi* and "normal people" could imply something bigger—that one understood that the norms had to be followed at
the ritualistic level, that this was no one's personal fault, and that one
should participate in these routine rituals to avoid causing problems to
the komsorgs, while the komsorgs worked in turn to reduce the load of
tedious Komsomol assignments given to the rank-and-file members.
However, if a person acted differently, not like one of *svoi*, putting others in a potentially unpleasant or risky position, the komsorgs could
penalize that person by insisting on a literal (constative) reading of Komsomol assignments.

Irina and other komsorgs had to conduct annual "Lenin examinations" (*leninskii zachët*) of the rank and file, at which a person could be
asked about his or her engagement in Komsomol work, knowledge of
the Soviet constitution, recent party decisions, events in the country, and
so forth.[44] In practice, however, most Lenin examinations, like other rituals, experienced a displacement to which I have referred as performative shift. At the level of form these rituals were meticulously reproduced
(in questions, answers, reports), but their constative meanings were profoundly unanchored and made potentially unpredictable or irrelevant.
When it was time to conduct examinations at the library committee, explains Irina, "we usually got together and discussed each person among
ourselves. We would say: 'Does everyone know that person?' 'Yes.' 'Is he
a good person?' 'Yes.' 'OK, then let's pass him.'" Then they called that
person for a short meeting to make sure that he or she understood that it
was necessary to perform the ritualized act of examination and to treat
the committee as *svoi*. Most people understood this and acted accordingly. However, if a person refused or failed to engage in authoritative

[43] Literally, "will hit her on the head."
[44] The tests were conducted by local Komsomol committees in form of interviews with
one person at a time; the questions for the examinations were sent from the raikom, and
the results submitted back to the raikom.

discourse under these conditions, either "out of principle" or because he or she was being irresponsible, the committee could take the ideological formalities literally, ensuring that the ritual was fulfilled and reported, the person was punished, and further transgression was discouraged. Thus, the committee could strategically adhere to the constative meanings of authoritative representations and rituals that were usually ignored, thereby drawing on the power delegated by the Komsomol to the committee as its authorized representatives. Often the ultimate punishment was to be expelled from *svoi* rather than from the state institution, although this punishment was administered by means of the power afforded by the state. This was yet another way in which state power became deterritorialized and deployed in unanticipated ways. According to Andrei: "All young people in our institute were *svoi* . . . [and] knew that the system involved many completely useless things. So, our committee tried to avoid torturing ourselves and others with unnecessary assignments. However, if the person was excessively lazy or defiant, we followed the ritual, urging him to change and in extreme cases issuing an official reprimand." In Irina's library, similarly, "how the committee treated a rank-and-file member depended on how that person behaved toward us." A problem arose if a person's actions caused problems for the committee members and if, on top of this, the person refused to treat the committee as *svoi*:

> For example, if after being hired someone forgot or neglected to register as a Komsomol member[45] in our library organization, we summoned him to the committee. If he was rude to us, we could easily issue him an official reprimand or even send his file to the raikom for further action. But if the person explained to us in a friendly manner [*po-druzheski*], "Guys, I just got caught up in things and did not find time to register," we would be understanding and would cover for him [*ponimali i prikryvali*].[46]

Speaking "in a friendly manner" (*po-druzheski*)—such as acknowledging that one recognized the predicament in which others found themselves and did not wish to aggravate their situation—was key for being

---

[45] Komsomol members were supposed to be "registered" as members of a primary Komsomol organization. Hence, when they changed place of employment or study they needed to "take themselves off the registration list" (*sniat'sia s ucheta*) in the old organization and register—"get on the registration list" (*vstat' na uchet*)—in the new one.

[46] Although this dynamic bears some similarity to the relations within Western bureaucracy, the difference is that in the Soviet context the reinterpretation of the meanings of assignments, rituals, and texts was the norm of practice rather than strategic deviation from it, which allowed for rather open arrangements between the leadership and the rank and file as to how to practice this reinterpretation.

111

able to belong to *svoi*. This discursive relationship was practiced between secretaries and the rank and file and between secretaries and the raikom. Remember that Andrei, in an example above, also talked to the raikom secretaries "in a friendly manner" (*po-druzheski*) to make sure that the raikom agreed that the assignment to organize a large number of political lectures in his institute was unrealistic, and therefore would not check too closely whether the lectures his committee reported were in fact conducted.

Whether a person would end up being one of *svoi* or not, in a concrete context, was often unclear in advance, and would emerge only in the course of interaction. It is commonplace that the meaning of discursive events cannot be understood outside of context, and that the context itself is not a static preexisting setting in which discourse takes place but is produced in discourse (Voloshinov 1986).[47] The ritualized acts of authoritative discourse that constituted the routine proceedings of every Komsomol organization—meetings, speeches, votes, examinations, reports—did not simply communicate static meanings, in a truthful or false manner, but were themselves dynamic, conflictual, and multivocal processes in which the meaning of everyday life of late socialism was shaped and displaced into something different. A typical event that took place in the library in the early 1980s demonstrates the indeterminate and emergent nature of the ritualized acts of authoritative discourse. A young library employee was offered a job as an instructor of Latin at the religious seminary. For a Soviet person, working in a religious institution meant disconnecting from the ideological dimension of life and withdrawing into a world that the state tolerated but viewed with suspicion and hostility. Since that employee was a Komsomol member, the raikom obliged the library committee to conduct a formal meeting, to examine his ideological loyalty, and to make a recommendation as to whether he should be expelled from the Komsomol.[48]

At first, the committee members were supportive of the man. He seemed like a normal person, not like a priest,[49] and there was nothing wrong with teaching Latin, especially considering he had a university degree in

[47] See, for example, Bill Hanks's analysis of the role played by the letters of Mayan elites to the Spanish crown in continuously shaping the meaning of "the Conquest" (2000, 104).

[48] The implications of being expelled from the Komsomol could be null, but they could also be substantial. This person might have trouble "returning" into a good, non-religious professional career, getting permission to travel abroad, and so forth.

[49] Being a priest or a student of a religious seminary was a position outside of the "normal people" (though not necessarily that of a dissident) because of the profound disconnection between the ideals and discourses of communism and those of religion. In practice religion was tolerated by the state but disconnected from state institutions (education, media, industry, public associations, army, bureaucracy, etc.).

classics. But their opinion unexpectedly changed in the course of the interaction. As Irina recalls:

> At first our committee was against expelling that guy. I personally respected him for his knowledge and interests. Considering his degree, it was obvious that teaching Latin was much more appropriate and interesting for him than doing tedious library work. However, the problem was that he refused to talk to us as normal people [*ne zakhotel razgovarivat' kak s normal'nymi liud'mi*]. He was arrogant and disrespectful and just tried to show that he couldn't care less what we had to say. And unexpectedly, several people in our committee began attacking him for being a "traitor of the motherland." One committee member even said, "And what would you do if you were offered a job by the CIA?" That was a ridiculous thing to say, of course, but at that point all of us started attacking the poor guy. We were not too kind to him.

Although the ritual was unavoidable and its topic fixed, what it would mean was not completely predetermined. Indeed, it ended up proceeding in the direction that the conveners wanted to avoid. Attacking the person against their initial inclination, the Committee members drew on the constative meaning of authoritative formulas to challenge not his ideological loyalty but his refusal to be one of *svoi*. For most of them such accusatory formulations as "a traitor to the motherland" or "a recruit for the CIA" were absurd (the constative meaning of these formulations was usually irrelevant). However, by reproducing these statements in a serious voice, in the context of the committee meeting, they, surprising to themselves, overidentified with the constative meaning of these formulas to withdraw the person, first and foremost, not from the ranks of that institution but from the ranks of *svoi*. It was on that decision that their recommendation to expel him from the Komsomol was predicated.

It was important to be linked with both authoritative discourse and the *svoi*. Remember that the secondary school secretary, Masha, made sure that students knew that her naming bad names in a speech was not to be taken too literally. She contacted them and explained this beforehand, establishing and drawing on an identity of *svoi*. At the same time, she also made sure that her speech was written in precise authoritative language and that her Komsomol work was meaningful to her and was seen as important by the Komsomol bosses and teachers. To do so, she drew on two types of performative power simultaneously: delegated to her, first, as an "authorized spokesperson" (Bourdieu 1991, 106) of authoritative discourse and, second, as one of *svoi*, as their authorized spokesperson who opened up and shifted the constative meanings of authoritative discourse,

113

enabling new meanings and forms of life. Her identity was constructed and empowered not just by one or the other of these discourses, but by both. Remember also the raikom secretary Sasha earlier in this chapter who helped his friends to write Komsomol speeches. In doing this, Sasha first joked around, then cleared his throat, and said "OK, let's start," before dictating the speech "in a well-trained voice." And recall the former party boss in Pelevin (2002) who, before launching into an imitation party speeches, also "coughed and said in a loud well-trained voice." The use of such discursive markers as joking, coughing, and switching to a well-trained voice, like a speaker at the imaginary podium, did not simply introduce a switch of genres from ordinary discourse to authoritative, but rather signaled their coexistence and mutual productiveness. These discursive markers allowed those who used them to draw on two types of power delegated to the these people as "authorized spokespersons" of two constituencies: that of Komsomol as state institution and that of *svoi*. Being "authorized spokespersons" of these two constituencies at the same time shaped these secretaries into who they were, allowing them to be neither completely "serious" nor completely cynical and uninterested about the constative meanings of Komsomol work.

This dynamic illustrates again that the Komsomol, or at least its lower hierarchical level, became articulated as a site in which both the Komsomol work and the sociality of *svoi* were produced. Before considering what the nature and the meaning of this sociality was, and what meanings, identities, relations and forms of life became produced in it, let us summarize the previous discussion on a more theoretical level.

Deterritorialization

The logic of the techniques of ideological production encountered so far in this chapter has hinged on the principle of performative shift—that is, the signifiers of authoritative discourse (how it represents) were meticulously reproduced, but its signifieds (what it represents) were relatively unimportant. One voted in favor, passed Lenin examinations, filed reports, repeated precise textual forms, and went to the parades, but without necessarily or usually having to pay close attention to the constative meanings of these ritualized acts and speech acts. At the same time, this routine replication of the authoritative symbolic system did not limit the realm of available meanings; on the contrary, it enabled new, unpredictable meanings that went beyond those that were literally communicated. For example, we have seen in this chapter how the routine replication of authoritative discourse enabled new identities, socialities, and forms of knowledge that were enabled but not determined by the authoritative rhetoric. (Below and in the following chapters we will see more examples.) This internal displacement of the system's dominant discourse was different from the dissident kind of opposition and was not articulated in oppositional terms; indeed, it did not preclude one from feeling personal affinity to many values that were explicitly and implicitly central to the socialist system. Rather, this displacing move was closer to what Deleuze and Guattari have called the strategy of deterritorialization.

Deleuze and Guattari provide an illustration of this process: the symbiotic relationship between an orchid and a wasp.[50] The wasp transports the orchid's pollen; the orchid feeds the wasp. The two processes are mutually constitutive and change the nature of each system: "The wasp is . . . deterritorialized, becoming a piece in the orchid's reproductive apparatus. But it reterritorializes the orchid by transporting its pollen" (Deleuze and Guattari 2002, 10). This strategy is not based merely on mimicry or imitation: the orchid does not imitate the wasp any more than the wasp imitates the orchid. Rather, this process amounts to "a capture of code, surplus value of code, an increase in valence, a veritable becoming, a becoming-wasp of the orchid and a becoming-orchid of the wasp." The orchid acquires some waspness and the wasp acquires some orchidness, which means that, depending on the perspective, one system is *deterritorialized* while the other is reterritorialized, and vice versa.

As we saw in the examples in this chapter, having to report the fulfillment of Komsomol assignments, write texts in the authoritative genre, or engage in other ideological activities, the secretaries, komsorgs, and rank-and-file members became involved in practices and strategies that resignified the meanings of these reports, texts, rituals, and assignments. These actors deterritorialized the authoritative discursive field that these reports, texts, rituals, and assignments, and the state institutions of the Komsomol constituted. Reproducing the forms of this discourse while unanchoring or ignoring their constative meanings enabled creative production of new meanings and forms of life. Between its fixed authoritative forms, this system was "injected" with elements of the new, unpredictable, imaginative, creative, "normal life" that was not limited to the constative meanings of authoritative discourse, even if enabled by its

---

[50] Such a symbiotic relationship between different "heterogeneous elements" forms what Deleuze and Guattari call a "rhizome." The term *rhizome* comes from botany, where it refers to an underground plant stem (e.g., of an asparagus or potato plant) that sends out roots and shoots as part of its reproductive apparatus. Deleuze and Guattari use this term as a metaphor for the interconnectedness of various cultural, linguistic, political, biological, and other systems of knowledge. Using this concept, they develop an approach that allows them to consider in one analysis multiple and nonhierarchical assemblages between data of different natures. See Deleuze and Guattari (2002, 3–25).

115

performative reproduction. The Soviet system was undergoing an internal deterritorialization, becoming something quite different, although at the level of authoritative representation this shift remained relatively invisible. Unlike the dissident strategies of opposing the system's dominant mode of signification,[51] deterritorialization reproduced this mode at the same time as it shifted, built upon, and added new meanings to it.

The Public of *Svoi*

The sociality of *svoi* became one of the central unanticipated products of this deterritorializing move within late-socialist culture. This sociality shared some characteristics with the forms of "publics" in other modern contexts, such as Western capitalism, but also had distinct features of its own. What kind of "public" was this and what discourses, cultural products, and forms of knowledge and imagination were produced within it? Discussing modern Western contexts, Michael Warner defines a "public" as a self-organized sociality that comes into existence by being addressed in a discourse; that public exists "independently of state institutions, law, formal frameworks of citizenship" and therefore can be "sovereign with respect to the state" (2002a, 51). This last claim is problematic. We should speak instead of relative independence and relative sovereignty of publics vis-à-vis the state—they are enabled by and impossible without the state and its laws, discourses, and institutions. According to Warner, since the exact composition of those addressed in a public discourse cannot be entirely known in advance, the public is an open-ended sociality that can include known persons and strangers (2002a, 55–56).[52]

Warner contrasts this self-organizing principle of a public in relation to public discourse with Althusser's interpellation (1971). For Althusser, the moment one recognizes oneself as the one addressed by a state institution, police officer, or other authority figure—the moment of turning around—is the moment that person is interpellated as a subject of the state. However, Althusser's model, limited to an isolated event, does not account for the operation of public speech. With public address, argues Warner, even while recognizing ourselves as the addressee, we also recognize that this discourse is "addressed to indefinite others; that in singling us out, it does so not on the basis of our concrete identity, but by virtue of our participation in the discourse alone, and therefore in common with strangers." Furthermore, unlike Althusser's account of personal address,

[51] Such strategies were much more visible to external observers, especially in the West.
[52] See also Calhoun (2002); Warner (2002b).

the outcome of a public address always involves a "partial *nonidentity* with the object of address" (Warner 2002a, 58).[53]

In the context of late socialism, the key public address that brought about the social totality of *svoi* was that made in authoritative discourse— in the endless texts and slogans hanging on façades, used during meetings and parades, and so forth—that everywhere punctuated everyday reality. This address took such forms as the public question "Who is in favor?"; the public slogan, "Our goal is Communism"; a speech delivered at a meeting in front of an audience; or a Lenin examination that one had to pass in front of a committee. However, because every instance of authoritative address in these contexts was subject to a process of performative shift—its ritualized forms were reproduced, and this performative reproduction enabled the creation of new meanings—the kind of public these addresses brought into existence was *nonidentical* with how the addressed public was articulated in authoritative discourse, such as the "Soviet people" or the "Soviet toilers."

When the Komsomol secretary Leonid, who spoke in an unusually activist voice (above), made claims in the name of his peers—"we, the young generation of the Komsomol . . ."—most of his peers identified with the "we" but understood it differently from the literal representation in the speech. Recognizing themselves as being addressed, they responded with impressively unanimous gestures to the vote that he called. However, they collectively responded not to the constative meaning of this question ("Do you support the resolution?") but to its performative meaning ("Are you the kind of people who understand that the norms and rules of the current ritual need to be performatively reproduced, that constative meanings do not necessarily have to be attended to, who act accordingly, and who, therefore, can be engaged in other meanings?") It is this latter address that the audience at the meeting recognized with an affirmative gesture and that therefore brought into existence the public of *svoi*—a kind of *deterritorialized public*.

This public should be distinguished also from a "counterpublic" that Nancy Fraser defines in the Western context as "a parallel discursive arena where members of subordinated social groups invent and circulate counterdiscourses to formulate oppositional interpretations of their identities, interests, and needs" (Fraser 1992, 123). Obviously, unlike a counterpublic, the public of *svoi* was self-organized not through an oppositional counterdiscourse of one's "interests and needs" but through the performative shift of authoritative discourse. Explicit opposition, just like explicit support, was avoided.

[53] This partial nonidentity can also be formulated as a public manifestation of the failure of interpellation to fully constitute subjects.

117

Russian sociologist Oleg Vite argues that from the late 1950s the public sphere of everyday Soviet life became increasingly reorganized into two public spheres: *publichnaia* (public sphere proper) and *privatno-publichnaia* (privately public sphere) (1996). These two distinct public spheres, according to Vite, were marked by distinct norms and rules according to which practices and relations were structured: the former was regulated by the written laws and rules of the state that Vite compares to "statute law"; the latter was regulated by unwritten cultural understandings and agreements that he compares to "customary law."

This discussion rightly unsettles the picture of a singular "official" Soviet public sphere. However, by describing the two public spheres as fixed, bounded, and autonomous topographical locales, governed by distinct sets of rules and codes, it produces a new dichotomy, downplaying the indivisible and mutually constitutive relationship between these rules, codes, spheres, and publics. It is more appropriate to speak of a process of deterritorialization in which multiple deterritorialized publics, not static public spheres, were continuously produced.[54] Through these processes, in different contexts and groups, but always in relation to authoritative discourse, one became included in or excluded from *svoi*, without being relegated to that identity once and for all.

"Normal Life"

Oleg, who was a student in the 1970s and 1980s, remembers his life at that time: "We had a normal life (*u nas byla normal'naia zhizn'*). We had friends; we studied, read books, discussed things; we went to exhibitions, traveled, had interests and goals. We lived a normal life (*zhili norma'noi zhizn'iu*)." However, Oleg was not keen on ideological activities and organizations, and distanced himself from the Komsomol. The "we" in Oleg's comment includes his peers, the normal people, *svoi*. The idea of "normal life," like the idea of "normal people," signified a life that was neither too activist nor too oppositional, implying instead that this life was interesting, relatively free, full, creative, and not reduced to an oppressed existence, ideological automatism or idealist activism. The collective performance of authoritative speech acts and rituals enabled the production not only of "work with meaning," described earlier, but also, more broadly, life with meaning, the "normal life," which went

---

[54] See Yurchak (2001a) for a discussion of *officialized* and *personalized* public spheres and how they reproduced from the Soviet to the post-Soviet contexts in Russia.

beyond the constative reading of ideological messages and was not determined by the dictatorship of the party.

The institutional power the Komsomol delegated to its authorized representatives was everywhere redeployed for the creation of "normal life." The Komsomol committees became sites for this production. Their members were increasingly chosen according to the principle of belonging to *svoi*. Irina describes the composition of her committee in the early 1980s:

> Anastasia, my close friend and a very energetic and bright person, was elected to the Komsomol committee. Soon she started feeling lonely there without me and decided to bring me in. So I ended up on the Komsomol committee "out of friendship" [*po druzhbe*]. Eventually, when Anastasia left to join the Communist Party . . . I started feeling lonely on the committee without her and arranged for my other friend Natalia to get elected to it too. After that we attracted another friend, and eventually built a fantastic Komsomol committee that consisted almost exclusively of friends. I have very warm memories of that committee.

Building the committee on these principles meant that its members shared an understanding that many texts and assignments were performed at the level of form, with the constative meanings ignored, and that critical discussion of this practice would usually be avoided—a practice that would be difficult to maintain if the committee included activists. Komsomol Committees therefore became sites of deterritorialization. Natalia recalls, "We liked to gather in the committee room for a meeting. Naturally, this took place during working hours. We would first quickly discuss some Komsomol issues, and then we would sit around for hours doing our own thing, chatting with each other, drinking tea, and generally avoiding regular [*obychnuiu*] [library] work."

Other places and positions in the Komsomol hierarchy served the same multiple functions as the committee room. One of them was the raikom of a local district, which committee members of primary organizations regularly visited to have discussions with their superiors, submit membership dues, collect documents, receive assignments, and so on. It was not uncommon for committee members to leave their institutes and factories during working hours in order to go to the raikom, where the committee members would often quickly finish their business, and then use the raikom visit as an excuse to take time away from work, hanging out with friends, going to museums, shopping, or whatever. The state's separation of the ideological and professional institutions made this strategy possible: one's bosses at work were unlikely to find out how much time one spent at the raikom.

119

Natalia and Irina even used a coded phrase, "to leave for the raikom" (*uiti v Raikom*), that only *svoi* understood: "If we wanted to go to an art exhibition or to a café during work, we told the chair of our department that we needed 'to leave for the raikom.' " These techniques of personalizing and domesticating the time, space, institutions, and discourses of the state, by citing authoritative forms, went on at all levels of the ideological hierarchy, including the Communist Party committees that were superior to the Komsomol committees. Occasionally this led to comical situations. Once, Natalia and Irina told the boss of their department at the library that they needed to leave for the raikom. Instead, they went to try out a new pizzeria that had recently opened in the neighborhood. An hour later, the department boss also showed up at the same pizzeria with another senior colleague. They were both members of the party committee and had also left work allegedly for urgent business at the local party raikom. After sitting down at a table they noticed Irina and Natalia. "It was very awkward," Natalia remembers, "I almost choked laughing. We were sitting at different tables and behaved in the most civilized way, as if everything was fine."

In her 1983 diary, Lena (born in 1963), a student in the journalism department at Leningrad University, described how an invented authoritative assignment was used by university students for truancy. On June 4, 1983, Lena and her friend Mila, also a student, were talking in front of the seminar room at the university:

Mila says: "Lena, let's not go to Irina Pavlovna's [Russian literature] seminar."

"I wonder how you plan to do that?"

"Let's say that we have an interview for the student paper with the secretary of the Komsomol committee of the Kozitsky television factory."

I laugh in response—this is our permanent excuse, since we can't be bothered to come up with a new one. Mila approaches Irina Pavlovna and with a very preoccupied expression starts: "Irina Pavlovna! In twenty minutes we have to be . . ."and so on.

I am standing nearby with a pitiful and slightly desperate expression, showing with all my posture that, of course, I would not give up the chance of going to my favorite Russian seminar for any riches of the world. But, alas, the reality is harsh. . . . What awful things realism does to people! Irina Pavlovna is moved (or pretends to be).

She says: "Of course, girls, you should go."

And, destroyed by sorrow, we slowly leave. The others stare at our backs with envy. Outside of the building we start jumping with joy.

"So," says Mila, "where should we eat?"

We are going to the café on the corner of Srednii Avenue and 8th Line Street.[55]

Lena's remark, "What awful things realism does to people!", summarizes the situation: the professor, just like the library bosses, would be unlikely to protest if the reason were described in terms of authoritative symbols—the raikom, the Komsomol secretary of a factory, or otherwise. The use of these symbols was more than trivial truancy and avoidance of work. By momentarily making a constative reference to the authoritative symbol (by presenting it literally, at the level of constative meaning), these people were able to draw on the institutional power delegated to authorized representatives of the Komsomol, to gain relative freedom from library bosses, university professors, the raikom itself, and the very state institutions (including the Komsomol) that authorized this power. In short, they were able to deterritorialize time, space, relations, and meanings of the socialist system by drawing on the system's principles.

Parades

May and November parades, which at one level were seen as unpleasant obligatory duties, often became appealing celebrations. With their massive scale, parades were a powerful machinery for the cultural production of the publics of *svoi*, creating temporary collectivities of friends and strangers who marched together through the streets, carried the same portraits and slogans, shouted "hurray" in response to the same appeals blaring from loudspeakers, and publicly displayed the same celebratory mood. Participating in these events reproduced the collectivity of belonging that was enabled by these slogans and portraits but no longer bound by their literal sense. Natalia went to the parades "because the Komsomol secretaries pleaded: 'Please, come!' The people who asked you were your friends and of course you always came. But, actually, I did not have a bad time there. It was a lot of fun to shout 'hurray' all together!" Andrei, the institute secretary, recollects:

The parade was simply one more celebration where you met your friends and acquaintances and had fun. It was not really experienced as an ideological event. . . . The May parade happened when the weather finally turned for the spring; it was warm and sunny. Everyone was in good spirits; everyone came to have a good time. There

[55] From Lena's personal archive, quoted with her permission.

121

were a lot of children. Children loved the parades. Imagine, a child gets three balloons or is allowed to carry a flag for a little bit. That was a lot of fun for the kids. As for the slogans on those flags, I don't think many people took notice of them.

Revolution Day, Labor Day, and many other celebrations became meaningful as rituals that reproduced the belonging to the massive publics of *svoi*. On these occasions people had celebratory dinners at home, with collective drinking, eating, and singing with relatives, friends, and colleagues. Millions sent greeting cards with good wishes on the occasion of these national holidays. The pictures on the postcards contained Soviet symbols: stars, banners, hammers and sickles, slogans, and Lenin portraits. On the postcards people typically wished each other health, happiness, success in work, and so on. They also used the occasion to exchange news with friends, relatives, and colleagues. The meaning of these massive discursive rituals, repeated a few times a year, shifted the constative dimension of authoritative messages, contributing instead to imagining and creating the publics of *svoi*.

Soviet Newspapers

In the fall of 1983, Lena worked at a local factory newspaper as part of her "practical training" (*uchebnaia praktika*) as a student of journalism. One day, the paper's editor Volodya gave Lena an assignment to write a story about the achievements of a large local vegetable warehouse (*ovoshchnaia baza*). According to standard procedure, she would write a generally positive article without ever visiting the place.[56] Both the editor and the journalist understood that the meaning of this piece was not supposed to be "literal," and both participated in techniques of producing it that saved them time and energy and minimized formulaic activities. But when Lena sat down to write, she became aware of the portrait of Lenin hanging on the wall looking at her, and she felt sudden embarrassment at the irony of the situation. Once again we see the image of "Lenin" playing the role of a key master signifier. Unlike most other representations and images of authoritative discourse, it could not be easily reduced to the performative dimension. Most of its powerful constative meaning was grounded outside the authoritative discursive field and therefore nonerasable, still referring to moral promise and the original purity of the communist ideal. This is why it was embarrassing and

---

[56] In a similar manner Soviet newspaper editors themselves routinely produced the "letters from the readers" that were published in their newspapers. See Humphrey (1989, 159) and Losev (1978, 242).

ironic for Lena to participate in converting these ideals and promises into pure "pro forma" under Lenin's gaze. In her diary, Lena described her exchange with the editor on September 19, 1983: "Volodya, I cannot work like this. He is looking me straight in the eyes." Encouraged by Volodya's understanding, ironic glance, Lena added that she would be equally embarrassed to write this formulaic report under the gaze of another person: "You know, my friend has a portrait of Vysotskii above her table. He is embracing his guitar looking with loathing [*s nenav-ist'iu*] as only he can look. I cannot sit at her table and concoct some silly reports under his gaze. I have to turn him away." [57]

Vladimir Vysotskii was a theater and film actor who gained immense popularity in the 1970s and 1980s as the writer and singer of songs that occupied an ambivalent niche in the Soviet culture. The state frowned upon most of these songs because they suggested alienating and dehumanizing aspects of Soviet reality, but it never explicitly outlawed them, since they were not openly dissident. During the Soviet period, most of Vysotskii's songs were never released by the state-run recording label *Melodiia*, nor were they played on Soviet radio. And yet they gained immense popularity circulating around the country in hundreds of thousands of privately made tape-recorded copies. These taped songs were popular among all strata of Soviet society, especially among the intelligentsia, including the state bureaucracy.

At the moment Lena mentioned Vysotskii to her editor, a mutual recognition of *svoi* occurred. They both liked Vysotskii, though both also wrote formulaic texts, were not completely cynical about the socialist ideals and ethics, and regularly had to attend Komsomol and party meetings:

> The editor looked at me thoughtfully and asked:
> "Does your friend like Vysotskii?"
> "Yes, I think so."
> "And what about you?"
> "I could also say that I do."
> He was quiet for a moment and then said: "OK, I need to go to the party committee. In the meantime, you may listen to this."
> He turned on the tape recorder. It was Vysotskii. He added: "When you get tired of it you can turn it off."
> How can I GET TIRED OF VYSOTSKII?!! (emphasis in original)

Lena wrote the article in the authoritative genre, in the context of ideological production, in the editorial office of a Soviet newspaper, under the portrait of Lenin, while the editor was leaving for a party committee meeting. At the same time, her conversation with the editor, and the

---

[57] From Lena's personal archive, quoted with her permission.

music they listened to, allowed them to recognize each other as *svoi*. Again, rituals of authoritative pro forma enabled the production of unpredictable and creative worlds, meanings, and publics.

Central Committee Analysts

This dynamic relationship with authoritative discourse continued all the way up the ideological hierarchy. Some of the younger employees of the CC—especially political analysts and speechwriters who occupied a privileged position—were also fans of Vysotskii and in the 1970s sometimes invited him to sing at their private gatherings. Vysotskii sang for them his legendary song "Wolf Hunt" (*Okhota na volkov*) (Burlatskii 1997, 261). This song tells the story of a young wolf running from his pursuers who are trying to encircle and kill him, which was a transparent metaphor of the oppressive episodes of Soviet history. The song contained such lines: "In my flight, sinews bursting I hurtle / But as yesterday—so now today / They've cornered me! Driven me, encircled / Towards the huntsmen that wait for their prey!"[58]

According to Fyodor Burlatskii, a CC speechwriter under Khrushchev and Brezhnev:

> Lev Deliusin, a [CC] specialist on the problems of China, was well acquainted with theater director Yurii Liubimov, Bulat Okudzhava, and Vladimir Vysotskii. He introduced them to other members of the group [of CC analysts]. Vysotskii sang to them "Wolf Hunt". Later he wrote another song about these events: "Big people are calling me over, they want me to sing them 'Wolf Hunt.' "[59] (1997, 261)

Another CC analyst and speech writer, Georgii Shakhnazarov, also knew Vysotskii and invited him to his apartment in the CC living block on Universtetskii Prospekt in Moscow to sing to Shakhnazarov's friends from the CC (Bogomolov 2001). When the group of young speechwriters in Yurii Andropov's International Department of the CC worked on the drafts of party documents and speeches at Burlatskii's CC dacha outside Moscow, they also often listened to tape-recordings of Vysotskii's songs.[60]

The production of new meanings, publics, temporalities, and spatialities of Soviet life were centered around the principle of the performative

[58] Official V. S. Vysotskii Foundation website: www.kulichki.com/vv/eng/songs/hamilton.html#wolf_hunt. Trans. Kathryn and Bruce Hamilton.
[59] *Menia zovut k sebe bul'shie liudi, chtob ia im pel "Okhotu na volkov."*
[60] Author interview.

shift. How the system signified was meticulously reproduced, but what it signified was unanchored and open to new interpretations. The late-socialist system became deterritorialized. This process was rooted not in mimicry or dissimulation of the system's constative meanings; instead it introduced into the system new meanings and possibilities. The system was internally mutating toward unpredictable, creative, multiple forms of "normal life" that no one anticipated. This deterritorializing move was a move toward greater freedom, but one that was not coded in the emancipatory rhetoric of grand narratives (such as "living in truth").

Chapter 4
Living "Vnye":
Deterritorialized Milieus

Like everyone else I have an angel
Behind my back she dances away
In the Saigon she orders me coffee
It's all the same to her, come what may
—Boris Grebenshikov[1]

Brodsky's Model

Writer Sergei Dovlatov wrote about the passions of the "sixtiers" (*shestidesiatniki*) generation[2]: "Neils Bohr used to say, 'There are clear truths and deep truths. A clear truth is opposed by a lie. A deep truth is opposed by another equally deep truth.' . . . My friends were preoccupied with clear truths. We spoke about the freedom of art, the right for information, the respect for human dignity" (1993, 23). This preoccupation with clear truths has also been called "the honesty psychosis" and "the active obsession with categorizing life choices as honest and dishonest" (Gessen 1997, 114). Dovlatov compares this concern with clear truths to an attitude that he first encountered in the mid-1960s, in which people did not evaluate Soviet life as moral or immoral, because they

---

[1] Boris Grebenshikov and his group *Akvarium*, from their 1981 album *Elektrichestvo* (trans. Melanie Feakins and Alexei Yurchak). The original Russian text is:

I kak u vsekh u menia est' angel
Ona tantsuet za moei spinoi
Ona beret mne kofe v Saigone
I ei vse ravno chto budet so mnoi.

[2] The "sixtiers" generation is ten to twenty years older than the last soviet generation. They came of age during Khrushchev's liberating reforms (late 1950s to mid-1960s) and identified with these reforms. Many of them started as young supporters of the party in what they saw as its sincere attempt to regain the original purity of Communist ideals distorted under Stalin. They later became disillusioned by the retreat from the reforms under Brezhnev. As a result, many of them developed a mixture of an affinity to Communist ideals with a critical outlook on the shortcomings of the Soviet system.

considered the events and facts of Soviet life around them to be relatively irrelevant compared to "deep truths." An extreme manifestation of this attitude was that of Leningrad poet Joseph Brodsky:

> Next to Brodsky, young nonconformists seemed like people of a different profession. Brodsky created an unheard-of model of behavior. He lived not in a proletarian state, but in a monastery of his own spirit. He did not struggle with the regime. He simply did not notice it. He was not really aware of its existence. His lack of knowledge in the sphere of Soviet life could appear feigned. For example, he was certain that Dzerzhinskii[3] was alive. And that Comintern[4] was the name of a musical group. He could not identify members of the politburo of the Central Committee. When the facade of the building where he lived was decorated with a six-meter portrait of Mzhavanadze,[5] Brodsky asked: "Who is this? He looks like William Blake." (Dovlatov 1993, 23)

Perhaps Brodsky's poetic intuition made him acutely aware that Soviet authoritative discourse had been distilled to what Jakobson called the "poetic function of language" (Jakobson 1960), which allowed him to read authoritative signifiers through his own universe of meaning. So profound was Brodsky's lack of involvement with the authoritative forms of everyday life that the Soviet state persecuted him for being a "loafer" (Dovlatov 1993, 23). But in the following decade, Brodsky's way of being became increasingly widespread among urbanites a decade younger than him—the last Soviet generation.

The previous chapter focused on the contexts and processes of the ideological production within the Komsomol, arguing that in addition to authoritative texts, reports, and rituals, it also produced new meanings and forms of temporality, spatiality, relations, discourses, and publics. This chapter takes this discussion outside that context of ideological production, focusing on the contexts that were in a peculiar relationship to the authoritative discursive regime—they were "suspended" simultaneously inside and outside of it, occupying the border zones between here and elsewhere. The above description of Brodsky's profound lack of concern with and ignorance of the facts and events of Soviet reality renders well this peculiar relationship. I refer to this relationship to reality by the term *vnye*. To be *vnye* usually translates as "outside." However, the meaning of this term, at least in many cases, is closer to a condition

---

[3] Dzerzhinskii was a Bolshevik leader, Lenin's comrade, and the founder of the ChK (the precursor to the KGB); he was well known as a legend of Soviet history. See also another reference to Dzerzhinskii in chapter 5.

[4] "Comintern" refers to the Communist International.

[5] Mzhavanadze was a member of the politburo in the mid-1960s.

of being simultaneously inside and outside of some context—such as, being within a context while remaining oblivious of it, imagining yourself elsewhere, or being inside your own mind. It may also mean being simultaneously a part of the system and yet not following certain of its parameters. For example, the phrase *vnye polia zreniia* (not within one's field of vision) is used when something is known to be *here*, but is invisible or obstructed from view by another object. This chapter argues that late socialism became marked by an explosion of various styles of living that were simultaneously inside and outside the system and can be characterized as "being *vnye*." These styles of living generated multiple new temporalities, spatialities, social relations, and meanings that were not necessarily anticipated or controlled by the state, although they were fully made possible by it.

I begin by concentrating on more "extreme" examples of such living, describing several milieus in Leningrad, from the 1960s to the early 1980s, where young people related to the Soviet system in this way. The chapter also describes more widespread examples, and ultimately argues that being *vnye* was not an exception to the dominant style of living in late socialism but, on the contrary, a central and widespread principle of living in that system. It created a major *deterritorialization* of late Soviet culture, which was not a form of opposition to the system. It was enabled by the Soviet state itself, without being determined by or even visible to it.

Inna and Her Friends

Inna (born in 1958) was a student in the history department of Leningrad University. The move from secondary school to the university, in the mid-1970s, was a big shift for her:

> When I was in school everything was still clear, of course. . . . I joined the Komsomol with great enthusiasm in the eighth grade [age fourteen, 1972–73]. . . . I also wanted to make a difference. I was the first person from my class to join. . . . But at home, even then, we heard a little bit of Galich and Vysotskii.[6] . . . By the ninth or tenth grade [ages

---

[6] Inna is referring to Alexandr Galich and Vladimir Vysotskii. Alexandr Galich (1918–1977) was a playwright, songwriter, and singer, and one of the founders of the Soviet "author's song" (*avtorskaia pesnia*) genre—poetic songs sung by the author to acoustic guitar. His songs were received with ambivalence by the Soviet state. After his 1968 song "In Memory of Pasternak," he was expelled from professional associations and his plays were no longer published. In 1974 he was exiled from the Soviet Union. He died and was buried in Paris in 1977. For more on Vladimir Vysotskii, see the end of chapter 3.

sixteen to seventeen] I had lost that [enthusiasm] . . . although I was still law-abiding, because I knew I had to be. But when I finished school I simply stopped participating in that life. I never went to the Komsomol meetings. I simply knew that I could avoid them without too many repercussions.

At the university, Inna met a group of friends who also lived this way, avoiding the system's ideological symbolism: "We never went to vote. We simply ignored elections and parades. . . . My only connection with Soviet life was through work and also through the university, which I rarely attended since I had no time." However, Inna stresses, their life was not colored by any anti-system discourse. They were equally uninterested in overt support of, or resistance to, the Soviet system: "None of my friends was any kind of *antisovetchik* [a person with an active anti-Soviet agenda]"; and, "We simply did not speak with each other about work or studies or politics. Not at all, which is obvious since we did not watch television, listen to the radio, or read newspapers, until about 1986 [the beginning of perestroika]." The discourse of the dissidents (before 1986) left them indifferent: "We never spoke about the dissidents. Everyone understood everything, so why speak about that. It was *not interesting* [*neinteresno*]."[7] This comment refers to the performative shift of authoritative discourse, suggesting that the meanings of authoritative symbols, acts, and rituals were not supposed to be read literally, as constative statements. Therefore discussing them made no sense and was considered a mistake and a waste of time. Instead, one could use the possibility afforded by their performative reproduction to be engaged with other meanings, including creating one's own. And so Inna and her friends quietly differentiated themselves from the dissidents, and the activists:

We had no attitude toward them. We were not them [*oni*]. We were here and they were there. We were different from them. We were different, because for us they were simply a change from plus to minus [*znaki meniaiutsia*]—the pro-system and anti-system types—they were all just Soviet people. And I never thought of myself as a Soviet person. We were *organically* different [*my organicheski otlichalis'*]. This is true. We were simply *vnye*.

[7] Emphasis added. Recollect also the words of Olesya in chapter 3, about being "uninterested" in the discourse of a dissident-like person who "is expecting some response from you, but you have nothing to say to him. Not because you are unable to analyze like him, but because you don't want to."

Inna's use of language is revealing of her position: when she uses the pronoun *oni* (them), she does not limit it to the party or state bureaucrats, but also includes the party's self-styled opponents. Inna's position is different from those who describe Soviet society in the terms of an us–them dichotomy. From the perspective of Inna and her friends, the voice of the dissidents belonged to the same authoritative discursive regime, even though the dissidents confronted that discourse. Sergei Oushakine argues that dissident discourse related to authoritative discourse of the state "intradiscursively rather than interdiscursively" and calls this form of dissident resistance "mimetic resistance." Although the dominant and dominated were differently positioned within the discursive field, they drew on "the same vocabulary of symbolic means and rhetorical devices. And neither the dominant nor the dominated could situate themselves 'outside' this vocabulary" (2001, 207–8).

Oushakine is right that most dissident and the activist discourses shared the same discursive field and rhetorical devices and that their relationship was intradiscursive. However, his conclusion that within that "'regime of truth' the dissident discourse that mimetically replicated . . . the discourse of the dominant was probably the only one that could be accepted in that society as truthful," is inaccurate (2001, 207–8). It is wrong to extend the argument about "truth" to the Soviet discursive regime as a whole, precisely because, as we have seen, the concept of truth became decentered and no longer anchored to constative meanings of the authoritative discursive field. For people like Inna and her friends, the location of "truth" was displaced into a realm that related to that discursive field neither "intradiscursively" nor "interdiscursively." Rather, it occupied a peculiar position in between. Recollect again Dovlatov's distinction between different types of truth: as in "clear truths" were constructed within the authoritative discursive regime (and related to its constative meanings), but "deep truths," with which people like Brodsky, Inna, and many of her peers became increasingly preoccupied, were articulated in a different vocabulary and a different discursive and ethical "dimension"—*not* the constative dimension of this discourse.

This dimension and vocabulary were neither "inside" nor "outside" authoritative regime, but in a peculiarly deterritorialized relation to it—that is, while the forms, acts and rituals of authoritative discourse were immutable and ubiquitous, the constative meanings of these forms were irrelevant to Inna and her friends. Instead, they injected their lives with new meanings, forms of sociality, and relations, adding a "surplus value of code" and making them something else, deterritorializing them (Deleuze and Guattari 2002, 10). It is not by chance that Inna and her friends talked about being "organically" different from Soviet people. They were *becoming*-different, as the orchid in Deleuze and Guattari's discussion above was becoming wasp-like.

Inna further elaborated this position: "We were strongly *vnye* any social status." She used the terms "Soviet person" (*sovetskii chelovek*) and "Soviet people" (*sovetskie liudi*) pejoratively to refer to any "organic" adherence to the authoritative discursive field, whether pro-Soviet or anti-Soviet. This distancing of herself and her friends from pro- and anti-positions parallels the feelings of dislike that many Komsomol secretaries and members had toward activists and dissidents, as described in chapter 3. Like the Komsomol members, Inna employed the term *svoi*. For example, she explained: "We did not consider Solzhenitsyn *svoi* [*ne schitali ego svoim*]. This was important. No, no, we were not anti-system like him." Inna's *svoi* encompassed neither anti-system nor pro-system people. Even when Inna and her friends paid attention to the dissident discourse (for example, she read samizdat and foreign publications of Solzhenitsyn), this literature helped them to position themselves in relation to both dissident and authoritative discourses. In her own words, these publications helped her to "understand where we in fact stood—*not in relation to power but in general*" (*Vazhno bylo poniat' gde my na samom dele nakhodimsia—ne otnositel'no vlasti, a voobshche*).[8]

Being *Vnye*

Inna and her friends, like the other groups and milieus described below, thought and spoke of everyone in their group as being *svoi*. As mentioned in the previous chapter, *svoi* was not a concept within a binary opposition between "us" (*svoi*, common people) and "them" (the state). This public, *svoi*, related to authoritative discourse neither supporting nor opposing it. Its location vis-à-vis that discourse was deterritorialized. This location was not invented by the last Soviet generation. It was inherent in what we called Lefort's paradox of Soviet ideology in chapter 1. However, it became a constitutive part of the subjectivity of these younger persons.

These publics of *svoi* were often organized in tightly knit networks of friends and strangers who shared some interest, occupation, or discourse. Such networks can be described as tight milieus[9] that were never

---

[8] Emphasis added.

[9] The term "milieu" is used here in the sense it has in cultural studies (see chapter 1, n 45). The use of this term in this chapter is indebted to Gladarev (2000).

completely bounded and isolated, and were always in the process of emergence and change, with an open-ended and somewhat shifting membership. Within these milieus, individual identities, collectivities, relations, and pursuits were shaped and normalized. To understand the nature of these milieus, consider again Inna's words: "We were very strongly *vnye* any social status"; "[w]e were organically different" from Soviet people, "We were simply *vnye*." Inna's use of the concept *vnye* suggests a particular relation to the system, where one lives within it but remains relatively "invisible." One employs discursive means that do not quite fit the pro/anti dichotomy in relation to authoritative discourse and cannot be quite articulated within the parameters of that discourse.

Instead of being explicitly involved with authoritative rituals and texts, as were the Komsomol secretaries and komsorgs in chapter 3, Inna and her friends found involvement with that discourse *neinteresno* (uninteresting). Considering something *uninteresting* and being *vnye* are related categories. Both refer to something that is irrelevant, because the person, although living within the system, is not tuned into a certain semantic field of meaning. In this sense it may be "uninteresting" to have to choose whom to support in a match between Juventus and Ajax if you never pay attention to European football, even if it sometimes plays on the television. This lack of preoccupation with certain parameters within the discursive field meant that instead of Havel's appeal "to live in truth" and Solzhenitsyn's appeal "to live not by lies" (*zhit' ne po lzhi*), Inna and her friends spoke of "living lightly" (*zhili legko*), "leading a very fun life" (*veli ochen' veseluiu zhizn'*), and "making merry in general" (*voobshche veselilis'*). These words are not about the nonseriousness of existence but about a replacement of Soviet political and social concerns with a quite different set of concerns that allowed one to lead a creative and imaginative life.

In Russia the more extreme examples of this type of living are sometimes described as "internal emigration" (*vnutrenniaia emigratsiia*).[10] This powerful metaphor, however, should not be read as suggesting complete withdrawal from Soviet reality into isolated, bounded, autonomous spaces of freedom and authenticity. In fact, unlike emigration, *internal emigration* captures precisely the state of being inside and outside at the same time, the inherent ambivalence of this oscillating position. Although uninterested in the Soviet system, these milieus heavily drew on that system's possibilities, financial subsidies, cultural values, collectivist ethics, forms of prestige, and so on. At the same time, they actively reinterpreted the cultural parameters of that world. The metaphor of internal emigration may apply less to other, less extreme but still related examples of this

---

[10] For example, Gudkov and Dubin (1994, 170).

lifestyle, when one is actually quite involved in many activities of the system, but nevertheless remains partial to many of its constative meanings—as were the Komsomol members described in chapter 3. In these more widespread cases the metaphor of internal emigration perhaps might be adapted to refer to certain dispositions and relations—for example, as emigration from the constative dimension of authoritative discourse, but not from all meanings and realities of socialist life.

Authors—Heroes of Everyday Socialism

The ontology of "being *vnye*" in relation to authoritative discourse was theorized in the early writings of Mikhail Bakhtin. Bakhtin's discussion will help us clarify what this relation stands for. However, we must first clarify an imprecision in the English translation of his text that obscures a central point for the purposes of our discussion. According to the translated version of Bakhtin's text, in a "fundamental, aesthetically productive relationship" between the author and the hero of a literary text, "the author occupies an intently maintained position *outside* the hero with respect to every constituent feature of the hero—a position *outside* the hero with respect to space, time, value and meaning" (Bakhtin 1990, 14).[11] The term "outside" in the English translation does not capture the Russian term *vnyenakhodimost'* coined by Bakhtin in the original. *Vnyenakhodimost'* is a compound of *vnye* (inside/outside) and *nakhodimost'* (locatedness). Whereas "outside" suggests a spatial location beyond a border, Bakhtin's term emphasizes a *relationship between* inside and outside. Therefore Bakhtin's original text would be more precisely translated thus: "a relation of intense *vnyenakhodimost'* of the author to all moments of the hero, *vnyenakhodimost'* of space, time, value, and meaning" (Bakhtin 2000, 40),[12] emphasizing an intense dialogic interrelationship between the author and hero positions, and the impossibility of dividing or splitting them into two separate selves.

This is not a relation between two bounded spaces or psyches but a dialogic simultaneity of several voices in one, where each continuously decenters the other. For Bakhtin, any subject simultaneously inhabits both the voice of the author creating a script and the hero following it, with neither position preempting the other in temporal, spatial, or thematic terms.

[11] Bakhtin's original essay, entitled *"Avtor i geroi esteticheskoi deiatel'nosti"* (Author and Hero in Aesthetic Activity), was written between 1920 and 1924 (see discussion in Clark and Holquist 1984, 353) and published in English in 1990.

[12] The original Russian reads, *"Otnoshenie napriazhennoi vnenakhodimosti avtora vsem momentam geroiia, prostranstvennoi, vrememmoi, tsennostnoi i smyslovoi vnenakhodimosti."*

This conception requires a particular understanding of the subject, one based not on a traditional binary "subject-object" relationship but on a *tripartite* relationship. The subject appears in a dual-unity (*dvuedinost'*) of a displaced "I and Other" or "author and hero," and only as such relates to an object (text).[13] In the analysis below, I refer to the relation of *vnyenakhodimost'* simply as being *vnye*.

This discussion has a direct bearing on the relation to Soviet reality described by Inna. As we saw in chapters 1 and 2, authoritative discourse during late socialism experienced a performative shift—that is, the position of its external "editor" disappeared and discourse became hypernormalized. It became important to participate in the performative reproduction of its fixed discursive forms, while not necessarily paying attention to the dimension of its constative meanings. This performative reproduction, however, had an important function of enabling new meanings, lifestyles, communities, and pursuits, all within the discursive field of the state but without being fully determined or controlled by it. Inna's relationship of being *vnye* the discursive field of late Soviet life was similar to the relationship of Bakhtin's author-and-hero of a text. In Inna's case, having this *vnye* relationship meant, on the one hand, acting as a "hero" of authoritative discourse who followed its script at the level of form, but, on the other hand, acting as "the author" of this discourse who invested that script with new meanings. In other words, the author's creative composition of new meanings was enabled by the hero's performative acts of reproducing authoritative forms, and vice versa. This complex relationship was obviously not a form, of opposition; it was rather the deterritorialization of Soviet life from within. It was the disappearance of the voice of an external "editor" of authoritative discourse that shifted the authorial voice onto every voice of the hero.

The Palace of Pioneers

Many of Inna's friends from her university years had known each other since secondary school, when they participated in different clubs at the Leningrad Palace of Pioneers. The time spent at the palace was formative for their personalities, friendships, and interests. The Leningrad Palace of Pioneers was run by the Soviet state under the auspices of the Komsomol. It was opened during high Stalinism, in 1937, in the magnificent Anichkov Palace on Leningrad's central street, Nevsky Prospekt. The famous poet Samuil Marshak spoke at the opening ceremony: "This is not simply a beautiful and rich palace, this is first of all a clever palace. . . . In it children

[13] See Mikeshina (1999).

will find the keys that open for them the doors to big science, technology, and art. . . . Here they will learn to work well and work as friends, cooperatively and collectively" (Marshak 1937). Marshak's words proved prophetic in both direct and ironic senses. During the Soviet period, the palace ran a large number of state-sponsored after-school societies, clubs, and events, from choirs, symphony orchestras, jazz groups, and dance ensembles to literary, mathematics, chess, and archeological clubs. Thousands of youngsters participated in these activities, among them future world-known figures.[14] The palace epitomized the familiar cultural paradox of Soviet socialism. It was housed in the headquarters of the city pioneer organization, whose announced goals were to bring up young pioneers to be "always prepared" to "struggle for the tasks of the Communist Party of the Soviet Union"[15] and to instill in children an interest in "socially useful activity" (*obshchestvenno-poleznaia aktivnost'*)—essentially, to bring them up as well-educated and devoted followers of the party. At the same time, however, some of the palace's clubs, also perfectly in line with the socialist values, actively promoted the types of knowledge, critical judgment, and independent thinking that taught children to question authority and ideological pronouncements.

Such after-school clubs and circles for children proliferated all over the country during late socialism—in schools, music schools, palaces of culture, palaces of pioneers, sports schools, amateur theaters, housing committee clubs, and so on. Much in this form of education depended on the teachers. For example, the Leningrad Palace of Pioneers attracted unusual teachers—among them the best writers, musicians, and historians—who worked there not necessarily for financial reasons (the salaries were lower than average) but because of their devotion to teaching and the considerable freedom to experiment that such "specialized" clubs offered in comparison with the more rigid, curriculum-bound, and hierarchical regular schools. Among Inna's friends, many belonged to one of two clubs—literary and archaeological—during their school years.

The Literary Club Derzanie

The Palace of Pioneers literary club Derzanie (meaning "dare") for schoolchildren interested in creative writing and poetry opened in 1937.

---

[14] For example, the opera singer Lena Obrastsova, the ballerina Natalia Makarova, and the world chess champion Boris Spassky. In the post-Soviet period, after the ideological Pioneer Organization had ceased to exist, the palace was renamed the St. Petersburg City Palace of Youth Creativity (*Sankt-Peterburgskii gorodskoi dvorets tvorchestva iunykh*).

[15] From "The Pioneers' Oath."

135

The club became particularly active and popular in the 1960s and 70s; it promoted open critical discussion about culture, literature, and society; its former students compare its free-spirited atmosphere with that of a "literary salon" and its classes to unstructured "improvisations" where most topics were allowed for discussion and most positions were openly questioned (Pudovkina 2000). A former member describes this atmosphere:

> We argued about everything, harshly and freely. We would invite schoolteachers and organize a dispute about the teaching of literature. We argued about the [Stalin's] cult of personality and supreme ideals, about poetry and science fiction. Teachers and students were disputing on an equal basis. No one made any distinction between who speaks—the authority of our teachers was *not* built on the understanding that only they knew the truth. Each of us doubted that, and was confident that the truth belonged only to him and no one else (Mark Maz'ia, quoted in Pudovkina 2000).

Despite the irrelevance of discussing political issues associated with the current Soviet context, discussions about Stalin's past were not irrelevant. This topic was seen as "history" that had links to the present, but was different from it. It was also possible to question the aesthetic canons of Soviet literature, provided one's argument was serious and sincere. Another participant remembers: "Some elements of the Soviet aesthetics were present there too, but in a maximally softened form. Importantly, even if you went beyond enlightened Soviet liberalism,[16] others did not reject you. The club valued talent and aspired to intellectual sincerity" (Lena Dunaevskaia, quoted in Pudovkina 2000). Another former student remembers that it was her club's poetry teacher who introduced her to the writings of Solzhenitsyn in the 1970s when his writings were outlawed in the Soviet Union (Nina Kniazeva, quoted in Pudovkina 2000). This student also describes cultural tours to old Russian towns organized by the teachers, where young clubbers learned details about Soviet history and literature that were not mentioned in the school curriculum: "In Tarusa[17] we met the daughter of Marina Tsvetaeva, Ariadna Efron, we visited the house of Konstantin Paustovsky, some of us spoke with Nadezhda Yakovlevna Mandelshtam" (Pudovkina 2000).

---

[16] This is a reference to belief in "socialism with a human face," which was common among the sixtiers generation. Going "beyond" this position meant being "uninterested" in socialism (being *vnye*).

[17] Tarusa, a small town on the Oka river near Kaluga, west of Moscow, was a favorite place for summer vacations among the Moscow intelligentsia. During the Soviet period, some artists and writers, many of them out of favor with the Soviet authorities, moved there permanently. At different times, Tarusa residents included such figures as Konstantin Paustovsky, Joseph Brodsky, Alexander Ginzburg, and Larissa Bogoras.

This emphasis on critical analysis of culture, sincerity of argument, respect for noncanonical positions, and collective access to forms of knowledge that were relatively inaccessible to the majority created among the club members a tightly knit milieu based on close friendship and a perception of themselves as different from "common" Soviet people. A former member describes that culture in the club as an "artificially created microclimate" where they "breathed a clear air, while a different life went on outside" (Nikolai Gol', quoted in Pudovkina 2000). Although this culture was not necessarily opposed to the goals proclaimed in the Soviet authoritative discourse, it was not necessarily in line with them either, rendering the club's name ironically fitting.

The Archaeological Circle

Some of Inna's new friends belonged to another club in the Palace of Pioneers that was started in 1972 and became known as the Archaeological Circle (*arkheologicheskii kruzhok*). By the late 1980s, several hundred schoolchildren had gone through its training as amateur archaeologists. They came from different social backgrounds, both intelligentsia and working-class families (Gladarev 2000). Most of them were first attracted to the circle by romantic ideas about adventures and traveling. However, thanks to the circle's teacher, the historian Vinogradov, these became linked with discussions about literature, poetry, history, and religion. Members of the circle went on archaeological expeditions in different parts of the Soviet Union, from the region of Leningrad to Tuva, Siberia, and the Caucasus. Sitting around bonfires, children of the circle recited the poetry of the Silver Age (*serebrianyi vek*) poets, Mandelshtam, Akhmatova, and Gumilev—who had been long unpublished by the Soviet state for ideological reasons[18]—and sang songs of Galich and Vysotskii, both of whom held an ambivalent status as "problematic" singer-songwriters in the eyes of the state. As in the literary club Derzanie these experiences helped to shape a tight milieu based on friendship and a mix of values from independence of spirit, tolerance of opinion, and suspicion of actively politicized positions to the feeling that they were

[18] Osip Mandelshtam, Anna Akhmatova, and Nikolai Gumilev—three great Acmeist poets—were associated by the Soviet state with counterrevolution, although they were not active dissidents. Mandelshtam (1891–1938) was arrested in the 1930s and died in a labor camp. Akhmatova (1889–1966) was persecuted and prevented from publishing. Gumilev (1886–1921), Akhmatova's first husband, was arrested and executed by the Bolsheviks in 1921, allegedly for participating in an anti-Bolshevik conspiracy, which later turned out to be a KGB fabrication (Volkov 1995, 537). Although largely unpublished until perestroika, their poetry was immensely popular among the intelligentsia throughout the Soviet period.

different from the regular *sovetskii obyvatel'* (Soviet philistine). A former member of the circle explains: "It was important that the person who was admitted [to the circle] was not simply a *sovetskii obyvatel'* but was different. Yes, consciously different" (Vasia, quoted in Gladarev 2000). They considered themselves neither anti-Soviet nor pro-Soviet but non-Soviet (*asovetskie*), uninterested in political and ideological topics (Gladarev 2000).[19]

Most former members continued to go on archaeological expeditions for years after leaving the circle. According to Inna, these expeditions were not strictly about archaeology but about developing a culture of independent thinking: "It was very important in these expeditions . . . that everyone developed in his own direction and no one stood in the way of another's thinking and feeling in his own way. That was very important. . . . It was like meditation."[20] The metaphor of meditation captures well the experience of living in deterritorialized worlds of friendship, poetry, and neverending discussions in the contexts of nature, bonfires, and hiking. The practice of meditation also stands for a particular relationship to the world—one stays acutely present in the world and yet uninvolved in its concerns, which is synonymous with the relationship of being *vnye*.

The Soviet state enabled this style of living, shared values, and collective pursuits with its educational system's emphasis on learning, cultural knowledge, collectivism, and nonmaterial values (*nematerial'nye tsennosti*). Like many others, members of the circle felt that monetary concerns were shameful, and they disparagingly referred to money as "vile metal" (*prezrennyi metal*) (Gladarev 2000). This rather widespread attitude was further reinforced by their teachers and heroes who belonged to the sixtiers or older intelligentsia. The same uneasy attitude toward money translated into an ambivalent relationship toward *fartsovshchiki* (black-marketers dealing in Western goods). The socialist state again enabled the development of these shared moral values not only through ideological rhetoric but also economically, subsidizing most social and cultural pursuits and organizations and also basic life necessities. As one member of the circle explains: "To be honest, no one [in the circle] was focused on making money. In those times that was not necessary. Any stable salary was enough not to die of hunger and be relatively well

---

[19] "Political activity" became relevant for the members of the Archaeological Circle only later, when the reforms of perestroika began and the discursive regime changed. In 1986 members of the circle formed "the group for saving the monuments of history and culture" (Gruppa po spaseniiu pamiatnikov istorii i kul'tury)—the first social organization in Leningrad organized "from below," without the sponsorship of the Komsomol or the party. Their first famous action was a campaign to save the house of Anton Del'vig (a close friend of the poet Alexandr Pushkin) and the Hotel Angleterre.

[20] Author interview.

dressed" (Tamara, quoted in Gladarev 2000). Instead, the main ethical and aesthetics values in the circle were based on constant interactions and conversations.

Theoretical Physicists

Different forms of living in a more or less deterritorialized reality were present in all contexts of late socialism, constituting one of the central principles of its culture. In the previous examples, the relation of being *vnye* was learned by children in contexts provided by the state. This form of relating to the system's discourse, being simultaneously internal and external to it, emerged in groups and collectivities that occupied privileged positions within the state—from engineers and students to film-makers and scientists. Even milieus of elite Soviet citizens that were insti-tutionalized, funded, and afforded privileges and high symbolic capital by the state created styles of living *vnye*, which the system enabled. A partic-ularly paradigmatic example was the milieu of theoretical scientists—for example theoretical physicists—who also developed a culture of being *vnye* enabled by the state's promotion of the values of science and knowledge. Many physicists worked in prestigious research institutes, received higher salaries and bonuses, and enjoyed considerable social prestige. One could pursue physics and shape one's research under con-ditions of relative independence from ideological, financial, or bureau-cratic constraints. As Nyíri and Breidenbach point out, "[A]rguing that advances in physics are often based on unexpected discoveries, [Soviet theoretical] physicists generally succeeded in convincing the leadership to let them conduct the research they wanted" (2002, 45). Physicist Boris Altshuler, who now lives and works in the U.S., describes what the research conditions were like for theoreticians at the Leningrad Institute for Nuclear Physics in Gatchina (LNPI) where he worked from 1978 to 1989, comparing those conditions with research conditions in the U.S. universities where he has been working in recent years: "We had no par-ticular obligations. We didn't have to teach, and we were basically free to decide what we wanted to work on. People in the U.S. can't imagine that kind of freedom. Here, you spend a lot of your time writing applications for grants that you may or may not get. In Leningrad, if you wanted to switch from solid-state to particle physics, no problem: all you had to do was perhaps move to another group" (Nyíri and Breidenbach 2002, 45).

As with previously discussed milieus, the milieu of theoretical physi-cists was produced through intense intellectual and cultural interac-tion, friendship, sharing of scientific ideas, and cultural pursuits outside physics, all organized as a philosophy of collective searching for what

139

was described in the beginning of this chapter as "deep truths" as opposed to "clear truths." Pursuing theoretical physics involved "intensive thinking ... and continuous dialogue with colleagues. ... Problems presented at seminars were jointly scrutinized from all possible perspectives. Ideas about 'hot' topics were thus rapidly shared, and the thinking of each individual built on that of many" (Nyíri and Breidenbach 2002, 47).

These discursive genres produced a collective world of being thematically, temporally, and spatially *vnye* authoritative discourse. This milieu's internal ideology, like that of the milieus discussed above, stressed its own uniqueness; and, like with the other milieus, the scientific discussions among its members "took place in a completely egalitarian and communitarian spirit, with everyone allowed to criticize" (Nyíri and Breidenbach 2002, 47). In this sense, collective research, intellectual excitement, cultural pursuits, and summer vacations were linked together, as with other milieus. The practices of going on expeditions, singing songs, reciting poetry, studying archaeology, writing music, or constantly interacting could not be divided into separate spheres but were productive of these milieus all together—and enabled by the state:

> Summer and winter schools of theoretical physics were orgies of undiluted physics-making. Events of the Leningrad Physico-Technical Institute (later the LNPI) took place in the countryside holiday homes of the Academy of Sciences. Yuri Dokshitzer, whose father had made him suffer through a rigorous musical education, played songs by Okudzhava,[21] Vysotskii, and Galich on his guitar. Alexei Kaidalov from ITEP[22] sang. The lifestyle of physics-making was punctuated by mountaineering and kayak trips and flavored by *samizdat* copies of poetry by Mandelshtam, Solzhenitsyn's prose, or Agatha Christie and Irving Stone novels bought during trips to the West. Physicists' flats housed readings by actors and concerts by bards Bulat Okudzhava and Vladimir Vysotskii, members of an emerging alternative to the totalitarian uniformity of culture (Nyíri and Breidenbach 2002, 47–48).

This description illustrates the importance of the creative, imaginative, collective, and relatively independent professional and cultural pursuits within this milieu. However, the final characterization, which makes a familiar division into "the totalitarian uniformity of culture" and "alternative culture," reproduces the problematic effect of a binary division, de-emphasizing the fact that the very existence of creative, dynamic, and relatively independent milieus of theoretical scientists and other cultural

---

[21] Bulat Okudzhava was a prominent member of the "author's song" genre.
[22] The Institute of Theoretical and Experimental Physics in Moscow.

producers[23] was an indivisible, if somewhat paradoxical, element of the Soviet state's cultural project, not its opposite (recall the CC speechwriters who listened to Vysotskii's recordings in chapter 3). The conditions that made the physicists' milieu possible and thriving, and enabled them to develop the styles of living *vnye*, were again provided by the state itself: from the immense prestige accorded to scientists in the Soviet society, state-sponsored academic institutions where scientists were relieved of teaching duties, relative financial and political independence, and freedom to choose research topics, to state-promoted discourse on the value of scientific and cultural knowledge, creative arts, music and literature, and so on. Indeed, outside of the Soviet state project, this milieu would have made no sense and would have failed to thrive.

Saigon

In the previous examples, the style of living by being *vnye* authoritative discourse was illustrated in the contexts that were strongly affiliated with state institutions. This however, was not the only possibility. Many similar collectivities emerged in various contexts with much looser connections to state institutions. Examples were various *tusovki*, a slang term referring to non-institutionalized milieus of people with some shared interest based on "hanging out" and interacting within such milieus.[24] These sprang up in the cities between the 1960s and the 1970s.

In the early 1960s, during Khrushchev's liberating reforms, many large Soviet cities, including Leningrad, experienced a cultural transformation that was minute in quantitative terms but enormous in cultural significance. The poet Viktor Krivulin called it "the Great Coffee Revolution" (*velikaia kofeinaia revoliutsiia*).[25] The revolution amounted to the creation of a few modest cafés in city centers that sold strong coffee and pastries and enabled new spatial and temporal contexts for interaction among large groups of young people. This interaction was similar to the interaction enabled by the previously discussed clubs but without their limited thematic focus, state institutional organization, and registered membership.

Although most of these cafés had no official names (the signs on the doors simply said "*kafe*"), many quickly acquired slang names, often

---

[23] See also Faraday (2000) for a discussion of cultural production among the tightly knit milieu of Soviet filmmakers.

[24] *Tusovki* (plural of *tusovka*) is from the verb *tosovat'*—"to shuffle."

[25] This is a play on the ubiquitous Soviet authoritative signifier, "The Great October Socialist Revolution," which referred to the Bolshevik Revolution of 1917 (Krivulin 1996).

141

based on "Western" locations (e.g., Evropa, London, Liverpul', Tel'-Aviv, Rim, Olster). By the late 1960s, one café known as Saigon,[26] emerged as a particularly important context for interaction. It opened on September 18, 1964, (its former regulars still celebrate the date) in an ideal central location in Leningrad.[27] The slang name Saigon symbolized the existence of a different dimension of discourse, *vnye* in a location. The name's strength was in its ubiquity and recognizability, created by the critical discourse in the Soviet media against the American "imperialist war" in Vietnam. In the new context the name was completely reinterpreted, losing its negative political connotations while preserving a recognizable reference to an exotic and decadent "Western" locale. Perhaps the negativity surrounding the name in the Soviet press made it particularly attractive to the café patrons as a gesture of jocular defiance; this possible meaning, however, was never explicitly discussed, consistent with the café-goers' "uninterestedness" in political topics.

Saigon soon acquired regulars who would stop in to talk to acquaintances and drink strong coffee and sometimes port wine clandestinely brought in from the outside (Krivulin 1996, 4–5). These regulars differed from random visitors off the street in that for them Saigon became not just a café but "a source of information, books and ideas; a territory where you established contacts with the opposite sex, a shelter from parents' moralizing, and a cover from the nasty Leningrad weather" (Zaitsev 1996). The regulars tended to form groups that did not mix with each other. Because of this diversity, one patron observed that "Saigon was reminiscent of an aristocratic English club through which alcoholics walked" (Grebenshikov 1996, 38). The poet Viktor Toporov, a graduate of the club Derzanie and a Saigon regular, describes the crowd as follows: "There was our group of poets, then a group of artists that were connected to us, then a group of drug addicts, then a group of blackmarketers and *fartsovshchiki* [blackmarketers buying clothes from Western tourists and reselling them to Soviet citizens] selling shoes" (Toporov 1996, 50). The nearby Palace of Pioneers fed Saigon's groups of literature lovers. For them the main attraction was the possibility of socializing in an atmosphere similar to that of the palace but even more mixed, open-ended, and unpredictable:

I still do not like going to private dinner parties or inviting people to my place precisely because of the predictability [*predskazuemost'*] of

---

[26] Today, memoirs and stories about Saigon are regularly published in St. Petersburg journals and newspapers, and in scholarly works (Zdravomyslova 1996, Boym 2001), and although the original café has ceased to exist, its name lives on in clones in St. Petersburg and other Russian cities.

[27] On the corner of Nevsky and Vladimirsky Prospekts.

FIGURE 4.1. Saigon. The Leningrad café. Drawing by Mikhail Petrenko, one of the café's regulars, 1979. (Petrenko is depicted on the right, with a moustache and wearing a beret.) Reproduced with permission of the artist.

the whole situation. But in Saigon the situation was open [*otkrytaia situatsiia*]. When I went there I never knew whether that evening would be extremely tedious or remarkably entertaining, who I would meet there, and whether I would end it in the police station or in the bar at the Hotel Evropeiskaia. I knew very well that if you came to Saigon around 2 P.M. you would definitely meet the person you were looking for, because he would also stop by. These were free people who were drinking and having conversations. Some of them wrote poetry, others drew pictures. (Toporov 1996, 50)

The centrality of open-ended and temporally unconstrained interaction, and the unpredictable and changing milieu of participants that it involved, became reflected in slang expressions. One could meet *v Saigone* ("in Saigon," that is, in its physical space) or *na Saigone* ("at Saigon," within the milieu of its regulars) (Fain and Lur'e 1991, 171). Like Inna's friends, Toporov's circle was more interested in talking, socializing, drinking, and reading early twentieth-century poetry than discussing politics. Their relationship to political dissidents was also one of quiet distancing; according to Toporov, "there were occasional dissidents

143

there . . . but for us this was uninteresting [*neinteresno*]. . . . In our circle no one got involved in dissident activities" (quoted in Zaitsev 1996, 51).

Even though "the dissidents" did not constitute a sizable group at the Saigon, their general presence, as well as the activities of others who were having long conversations and exchanging books, made the café an ideal place for KGB operatives to keep an eye on the general atmosphere among such milieus in the city. Partly because of the usefulness of the café for KGB monitoring, the place never closed down and remained relatively unbothered by the police, which allowed its milieus to thrive and grow. Viktor Krivulin claimed that most people at the Saigon did not worry too much about the KGB precisely because political concerns were for them relatively irrelevant. At the same time, he and his friends were occasionally summoned "to the organs" for questioning. Krivulin recollected that in the late 1960s, he recognized a man drinking coffee next to him at the Saigon as a KGB operative. The commonly understood presence of clandestine figures and potential threat, "added some feeling of romanticism and adventure" (Krivulin 1996, 7–8). This relationship between the milieu and the state "security organs" illustrates how the state enabled such milieus, which is why the KGB was not a profound concern for most members of these milieus.

Inna, whom we encountered above, began frequenting Saigon in the late 1970s. She and her friends "sat on the windowsills, drank coffee, and talked about various things. . . . Here one could always find someone to talk to. If you came to Saigon you would definitely find someone. *Obshchenie* [interaction, chatting, being together] was the most important thing." They read "various books which one could not buy anywhere. . . . We read a lot of poetry from the turn of the century. . . . We also read French poetry. . . . We read works in classical physics [foundational texts in mechanics and thermodynamics]. We read Beckett and Ionesco" (see figure 4.1).[28] Although this reading list may seem an incoherent mix, all these texts in fact shared the important feature of being temporally, spatially, and thematically *vnye* to the "uninteresting" social and political issues of the Soviet discourse.

In the early 1980s, many of the works of poetry and fiction read by these people had not been published for decades, and some of their authors had either been repressed or were out of favor with the party. However, in line with the cultural paradox of socialism, many of these works had never been made fully "illegal," so that students and people with contacts could still access their earlier Russian and limited Soviet editions, say, in research libraries. Inna's part-time job at the university

[28] Author interview.

library provided such access: "We could come to the reading room and read the kind of books that we could not get anywhere else. For example, we read [old Russian editions of] Gumilev, who was no longer published or sold in shops." Despite their reading, discussing, and exchanging of these books, Inna and her friends were also not particularly worried about the KGB:

> We always had bags full of literature. So we were taking little risks. But we also understood perfectly well that no one was terribly interested in us. Why would they be? At most, we had a typed song by Galich or a poem by Brodsky. And, of course, we exchanged this stuff. But as far as arresting us for this—who would do that? This was not serious stuff. As for signing dissident letters or getting involved in other [dissident] activities, we never believed in that.

According to St. Petersburg cultural historian Lev Lur'e, himself once a frequenter of several literary milieus and the café Saigon, the authors that circulated among their members also included Andrei Platonov, Mikhail Bulgakov, Marcel Proust, James Joyce, and Arthur Miller (Lur'e 2003). As a result, "in the 1970s you could receive a better literary and philosophical education in the Saigon than in the departments of philology or history of Leningrad University," which is why the café's milieus played an important role in educating and preparing the future post-Soviet founders of private publishing houses, as well as their editors, translators, and readers (Lur'e 2003).

The venue of cafés naturally begs some comparison with Habermas's "public sphere," which emerged during early capitalism, when individuals constituted themselves as a "public" through critical and rational debate about political and social issues in bourgeois cafés and salons (Habermas 1991). Drawing a parallel with this discussion of "public sphere" in the bourgeois context, Russian sociologist Elena Zdravomyslova argues that the phenomenon of Saigon "can be interpreted as a certain form of collective protest . . . a neverending strike of young Soviet intelligentsia against the regime [and] . . . a political protest" (1996, 39–40). However, the problem with using the concept of "public sphere" is precisely in the unfortunate binary models and metaphors of protest and political opposition that it drags out. Describing the cultural logic of milieus in this way obscures the crucial fact that they explicitly distanced themselves from dissident discourses or political protests. Like other milieus of the 1960s and 70s, Saigon did indeed breed certain kinds of publics of *svoi*. However, as we saw in the previous chapter, within these publics Soviet reality was not resisted but deterritorialized. Not surprisingly, for members of these milieus critical debates about Soviet political and social issues were considered "uninteresting." The relation of these publics to authoritative

145

discourse was one of neither opposition nor support, but of being *vnye*. As part of this relationship, one could avoid authoritative rituals and texts of the system but continue to be involved in many of the system's cultural ideals and pursuits. The latter were especially strengthened by the presence in the milieu of people of the sixtiers generation (poets, literary club teachers, etc.), with their more idealist relationship to the promises of socialism. It is not by chance that the discourse of "fun living" played a dominant role in that circle. The poet Krivulin summarized the atmosphere at Saigon: "We lived a fun life" (*my veselo zhili*) (Krivulin 1996, 7–8). The reference to "fun life"—like Inna's references (quoted earlier) to "living lightly" (*zhili legko*) and "leading a very fun life" (*veli ochen' veseluiu zhizn'*)—refers to a kind of "normal life" in everyday socialism, a life that had become invested with creative forms of living that the system enabled but did not fully determine.

Music *Tusovka*

Leningrad amateur rock musicians, who in the late 1970s and early 1980s also constituted a *tusovka*, insisted that they too were "uninterested" in politics and did not consider the state's critical campaigns directed at rock music to be particularly dangerous. Sociologist Thomas Cushman discovered that in the *tusovka* of Leningrad rock musicians in the 1980s:

> the practice of acquiring [recorded] music, sharing it, and, ultimately, playing it simply went on with little conscious thought about whether or not such acts would be considered politically deviant. While the political circumscription of rock music [by the state] was quite strong, such circumscriptions were often ignored, or seen simply as an inconvenience by musicians. . . . Indeed, what is striking . . . is not just the lack of discussion about politics per se, but the complete dearth of any expression of fear on the part of rock musicians, either of the state in the abstract sense, or of the actual potential of it to intrude directly into their lives. (Cushman 1995, 93–94)

According to Cushman, when talking about their artistic interests, rock musicians distinguished between two Russian concepts for "truth"— *pravda* and *istina*—a parallel to Dovlatov's distinction between "clear truths" and "deep truths" discussed earlier in this chapter. Rock musicians saw their pursuit of music "as expressions of *istina*, as the embodiment of elemental truths about the human condition," and were utterly uninterested in the political stance that searching for *pravda* implied (Cushman 1995, 107–8). One musician explained: "We're interested in universal problems which don't depend on this or that system, or on a particular time. In other words, they were here a thousand years ago, and they still exist—relations between people, the connection between man and nature" (Cushman 1995, 95). And yet Cushman, like Zdravomyslova above, draws on Habermas to describe this apolitical stance as a form of rock *tusovka*'s "counterculture" that was based on "a stock of knowledge which, quite literally, runs counter to the dominant stock of knowledge in society" (Cushman 1995, 8). The insistence on this binary scheme again de-emphasizes the crucial difference between being in opposition and being *vnye*.

The discussions of timeless and universal problems that preoccupied members of the *tusovka*—such as Inna and her friends' interests in ancient philosophy, early twentieth-century poetry, and theoretical physics—continuously deterritorialized the temporal, spatial and thematic parameters of this milieu's life in relation to authoritative discourse. This allowed the musicians to lead creative lives that were made possible by the political system but not quite constrained by it. The profound irrelevance of political issues was in fact not just a cultural reality of such milieus, but also their explicit ideology. Political themes were not only considered uninteresting and banal, but any hint of raising such topics was met with explicit sarcasm. Alik Kan, a music critic and close friend of many members of the rock and jazz *tusovka*, recollects an episode that illustrates this. In 1982, he was sitting in the foyer of the Hotel Leningrad with Boris Grebenshikov, Sergei Kuryokhin,[29] and a British friend who lived in Leningrad and was about to go to London for a few days. "I asked him," said Alik, "to bring back some British newspapers and magazines. . . . To this Kuryokhin and Grebenshikov ironically exclaimed: 'Alik, are you still reading newspapers? What, you are still interested [in political issues]!?' [*Alik, ty eschë chitaesh' gazety? Tebe chto, eshchë interesno?*]"[30]

Even though the newspapers were foreign, Alik's interest in their political analysis of the Soviet situation was inappropriate in that milieu. The sarcastic tone of the comments was a common mode of conversation in the *tusovka* about other topics too, including music and culture. "They joked a lot," Alik explains, "in a sarcastic way [*iazvitel'no*], as if sharpening their sarcasm on each other. It was neverending. The main texture of the communication in the rock *tusovka* was sarcasm and a lack of any political themes."[31] This ritualized discursive genre performatively produced the *tusovka* as a tight milieu of *svoi* whose ambiguous relation of

[29] Two famous figures of the Soviet "amateur" rock scene. Boris Grebenshikov was and remains the leader of the group Akvarium; Sergei Kuryokhin was a jazz pianist and leader of the group Popular Mechanics (*Populiarnaia Mekhanika*).

[30] Author interview.

[31] Author interview. See the discussion of irony during this period in chapter 7.

being *vnye* authoritative discourse was strictly monitored through public sarcasm directed at its members. This is also why, in contexts that were not directly linked to the milieu, some people could consider political and other themes more relevant. According to Alik, although "it was considered bad form [*plokhoi ton*] to talk on any political or social topics in the *tusovka*," speaking with Kuryokhin one-on-one, "we could have very long and serious discussions" about the Soviet system, the West, and anything else.

Obshchenie

All these milieus, from those that were institutionalized by the state to those that were spontaneous, were not static social spaces; they were continuously reproduced through repeated performative genres known as the practice of *obshchenie*, a term that has no adequate equivalent in English.[32] It refers to "communication" and "conversation" but in addition involves nonverbal interaction and spending time together or being together. It is different from just "hanging out" with friends, as used in the United States, because it always involves an intense and intimate commonality and intersubjectivity, not just spending time in the company of others. The noun *obshchenie* has the same root as *obshchii* (common) and *obshchina* (commune), stressing in the process of interaction not the exchange between individuals but the communal space where everyone's personhood was dialogized to produce a common intersubjective sociality. *Obshchenie*, therefore, is both a process and a sociality that emerges in that process, and both an exchange of ideas and information as well as a space of affect and togetherness. Although *obshchenie* is an old cultural practice in Russia, during late socialism it became particularly intense and ubiquitous and acquired new forms, evolving into a dominant pastime in all strata of Soviet society and in all professional, ideological, public, and personal contexts (Vail and Genis 1996, 69).[33] According to cultural critics Petr Vail' and Alexandr Genis, in the 1960s and 1970s *obshchenie* emerged as a new "cult" (1991, 242); philosopher Iakov Krotov called it a "new fetish" (1992, 247).

Obshchenie could not proceed in authoritative discourse, but it was as common in the contexts where authoritative discourse was produced (e.g., in Komsomol committees) as it was elsewhere. It was not limited to friends and acquaintances, and could include complete strangers. It

[32] Pronounced: *ob-SHEH-nee-yeh*. Similarly, its near opposite, the English-language concept of "privacy," has no exact equivalent in Russian (Boym 1994, 3). See the discussions of *obshchenie* in Pesmen (2000) and Nafus (2003a).

[33] In the post-Soviet period, one regularly hears regrets that the times and spaces of *obshchenie* are shrinking, that there is no longer enough of it.

could last just the length of an evening or a train ride, as long as the person participated in a kind of interaction that was recognizable as a form of *obshchenie* that, if circumstances permitted, could be repeated. Anyone could become *svoi* through *obshchenie*, and, conversely, was not *svoi* if they refused to participate in *obshchenie*. Krotov remarks that "a person who was always ready to have a chat [*poboltat'*] and to drink a bottle [*razdavit' butylochku*] with friends was never regarded as criminal and evil, whatever society thought of him. But a person who was too reserved, who 'thought of himself too highly,' who avoided *obshchenie*—whether he was . . . a dissident or a member of the KGB [*gebist*]—looked suspicious and evil, almost like Judas" (1992, 249).

Practices of *obshchenie* during late socialism became particularly ubiquitous and open-ended. Through these practices the temporality and spatiality of, and the social relations and personal identities within, state socialism were being reshaped and reinterpreted. Krotov describes some of these practices: "Endless *zastol'ia* [around-the-table drinking-eating-talking], *posidelki* [casual sitting and talking where the topic is open-ended and is less important than the process], *trepy* [chatting], *vypivony* [drinking and talking with friends or strangers] . . . constant anniversaries and birthdays celebrated both at work and at home" (1992, 248).[34] For many people, belonging to a tight milieu of *svoi*, which involved constant *obshchenie*, was more meaningful and valuable than other forms of interaction, sociality, goals, and achievements, including those of a professional career. In many cases, the *obshchenie* of professional and nonprofessional types became tightly intertwined, as with the theoretical physicists above whose milieu was organized on principles that went well beyond physics and institutions. According to Vail' and Genis, in the 1960s the "ephemeral joys of *obshchenie* were valued incomparably higher than the more real, but also more cumbersome achievements in the form of one's career or salary. To be one of *svoi* [*byt' svoim*] seemed and indeed was more important than any official gains. . . . Friendship—the emotion that occupied the 1960s—became the source of independent social opinion. . . . Ostracism of one's friends became a more vicious force than problems at work" (1991, 242).

In multiple forms of *obshchenie*, including judging and controlling who belongs to *svoi*, these milieus became produced. Nancy Ries captures the performative nature of "talk" in Russia, arguing that it is "not just an activity during which value creation is described, but one in which, during which, and through which value is actually produced" (1997, 20–21). This point can be expanded to all forms and practices of *obshchenie*, including those that did not involve talk and were not confined to informal

---

[34] See also Pesmen (2000, 165) for a discussion of different practices of *obshchenie*.

or private interactions. For all the milieus discussed in this chapter, it was important not only to read certain books, discuss certain ideas, and listen to certain music, but, above all, to remain involved in the neverending and open-ended *obshchenie* with or without these books and ideas in mind. The open-ended and unplanned nature of the time spent together was more important than any concrete discussion. For members of the Archaeological Circle, "[o]bshchenie in its various forms became a goal in itself" and they "devoted all their free time to it" (Gladarev 2000). In the café Saigon it was the same. It provided *obshchenie* as an abstract entity that had value in itself; here *obshchenie* was particularly open in terms of topics, participants, time spent on it or results achieved. In the literary club Derzanie, among the theoretical physicists, and in the rock music *tusovka* these characteristics of *obshchenie* were equally important.

The "value" produced in such practices went beyond just milieus of friends; it included the production of particular worlds that were spatially, temporally, thematically, and meaningfully *vnye* the regime of Soviet authoritative discourse. It is not by chance that members of these circles engulfed themselves in ancient history and foreign literature, pre-Soviet architecture, and Russian Silver Age (early twentienth-century) poetry, theoretical physics and botany, archaeology and Western rock music, Buddhist philosophy and religion. Remember that café Saigon regulars were as interested in reading French poetry as works in classical physics, while avoiding political issues. And this is how Inna describes the practices of *obshchenie* among her friends:

> We talked about aesthetics, about Tolstoy and Pushkin, about poetry, about Brodsky, about Sosnora.[35] . . . We talked a lot, we just talked a lot. We walked around the city and talked about architectural styles, about *moderne*.[36] We walked around courtyards and climbed around rooftops, and we discussed everything. . . . Around 1981–82, we became interested in religious topics and discussed that too. Some people slowly started getting baptized. We also discussed various crazy historico-philosophical topics and religious topics, and we argued a lot. . . . We read Berdyaev's [1923] *The World View of Dostoyevsky*. It was also important to copy everything by hand [since copies of these books were rare] from old editions, keeping the old alphabet, spelling system, punctuation. . . . We also talked about plants and flowers, for

[35] Viktor Sosnora is a St. Petersburg poet, better known among poetry connoisseurs than the general public. He was practically unpublished during the Soviet period. His poetic style is known for its delicate grace and disrespect for canons. In the 1960s and 1970s, Sosnora led a literary circle for young poets (*LITO Sosnory*).

[36] *Moderne* is another name for the Art Nouveau style, a French architectural style of the turn of twentieth century that is well represented in St. Petersburg.

example. Not to withdraw from life or to hide away, but simply be-cause other things were unimportant to us.

It was important to engage personally with these distant topics—for ex-ample, to copy old texts by hand, to use old editions, to write in old Russian or foreign alphabets and spelling systems. All these various top-ics and representations of distant histories, foreign codes, ancient alpha-bets, and natural and physical worlds were interesting and meaningful not only *in themselves* but because they "injected" various temporal, spatial, semantic, linguistic, scientific, biologic and other "elsewheres" into the here-and-now of one's personal life, producing the intense rela-tion of "being *vnye*" the Soviet universe. These acts and processes can be compared with shamanic rituals that add otherworldly realities to the present world through the processes that William Hanks calls "transpo-sition"—a multiplex linking of the local world and people with distant and imaginary worlds (2000, 237).

Obshchenie was far more than communication between separate indi-viduals; it produced a form of sociality and a form of personhood that transcended the personal and the social (Rosaldo 1982; Strathern 1988). In this process, *svoi* acquired the features of a dispersed personhood, as the lives of participants became tightly intertwined through togetherness that was a central value in itself. This was not simply close friendship, but kinship-like intimacy. A former member of the Archaeological Circle describes his relationship to that milieu: "This was like a family atmo-sphere, like people from your kin [*rodnye liudi*]. Simply *svoi* people. . . . Not just relatives, but intimate and dear people. And everyone is ready to do anything for the others" (Yana, quoted in Gladarev 2000). Another member of the circle remembers: "I had developed a very strong feeling towards these people as to very close people who are related to you. I feel this closer than family ties. While I have actual brothers and sisters whom I haven't seen for a thousand years and don't even know where they live" (Tatyana, quoted in Gladarev 2000). A third explains: "We are almost like relatives. . . . they are just *tvoi* people ["your people"], this is a very different level of relations" (Stas, quoted in Gladarev 2000).

Boiler Rooms

During late socialism, especially in the 1970s and early 80s, it became increasingly common among some groups of the last Soviet generation, especially children of intelligentsia families, but also some from working-class backgrounds, to give up more sophisticated professional careers for occupations that offered more free time. The more extreme and telling

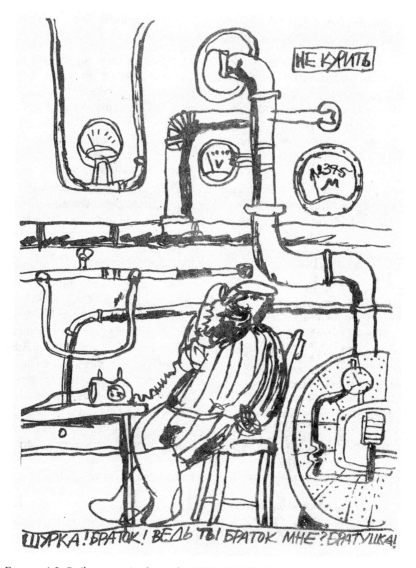

FIGURE 4.2. Boiler room in the early 1980s (1990). Alexandr Florenskii.

examples of such jobs included boiler room technician (*kochegar*), warehouse watchman (*storozh*), freight train loader (*gruzchik*), and street sweeper (*dvornik*).[37] These jobs kept them busy for only two to three night shifts a week, leaving them plenty of free time for *obshchenie* and

[37] Havel describes a similar tendency in Czechoslovakia (Brodsky and Havel 1994).

for pursuing other interests. One's obligations were minimized because the work was undemanding, because it was organized in long shifts with breaks in between, and because one was spared the need to attend meetings, parades, and other public events (since only people with stronger institutional affiliations were required to attend such events through their jobs).

"Boiler rooms" (*kochegarka* or *kotel'naia*) were local technical hubs of the centralized heating system in the district: rooms with valves and control mechanisms for the district's hot water pipes. The jobs of boiler room technicians amounted to keeping track of the pressure in the pipes, turning on and off hot water and cold water, calling a repairperson in case of trouble, and so on. The technicians were required to be present in the room during their shifts, but they rarely had to do much work. They usually worked one twenty-four-hour shift every four days (*sutki cherez troe*). Although the salary was very low (sixty to seventy rubles a month, the lowest official wage), the job allowed a large amount of free time.

These jobs became attractive for some individuals because of the performative shift of authoritative discourse. The state's law of mandatory employment was reproduced purely performatively, at the level of form (its constative meaning of having a job became shifted almost beyond recognition), and this performative reproduction enabled new meanings, temporalities, communities, pursuits, interests, forms of aesthetics and expertise—in short, a whole universe of meaning. The state again enabled it, without quite being able to control or account for it. Such occupations allowed the person to pursue various interests and amateur careers, from scholar of ancient languages to rock musician. One could be a writer who was unrecognized by the state's union of writers and therefore unpublished and in need of official "employment" (Brodsky was a case in point). Many "amateur" rock musicians were employed in such occupations; they came to be referred to in slang as "boiler room rockers" (*kochegary-rokery*).[38] Having no professional status as musicians, they could not make a living playing music and so sought out employment that would provide some money, satisfy the law of mandatory employment, and allow as much free time for music as possible.

These occupations became so commonplace that the famous band Akvarium sang about their peers as "the generation of yard sweepers and night watchers" (*Pokolenie dvornikov i storozhei*).[39] By the early 1980s, it became difficult to find a vacancy in such jobs. Milieus of *svoi* that emerged in these contexts tried to hire only those who belonged. This

[38] Cushman (1995, 57–58).

[39] From the song "Pokolenie dvornikov i storozhei" by Boris Grebenshikov. See Yurchak (1997a).

allowed them to concentrate on joint pursuits in art and philosophy[40] and to guarantee a system of substitution at work since many were in fact busy with vocations outside of their employment. In the early 1980s in Leningrad, one often needed connections within these milieus to be hired at such jobs. Inna's friend, who was trying to get a position in a boiler room, was asked what she "also" did. When she said she was a medieval historian, they replied: "What? A medievalist? Oh, no, no. Here everyone is a legal scholar. Two PhDs [*kandidaty*] and the third is defending soon."[41] These legal scholars needed free time to engage in research that was unconstrained by work in law institutions and that allowed one to spend time reading and writing, often on topics that went beyond those accepted in Soviet publications. Essentially, their boiler room wages functioned as academic research grants that enabled scholarly pursuits and did not constrain the topics they pursued. However, they operated as such primarily in the world of *vnye* (one could not necessarily publish in the state owned journals). As a context for research that did not require teaching (like the theoretical physicists above), such employment was a *vnye* imitation of employment in academic institutions.

Such employment also allowed for engagement with cultural, philosophical, or religious topics that one could not pursue at all in Soviet institutions such as, Buddhism, Western jazz, existential philosophy, and so on. Although the salaries for boiler room jobs were lower than for most other occupations, one could easily survive because meeting one's basic needs in the Soviet Union was inexpensive. According to one rock musician, "before the advent of glasnost and perestroika he could live on three rubles per week, or roughly, at official exchange rates of the time, for about $1.80" (Cushman 1995, 57). Rent, food, transportation, clothes, books, theater, cinema, and museums were all very cheap; medical care and education were free. In addition, the socialist state in fact subsidized these occupations. Therefore, a vibrant culture of artistic and philosophical milieus came about through the support of the state, pursuing many forms of knowledge that the state had never anticipated. Boiler rooms were literally *vnye*—inside and outside—the system. Their valves and heat pipes reached like arteries into thousands of apartments in the district embedding these boiler rooms inside the very entrails of the system, simultaneously providing utopian amounts of time, space, and intellectual freedom from its constraints. These were temporal, spatial, and thematic zones of *vnye* par excellence.

[40] For example, in one Leningrad boiler room in the 1970s and early 1980s, Boris Ostanin and Boris Ivanov worked on a multivolume history of St. Petersburg cemeteries and churches that was eventually published during the post-Soviet period (Lur'e 2003).
[41] Author interview.

Although only a small minority actually gave up their professional careers for such occupations, these examples were extreme manifestations of a common tendency of deterritorializing the system. By the early 1980s, it became common practice in all jobs—at factories, institutes, libraries, Komsomol committees, or wherever—to expect a payment or a bonus day off *(otgul)* in exchange for participation in certain formal activities such as going to a *subbotnik* (an allegedly voluntary unpaid Saturday work day),[42] "helping the agriculture" in the fields of suburban collective farms, or going to November or May parades. All these activities were represented in reports and in the press as voluntary and unpaid; however, since local chiefs and party secretaries were responsible for big turnouts, they relied on the local systems of bonuses to guarantee participation. Even though not all jobs or departments provided these bonuses for the same functions, virtually all provided them for some of them, and, importantly, everyone was well aware of this fact. In the 1970s and early 1980s, great numbers of shops and services on any given day were closed "for technical reasons" *(po tekhnicheskim prichinam)*, "for cleaning" *(na sanitarnyi den')*, "for repairs" *(na remont)*, or "for inventory" *(na pereuchët)*. One often expected a shop, café, or a public office to be closed rather than open. Bureaucrats, administrators, and secretaries became legendary figures of urban folklore who were permanently away from their desks. Soviet jokes did not fail to note the situation: "An epitaph on the tombstone of a bureaucrat reads [in the familiar clichéd formula of an office door sign]: 'I'm not in, and I won't be back' [*menia net i ne budet*]."

Spatiality and Temporality

Each of these multiple strategies and practices shifted the temporality of state socialism. It has been argued that socialist states monopolized citizens' time (Verdery calls it "etatization of time"[43]), and that citizens employed various counter-measures to slow time down (Borneman 1998, 100). We should add that the opposition implied in the concept of "slowing down" time was not a central process of temporal reinterpretation, but only one of many processes of reinterpreting time. Soviet citizens also sped up time by cultivating networks of *blat*[44] and arrangements such as those in the Komsomol committees discussed in chapter 3

[42] See chapter 3, n. 18.

[43] Verdery (1996, 39–57). See also Hanson (1997) and Buck-Morss (2000) for discussions of the socialist state's control over time.

[44] Informal networks for procuring products, finding resources, providing assistance, and so on. See Ledeneva (1998).

to avoid spending time in lines, on waiting lists, or on "pro forma" mandatory activities; turned time into an expandable and exchangeable resource; rendered time indeterminate by engaging in *obshchenie* in all professional contexts, as when Komsomol committees and physics labs were turned into milieus of *svoi*; created free time by taking undemanding jobs with multiple sickness leaves, bonus days off, and so on; and, above all, shifted the parameters of temporality altogether by engaging in temporally "distant" activities such as pursuing ancient history or engaging in archaeological expeditions and trips into remote, "time-less" areas of the state. Indeed, these various pursuits and employments did not just provide "free time," but rather deterritorialized temporality, filling it with busy lifestyles, intense interaction, and the pursuit of "unusual" interests. This temporality often contained no time for "regular" Soviet concerns. Recall Inna's remark at the beginning of the chapter that she rarely attended the university "since I had no time." Most of these practices of deterritorializing temporality, as we have seen, were enabled by the Soviet state itself. Besides subsidizing much of social life and services, it emphasized in its ideology the value of education, pursuit of knowledge, science, art, creativity, and community, usually requiring the fulfillment of goals and norms only in form.

As pointed out earlier, the times and activities of *obshchenie* and being *vnye* within various milieus should not be seen as spaces of authenticity and freedom that were clandestinely "carved out" from the spatial and temporal regimes imposed by the state. They were not exceptions to the system's dominant spatial and temporal regimes but, on the contrary, were paradigmatic manifestations of how these regimes functioned during late socialism. The forms of existence of even the most esoteric milieus discussed earlier illustrate the principles that were central to the functioning of late Soviet system, not to being in opposition to it.

The ontology of the relationship between the times and spaces of *vnye* and the authoritative times and spaces of the state was reversed from how the dominant models of Soviet reality portray this relationship. To grasp this reversal let us consider what Marilyn Strathern calls a "phenomenological reversal" between the particular and the general in her discussion of the relationship between place and space. Despite a widespread "naturalistic view of space as the prior background against which we are invited to see individual places 'in' it," argues Strathern, our actual experiences of space are always emplaced. This is why, in fact, "[f]ar from being suspended in space . . . a place contains space within itself, as it does time, journeys, and histories" (Strathern 2002, 91–92). In other words, the place is not a segment of generalized space but its condition of possibility. The same is true about time: conceptualizing intervals of time as if they were carved out of some infinite expanse is a particular

(Euro-American) conception of linear time that is historically shaped within the temporal ideology of the nation-state (Strathern 2002, 91).[45] In fact, however, in our experience of time, linear time emerges out of ordering particular "segments, intervals, and moments," not the other way around.

Instead of thinking about various local milieus of *svoi* and their practices as periods and spaces of authenticity and freedom that were "carved out" of and suspended outside state socialism, and from which that system was resisted and opposed, we should rather consider them as phenomena that were actively engaged in and productive of a shifting socialist system. These milieus and practices demonstrate that the supposed spatial and temporal linearity and totality of late socialism became everywhere injected with new forms of diversity, plurality, and indeterminacy. The temporal, spatial, and semantic regimes of late socialism became deterritorialized from within as the very logic of the system's existence. The constant refrain in all these milieus that they were profoundly uninterested in anything political was, of course, not a nihilistic position, but a kind of politics that refused heroic "clear truths." This was a politics of "deep truths" that were grounded in deterritorialized spaces and times.

[45] In this argument Strathern draws on Casey (1996) and Greenhouse (1996).

Chapter 5

Imaginary West:
The Elsewhere of Late Socialism

> I am often asked what does this Zone stand for. There is only
> one possible answer: the Zone doesn't exist. Stalker himself
> invented his Zone. He created it, so that he would be able to
> bring there some very unhappy persons and impose on them
> the idea of hope. The room of desires is equally Stalker's
> creation, yet another provocation in the face of the material
> world.
> —Andrei Tarkovsky[1]

Zagranitsa

A joke popular in the Soviet Union in the 1970s went like this:

One man says to another: "I want to go to Paris again."
The second one exclaims in disbelief: "What!? You've been to Paris be-
fore?"
The first one replies: "No, but I have wanted to go before."

The joke exploited the profound paradox within the concept of *zagranitsa*, which literally means beyond the border and in practice means
"that which is abroad." *Zagranitsa* came to reflect the peculiar combination of insularity and worldliness in Soviet culture. Most Soviet people
believed that the communist ideals and values they represented to the
world were fundamentally "internationalist" and outward looking,[2] and
yet they were also aware that travel to that world beyond the border was
in fact impossible.

---

[1] Andrei Tarkovsky commenting on his 1979 film *Stalker* (quoted in Slavoj Žižek 1999).

[2] That internal worldliness and internationalism of Soviet culture was reflected in the
fact that the Soviet person was, in the words of Viktor Krivulin, a "deeply historical being"
(*sushchetsvo gluboko istoricheskoe*) who lived not simply in a country but in an "international and historical process" and experienced events in the world on an existential level,
as part of his or her own personal life (author interview). This intrinsic worldliness of the
Soviet identity was also boosted by the vastly multicultural experience of being Soviet. As

Zagranitsa lay at the intersection of these two attitudes toward the wider world, signifying an imaginary place that was simultaneously knowable and unattainable, tangible and abstract, mundane and exotic. This concept was disconnected from any "real" abroad and located in some unspecified place—over there (*tam*), with them (*u nikh*), as opposed to with us (*u nas*)—and although references to it were ubiquitous, its real existence became dubious. In the 1980s, the clowns from the famous troupe Litsedei made their audiences roll in the aisles with laughter by re-marking that, in reality, *zagranitsa* did not exist; foreign tourists on the streets of Soviet cities were dressed-up professional actors, and foreign movies were shot in a studio in Kazakhstan. In a short story by Mikhail Veller the protagonist from a small city in the Urals in the 1970s has an impossible dream—just once in his life to have a glimpse of Paris. Having failed in endless attempts to get permission to travel overseas, the hero fi-nally, when getting close to retirement age, is allowed to join a group of factory workers going on a rare voyage to France. After a few euphoric days spent in the French capital, he grows suspicious:

> The Eiffel Tower could not possibly be three hundred meters. It was perhaps not higher than the television tower in their hometown, a hun-dred and forty meters at the most. And at the base of its steel leg Ko-ren'kov spotted the branding of Zaporozhie Steel Factory. He walked further and further . . . and was suddenly stopped by an obstruction that extended to the left and to the right, as far as the eye could see—a gigantic theatrical backdrop, a painted canvas strung on a frame. The houses and the narrow streets were drawn on the canvas, as were the tiled roofs and the crowns of chestnut trees. He set his lighter on maxi-mum and moved the flame along the length of the deceitful landscape. Paris simply did not exist in the world. It never had (Veller 2002, 291).

These narratives and jokes, of which there were many in late Soviet times, depict *zagranitsa* as a Soviet imaginary "elsewhere" that was not necessarily about any real place. The "West" (*zapad*) was its archetypal manifestation. It was produced locally and existed only at the time when the real West could not be encountered. We will call this version of the elsewhere, the Imaginary West (Yurchak 2002b).

This chapter continues the discussion of the internal deterritorializa-tion of Soviet culture during the period of late socialism. It builds on the previous two chapters: chapter 3 analyzed the publics of *svoi* that emerged

---

Caroline Humphrey points out, the very real practice of multicultural Soviet life, coupled with the ideologies of collectivism and equality of different ethnic groups, generated the kinds of desires and temptations that provided for a very "cosmopolitan" identity (2002a).

as a deterritorialized sociality of late socialism; chapter 4 focused on tight milieus that were living in the temporal and spatial *vnye* (inside-outside) of the Soviet system. The current chapter ventures into the larger realm of the imaginary, arguing that among the great number of imaginary worlds that were both internal and external to late Soviet culture, the Imaginary West was perhaps the most significant. The emergence of the Imaginary West was not in contradiction with the ethics and aesthetics of state socialism; on the contrary, and somewhat paradoxically, cultural products and forms of knowledge on which the Imaginary West was based were explicitly produced and implicitly enabled by the socialist project itself.

The Zone

The presence within the Soviet universe of spatially and temporally distant worlds was manifested by the explosion of interest in the 1960s in various cultural and intellectual pursuits based on the experience of a faraway "elsewhere"—foreign languages and Asian philosophy, medieval poetry and Hemingway's novels, astronomy and science fiction, avant-garde jazz and songs about pirates, practices of hiking, mountaineering, and going on geological expeditions in the remote nature reserves of Siberia, the Far East, and the North. Vail' and Genis referred to these Soviet worlds of the 1960s as "some unknown and wonderful country of Dolphinia (*strana Del'finiia*) . . . [that] could exist anywhere—in other galaxies, as in science fiction books, or in one's own room, separated from the surrounding world with something private—usually, in a typical Russian way, with books" (Vail' and Genis 2000, 137–38).

The emergence of these imaginary worlds in Soviet life was investigated in Soviet literature and film of the period. A popular Soviet science fiction novel *Roadside Picnic* (*Piknik na obochine*) by the famous writers brothers Boris and Arkadii Strugatsky (1972) and its equally popular film version *Stalker* by Andrei Tarkovsky (1979) involve a mysterious world called *Zona* (the Zone). The story takes place in an unnamed country twenty years after it served as a picnic stop for an alien spaceship. The spaceship left behind some debris around which the Zone had formed. The Zone is dangerous and can cause death to anyone who ventures in; the state declares it off limits and installs special armed forces to guard it. But the Zone is also a site of mysterious powers. Adventurous individuals, called stalkers, bring people to the Zone for a fee, leading them to the room at the Zone's center where one's deepest desire is granted. It is widely recognized in Russia that the Strugatskys meant their book to be a metaphor of late Soviet reality. The Zone did not imply any concrete "real" territory; it referred to a certain imaginary space that was simultaneously internal and external to late-socialist reality. Crucial was its paradoxical status—intimate, within reach, and yet unattainable. The Zone could only exist as an imaginary construct that could not be encountered in reality. When the characters of the Strugatskys' book reach the room, they find to their surprise nothing extraordinary there. But the stalker who brought them there insists that this news should be kept from the others in order not to destroy their hope, as the Zone was constitutive of their reality.[3]

What I call in this chapter the Imaginary West was, like the Strugatskys' Zone, a kind of space that was both internal and external to the Soviet reality. This space was neither explicitly outlined or described in the Soviet Union as a coherent "territory" or "object," nor referred to by the name Imaginary West. However, a diverse array of discourses, statements, products, objects, visual images, musical expressions, and linguistic constructions that were linked to the West by theme or by virtue of their origin or reference, and that circulated widely in late socialism, gradually shaped a coherent and shared object of imagination—the Imaginary West. An analysis of how this entity emerged and functioned in late Soviet reality provides another perspective on the paradoxes and internal displacements of that reality.

This analysis starts with a genealogy (Foucault 1972) of the Imaginary West, considering late socialism as a particular discursive formation within which the Imaginary West emerged as an indivisible and constitutive element of Soviet reality. Foucault's concept of "discursive formation" stands for a dispersed milieu of statements, concepts, enunciative modalities, and thematic choices that coexist in a certain historical period and concern a concrete topic (e.g., madness, sexuality) but are neither organized into a singular unified discourse on this topic nor limited to shared commonsense understandings about it. These statements, enunciations, and thematic choices may be produced by diverse authors in

---

[3] See Žižek (1999) for a discussion of Tarkovsky's *Stalker*. Agamben argues that in the constitution of any modern sovereignty an essential role is played by such imaginary and unlocalizable spaces (the "zones of indistinction") that always remain on the border "between outside and inside" of law, between "chaos and the normal situation" (1998, 18, 19). See also Carl Schmitt for a discussion of sovereignty (1985). In the essay "Different Spaces," Foucault similarly argues that such imaginary spaces as the "space of the mirror" are crucial for the constitution of a sovereign subject: the mirror "makes this place I occupy at the moment I look at myself in the glass both utterly real, connected with the entire space surrounding it, and utterly unreal—since, to be perceived, it is obligated to go by way of that virtual point which is over there" (1998c, 179). This simultaneously real and unreal, internal and external status of perceiving oneself allows for the self to be constituted. Similarly, it was the zones of internal exteriority—occupied by the world of *vnye* and by the Imaginary West—that allowed for the constitution of a particular, deterritorialized space of everyday socialism.

different voices and may involve things spoken and unspoken, supported and rejected, compatible and inconsistent with each other. And yet, this discursive milieu contains coherent regularities and principles of organization as a result of which certain concepts and understandings become gradually shaped within it. In Foucault's examples, one concept that emerged in this way, in seventeenth- to eighteenth-century Western Europe, was the modern understanding of "madness" as a form of "mental illness." Thinking about madness as illness had been neither commonsensical nor explicitly articulated in any one discourse; rather this concept became constituted as a result of diverse and not necessarily consistent statements, enunciations, voices, and assumptions on the topic of madness in the discourses of medicine, religion, jurisprudence, citizenship, and so forth.[4]

Late socialism can be considered a particular discursive formation that was organized around certain unspoken principles and regularities, some of which we analyzed in the previous chapters—including the disappearance of a metadiscourse on ideology, the hypernormalization of authoritative form and a subsequent change in the role authoritative discourse played in everyday life. Within this discursive formation of late socialism, diverse public statements that might seem contradictory in fact coexisted as logically linked and mutually productive. Western cultural influences were both criticized for bourgeois values and celebrated for internationalism, circulated through unauthorized networks and official state channels, transported from abroad and invented locally. It was within this dispersed discursive milieu between the 1950s and the 1980s that the entity of the Imaginary West emerged as an internal "elsewhere" of late Soviet culture and imagination.

Cosmopolitanism and Internationalism

One of the conditions that enabled the formation of the Imaginary West was a persistent but ambivalent distinction that the Soviet state made between good and bad forms of international culture. As chapter 2 argued, in the late 1940s, Stalin's intervention into political, scientific, and aesthetic spheres opened up an internal paradox within Soviet ideological discourse. For example, in his critique of linguistics Stalin started with attacking "vulgar" Marxist theories of language that saw language as a product of social class. Instead, he argued, linguistics needed to study the "objective scientific laws" that governed human language (the laws of psychology, physiology, cognition, etc.) and were rooted not in social

---

[4] Foucault (1998b, 312). See also Foucault (1972, 109); Dreyfus and Rabinow (1983, 181); Hall (1988, 51).

class but nature. These laws, went the argument, so far remained insufficiently understood. The same argument for a need to shift to objective scientific laws was extended to other sciences. The ultimate effect of that shift was the growing indeterminacy of a Marxist-Leninist "canon" that was external to discourse and against which all formulations could be evaluated as politically correct and incorrect. This shift introduced a profound ambiguity into the Soviet authoritative discourse, making it impossible to know for sure whether any given formulation was right or wrong. Ultimately, as chapter 2 demonstrated, this ambiguity led to the internal hypernormalization of authoritative discourse.

A parallel transformation at the same time took place in the realm of cultural production. It concerned the evaluation of cultural and artistic forms as correct and incorrect from a political standpoint. This shift affected the views about foreign influences in art and culture and became manifest in 1948 in the campaign against "cosmopolitanism" (*kosmopolitizm*) in its Soviet definition. Cosmopolitanism was described as a product of Western imperialism, which, in pursuit of its imperialist goals, strove to undermine the value of local patriotism among the peoples of the world, thereby weakening their national sovereignty.[5] The opposite of cosmopolitanism was not nationalism, an equally dangerous enemy, but internationalism. Cosmopolitan influence in national art and culture was bad because it undermined them; internationalist influence, on the contrary, was good and enriching.

This campaign had a direct impact on all spheres of Soviet cultural and artistic production. Addressing the conference of Soviet music workers in 1948, Minister of Culture Andrei Zhdanov celebrated the examples of internationalism in Soviet music: "Our internationalism in music and respect for the creative genius of other nations is . . . based on the enrichment and development of our national musical culture, which we can then share with other nations" (Zhdanov 1950, 62–63). These good internationalist influences in music "inspire the working people of Soviet society to great achievements in labour, science and culture" (1950, 74). At the same time, Zhdanov attacked the examples of bad cosmopolitanism in music for introducing bourgeois aesthetics into Soviet life. He singled out the work of composers Sergei Prokofiev and Dmitrii Shostakovich, arguing that cosmopolitan influences led them to write flawed music that was "unharmonious" and "unmelodious," violated "the fundamental physiology of normal human hearing," and disturbed "the balance of mental and physiological functions" (1950, 72, 74). Zhdanov's discourse represented an attack from the "objective scientific" or socialist-realist position on the remnants of the revolutionary avant-garde

[5] See Dunayeva (1950, 18).

163

in music and art.[6] According to Zhdanov, the writing of such unnatural music inspired by "rootless" cosmopolitanism became possible because Soviet science and art specialists disregarded the objective scientific laws of musical perception. This was caused by a general lack of a scientific "theory which deals with the physiological effect of music on the human organism"; such a theory "so far unfortunately ... has been insufficiently developed" (1950, 72, 74).

Zhdanov's argument can be summarized as follows: foreign musical influences could represent bad cosmopolitanism or good internationalism; the former was a bourgeois product of imperialism, the latter was a product of progressive people's culture; the former was unnatural because it violated human physiology, the latter was realistic and natural; the evaluation of cultural forms as progressive or bourgeois had to be done not according to the subjective opinion of some external arbitrator but according to objective scientific laws of the physiology of human musical perception; however, these objective scientific laws had been so far insufficiently developed. This line of argument, similar to the one made by Stalin in linguistics and in other sciences, led to a paradoxical effect: since the objective canon against which to compare was not known, it could not be certain whether a concrete foreign influence in music was a manifestation of good internationalism or bad cosmopolitanism, and therefore each concrete case was potentially open to interpretation.

This ambiguity in the judgment of foreign influences in music, art, and culture in general opened up a space of interpretation of what concrete foreign cultural forms might mean in different contexts, and contributed to the emergence of the Imaginary West during the late Soviet period. It became possible to interpret the same foreign cultural influences in some contexts as representing bad cosmopolitanism and the values of bourgeois classes but in other contexts as representing good internationalism and the realism of common people's culture.[7] This ambiguity became an indivisible element of late-socialist culture and led to a persistent oscillation between different interpretations of the same aesthetic phenomena in all fields of cultural production. Take the case of the relationship of the Soviet state to Pablo Picasso. In September 1961, the General Secretary

[6] This "unrealistic" music was related to the earlier avant-garde experiments of Alexandr Scriabin, Igor Stravinsky and Mikhail Matiushin, such as, Matiushin's chaotic score to the futurist opera *Victory over the Sun* (1913), performed in St. Petersburg in 1913, for which Alexei Kruchenykh wrote nonsensical text and Kazimir Malevich designed avant-garde costumes (Hunter 1999; Fauchereau 1992).

[7] Some aspects of this paradoxical relation to "the West" have deep roots in Russian culture and for at least three centuries have manifested themselves in the split between the Slavophiles and the Westernizers. My focus here, however, is on how old and new aspects of this ambiguous relationship took new form during the late socialist period playing up the paradoxes of the socialist project.

Nikita Khrushchev publicly ridiculed Picasso's abstract art displayed in an exhibition at Moscow's Sokolniki Park for its bourgeois lack of realism. In May 1962 however, Picasso was awarded the Lenin Peace Prize for the progressive internationalism of his work as a Communist artist (Egbert 1967, 361). Another example was the official discourse about American jazz: between the 1940s and 1970s jazz was continuously praised for its roots in the creative genius of the slaves and the working people *and* condemned as bourgeois pseudo-art that lost any connection to the realism of people's culture. Or consider the cultural policies of the Soviet film industry. The state bureaucrats who managed Soviet cinema constantly "fostered the cult of the autonomous artist by upholding its ideological value" in public pronouncements, awards, and prizes; at the same time, they attempted in practice to prevent the work of the artists who were becoming truly autonomous and individually recognized (Faraday 2000, 12).[8]

This ambiguity in the interpretation of the true meaning of cultural forms once again recalls "Lefort's paradox" from chapter 1—the paradox between the goal of a total liberation of culture, and the means of achieving it through subjecting culture to total control by the party. When the external Marxist-Leninst canon for evaluating good and bad cultural forms became no longer determinate and authoritative discourse experienced performative shift, the constative meaning of these cultural forms as it was described in authoritative discourse became unanchored from form and could then change. Ultimately, this meant that one did not have to think of "socialist" and "bourgeois" cultural forms as inherently incompatible because their meanings could shift depending on how and where these forms were used. It also meant that being and seeing oneself as a good Soviet citizen who lived in harmony with the general values of socialism did not necessarily require one to agree with every authoritative critique of concrete cultural forms that appeared in the Soviet press. To analyze the ultimate effects of this open-endedness of meaning on the culture of late socialism we will trace its developments in different historical periods from the 1950s to the 1980s and in different forms of cultural production, showing that foreign cultural forms in jazz, radio broadcasts, fashion, film, language, rock music and so forth were simultaneously critiqued and promoted, attacked and allowed to develop by the Soviet state. Because of this ambiguous dynamic, in the 1970s and 1980s, the Imaginary West had become an indivisible and constitutive element of late Soviet culture that contributed to its further internal deterritorialization—deterritorialization that remained relatively invisible to those living in that system until it "collapsed."

---

[8] See in particular Faraday's discussion of Andrei Tarkovsky.

Contradictory West

During World War II the Soviet experience acquired new worldly dimensions, which had important implications for the development of the Imaginary West. The dominant image of the United States during the war and in the first postwar years was that of an ally who supported the Soviet people through the lend-lease program that started in 1941.[9] With the opening of the British and American "second front" in 1944, and the meeting of Soviet and American troops in Germany, American jazz became associated with the nearing victory over the Nazis. In liberated Krakow and Prague, Red Army orchestras entertained the locals on the streets by playing American tunes "Chattanooga Choo-Choo" and "In the Mood."[10] After the war, the army musicians brought these tunes to the dance halls and restaurants of Soviet cities. For example, in the *Krysha* restaurant on the roof of Hotel Evropeiskaia in Leningrad the Yosif Vainshtein orchestra played American swing melodies learned from the Allies at the front.[11]

Despite this temporary postwar openness, jazz soon came under attack during the campaign against cosmopolitanism. Orchestra director Boris Khainkin announced at a meeting of music workers in the party CC that the original roots of jazz among the working people "have been long lost and have since been replaced by trashy philistine motifs" that no longer provide anything "for the heart and mind of the Soviet person" (quoted in Feiertag 1999, 66).[12] Despite its literal meaning this argument also implied that since cultural forms at times could be considered proletarian and at other times bourgeois, they were not necessarily defined by class. (This point parallels Stalin's argument about the classless nature of science and language in chapter 2.) It followed that the meaning of cultural forms depended on who practiced them, how, and in what context.[13] Therefore, if jazz was clearly an example of bourgeois culture in some contexts, it did not necessarily

[9] Turovskaya (1993a). U.S. assistance to the Soviet Union in food, equipment, and other materials began after the Lend-Lease Act of March 1941. See Munting (1984) for a discussion of the Lend-Lease program.

[10] Starr (1994, 205); Chernov (1997a, 32).

[11] Chernov (1997a, 32); Feiertag (1999, 65).

[12] The same critique was directed against Western rock music in the 1970s and 1980s (see chapter 6).

[13] The distinction drawn between the culture of rich and common Americans was a case in point. In Alexandrov's 1949 film *Vstrecha na El'be* (Meeting on the Elbe) American generals in occupied Germany are shown as capitalist profiteers who sell defeated German people food and cigarettes at a high interest. However, lower-rank American officers and soldiers of common origin are shown to be appalled by this colonialist attitude of their commanders as are the Soviet soldiers stationed nearby.

have to be so in all contexts. This is why jazz was criticized but also tolerated. It managed to survive denunciations in the press by being creatively adapted to fit the Soviet context. Even during the years when jazz was under extreme attack Soviet orchestras occasionally played jazz tunes that were arranged in the style of Soviet "light music," changed their names, inserted them among Soviet compositions, and, in these reinterpreted forms, jazz continued to be heard in restaurants and dance halls, and occasionally even at the concerts of state philharmonic orchestras.[14]

Jazz could also be heard at the "student recreational evenings" organized by Komsomol committees in colleges and universities as part of their cultural work with the young. Because of the "amateur" status of student bands they were not registered in state philharmonic societies, which meant not only that they could not make money on performances, but also that their repertoire was less subjected to state control. This made it easier for them to play occasional jazz tunes, but also put them in an ambiguous situation. Vladimir Feiertag, the leader of a student jazz band at Leningrad University remembers that in the 1950s, at a student dance, they "repeated 'In the Mood' three times in a row . . . at the request of the excited Komsomol members, who lost all self-restraint" (Feiertag 1999, 69–70). And although the university party committee usually tolerated the performances of such bands, this time, because of the explicit manifestation of the students' excitement about that music, the party committee decided to denounce the dance. The band was issued an official warning: if they continued to play "low-taste American music alien to Soviet youth" they would be expelled from the Komsomol and the university. The problem, it seemed, was not so much in the music that the band played but in the overly excited reaction it elicited from the students—that is, the problem was not in the form but in its interpretation.

As with music, the situation with Western films was also ambivalent. In the postwar years, American and German films became Soviet box office hits, thereby introducing new styles of music, dress, language, and behavior to Soviet life.[15] A trendy young macho man became known in slang as *tarzanets*—a reference to the American movie *The Adventures*

[14] Kaplan (1997a, 46), Feiertag (1999).

[15] German films were shown in the Soviet Union as part of the reparation payment by Germany. On August 31, 1948, the politburo gave permission to release American and trophy German films in Soviet distribution. The most popular German film, out of several dozen German films in Soviet distribution, was *Devushka moei mechty* (The Girl of My Dream, or in the original, *Die Frau meiner Träume*), starring the Hungarian singer and actress Marikka Rökk. See Turovskaya (1993a, 104), Stites (1993, 125), Graffy (1998, 181), Bulgakova (1995).

167

of Tarzan.[16] Lovers of jazz imitated the body language from American films. Efim Barban, a founder of the Leningrad Jazz Club, listened to American jazz and put his legs up on the chair in front of him, imitating American actors; when someone rebuked him for uncultured manners, he replied: "American music must be listened to in the same way as it is listened to in America" (Feiertag 1999, 81).

At first foreign films were widely shown, then criticized, then banned, and then shown again (Turovskaya 1993a and 1993b). Although concrete historical events provoked these waves, it was the deeper paradox of the socialist system that made these waves of cultural policy possible. Some films were promoted in one context and criticized in another. In 1947 the state-run weekly newspaper of art and literature *Literaturnaia gazeta* attacked Soviet photographers who "speculate on the Soviet people's love for the cinema" by printing the portraits of smiling American film stars "on thousands and thousands of postcards that pile up in newsstands, kiosks, and bookstores," and charging even for their small black-and-white copies three to five rubles each, compared with fifty kopecks charged for larger colored postcards with the reproductions of the best Russian artists from the Tretiakov Gallery.[17] This criticism focused not on the films' popularity among Soviet audiences, but on the photographers' speculation on this popularity. But there was again ambivalence. Although this article presented American films as low culture, opposing them to the high-culture canon of the Tretiakov Gallery, in another article in the same newspaper journalist Ilya Erenburg explained that American cinema "gave the world outstanding masters. . . . Charlie Chaplin is loved on all five continents. I saw wonderful films by [John] Ford, [Lewis] Milestone, [Rouben] Mamoulian. The films of the Marx brothers are full of good simple humor. Disney's animations are the poetry that is able to touch a person whose life has lost all lyricism."[18]

The paradox in interpreting the meaning of cultural forms translated into a general tendency of the state's critical attacks to focus on "extreme" manifestations of Western cultural influences as bourgeois, while tolerating more common and less conspicuous tendencies among wider groups of "normal" citizens as good internationalist or aesthetic pursuits. This tendency manifested itself, for example, in the representation of material commodities. Even during the Stalin years, as Vera Dunham famously demonstrated, the Soviet person was encouraged to enjoy consumption of personal "bourgeois" pleasures (dresses, wristwatches, lipstick) as long

[16] Stites (1993, 125).

[17] *"Doloi poshlost'!"* (Down with philistinism). *Literaturnaia gazeta*, November 19, 1947.

[18] Ilya Erenburg, "Amerikanskie vstrechi" [American Encounters]. *Literaturnaia gazeta*, November 16, 1947, 2.

as they were used not for egoistic goals of social prestige, careerism, and so forth, but as elements of "cultural life" and due rewards for hard work.[19] With the shift in authoritative discourse toward new hypernormalized form, especially after Stalin's death and during the reforms of Khrushchev's thaw, the discourse about the acceptable and unacceptable ways to enjoy material and cultural products developed further. It became apparent, for example, that there was nothing wrong with admiring bourgeois luxuries of Western life as long as admiration focused on aesthetic beauty, technological achievement, and the genius of the working people who created them. By explicitly crediting the artisans *Literaturnaia gazeta*, with unconcealed admiration, described the opulence of luxurious Parisian shops:

> Place Vendome is the heart of luxury trade. Like the street Faubourg Saint-Honore it gives an impression of what fashion is all about (including the fashion for precious jewelry and golden and silver artifacts): this is a constant innovation of tastes and vitality of imagination. . . . Today this street demonstrates the skillfulness of Parisian artisans—masters of furniture, tailors, jewelers, and decorators who turn every window display into a brilliant canvas that is constantly changing.[20]

In addition to providing this knowledge about the West, newspaper articles also reminded their readers that any Soviet person who aspired to be "cultured . . . should be fluent in one or several foreign languages."[21] The knowledge of languages implied that it was perfectly congruent with the good Soviet identity to desire to learn more information about the West on one's own as long as one learned about the right information and did so with a critical eye. The good information could include scientific and technological examples, and those of high culture. An engineer from a technical institute explained on the pages of *Literaturnaia gazeta*: "I have come to the conclusion that the knowledge of English, German, and French languages is mandatory to anyone who wants to be technically creative. Having learned these languages I regularly read foreign magazines, newspapers, and advertising booklets."[22] An academician added that foreign languages are "necessary not only for economic communication but also for the broadening of one's cultural

---

[19] Dunham (1976).

[20] Dominika Dezanti, "Parizh i parizhane" [Paris and Parisians]. *Literaturnaia gazeta*, April 28, 1956.

[21] A. Chakovskii, "Ot slov k delu" [From Words to Deeds]. *Literaturnaia gazeta*, March 22, 1956.

[22] E. Kazakovskii, "Dlia tekhnicheskogo progressa" [For Technical Progress]. *Literaturnaia gazeta*, March 22, 1956.

horizons. . . . How much thrilling pleasure one feels being able to appreciate the splendor of Burns's poetry . . . in the original. The power of sarcasm and the rhythmic tenderness of Heine's poetry are inevitably somewhat lost even in the best translation."[23]

All these articles, stories, and pronouncements fed the imagination of Soviet readers, suggesting that a well-rounded Soviet person should be able to admire Western cultural forms as long as he or she looked at them critically, distinguishing between the creativity and imagination of the working people and the materialism and philistinism of the bourgeois classes. Ultimately, it became apparent that there was nothing intrinsically wrong with being a fan of Western jazz, a follower of Western fashion, or a person interested in the foreign press if one was also a Soviet patriot. Natan Leites, the founder of the Leningrad jazz club Kvadrat in the early 1960s, captured this ambiguity perfectly. An avid lover of American jazz he also thought of himself as, "quite a red person. At least, I believed in socialism." According to him, most of his friends among musicians and jazz fans were similar.[24] Jazz organizer Feiertag, who believed that in the West jazz indeed represented bourgeois tastes, was also confident that in the Soviet context jazz was different and "could not be harmful to my unbeatable motherland" (Feiertag 1999, 68).

Stylization

Fashion and style, like film and music, became important arenas for producing new worldly identities and imaginations, contributing to the emergence of the Imaginary West. Here too the state's ambivalent cultural policy was reflected in the same tendency to critique extreme manifestations of "bourgeois" influences, while tolerating or overlooking more common and less conspicuous tendencies among wider groups of youth. An example was the state's attitude to the subculture of trendily dressed youths, the *stilyagi* (from *stil'*—style), which emerged in the 1940s.[25] The *stilyagi* were a relatively small subculture, but they were a symptom of a much bigger emerging importance of Westernized imaginations among millions of regular Soviet youths, most of whom actually looked at the *stilyagi* with disdain.

Stilyagi's aesthetic was influenced by the American films shown in Soviet cinemas. A Leningrad *stilyaga* Valentin Tikhonenko, in the 1940s,

[23] V. Engelgardt, "Pod gipnozom grammatiki" [Under the Hypnosis of Grammar]. *Literaturnaia gazeta*, March 22, 1956.

[24] Interview with Natan Shamovich Leites. "Klub 'Kvadrat': Dzhaz-shmaz i normal'nye liudi" [" 'Kvadrat' Club: Jazz-shmaz and Normal People"]. *Pchela* 11 (1997): 37.

[25] Troitsky (1988); Stites and von Geldern (1995); Edele (2003).

170

copied his style from the protagonist of the movie *Secret Agent*, an American spy who during the war infiltrated the German Gestapo and therefore was seen in the Soviet context as a positive character. Like him, Tikhonenko grew long sideburns, a thin moustache, and arranged his hair in a pompadour. He assembled a wardrobe out of American lend-lease clothes available through state-run secondhand shops: "stylish pants with foggy-silvery-white stripes," an English woolen suit, white shirts, white sweaters, a bow tie, and a large suede hat (Guk 1997, 24–25). *Stilyagi* all over the country also made their own clothes, including colorful knitted sweaters, tailored pants and home-sewn ties ornate with various pictures including "a silver spider web design, . . . palm trees, monkeys, even girls in bathing suits" (Troitsky 1988, 2–3).[26]

These experiments with style were not limited to small privileged groups from Moscow and Leningrad. In the 1950s, in Penza, four hundred miles southeast of Moscow, a group of stylish youths, mostly children of local factory workers and collective farmers, made their own trendy clothes or purchased "real" Western ones from local black marketers who brought them from contacts in Moscow, and danced the twist and boogie-woogie in state-run cultural centers. One of the Penza youths, Vitalii Sinichkin, in the 1950s "arranged his blond curls in a pompadour a la Elvis Presley" by "raising his long forelock over his forehead and fixing it" with sugar syrup, because "hair spray or mousse . . . were unavailable in the USSR." He wore "a stylish jacket of light cocoa color, with vertical crimson stripes (made in France), yellow shoes on a very thick white sole . . . and with heavy buckles (also French), green trousers, and a wide tie hanging below the waist." Some of the Penza youths traveled to the summer resorts on the Black Sea where hundreds of thousands of young people from all corners of the Soviet Union spent holidays, bringing back to their hometowns the latest trends. In the early 1960s, at the twist contests organized by the public parks in the Black Sea resort town of Sochi, a visitor from Penza learned firsthand that not only small groups of *stilyagi* but "the whole country was infected" with the twist. In the context of "summer vacations" these dances were not only more openly tolerated but even explicitly taught. The dancing floor in the park *Riviera* organized a twist contest: "one had to jump for seven to ten seconds on one leg, while making with the other leg five original moves, all different from each other."[27]

In its attacks on the *stilyagi*, the Soviet press portrayed them as a small and insignificant group of deviationists, bourgeois sympathizers, and

[26] Also Aksyonov (1987, 13).
[27] Rita Mohel', "Konfetnyi mal'chik" [Candy Boy]. *Moskovskii Komsomolets*, August 23, 1999.

Достиг
Ведущей
Роли,
Но
        только
        в... рок-н-ролле.

FIGURE 5.1. Leading loafer. He got a leading role, but just in rock and roll.
S. Smirnov. *Krokodil* 35 (1958): 3.

uneducated loafers (see figure 5.1). Newly established "Komsomol pa-
trols"[28] on the streets focused on those young people who had a
"provocative look" (*vyzyvaiushchii vid*). One Leningrad *stilyaga* was detained for wearing a "loud" American jacket with a large logo of "Dun-
lop" on which "bright yellow-red tigers were jumping across pitch black
tires" (Kaplan 1997b, 30). Another one was detained for the "parrot"
(*popugaiskii*) look of his bright clothes and an extravagant hairdo
(newspaper *Smena*, May 29, 1954, quoted in Lur'e 1997, 19). The *stilyagi*
were also referred to as canaries and monkeys (see figures 5.2 and 5.3).
The media associated this abnormal look with deficient education. The
state-run satirical magazine *Krokodil* wrote: "The *stilyaga* knows the
fashions all over the world, but he doesn't know Griboyedov. . . . He's
studied all the fox trots, tangos, rumbas, and lindy hops in detail, but he
confuses Michurin with Mendeleev, and astronomy with gastronomy.
He's memorized all the arias from *Sylvia* and *Maritza*, but does not

[28] They consisted of a group of young men, members of the Komsomol, designated by
local enterprises and police to walk on the streets of their districts "keeping the order."

FIGURE 5.2. Monkeys. L. Khudiakov. *Krokodil* 2 (1957): 7.

know who wrote the operas *Ivan Susanin* and *Prince Igor*" (March 10, 1949, quoted in Stites and von Geldern 1995, 452).[29]

Such descriptions presented the *stilyagi* as small and isolated groups of deviationists that had nothing in common with the masses of good

---

[29] Alexander Griboyedov was a classic Russian writer and poet of the early nineteenth century, whose works were part of the official school curriculum. Ivan Michurin was a Soviet

FIGURE 5.3. God, what nonsense!—So, do you like it now? A. Bazhenov. *Krokodil* 7 (1957): 14.

Soviet youth. As a result, young people who were interested in Western fashion, music, and films but *also* in high culture, literature, classical music, and science did not necessarily see themselves as the target of that

botanist and agronomist, whose work was also part of the official school curriculum. Dmitrii Mendeleev was a Russian chemist and discoverer of the periodical table of elements, also studied in school. *Sylvia* and *Maritza* were foreign "light-genre" operettas by Imre Kalman. *Ivan Susanin* and *Prince Igor* were Russian patriotic operas by Glinka and Borodin about Russia's struggle against Napoleon and the Tatar invasion respectively.

criticism and often themselves disapproved of the *stilyagi*. For example, a young Leningrad engineer Vladimir, in the mid-1950s, liked to attend youth dances at which the Panarovsky Orchestra often played American tunes inserted among more numerous Soviet ones. The frequenters of these dances, his colleagues and friends, liked these American tunes; at that time Duke Ellington's "Caravan" was particularly popular: "When they played these tunes everyone would run out on the dance floor. Panarovsky became a cult figure among Leningrad youth." However, Vladimir and his friends, who were keen on science and professional careers, distinguished themselves from the *stilyagi* and "wanted to have nothing to do with them" (author interview).

Valerii Popov and a group of his friends also danced in the 1950s to American jazz and paid as much attention to the Western clothes that they bought on the black market as most *stilyagi*. However, unlike the "uneducated" *stilyagi* of the Soviet press, they read serious literature and discussed theater and poetry. They regularly came to the restaurant Krysha, on the roof of the Hotel Evropeiskaia—the restaurant most popular among *stilyagi*—to listen to music, talk about literature, and share with each other their first literary experiments (Popov 1996, 25). In Popov's words, they saw themselves as the new Soviet youth, for whom the 1950s was a time "loaded with happiness," in which Soviet hopes for the future incorporated creative experiments with literature, poetry, Western music, and foreign clothes, creating a mix of Soviet and Western imaginations (26). Ultimately, the state's authoritative critique of uncultured deviationists only contributed to normalizing Western influences among the masses of educated Soviet youth: by focusing its attacks on an isolated phenomenon, the state made the more common and less extreme manifestation of Western symbols and tastes appear even more natural and congruent with the identity of a good Soviet person.[30]

Shortwave Radio

The internal paradox of the state's policy toward Westernized cultural forms and ideas—its promotion of an internationalist outlook and cultural education and its attacks on bourgeois philistinism and unculturedness—also meant that the state introduced various new technologies that contributed to the production and dissemination of these cultural forms and ideas, while at the same time trying to contain their negative effects. One

[30] This division into "extreme" and "normal" is reminiscent of how the British media in the 1970s treated punk as opposed to other forms of youth culture (Hebdige 1988, 97).

175

of these technologies was shortwave radio. Although its role in the Soviet context is well known, its uniqueness is sometimes misinterpreted. In the West, television and FM and AM (mediumwave and longwave) radio have long been the dominant types of broadcast media that provide access almost exclusively to the information produced and rebroadcast locally.[31] In the case of shortwave radio, by contrast, the signal may originate thousands of miles away, allowing for programs that are produced abroad to be consumed locally. This made shortwave radio as a technology of cultural production incomparably more important in the Soviet context than in the West.[32] As with the previous forms of information and culture, the relationship of the Soviet state to shortwave radio was ambiguous. The shortwave radio as a tool for exploring the world was important for the state's project of enabling the development of an educated and internationalist Soviet person. Listening to foreign broadcasts was acceptable and even encouraged, as long as these qualified as good cultural information and not bourgeois or anti-Soviet propaganda. However, the gray area between the two was immense for the same reason as discussed earlier—much cultural information on the radio (popular music, international news, stories about foreign countries, language lessons) did not have a well-defined bad or good meaning. This ambivalence made listening to most shortwave broadcasts, at least during the period of late socialism, seem perfectly acceptable.

With the invention of the transistor, the Soviet industry started mass production of portable sets that were smaller and cheaper.[33] Shortwave sets became available to more and more people. From the late 1950s until the mid 1980s, the production of portable shortwave sets steadily increased. This technological tool allowed listeners all over the vast Soviet Union, including remote areas, to tune into various Soviet stations. However, shortwave receivers were designed to fulfill much more than that; shortwave radio became promoted as a cultural tool of an internationalist outlook on the world, which was reflected even in the design of the sets. As in the West, the tuning dials of many Soviet sets listed not only meter bands and frequencies but also names of foreign cities—Rome, Paris, Stockholm, London, Prague, Tokyo—inviting particular forms of listening and imagining.

[31] This is changing today with satellite television and the internet. However, even in these cases it is the local satellite and internet providers who control access.

[32] In the United States most people have no personal experience of shortwave radio and often are uncertain about what exactly it is. Even the BBC World Service is known in the United States almost exclusively through rebroadcasts on local National Public Radio (FM) stations.

[33] The first mass-produced portable shortwave set was Spidola, manufactured by VEF Radio Factory in Riga around 1960.

The state's ambivalent relationship to shortwave radio translated into the technical specifications devised by the Ministry of Communications for Soviet-made shortwave receivers. Soviet sets available in the Soviet Union contained meter bands starting with 25 meters and longer (31, 41, 49, etc.) but not the four shortest bands (11, 13, 16, and 19 meters).[34] This peculiar standard had political reasons: by cutting off several bands used for daytime reception of distant stations, the state made it easier to monitor or jam the unwanted foreign broadcasts on the remaining bands. At the same time, it still allowed reception of distant stations on the remaining bands. In fact, the 25 and 31 meter bands that Soviet shortwave receivers had are the most common bands for international broadcasting. In other words, shortwave reception was not banned altogether but restricted partially, while its promotion and the production of radio sets constantly increased. The basis of these ambivalent specifications, like with other ambivalent forms of the state's cultural policy, was once again the state's wish to continue endorsing international cultural knowledge while trying to contain its unwanted effects.

Not surprisingly, this ambivalent goal had mixed results. First, these conflicting measures made most shortwave listening appear acceptable. Second, the relentless promotion of radio technology by the state undid many of its efforts to contain the use of this technology in ways the state deemed inappropriate. For example, from the 1950s the state increased dramatically the number of radio and telecommunications departments in Soviet technical schools, colleges, and universities; the number of radio technicians and engineers trained in these departments also grew dramatically. Thousands of amateur radio clubs emerged all over the country. In the 1940s, the state established a monthly magazine *Radio* that targeted fans of radio technology and regularly published articles and circuitry designs explaining how to build one's own shortwave receivers.

In many cities special shops selling electronic parts for radio amateurs opened. In front of these shops black markets of parts and circuit diagrams—most carried out from state factories—thrived. In Leningrad, fans of shortwave reception gathered outside the shop Young Technician (*Iunyi Tekhnik*) and a secondhand radio store in the Apraksin Dvor shopping arcade. Visitors from smaller towns came there to purchase radio parts for resale at home. For a fee, radio engineers offered techniques on how to go around the limiting technical specifications introduced by the

[34] In the 1980s, I worked as a scientist in the Popov Research Institute of Radio Reception and Acoustics in Leningrad and had personal knowledge of industrial standards and specifications. The 11, 13, 16, and 19 meter bands are particularly suitable for the reception of distant stations during the light hours of the day, when the lower edges of the ionosphere, from which short waves reflect, are much more ionized and rise higher above the ground.

state, including equipping your set with the missing 11, 13, 16, and 19 meter bands.

The ambivalence also translated into the notorious practice of "jamming" foreign broadcasts—another practice of the Soviet state that is sometimes misinterpreted.[35] The Soviet state jammed only certain stations (designated as anti-Soviet) among those that broadcast in Russian and other Soviet and Eastern European languages. This meant, for example, that CIA-funded Radio Liberty was always jammed;[36] the Russian services of the Voice of America (VOA), BBC, and Deutsche Welle were jammed in certain periods;[37] the Russian Service of Radio Sweden and a few others were not jammed at all; and, importantly, the broadcasts in languages other than those spoken in the USSR and Eastern Europe were *never* jammed. The broadcasts that were never jammed included endless stations transmitting in world languages, among them the BBC World Service, VOA in English, Radio France International in French, and so on. Their broadcasts gave Soviet listeners an opportunity to become interested in jazz and rock and to study foreign languages. Thousands did just that, following the abovementioned appeal of Soviet newspapers that a cultured person should speak multiple foreign languages.

Listening to shortwave radio became a common pastime around the country, and in the case of broadcasts in foreign languages it was done

[35] The legality of radio broadcasting and radio jamming in different contexts has been a topic of intense contestation in international law. The United States has maintained until recently that it has a right "to broadcast putatively objective radio programs abroad, and any interference with these transmissions [is] a breach of international law"; the Soviet Union and the socialist camp between the 1950s and 1980s, as well as many postcolonial countries in different periods maintained that provocative transmissions directed against their governments breached the international law protecting "state sovereignty" and therefore "jamming was a legitimate . . . countermeasure." Using the same legal reasoning, the United States has practiced jamming in some parts of the world as part of "combat and psychological warfare" to protect national interests. See Jamie Frederic Metzl, "Rwandan Genocide and the International Law of Radio Jamming." *American Journal of International Law* 91, No. 4 (October 1997): 628.

[36] Radio Liberty broadcast exclusively for the Soviet Union in the Soviet languages and was the most openly anti-Soviet of Western stations. It started regular Russian broadcasts to the USSR on March 1, 1953, from its headquarters outside Munich, Germany (Sosin 1999). Other languages followed. Its second branch Radio Free Europe broadcast in the Eastern European languages exclusively to the socialist countries of the Soviet bloc. Both were founded as "propaganda stations" and were partly funded through the CIA, which distinguished them from the official station of the U. S. government, the Voice of America.

[37] Their jamming stopped in 1956 after the Twentieth Party Congress, resumed in 1968 during the Soviet intervention in Czechoslovakia (Friedberg 1985, 18), and ceased altogether in 1988. For a memoir of how a jamming station worked in Soviet Estonia see "Radio Jamming," www.okupatsioon.ee/english/mailbox/radio/radio.html.

Нашли общий язык...   Рисунок Л. СОЙФЕРТИСА

FIGURE 5.4. They have found common language. L. Soifertis. *Krokodil* 14 (1970): 7.

quite openly. During the summers on the Black Sea resorts one could hear foreign music and speech coming from small transistor sets on the beaches and in the parks. When criticism of this practice appeared in the press, it sounded misplaced. A cartoon in the satirical magazine *Krokodil* showed three youngsters standing next to each other on a beach and listening each to their own individual set (the protruded aerials suggested shortwave radios) (see figure 5.4). The sarcastic caption—"They have found common language"—was a pun ridiculing their individualized practice of listening and doing it in a foreign language, instead of communicating with each other in one common language. As with lovers of trendy clothes and jazz, most listeners of foreign stations would not recognize themselves in such critical images.

Foreign radio broadcasts had a huge impact on the development of the local Soviet jazz and rock scenes.[38] In the early 1950s, Yurii Vdovin, as a schoolboy who would later become a jazz musician, tuned his prewar Soviet lamp receiver SVD-9 to the English-language programs of the BBC and VOA: "I studied in school during the second shift and in the morning always listened to the BBC. They constantly played jazz. . . . Then in the mid-1950s, Willis Conover appeared on the air. The VOA broadcast his *Time for Jazz*[39] from 10 P.M. till midnight. The first hour was swing and the second was bebop, although at that time we did not know what it was" (Kaplan 1997a, 46). Conover's program on the English Service of the VOA ran for almost forty years, creating jazz fans all over the world (he is virtually unknown in the U.S. because the VOA did not broadcast domestically except on shortwave).[40] Conover's slow manner of speaking and the scripts written in "special English"[41] made his programs more widely accessible, further promoting jazz and American English among the young. Feiertag remembers that in 1953 "my first English words and phrases I learnt from Conover. He spoke slowly and clearly, repeating certain turns of phrase day after day. I think that Conover became the teacher of English for the whole generation of jazz lovers" (1999, 69). Writer Vassily Aksyonov, himself an avid Conover listener, nostalgically remarked: "How many dreamy Russian boys came to puberty to the strains of Ellington's 'Take the A Train' and the dulcet voice of Willis Conover, the VOA's Mr. Jazz" (Aksyonov 1987, 18).[42]

[38] This impact was comparable to the influence that the American Forces Network (AFN) had on the development of the British rock scene in the 1950s. The AFN in Britain consisted of small AM stations that broadcast from U.S. military bases the music that the U.S. troops were accustomed to hearing (blues, R & B, rock and roll, jazz, etc.). Situated in the U.S. bases, these stations were "suspended" outside of the British cultural context and did not target that audience. However, their broadcasts could be received by British listeners living near the bases, providing them with access to musical information that was unavailable in Britain otherwise. In the late 1950s, these broadcasts brought up a whole generation of future British rock musicians. See David Bowie, "Stardust Memories," *New York Times Magazine*, March 19, 2000, 38.

[39] In fact, Conover's program was called *Jazz Hour*, but he always opened it with the phrase "Time for jazz."

[40] After Conover's death in 1996 radio listeners from South Africa, Japan, Poland, Latin America, and elsewhere sent testimonies. See "Some Testimonies to Willis Conover," part of the University of Maryland project, "The Beat Begins: America in the 1950s." www.inform.umd.edu/EdRes/Colleges/HONR/HONR269J/.WWW/archive/conover2.html.

[41] VOA started broadcasting some programs in slow-paced "special English" with simplified vocabulary and grammar in 1959, to facilitate comprehension among the nonnative speakers of English in its audience around the globe. See VOA History, www.voa.gov/index.cfm.

[42] According to Harrison Salisbury, the *New York Times* correspondent in Moscow in the 1980s who interviewed Yurii Andropov at his dacha, Andropov was also a frequent

Conover's popularity among Soviet jazz lovers was staggering, which indicated how widespread shortwave listening in English was. In 1967, the Charles Lloyd Jazz Quartet performed at the Tallinn jazz festival in Soviet Estonia. Willis Conover accompanied the quartet on this tour. As regular tourists, they also visited nearby Leningrad and were clandestinely brought by Leningrad musicians to a concert of the local Vainshtein Orchestra in the Leningrad Jazz Club. The hall was packed but the audience did not know of Conover's presence. One of the organizers suggested that Conover announce the next composition. Yurii Vdovin remembers: "No one knew him by sight, but his voice was definitely familiar to everyone in the audience. When he came up to the microphone and announced the next number something unbelievable happened—the entire crowd charged toward him. Here was the man who single-handedly educated the Russian jazz audience" (quoted in Kaplan 1997a, 46–47).

The state's ambivalent policies toward radio—its promotion of shortwave technology, the focus of its criticism only on foreign propaganda stations in certain languages, the ever-growing production of Soviet shortwave sets, the ambivalent policies of jamming and of technological specifications—all resulted in normalizing the practice of shortwave reception among the majority of Soviet people. Listening regularly to all sorts of foreign stations was not necessarily perceived as in contradiction to being a good Soviet person.[43] This allowed for shortwave radio to emerge as one of the most important tools for cultural production in the late Soviet context. This tool was completely enabled by the state, but its meaning was not determined by the state in any predictable way. The forms of cultural production that this tool influenced included a huge explosion in the popularity of Western jazz, rock and roll, foreign languages, and general knowledge about the world.

Rock on Bones

In the 1950s, the demand for Western jazz and rock and roll boosted by shortwave radio and films and the virtual absence of this music on Soviet state-produced records led to the invention of an independent technology for copying music—the homemade gramophone record. Original Western

listener of Conover's programs. Edward Jay Epstein, "The Andropov Hoax," *New Republic*, February 7, 1983.

[43] The father of literary critic Evgenii Dobrenko, who joined the party on the front during World War II and was a devoted Communist all his life, was also an avid listener of the Russian service of the VOA. Author interview. On a similar mixing in the family of a dissident, see Smith (1976).

records with jazz and rock and roll (and also samba, tango, and spiritu-als[44]) were copied on used plastic x-ray plates, which gave them their in-triguing slang names—"rock on bones" (*rok na kostiakh*) and "rock on ribs" (*rok na rebrakh*).[45] Music journalist and producer Artemii Troitsky explains: "These were actual x-ray plates—chest cavities, spinal cords, broken bones—rounded at the edges with scissors, with a small hole in the center and grooves that were barely visible on the surface. Such an extrav-agant choice of raw material for these 'flexidiscs' is easily explained: x-ray plates were the cheapest and most readily available source of necessary plastic" (Troitsky, 1988, 7–8).

Among inventors of the x-ray record technology were students in engi-neering colleges. The state's promotion of science, technological ingenuity, and experimentation made this invention appear perfectly compatible with the Soviet student culture. Students of the Leningrad Shipbuilding Institute designed a technique in the institute's laboratory, as part of their practical training in electronic and radio design. The technology involved two con-nected turntables: the original record was played on the first turntable; the electrical signal was amplified and set to control the movements of a heated sapphire needle on the second turntable that cut the grooves on the hard glossy surface of the plastic plate. In Leningrad, they were sold clan-destinely in front of the central music store Melodiia, at the city markets, and near radio shops; before the financial reform of 1961 one record cost around ten rubles. The low quality and relatively high prices did not affect the records' popularity. According to Rudolf Fuks, one of the first practi-tioners of this technology: "In the late 1950s and early 1960s, Elvis, Little Richard, and rock and twist were in such crazy demand that all our home-made records were sold out in a second" (see figures 5.5 and 5.6).[46]

The peculiar materiality of the "rock on bones" and the obvious meta-phors these x-rays invited were not lost on Soviet fans. The records prompted a jocular discourse that fostered imaginations of the West in two ways. By providing images and sounds that were inaccessible to nor-mal human senses except by means of special technologies—x-ray pho-tography, ingenious copying devices—the records represented something that was simultaneously visible and invisible, real and virtual. And by further mixing these real-virtual Western sounds with the clearly visible Soviet innards, they created an uncanny kind of intimacy: one both saw

[44] *Pchela* (October 1996): 22.

[45] It was also known as *roentgenizdat* from the Russian term for x-ray (after Wilhelm Conrad Roentgen the German physicist who discovered x-rays). See Starr (1994, 241); Troitsky (1988); Aksyonov (1987). According to Starr, similar bootleg technologies existed in other countries. See "Disc Bootleggers Are Waxing Fat on Stolen Goods," *Down Beat*, June 16, 1950, 10.

[46] Interview with Rudolf Fuks, one of the x-ray disk producers, in Fedotov (2001).

FIGURE 5.5. X-ray record of Bill Haley, "Rock around the Clock" (around 1954). Photograph by author.

and heard what was personal, tangible, and yet imaginary.[47] The intimate space that the bones and arteries of the Soviet body on these images provided to the sounds coming from elsewhere was parallel to the intimate space that the boiler room pipes and valves within the entrails of the system afforded to new meanings, pursuits, and forms of knowledge also coming from elsewhere. X-ray records and boiler rooms were metaphors par excellence of imaginary elsewheres—the ingenious experimental cultures that were both internal and external to the body of the Soviet state, located in its zones of *vnye*.

[47] This potentially powerful intimacy of an x-ray image is captured in Thomas Mann's *Magic Mountain*. In one scene the book's hero "flung himself into his chair, and drew out his keepsake, his treasure . . . a thin glass plate, which must be held toward the light to see anything on it. It was Clavdia's x-ray portrait, showing not her face, but the delicate bony structure of the upper half of her body, and the organs of the thoracic cavity, surrounded by the pale, ghostlike envelope of flesh. How often had he looked at it, how often pressed it to his lips" (Mann 1980, 348–49).

183

FIGURE 5.6. X-ray record of Little Richard, "Tutti Frutti" (around 1955). Photograph by author.

Recorderfication

Another technology that was introduced by the state and had similar effect as the shortwave radio was the tape recorder. Soviet industry began production of the first consumer reel-to-reel tape recorders (*katushech-nye magnitofony*) in the early postwar years, but the production reached a mass scale in the 1960s. Tape recording, which offered a technique of music reproduction that was cheaper, more efficient, and of higher quality than x-ray plates, quickly displaced the latter. As with the radio, the state tried to promote the use of tape recorders for the pursuit of "good" music, including certain foreign varieties, while also trying to restrict exposure to undesired musical influences. In fact, as could be expected, the circulation of Western music in the country increased exponentially.

As earlier, the criteria for good and bad music remained ambiguous and open to personal interpretation—good music was related to the healthy culture of common people, and bad music provoked in human beings unhealthy bourgeois instincts. In 1961, composer P. Kantor wrote in a widely published calendar: "We are not against good foreign songs" such as "genuine light music [*nastoiashchaia legkaia muzyka*] [that] should be joyful, gracious, and melodic" and "good jazz when it is playing beautiful folk tunes." However, one should distinguish them from bad foreign songs, such as "the wild music of rock and roll and other such works of the bourgeois 'art'" with their "distasteful songs full of wild sounds, convulsive rhythms, and repulsive moaning" that only "wake up in human beings excessive frivolity and gloomy indifference."[48] In 1965, another composer, Ivan Dzerzhinskii, writing in *Literaturnaia gazeta* bemoaned the potential dangers of tape-recording, this time referring to amateur Soviet songwriters whose songs circulated in taped form: "The bards[49] of the 1960s are armed with magnetic tape. This presents . . . a certain danger since distribution becomes so easy. . . . Many of these songs invoke in us feelings of shame and bitter offense, and greatly harm the upbringing of youth" (quoted in Vail' and Genis 1988, 114).

As before with *stilyagi*, some instances of the state's critique portrayed the fans of tape-recorded Western rock music as lazy, selfish, and immoral. In the mid-1970s, a cartoon in *Krokodil* showed a young woman dressed according to the latest Western fashion, wearing bell-bottoms and platforms, smoking, and listening to a tape recorder; on the wall behind her are photographs of rock stars. An old peasant woman is asking

---

[48] P. Kantor, "O legkoi muzyke" [On Light Music], daily tear-off calendar, October 30, 1961, quoted in *Ptiuch*, December 1998, 21.

[49] *Bard*: an amateur poet singing to an acoustic guitar.

- Помогла бы, внучка, репку вытянуть...
- Так у вас же мышка есть!

Рисунок Г. АНДРИАН

FIGURE 5.7. Could you help us to pull out the turnip, granddaughter? . . . —But you have a mouse, don't you? G. Andrianov. *Krokodil* 34 (1977): cover.

her, "Could you help us to pull out the turnip, granddaughter?", while in the field outside an old man is pulling on a giant turnip. The granddaughter responds with arrogance: "But you have a mouse, don't you?" The cartoon drew on a Russian fairytale, in which an old woman, an old man, their granddaughter, a dog, and a cat try to no avail to pull a giant turnip out of the ground—until a tiny mouse comes to their assistance. As with the criticisms of clothes and radio listening above, the majority of fans of the tape-recorded music did not identify with these images of lazy, immoral, and arrogant grandchildren who were supposedly living at the expense of their aging parents and grandparents.

Despite the critique, state production and promotion of tape recorders steadily increased. In 1960, Soviet industry produced 128,000 recorders; in 1969 it was producing more than 1 million recorders annually; and by 1985 the production grew to 4.7 million annually. Between 1960 and 1985 Soviet people purchased about 50 million recorders.[50] Between 1960 and 1985, the population of the Soviet Union grew from 216 million to 280 million, of which around 90 million in 1985 were young people between ages 15 and 34[51]—the main users of tape recorders. Clearly, most young Soviet people growing up in the 1960s to early 1980s, even if they did not own tape recorders personally, were regularly exposed to tape-recorded music at private parties, birthdays, weddings, dances, summer camps, and elsewhere. In those fifteen years the Soviet Union underwent a major cultural transformation that Vail' and Genis aptly called the "*magnitofikatsia* (tape-recorderfication) of the whole country" (Vail' and Genis 1988, 114).[52]

The main result of this transformation was that the last Soviet generation appropriated Western jazz and rock as its own cultural forms. This music became not only ubiquitous but also intensely personal, invested with local meanings and cultural values, and contributing to the production of a whole generational identity. Cultural critic Tatyana Cherednichenko argues that the generation that was growing up in the 1960s and 1970s, unlike all previous Soviet generations, "consolidated not on the basis of some epochal achievements, but on the basis of age as such," which made the "tape-recording of Western albums" a constitutive element of their identity (Cherednichenko 1994, 225). Foreign records that were copied were brought into the country through port cities by sailors and diplomats, sold through networks of music lovers, and then tape-recorded thousandfold throughout the country. Viktor (born in 1959) became exposed to Western rock in 1972, as a thirteen-year-old school

---

[50] *Narodnoe Khoziaistvo SSSR v 1985g. Statisticheskii Ezhegodnik* [People's Economy of the USSR in 1985: Statistical Annual]. Moscow: Central Statistical Department of the Council of Ministers, 169; *Narodnoe Khoziaistvo SSSR v 1970g. Statisticheskii Ezhegodnik* [People's Economy of the USSR in 1970: Statistical Annual]. Moscow: Central Statistical Department of the Council of Ministers, 251.

[51] "Vsesoiuznaia perepis' naseleniia 1989-go goda" [All-Union Census of 1989]. *Vestnik statistiki* [Review of Statistics]. 9 (1990): 75–79.

[52] They allude to Lenin's famous slogan: "Communism means Soviet Power plus the *electrification* of the whole country."

boy in the town of Smolensk. Every Sunday, recalls Viktor: "I walked with my huge 'Kometa' reel-to-reel recorder across town to the apartment of an older guy who always had new records. I recorded Black Sabbath, Alice Cooper, Bryan Ferry, paying him two and a half rubles per record. Most other people at that time liked the Beatles, but I did not care for them—who were they compared to Ozzy [Osbourne]?!" Most records reached Smolensk from Riga, a Soviet port on the Baltic Sea. In 1974, at the age of fifteen, Viktor started traveling to Riga himself: "The trip from Smolensk to Riga took one day by train. In Riga I went to the music *tolchok* [flea market]. . . . The first record that I bought there was Credence Clearwater Revival, for which I paid fifty rubles."[53] He brought records to Smolensk, copied them for himself, and resold them for a similar price, sometimes cheaper because "the point was not to lose [too much] money so you could continue collecting."

The state's critique of such flea markets was rare and, again, ambiguous. A typical cartoon showed a seller of music records, hiding them in special pockets inside his jacket; he opens it to display the records to his customer (an actual technique that allowed the process to be less visible to the police). The records bear the names of Western bands: Kiss, Abba, Eagles, BM (Boney M), the Beatles. The caption reads "Discobolus," playing on the two meanings of the word "disk" in sport and music (see figure 5.8). The cartoon did not clearly articulate particular problem with being interested in Western music per se; instead it made a vague ridiculing comment about naïve customers fascinated with Western music and black marketers who capitalize on this fascination.

In fact, the state forms of control over these markets and record collectors were usually not very strong. According to Viktor: "the police [in Smolensk] in theory controlled the activity of buying and selling records, but in practice they mostly did not care." In Leningrad, one musician similarly remembers: "Nobody permitted it, nobody prohibited it." According to another musician, the relative control of this music resulted in its shortage but was not dangerous otherwise (Cushman 1995, 97, 208). These half-hearted forms of control enabled not only the ubiquitous spread of Western music throughout the country but also the experience that it was a normal element of Soviet reality.

Young music lovers from different cities sent tapes to each other through Soviet post and exchanged letters about their hobby. In 1976, even in the remote Siberian town of Yakutsk, where records could only arrive by air from distant centers, school students recorded albums that had been released in the West the same year or a few years earlier. Older

[53] Author interview. See also Humphrey (1995, 62–63), for a discussion of *tolchok* in general.

ДИСКОБОЛ   Рисунок Е. ШАБЕЛЬНИКА

FIGURE 5.8. Discobolus. E. Shabel'nik. *Krokodil* 26 (1981): 13.

albums were less desirable and labeled *starina* ("ancient stuff"). On March 11, 1976, Leonid, a seventeen-year-old schoolboy from Yakutsk, responded to a letter about music from his Leningrad friend Nikolai, describing what he and his school friends listened to in Yakutsk:

> I got paid for a month of winter practical work [as part of the school's professional training]—128 rubles, which is great! So, I bought myself a second tape recorder, "Jupiter 1201." Not at all a bad machine, it works great! . . . I am very keen on getting the newest recordings, even though I haven't been collecting them for long. But I already have some stuff:

Alice Cooper's 1975 and 1976 albums, the Bee Gees, Deep Purple's *Made in Japan* album [1972], their songs "Smoke on the Water" [1972] and "Child in Time" [1970], Deep Purple's *24 Carat* album [1975]. I also have some *starina*—the Beatles, McCartney, and *Band on the Run* [1973] by Wings, etc. Also two albums by Uriah Heep. As for their song "July Morning" [1971]—over here it is already considered *starina*. Concerning J. S. Bach—he is indeed great, we also love him over here, especially his organ music. I wanted to ask you to *dostat'* [obtain through unauthorized channels] Credence [Clearwater Revival] for me, and also something new that you have over there. I'll send you money later.[54]

For these young lovers of rock music, the symphonic sound of the 1970s British bands and the organic drive of the classical music by J. S. Bach were of equal interest. Clearly, they would hardly recognize themselves in the critical portrayal of the fans of Western rock as people with no education or interest in high culture.

Translation

Although the state occasionally criticized Western rock music for its harmful bourgeois influences, it also provided limited access to this music through its own media. The state record company Melodiia released occasional rock and pop numbers from the West in compilation series entitled *Around the World* (*Vokrug sveta*).[55] The world on these collections was mostly represented by the socialist countries of Eastern Europe, remembers musician Andrei Makarevich, with the order of musical tracks typically representing the following places: "Bulgaria, Poland, Czechoslovakia, again Poland, again Bulgaria, sometimes France, and in the end something American or English, just one track." This one "bourgeois" track was commonly renamed and its attribution changed, to make it appear more appropriate for the Soviet listeners. For example, in the 1950s, Melodiia renamed the U.S. jazz composition "American patrol" as "On Guard" (*Na zastave*) to avoid the word "American."[56] In the 1960s and 70s, many Western tracks on pop compilations were identified either as a "folk tune" (*narodnaia pesnia*) or a "song of protest"

---

[54] Letters from the personal collection of Andrei A, one of the friends of the correspondent, quoted with permission.

[55] See McMichael (2005a; 2005b) about the music series *Krugozor* in the 1970s.

[56] Feiertag (1997, 35). Recall the similar technique above of renaming jazz songs employed by Soviet orchestras in the 1950s.

[57] Makarevich (2002, 53–54).

(*pesnia protesta*). A 1968 compilation included the Beatles' "Girl" with the attribution "English folk tune."[57]

The categorization "song of protest" allowed for it to be released on Soviet records. When Melodiia issued Merle Travis's "Sixteen Tons," it was also attributed as a "song of protest." In the context of the McCarthy's era of the late 1940s, that song indeed functioned as a protest. The FBI advised radio stations not to play it, and Travis was called a "communist sympathizer."[58] It was precisely this history that made the song acceptable for the Soviet release. However, young Soviet audiences ignored this information. What mattered was the song's dancing rhythm, non-Soviet sound, and American English. It was not only "played in all dancing halls and worn to the holes" but also "some unbelievable Russian words were written to it" that had nothing to do with any protest (Makarevich, 2002, 54).

The literal meaning of these songs was irrelevant. What was important was their Western origin, foreign sound, and unknown references that allowed Soviet fans to imagine worlds that did not have to be linked to any "real" place or circumstances, neither Soviet nor Western. Studying in school in a small town in middle Russia, in the early 1970s, future film actor Alexandr Abdulov and his friends constantly listened to the tape-recordings of the Beatles, inventing their own elaborate translations and stories for their songs. When in the post-Soviet 1990s printed translations of these songs became available, Abdulov discovered "that they sang about something completely different than we imagined."[59] In making Western music their own, the last Soviet generation engaged in a complex process of cultural translation.[60] When artist Dmitry Shagin painted a picture that was meant to represent the collective identity of that generation, he drew just two words on a canvas—TXE BEATJIE3—

---

[58] The song told a bitter story of the lives of Kentucky coal miners, including Travis's father. Miners were paid in scrip, which they could spend only at the company store with inflated prices. Most miners' families lived in permanent debt to the company. The lyrics described this: "You load sixteen tons, what do you get? / Another day older and deeper in debt / Saint Peter don't you call me 'cause I can't go / I owe my soul to the company store." Published interview with Travis's producer, Ken Nelson. See "Sixteen Tons—The Story behind the Legend," www.ernieford.com/sixteen%20tons.htm

[59] Author interview with Alexandr Abdulov. See also Vladimir Kozhemiakov, "Uzhe ne trubadur, eshche ne korol' [No Longer a Troubadour, Not Yet the King]." *Moskovskii komsomolets*, August 28, 1999.

[60] These acts of appropriating and reinterpreting musical records can be compared with the cultural techniques used in the style of hip-hop that originally emerged in poor urban neighborhoods where music instruments were unavailable because of their high price (Gilroy 1984). In that style "[r]ecords are deprived of the authority and reverential treatment appropriate to a fixed and final artistic statement. They become little more than a basic tool in complex processes of creative improvisation" (Gilroy 1991, 211).

[61] Dmitry Shagin was a member of the artistic group Mit'ki. See chapter 7 for more about this group.

a jocular, nonstandard, Cyrillic transliteration of the English words "the Beatles" that was meant to convey a Russian accent.[61]

The processes of cultural translation and appropriation of Western rock affected the development of a local rock scene among the last Soviet generation. In the late 1960s and 1970s, rock bands appeared in schools, residential clubs, palaces of pioneers, summer camps, colleges, and institutes all over the country. The status of these bands was "amateur," which meant that they were not registered as musical groups by the state, unlike "professional bands" and orchestras, and could not play for money or in large concert halls. Similar "amateur" bands existed in the era of jazz in the 1950s, as described earlier. According to Frederick Starr, in the early 1970s, "there was not a high school, institute, or factory in Moscow without at least one rock band, bringing the total to several thousand and meaning that several thousand private and independent [i.e., "amateur"] producers were operating in the field of popular culture" (Starr 1994, 301). Having no access to professional studios the more serious of these bands began recording their own "tape-albums" (kassetnyi al'bom) on reel-to-reel recorders. These tape-albums dispersed around the country; and the method of their production became known in slang as magnitizdat [tape recorder publishing].[62]

The state's promotion of the values of creativity, internationalism, cultural erudition, science, and technology, its increasing production of radios and tape recorders, and its ambivalent attempts to control the unwanted effects of these values and technologies produced unanticipated results—one of which was a feeling that rock music, like jazz, was compatible with socialism. These ambivalent policies also translated into the creation in 1981 of Leningrad Rock Club, an association of "amateur" bands that was officially run under the auspices of the Komsomol and with unspoken supervision by the KGB.[63] This arrangement, argues a music critic, "was advantageous for both" amateur rock musicians, "who were given relative freedom (e.g., to issue printed materials, organize exhibitions, concerts, places to meet)," and the state, which could monitor the growing amateur rock community (Chernov 1997c, 12–13). The special status given to the bands registered in the club imposed on them new forms of control as it provided new forms of freedom. On the one hand, the fact that the club's concerts were not advertised in the press greatly

[62] From the Russia word magnitofon (magnetic tape recorder) and, by analogy with samizdat and roentgenizdat (n. 45 above).

[63] The involvement of the KGB in the control of the rock club was revealed publicly during perestroika, in the late 1980s. Later, on January 14, 1995, the former KGB general Oleg Kalugin described it in more detail in an interview on the RTR television channel. This form of KGB control (limited permission to operate) also extended to other amateur publications such as the Leningrad literary journal Chasy (Clock).

reduced the potential audience; on the other hand, this contributed to the production of an intense and relatively independent milieu of rock music *tusovka* (see chapter 4 for a discussion of this term). And although the lyrics of all songs had to be approved beforehand by the club's state-appointed censor, the relative isolation of the club's auditorium allowed the groups to alter these preapproved lyrics during performances (Chernov 1997c, 12–13; Cushman 1995, 207). Ultimately the state's attempt to control the development of bands by concentrating them in one place and semi-legalizing them contributed to the development of a vibrant local rock subculture in the Leningrad of the 1980s. This effect was a stronger version of what happened with the milieu of the café Saigon, discussed in chapter 4, which was left relatively free to develop and grow partly because it was useful for the KGB to observe certain characters.

In this context of partial state control a certain critical tongue-in-cheek ethos was allowed to emerge, and transparent irony about various absurdities of everyday Soviet life became common.[64] Dmitrii, a club regular in the early 1980s, remembers that the concerts took place in a "strange atmosphere of buffoonery (*skomoroshestvo*)," of which a good example was the band Strannye Igry (Strange Games): "They were tongue-in-cheek about everything. To me it still remains an enigma how they were allowed to come out on stage in the first place. I heard that sometimes they had problems, but still their concerts continued to be organized."

Naming

Symbols of the Imaginary West also spread widely in language, and in the sphere of colloquial naming in particular. In the 1950s, *stilyagi* referred to central streets in Soviet cities as *Brod* or *Brodvei*[65] and called each other by such English nicknames as *Dzhon* (John), *Dzhim* (Jim), and *Meri* (Mary).[66] In the 1970s and 1980s, such nicknames were commonplace in schools and colleges, where students called each other Mike (for Mikhail), Alex (for Alexei), Bob (for Boris), Madeleine (for Elena),

---

[64] See a discussion of the irony of *stiob* and other tongue-in-cheek genres in chapter 7. Compare also with the practices of causticity among the rock music *tusovka* in chapter 4.

[65] In Leningrad, a stretch of Nevsky Prospekt from the Passage department store to Liteinyi Prospekt was called *Brod* (Krivulin 1996, 6). In Moscow, the right side of Gorky Street from Pushkin Square to Hotel Moskva was called *Brodvei* (Troitsky 1988, 3). The same phenomenon occurred in many other cities (Skvortsov 1964; Fain and Lur'e 1991, 172).

[66] Rita Mohel', "Konfetnyi mal'chik" [Candy Boy]. *Moskovskii Komsomolets* August 23, 1999.

Margo (for Margarita)—nicknames that were not standard in Russian and recognizably Western. Many "amateur" rock bands in the 1960s and 70s were named in that manner as well.[67] The famous band Mashina Vremeni (Time Machine) started in the mid-1960s as an "amateur" school band with an English name, The Kids (Makarevich 2002, 109). The collector of Western rock recordings Viktor (encountered earlier in this chapter) played in the mid-1970s in a Smolensk school band with an English name, Mad Dogs.

By the 1970s Soviet urban space was peppered with slang names that indexed a vibrant Imaginary West. Cafés in Leningrad were state owned. They were either named simply Kafe or had one of several predictable "nice" names without reference to place or event: *Ulybka* (Smile), *Skazka* (Fairytale), or *Rainbow* (Raduga). In slang, however, many cafés became known as *Saigon*, *Ol'ster* (Ulster), *Liverpul'* (Liverpool), *London*, *Rim* (Rome), *Vena* (Vienna), *Tel'-Aviv*, and so forth.[68] These names gained public recognition in the Soviet press in association with some cultural or political event in the foreign world—e.g., the Vietnam War, the conflict in Northern Ireland, the Beatles. However, they functioned not as references to concrete events but as recognizable signs of the West but without overt political commentary.[69]

Most students living in dormitories of Leningrad University and other colleges during the late 1970s or early 1980s decorated the walls in their rooms with photos of foreign places, music personalities, and sometimes "prints of avant-garde artists that were not represented in Soviet museums" (Dmitrii, born in 1964). In the diary of her stay in the dormitory of Moscow University in 1978, American student Andrea Lee writes about her surprise that even an ardent Komsomol activist, Grigorii, decorated his room with images of Western commodities that did not exist in the Soviet context: "The walls of his small green cubicle . . . are decorated, almost papered, with liquor and automobile advertisements cut carefully from the American magazines Grigorii has received as presents from other foreign acquaintances" (Lee 1984, 12). Young people in all corners of the country used empty Western liquor bottles, beer cans, and cigarette boxes to create a kind of "still life" installation on the bookshelves and cupboards in their rooms.

---

[67] Mikhail Naumenko, who in 1980 founded the famous Leningrad rock group Zoopark, was better known by his anglicized stage name Maik (Mike), and Boris Grebenshikov, the founder and leader of the legendary Leningrad band Akvarium, is known to millions of fans by the nickname Bob.

[68] Fain and Lur'e (1991, 170); Krivulin (1996); Yurchak (2000a).

[69] "Nevskii do i posle velikoi kofeinoi revoliutsii" [Nevsky before and after the Great Coffee Revolution] (Krivulin 1996, 7).

Most of these packages and bottles were empty—they could not be purchased in regular Soviet stores and often circulated as pure packaging free of original products. However, this empty status did not matter because their original meaning as consumable commodities (the actual liquor, beer, or cigarettes) was largely irrelevant. They were not commodities but shells of commodities whose role was to link the here and now to an "elsewhere." The materiality of these objects, and the fact that they were unmistakably "Western" in origin, endowed them with great power for doing this work of linking. The link they established was simultaneously real (the objects were right here) and abstract (the "elsewhere" to which they linked was imaginary). In this way they injected an imaginary dimension into the space of one's room, reinterpreting and deterritorializing the meaning of that space.

A symbol such as an unknown, misspelled, and invented "English" word worked perfectly well regardless of whether its literal meaning was understood. A student at a Leningrad technical college, in the early 1980s, carried an American plastic bag acquired on the black market. Its literal meaning—the name and address of a Manhattan laundromat—was irrelevant for the students, who were unfamiliar with the concept of street laundromats, even if they understood English. However, such bags were extremely popular, meaningful, and powerful. This bag, with its tangible foreign materiality, texture, color, and English script provided a link with the Imaginary West. Foreign tourists visiting Soviet cities in the 1980s became familiar with a peculiar sight: Soviet pedestrians, not only young but also of older age and conservative style of dress, carried around foreign plastic bags printed with frivolous pictures of topless models in tight jeans. What seemed incongruous from the outside seemed perfectly normal to the participants in the Soviet context. What was depicted on these bags was irrelevant—their images were "transparent"—but the bags, images, and textures were important for the link they established to the Imaginary West.

Authentication

These and earlier examples demonstrate how the state's ambivalent cultural policy contributed to the production of particular forms of imagination, especially among Soviet youth. These forms linked their socialist realities with the world of the Imaginary West, which they produced locally, drawing on foreign symbols, alphabets, and images, profoundly reinterpreting them in the process. Another ubiquitous symbol in this form of creative imagination, from the 1960s to the 1980s, was a physical marker worn on clothes and personal possessions and known in youth slang as *leibl*, from English "label" for a tag or brand name. A *leibl* came in various incarnations, from authentic Western labels, to imitations, to pure local inventions. In 1985 *Literaturnaia Gazeta* described a dispute about fashion that occurred in a Soviet school, during which one student argued that what made clothes *firmennyi* (of a "brand" make, slang for "trendy" or Western) was the presence of a *leibl*. The student explained that "*leibl* is a little tag that is put on every *firmennyi* thing, and that this year she was given a foreign coat as a gift and it had a *leibl*" (quoted in Kostomarov 1994, 94).

A piece of clothing was *firmennyi* not because it was of a known Western brand but simply because it was "Western" at all. In the 1970s, the difference in price between famous brands of American jeans bought on the black market (Lee, Super Rifle, Wrangler) and Soviet pants or Polish *Odra* jeans sold in regular Soviet stores was huge—the former cost between 100 and 180 rubles, the latter cost around 20.[70] At the same time, the difference in price between famous American brands and completely unknown but authentic Western jeans (which were even more numerous than known brands) was negligible. The high price was paid more for the authentic Westernness than for a concrete brand. The same was true for jackets, coats, and women's boots.

Because of the high prices, there emerged an underground production of fake Western jeans. According to Lyuba, good fakes of Lees and Wranglers were almost indistinguishable from the real thing. They were made locally from denim fabric brought from Italy, with real designer labels, buttons, and zippers, and were "sewn according to the original cuts, with overlock seams, the whole thing." Lyuba herself once made a mistake: "My husband and I bought a denim dress for me because we thought that it was a *firmennoe* [authentic Western] dress—it was perfect and had a Wrangler label. We were very disappointed when it turned out to be a well-made fake." To ensure that clothes were really Western, sophisticated techniques of authentication emerged. Lyuba explains: "People looked carefully at every seam, turned the pants inside out, rubbed the fabric with a moistened match to check the coloring, tested every button, label and zipper. If you saw that they were not *firmennyi*, you would not pay 180 rubles even if the jeans were perfectly well made and indistinguishable from authentic jeans." Something was *firmennyi* because it was manufactured elsewhere and therefore established an authentic link with the Imaginary West.

Checking the denim dress, Lyuba was verifying the authenticity not of a particular brand but of a Western origin in general. When youngsters

---

[70] The average monthly salary at the time was around 150 rubles; a student's stipend was 40 to 75 rubles.

from the provinces asked their friends in big cities to send them jeans (which traveled around the country like tape-recorded music), they also did not specify the brand. The jeans could be of any brand, including unknown ones, as long as they were *firmennyi*. On May 12, 1975, a sixteen-year old Alexei, from the remote Siberian town of Yakutsk, wrote to his friend Nikolai who had recently moved to Leningrad asking him to send Western jeans, which were much easier to come by in Leningrad:

> How are you, Kol'ka [friendly version of Nikolai]? How's life? What's the climate like in Leningrad? Have you managed to obtain any new records [with Western music]? Kolya, I apologize for my importunity, but I wanted to ask you again about the jeans. Is it possible to buy them over there or not? You understand yourself, Kol'ka, that the summer is approaching, and during the summer jeans are indispensable. If it is possible to obtain them [*dostat'*—to obtain through contacts], could you buy and send them, please? I will send you a money order right away. Just in case, I repeat: my size is 48, length is 4 or 5.

Another friend, Alexandr, wrote to Nikolai from Novosibirsk two years later, on July 10, 1977, also reminding him about his request to get him *firmennyi* jeans:

> Nikolai, in the previous letter you mentioned that jeans will cost me "18.00." I did not understand—if you meant 18 rubles, then this is too cheap, but if you meant 18 tenners [*chervontsev* or 180 rubles], this is too expensive. I'll be able to buy them for this price over here. As far as I remember we have agreed that you will help me to obtain [*dostat'*] them cheaper, so, please, write in more detail. I'll be waiting![71]

All these labels, symbols, clothes, visuals, names, musical recordings, and linguistic expressions served as markers that introduced into the Soviet reality an abstract imaginary dimension, what I am calling the Imaginary West. A certain semiotic "bareness" of many of these symbols and artifacts (empty beer cans, "transparent" images, uninterpretable lyrics, non-existent goods, unknown brands) made them all the more powerful for the creative production of an imaginary world. Their immense appeal to Soviet youth was in their promise of personal creativity and the possibility of creating a vibrant and shared world that was neither Soviet nor foreign but was nevertheless tightly interwoven throughout their Soviet reality.

The profound disconnectedness of these symbols from the literal meanings they had in the Western context made it possible for them to coexist in the same room with the symbols of Russian high culture (a

---

[71] Letters from Andrei A.'s personal collection, quoted with the permission of the letters' authors.

bust of Chekhov, a picture of Tchaikovsky) and Soviet ideology (a book by Lenin, a picture of a revolutionary hero). One young man in Dmitrii's dormitory had on the wall in his room photos of English rock bands Police and Madness next to a portrait of Felix Dzerzhinsky, a Bolshevik leader and the first chief of the ChK. That same young man was a few years older than Dmitrii and before university had served in the Soviet army fighting in Afghanistan—the experience to which he referred when explaining his respect for Dzerzhinsky.

Ethical Dilemmas

As in the earlier examples of music and style, Soviet media criticized not the general interest in using Western symbols, labels, and brands among the Soviet youth in the 1970s and the 1980s but the extreme manifestations of this interest, equating it with low moral values, egoism, and laziness. And, as earlier, this ambivalent criticism had mixed results. A 1974 cartoon in the satirical magazine *Krokodil* showed two long-haired youngsters wearing bell-bottoms, smoking cigarettes, and holding guitars (all signs of aimless asocial behavior). One of them asks the other, pointing to the label on his pants: "Where did you get such a cool patch?" The patch reads "*cowboy*," suggesting that the boy attached it himself to "Westernize" his pants. Such cartoons ridiculed the youths as aimless loafers who blindly follow bourgeois influences (figure 5.9).

Another cartoon published in *Krokodil* shows a histrionic youth, with tears streaming from his eyes, announcing to his elderly mother: "Either Super Rifle jeans or I go on a hunger strike" (figure 5.10). In another a grown-up son impudently questions his elderly mother: "Why did you give me life, mother, if you aren't giving me money for life?" (figure 5.11). None of the clothes he is wearing or symbols that surround him came from regular Soviet shops: Lee jeans, foreign liquor bottles, a Pepsi-cola advertising logo, a frivolous Western poster of a woman in a bikini with the word "drink." There is a shortwave receiver by the bed, too—this young man listens to foreign broadcasts.

These cartoons portrayed spoiled youths who blindly follow bourgeois influences, exploiting their hard-working parents and the older generation. As before, this criticism helped to normalize the use of Western symbols among Soviet youth who were interested both in having Western music and clothes *and* in work, study, and many other pursuits. They would not have recognized themselves in these images of insolent loafers. Indeed, for many of them, Western clothes and music were part of a different ethics, whose roots were just as socialist as they were capitalist, and this caused a peculiar ethical dilemma. It was not

— И где ты такую заплатку оторвал?!.

FIGURE 5.9. Where did you get such a cool patch?! B. Starchikov. *Krokodil* 28 (1974): 9.

—Или джинсы «Супер-Райфл», или объявляю голодовку...

Рисунок Е. ГОРОХОВА

FIGURE 5.10. Either Super Rifle jeans or I go on a hunger strike. *Krokodil* 23 (1978): 4.

uncommon to buy these products but also to dislike the types of people who supplied them through black market channels, nor was it uncommon to feel ashamed by having to deal with them. Dmitrii (born in 1964) from the town of Zaporozh'e in the southeastern Ukraine, who studied at Leningrad University in the early 1980s, described this ambivalence:

FIGURE 5.11. Why did you give me life, mother, if you aren't giving me money for life? I. Semenov. *Krokodil* 13 (1981): 5.

There were channels for getting foreign clothes, but for a person like me they were off limits. Apart from having money you needed to be pushy and crafty [*pronyrlivyi*]. The person who sold the jeans [at the university dormitory] was absolutely uninteresting and unpleasant to me. I did not want to have anything to do with those types. I did have a certain taste in clothes and wanted certain stuff that was hard to get, like jeans, but wouldn't go out of my way to fulfill that desire. The majority of the people around me felt that way. Very few people knew *fartsovshchiki* [black marketers of foreign clothes and goods] personally or wanted to interact with them.

The black marketers constituted a small group and were recognized as being different from most people in their unapologetic interest in money and material possessions. This made them much closer to the images in the *Krokodil* cartoons and different from most young people. Andrea Lee describes an encounter with a black marketer in 1978 at Moscow

University. She exchanges her American clothes for Russian icons and antique lacquer boxes with a woman called Olga:

> Within a few minutes Olga was running her small white hands with their pink polished nails over my jeans and dresses, checking seams and the quality of the material, and offering a running commentary which taught me more than I ever wanted to know about the black market. . . . "*Ochen krasiva* [sic] very pretty," she said, holding up a denim blazer. You could get two hundred for this, maybe two-fifty. . . . "What are these—underpants? My dear, you could get twenty or thirty apiece for these. Russian girls are desperate for pretty underwear. And if you're interested in selling your eyeglass frames or that nice little umbrella." . . . We went through Tom's closet, through my cosmetics, through our books and records. Everything had its inflated price (records were from fifty to seventy-five rubles), and everything quite obviously awakened in Olga a kind of lust that went far beyond a businesslike interest. As I stood close beside her, breathing in her delicate scent of perfume and watching her busy hands and glittering eyes, I experienced a complicated mixture of feelings; annoyance at having allowed myself to be victimized, a guilty pride at being so rich, and an intense repulsion at the obsessive materialism I saw in Olga (Lee 1984, 24–25).

It was this recognized association with materialism and greed that made many of Dmitrii's peers experience intense discomfort when encountering *fartsovshchiki* and made most of them avoid or minimize such encounters. Dmitrii desired American jeans, but without that association of "obsessive materialism" and abuse of others. When he finally bought a pair it was from a friend, which spared him the unpleasant interaction with a crafty dealer and the risk of appearing the same in the eyes of others. Buying occasional black market goods but avoiding association with the black market ethos was a common feature of this generation and says much about the local meanings of the Imaginary West.[72]

Real Contact

The abundant circulation of Western cultural symbols and forms of imagination during late socialism is sometimes interpreted as a sign of resistance to the Soviet state, a desire to flee from it to the West, or a

---

[72] This ethical tension is also reflected in a particular form of the "misrecognition" of *blat* (the Soviet informal economy of favors) that is central to its functioning. See Ledeneva on "misrecognition as a system of denial" (1998, 60–63).

manifestation of Soviet youth's consumerism and materialism.[73] Such readings are related to a broader view that, in today's globalizing world, the agendas of those who appropriate transnational cultural messages on subnational and local levels contradict and undermine the agendas of the nation-state, challenging its cultural hegemony (Appadurai 1990). However, this view has two problems: first, it posits transnationalism and the nation-state as mutually exclusive, bounded entities that compete with each other; and second, it locates people's agency and resistance in a cultural sphere somehow suspended outside the nation-state.[74]

As this chapter has argued, "Western" cultural symbols and forms of imagination that circulated in the Soviet Union during the late-socialist period were neither necessarily external to the agendas of the Soviet state nor necessarily incompatible with the values of socialism. Perhaps the most intriguing aspect of these symbols was that, despite the Soviet state's regular attacks on the bourgeois influences these symbols helped to shape, the state also promoted and enabled their proliferation. This made most Western influences in Soviet life not only perfectly compatible with the Soviet state's vision of socialist culture but also allowed them to be profoundly reinterpreted in local terms and to become a constitutive part of late Soviet culture. The symbols of the Imaginary West did not necessarily represent the "real" West and its "bourgeois" values; rather, they introduced into Soviet reality a new imaginary dimension that was neither "Western" nor "Soviet."

Rosemary Coombe has argued that a commodity brand has two meanings: it serves as evidence of the product's authenticity (the brand demonstrates that it is a true or accurate copy), and as testimony of real contact with the moment, place, and person of production, acting as a kind of "fingerprint" (Coombe 1998, 169).[75] This distinction is obvious between two copies of the same book, one of which has been autographed by the author and the other not. They are identical accurate copies but different testimonies of a real contact (which may translate, for example, in the difference in prices of desires invested in them). It is the second meaning—its role as testimony or real contact with a "distant" moment, place, person—that was central to the symbols of the Imaginary West in late socialism. These symbols were desirable, first and foremost, not as authentic famous brands, real drinks, or literal values coming from the West but as links to imaginary worlds that were spatially, temporally, and meaningfully "distant," as "fingerprints" of these imaginary worlds on the sur-

[73] For example, Borneman (1998, 101), Cushman (1995, 7–8).

[74] See Cheah (1998, 296–97), Schein (1998), Gupta (1995), Taussig (1992), Clifford (1992), Bhabha (1984; 1997).

[75] Coombe draws on Taussig (1993, 220) and Benjamin (1969b).

face of Soviet life. Thus Western jeans of an unknown brand that did not work as an "accurate copy" (i.e., not an accurate copy of "real" Levis but a cheap imitation) still worked as "real contact."

Indeed, many of these symbols were not "real" commodities, but stripped-down versions of the latter, empty husks, from which the original literal meanings were drained. The "emptiness" of these commodities is clearly seen in the earlier examples of empty beer cans, empty cigarette boxes, reinterpreted "songs of protest," invented translations of lyrics, "invisible" pictures on plastic bags, and so forth. Most members of the last Soviet generation cared deeply about the visibility of Western labels in their lives: they sewed foreign tags on their pants and jackets, knitted sweaters and winter ski hats with English words, carefully checked labels, tags, buttons, seams, and textures of foreign clothes, invented foreign nicknames for places and people, and so on. The acts of citing these symbols, markers, and names on clothes, bags, pictures, in language, and in music recordings, continuously introduced a shared imaginary world into the Soviet reality, deterritorializing it, making it neither Soviet nor Western. It was not the literal meaning of all these symbols that mattered most but their linking of the here and now to an imaginary "elsewhere."

Clearly, the symbols of the Imaginary West were not just manifestations of consumerism and materialism of the Soviet youth. Indeed, they can be compared with some "anti-consumerist" practices in the West. For example, in the 1980s, it was popular among some U.S. students to cut off visible labels from designer jeans and sweatshirts. This eradication of labels was described as resistance to the homogenizing consumerism and branding of capitalism. Such acts may add elements of personal agency to the "agentless" context of inescapable brand hegemony (see Willis 1990); however they do not undermine the brand's role in shaping desire (these youngsters continued wearing designer jeans with cut-off labels, instead of not wearing them at all). The Soviet acts of inventing and adding labels were performed within the context of the hegemony of authoritative form. By using Western brands and labels in the Soviet context they also infused that context with agency, refusing the literal readings of authoritative discourse, but without necessarily refusing the broader cultural context of socialism, its realities, possibilities, and values.

As we will see in the next chapter, it became perfectly appropriate to reproduce the form of authoritative discourse (write speeches, vote in favor, participate in Komsomol meetings) while wearing Western jeans, playing Western music, and having a Westernized nickname. The two signifying systems were not in contradiction but were, in fact, mutually constitutive. Without the hegemony of the authoritative rhetoric, the Imaginary West would not exist, and vice versa, without such imaginary worlds, the hypernormalized authoritative discourse could not be reproduced. However, this process was neither circular nor innocent: the development and further spread of the imaginary worlds within the fabric of socialist society gradually changed the very cultural logic of the Soviet system, deterritorializing it and rendering it increasingly incongruous with the descriptions it made of itself.

When, in the late 1980s, during the reforms of perestroika, the sacred Soviet *granitsa* (the border) suddenly became crossable, it became obvious that the Imaginary West was something very different from the "real" West. That construction quickly lost its status as an internal Soviet production intrinsic to and constitutive of late Soviet reality. As a result, it experienced the same sudden collapse as the greater system within which it developed. For members of the last Soviet generation the discovery of that link between their collapsing state and their imaginary world came as a stunning surprise. When many of them first traveled to Western Europe, between 1988 and 1990, they were particularly impressed not by a glimpse of Western cars or the variety of food in shops, as the West had expected, but by a sudden realization that the real West was somehow "ordinary." Marat (born in 1956) visiting London in 1989 was mesmerized by the dust on the streets, clothes hanging to dry in the backyards, and cats sitting on windowsills. Ekaterina was astonished to see endless birch trees in West Germany—the tree that in the Soviet context had been constructed as an archetypal symbol of Russianness.[76]

Vassily Aksyonov wrote about a similar surprising discovery experienced by the Soviet émigrés of his generation a decade earlier, when they encountered the "real" America. The imaginary America with which they had lived in the Soviet Union was a whimsical, adventurous space, full of fanciful names, sounds, images, and knowledge. It was imagined as "the utmost crossroads of universal cosmopolitanism" where "the weather report on the TV would certainly mention the water temperature in Nice and the depth of snow on Kilimanjaro, and the news would discuss the new shoes of the Spanish king, the courtly intrigues in the Central Committee of the Chinese Communist Party, and the movement

[76] Author interviews. Also memories of art curator Ekaterina Degot'. Round table discussion, Conference on Russian Art, White Chapel Art Gallery, London, March 2003. There were plenty of other stories about the "encounter." For example, that Western drinks had an "imaginary" dimension constructed in the Soviet period was revealed in the first post-Soviet years, when they became available. In the 1990s, Western beer in Russia generated a short-lived euphoria of consumption but quickly fell out of favor. A newly widespread discourse suggested that the "reality" turned out to be less interesting than what was once "imagined." Most people quickly switched to local beers. Today foreign brands account for just 1 percent of beer consumption in Russia ("Beer Is Booming in Russia," *Alfalaval International Customer Magazine*, March 2003). The phenomenon of being disillusioned with Western foodstuffs after they "failed" to meet expectations is a widespread phenomenon in Russia (see Humphrey 1995 and 2002b).

of Marxism deep inside New Guinea. . . . Boredom was the last thing they feared, if this word came to mind at all." What came to mind were mysterious names that "sounded like pure silver": "How can one be bored in a town called Indianapolis or in a state with such a name as Minnesota that sings like the wind of adventures? And those islands of service burning in the night: Pizza Hut, Burger King, K-Mart, Grand Union." But upon the encounter with the "real" world, one unexpectedly discovered "that all this is the sticks, routine, solitude" (Aksyonov 1987, 35–36).

Later, such discoveries were more profound. They revealed that the Imaginary West was no longer to be found anywhere and was lost forever—and that with it were lost all those intimate worlds of meaning and creativity that were so indivisible from the realities of socialism and so constitutive of its forms of "normal" life. The greatest discovery of all was that one could now turn back to the Soviet past with an equally astonished glance. The protagonist of Victor Pelevin's "Generation P," recollecting the recent Soviet past from the perspective of the post-Soviet 1990s, feels regret at the passing of these internal imaginary worlds that he calls the "parallel universe." He suddenly realized that "a great deal of what he had liked and been moved by had come from that parallel universe, which everyone had been certain could never come to any harm; but it had been overtaken by the same fate as the Soviet eternity, and just as imperceptibly" (Pelevin 2002, 29–30).

Chapter 6

The True Colors of Communism:
King Crimson, Deep Purple, Pink Floyd

In those days, however, language and life both abounded in the strange and the dubious. Take the very name "Babylen," which was conferred on Tatarsky by his father, who managed to combine in his heart a faith in communism with the ideals of the sixties generation. He composed it from the title of Yevtushenko's famous poem "Baby Yar" and Lenin. Tatarsky's father clearly found it easy to imagine a faithful disciple of Lenin moved by Yevtushenko's liberated verse to the grateful realisation that Marxism originally stood for free love, or a jazz-crazy aesthete suddenly convinced by an elaborately protracted saxophone riff that communism would inevitably triumph. It was not only Tatarsky's father who was like that—the entire Soviet generation of the fifties and sixties was the same. This was the generation that gave the world the amateur song and ejaculated the first sputnik—that four-tailed spermatozoon of the future that never began—into the dark void of cosmic space.
—Victor Pelevin[1]

Ideological Weapon

Western rock and roll had a phenomenal appeal to the Soviet youth coming of age in the 1970s. This music became such a ubiquitous and vibrant part of Soviet youth culture that the party sought a more nuanced understanding of its effects on ideological convictions. In the early 1980s two famous sociologists of youth who were both ardent party members of an older generation organized debates with young Soviet audiences around the country, intending to explore the extent of Western mass culture's influence on the lives of Soviet youth. In the debates, the sociologists provoked their audiences by arguing that in the contemporary world the ideological struggle between capitalism and socialism was at its peak, and that rock music had transformed into an ideological tool that capitalism employed in this struggle. As testimony of this development they

[1] Pelevin (2002, 2).

presented the alleged conversion of many formerly progressive Western artists to conservative bourgeois values. For example, they argued, the folk singer Joan Baez, who had previously been associated with progressive "songs of protest" opposing the Vietnam War, had now moved into the anticommunist camp. However, to the sociologists' distress, young Soviet audiences were left unmoved by these arguments and typically reacted with a comment: "Why should we worry about any connection between music and politics?" (Ikonnikova and Lisovskii 1982, 96–97). Indeed, as we saw in chapters 3, 4, and 5, Soviet youth tended to ignore any explicit political connection as uninteresting and irrelevant and, moreover, was not particularly interested in the literal meaning of Western songs. The two sociologists pessimistically concluded that Soviet youth had become precariously naïve, failing to recognize the direct link between bourgeois mass culture and the politics of anticommunism.

On one level, this pessimistic conclusion was a shift from the earlier critique of Western cultural influences that concentrated on relatively small and isolated groups of deviationists, such as the subculture of trendily dressed youths above, the *stilyagi*, whom satirical articles and cartoons presented as immoral and uneducated loafers. The new critical campaign seemed to acknowledge that Western influences had become common and widespread among the masses of the ordinary Soviet youth. With that apparent change in the focus of the critique, how it portrayed its target also seemed to change. It now attacked Western "mass culture" not simply as a manifestation of decadent and bourgeois tastes, but as an insidious ideological weapon that the bourgeois world employed in its broad struggle with socialism.

Critical articles in the Soviet press at the time reflected this apparent change in focus. In 1981, the newspaper *Komsomol'skaia Pravda* published an article entitled, "Popular Music in the West Has Hit the Wall," explaining that the music of new trendy Western pop stars "almost completely lacks an uncompromising attitude toward the vices of the bourgeois world." This music had become an arm of bourgeois ideology, leading "the listeners away into the world of unrealizable illusions" and acting like "music-drug [*muzyka-narkotik*], music-sleeping-pill [*muzyka-snotvornoe*], music-deceit [*muzyka-obman*]." This was, the article concluded, an inevitable development in Western bourgeois mass culture because it was nothing but "the deformed offspring of an unequal marriage between art and business."[2]

On another level, however, this critical campaign was not that different from the previous ones mentioned in chapter 5. As before, the criticism

---

[2] V. Barko. "Pered stenoi okazalas' segodnia populiarnaia muzyka na zapade" [Popular Music in the West Has Hit the Wall]. *Komsomol'skaia Pravda*, March 19, 1981.

focused on the issues of personal character and morality. And, as before, the "problem" of Western cultural influences among Soviet youth was presented in terms of moral corruption or dangerous political naïveté.[3] The only difference was that now critical discourse concentrated not on a few deviationists but on broader masses of Komsomol members.

The previous chapter traced the emergence of the construct of the Imaginary West from the postwar period to the 1980s, analyzing how internal conditions and paradoxes of the late Soviet system enabled that development. The current chapter builds on this analysis to demonstrate how even the most active Komsomol secretaries and sincere young communists managed to integrate the cultural symbols and forms of aesthetics of the Imaginary West with the values, ideals, and rhetoric of communism, creating an imagination of the communist future that differed from its description in the authoritative rhetoric of the party. This chapter starts by demonstrating that the official critical campaigns were not only misleading but also self-destructing—by failing to recognize the nature of the cultural change within Soviet society they boosted this change further. The chapter focuses on active and conscientious Komsomol secretaries who were deeply involved with both the Communist ideology and "bourgeois" culture and who considered themselves to be conscientious, ethical, and creative Soviet citizens invested in communist ideals and the common good. The second part of the chapter focuses on a young man called Alexandr, who, the chapter argues, was a perfect product of the Soviet system and of the internal paradoxes of its discourses and messages. He was well educated, valued independent thinking, pursued diverse cultural interests, and was devoted to ethical and moral principles and values of communism—all of which made his passionate interest in the Western "black market" rock music perfectly logical. The result of the activities of people such as Alexandr was yet another kind of profound deterritorialization of the Soviet system—a deterritorialization that was performed paradoxically in the name of Communism.

Opportunist

The critical discourse that focused on personal moral corruption singled out certain "duplicitous" Komsomol members as the central problem.

[3] With this conclusion in mind, from the late 1960s, Soviet sociology of youth began serious studies of "deviant behavior" (*deviantnoe povedenie*), which was seen as a growing problem among the youth. See Ikonnikova and Lisovskii (1969), Lisovskii et al. (1978).

These individuals, it was claimed, hid their true inclinations as fans of bourgeois Western values and commodities behind the mask of devoted communists. It was such immoral individuals who were at the root of the problem, went the critique. By locating the dangers of bourgeois culture within the duplicitous psychology of such individuals, this discourse misrepresented "the problem" in the same way as did earlier critical campaigns (such as those discussed in chapter 5). It did not recognize the fact that Western cultural influences in the Soviet context were enabled by the contradictions of the state's cultural policy, that they were part and parcel of socialist realities, and that "bourgeois" aesthetics could acquire specific meanings in the Soviet context and did not necessarily have to contradict the values and realities of socialism. The critique read the symbols of bourgeois mass culture literally, failing to consider the complex translation and appropriation of that culture by Soviet youth in ways that were substantially different from that literal reading.

An example of this critical misreading is a poster published in the mid-1980s by the Komsomol to be posted in colleges and in offices. It read: "The opportunist changes faces—expose him!" (figure 6.1).[4] The light-colored square (red in the original) represents the context of authoritative discourse within which the person wears the mask of a good Komsomol secretary: he is passionately addressing the audience; he is dressed in a formal Komsomol suit, with a Komsomol badge on the left lapel; his pose is upright and confident, and his speech is peppered with the Communist phraseology represented by the names of "heroic" construction projects—*BAM, VAZ, Urengoi, KAMAZ, Katek*[5]—political campaigns—*glasnost', khozraschet, kooperativ*[6]—and scientific achievements—EVM, GES.[7]

Outside authoritative discourse, in the black frame that surrounds the box, this opportunist is revealing his "true face" as a materialistic bourgeois sympathizer, reminiscent of the images we saw in the cartoons in chapter 5. He is wearing American jeans, with an image of the American flag sewn above his right knee. He is also wearing Western-style sneakers and is standing in a relaxed, "unprincipled" pose with his legs crossed. This dark space is filled with bourgeois discourse represented by foreign names of Western commodities and brands written in the Latin script, as opposed to the Cyrillic script in the red square.

[4] *Prisposoblenets meniaet lichinu—razoblachi!*

[5] Komsomol participated in the construction of Baikal-Amur Railroad (BAM), the Volga Automobile Plant (VAZ), Kama Automobile Factory (KAMAZ), the Kansko-Achinsk Fuel and Energy Complex (KATEK), and gas pipeline in northwest of Siberia (Urengoi).

[6] Communist party political campaigns meaning openness, industrial self-accountability, and cooperatives, respectively.

[7] Computers (EVM) and hydropower stations (GES).

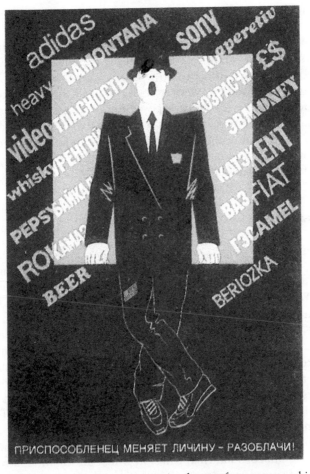

FIGURE 6.1. Political poster. The opportunist changes faces—expose him! A. Utkin.

This bourgeois discourse literally underlies the Soviet one, presenting its "true" hidden nature; the words in the red square morph into the words in the black square: *BAM* turns into *Montana* (a brand of Western jeans popular among the Soviet youth), *Kooperativ* turns into *aperitiv* (a Western drink), *EVM* becomes *money*, *GES* becomes *Camel*, *VAZ* becomes *FIAT*, *Urengoi* becomes *whisky*, and so on. Bourgeois symbols also include Pepsi, beer, Adidas, video, Kent, Sony, heavy (for heavy metal), dollar and pound sterling signs (archetypal signifiers of capitalism), and Beriozka (a Soviet chain of stores selling Western goods to Western tourists for hard currency). The poster's

211

message is clear: this Komsomol activist is an immoral opportunist who wears the public mask of a good communist, behind which he hides his corrupt bourgeois face. This representation is clearly a departure from the representations of cultural deviationists, such as *stilyagi*, who were portrayed as having nothing to do with Komsomol activism.

Contrary to the message, Western rock and other forms of "bourgeois" culture were neither necessarily opposed to nor necessarily divided from the dominant socialist culture but were thoroughly integrated into it. How this integration went on at the level of the most active and idealistic participants in the communist project is particularly revealing for our investigation of late socialism.

Approximate List

In the beginning of the perestroika reforms, the Komsomol leadership admitted its failure to curb the bourgeois cultural influences among the Soviet youth and tried to propose new measures to solve this problem. The journal *Young Communist* (Molodoi Kommunist), published for local Komsomol leadership and activists, wrote that the organization had not recognized how widespread the circulation of the tape-recorded music was around the country. This phenomenon, the article pointed out, contributed to the emergence of a nationwide subculture that shared interests, practices, and information, while remaining almost completely misunderstood by the Komsomol leadership that was supposed to organize and lead youth culture in the country. The article wrote: "Today we do not know the real scale on which taped music is distributed. The current exchange of tapes is very intensive and widespread. There have emerged spontaneous informal clubs, in which information, advertising, and exchange unite young workers and students of colleges and schools" (Makarevich 1987, 21).[8] The informal links in the communities of rock fans had become so well developed, argued the article, that there had even emerged well-informed independent journals written on typewriters (such as *Ukho* [Ear], *Roksi*, and *Kot* [Cat]). They published "amateur" journalists who wrote about tape-recorded music and provided translations from Western music media and information about local bands. These journals were copied again and again by retyping and rephotographing (photocopying equipment was strictly controlled by the state and usually unavailable), and these copies, like taped music, circulated throughout the country. The *Young Communist* urged the leadership to improve control over the national spread of taped rock music: "We must

[8] No relation to the songwriter Andrei Makarevich cited in chapter 5.

212

foresee things long in advance. Let us not repeat our mistakes" (Makarevich 1987).

Having admitted its failure to curb the spread of Western music, the Komsomol nevertheless did not analyze why it was so popular and what it meant in the lives of Soviet youth. Instead, it continued insisting that this music should be interpreted at the constative level of discourse—that is, as a literal manifestation of "bourgeois values" among naïve or morally corrupt groups of youth. Principles of authoritative discourse determined this lack of flexibility in the critical rhetoric. The only rhetoric the Komsomol authors had at their disposal was one in the authoritative genre—that is, as we saw in chapter 2, Komsomol speech was constrained by the rhetorical circularity of that discourse. To solve the problem local Komsomol bosses needed to apply more vigorously the kind of measures that had already failed in the past. The rhetorical possibilities of that discourse could change only if the whole discursive regime of socialism experienced a rupture, breaking out of the circularity. This rupture did eventually occur in the late 1980s, quickly undermining the socialist system beyond repair.

Before then, however, the attempts by the Komsomol to curb the spread of Western rock music within the same discursive parameters included sending Central Committee instructions, in the early 1980s, to the local city committees and raikoms of Komsomol, requiring them to intensify control over the repertoires of the discotheques in their regions. One such directive, entitled "The approximate list of foreign musical groups and artists, whose repertoires contain ideologically harmful compositions,"[9] was sent in January 1985 by the *Obkom* (regional committee) of the Nikolayev region in Ukraine to city and district committees in that region (see figures 6.2 and 6.3). The document, like other instructions sent to local Komsomol raikoms from superiors, was marked "for internal use only" (*dlia sluzhebnogo pol'zovaniia*), making this discourse invisible to the general public. Indeed, the very fact that the Komsomol issued such instructions was generally unknown until the 1990s. The document identified thirty-eight problematic Western bands and pop artists whose music circulated among the Soviet youth in tape-recorded forms.

The list described a concrete ideological problem associated with each band and artist. However, in a familiar paradox of Soviet cultural policy, with its attempts to do two things at once—allow cultural innovation and creativity but contain their unwanted results (see chapter 5)—the list

---

[9] *"Primernyi perechen' zarubezhnykh muzykal'nykh grup i ispolnitelei, v repertuare kotorykh soderzhatsia ideino vrednye proizvedeniia."* Reprinted in *Novaia gazeta*, no. 45, July 26, 2003.

Приложение к письму
от 10 января 1985 года

Пролетарии всех стран, соединяйтесь!
**ВСЕСОЮЗНЫЙ ЛЕНИНСКИЙ КОМ-
МУНИСТИЧЕСКИЙ СОЮЗ МОЛОДЕ-
ЖИ
НИКОЛАЕВСКИЙ ОБЛАСТНОЙ КО-
МИТЕТ ЛКСМ УКРАИНЫ**

Примерный перечень зарубежных музыкальных групп и исполнителей, в репертуаре которых содержатся идейно вредные произведения

Название коллектива   Что пропагандирует

Для служебного пользования
Секретарям ГК, РК ЛКСМ Украины

Направляем примерный перечень зарубежных музыкальных групп и исполнителей, в репертуаре которых содержатся идейно вредные произведения, а также список тарифицированных вокально-инструментальных ансамблей СССР.

Рекомендуем использовать эти сведения для усиления контроля за деятельностью дискотек.

Данной информацией необходимо обеспечить все ВИА и молодежные дискотеки района.

Секретарь обкома
комсомола   П. Гришин

№	Название	Что пропагандирует
1.	Секс Пистолз	панк, насилие
2.	Б-52	панк, насилие
3.	Меднесс	панк, насилие
4.	КЛЭШ	панк, насилие
5.	Стрэнглэрс	панк, насилие
6.	Кисс	неофашизм, панк, насилие
7.	Крокус	насилие, культ сильной личности
8.	Стикс	насилие, вандализм
9.	Айрон Мейден	насилие, религиозное мракобесие
10.	Джудас Прист	антикоммунизм, расизм
11.	Ай Си Ди Си	неофашизм, насилие
12.	Спаркс Спаркс	неофашизм, расизм
13.	Блек Сабат	насилие, религиозное мракобесие
14.	Элис Купер	насилие, вандализм
15.	Назарет	насилие, религиозный мистицизм, садизм
16.	Скорпион	насилие
17.	Чингиз Хан	антикоммунизм, национализм
18.	Уфо	насилие
19.	Пинк Флойд (1983)	извращение внешней политики СССР («Агрессия СССР в Афганистане»)
20.	Толкинхедз	миф о советской военной угрозе
21.	Перрон	эротизм
22.	Боханнон	эротизм
23.	Ориннджинелз	секс
24.	Донна Саммер	эротизм
25.	Тина Тернер	секс
26.	Джаниор Энглиш (Регги)	секс
27.	Кенед Хит	гомосексуализм
28.	Манич Мешин	эротизм
29.	Рамонэ	панк
30.	Бан Хейлен	антисоветская пропаганда
31.	Хулио Иглесиос	неофашизм
32.	Язоо	панк, насилие
33.	Данич Мод	панк, насилие
34.	Вилидж Пипл	насилие
35.	Тен Си Си (10сс)	неофашизм
36.	Стоджис	насилие
37.	Бойз	панк, насилие
38.	Блонди	панк, насилие

«ВЕРНО»
зав. общим отделом
обкома комсомола   Е. Пряжинская

FIGURE 6.2. The approximate list of foreign musical groups and artists whose repertoires contain ideologically harmful compositions (1985). From *Novaia Gazeta*, July 26, 2003.

APPROVED COPY	Approximate list of foreign music groups and artists whose repertoires contain ideologically harmful compositions	
Workers of the world unite! ALL-UNION LENIN COMMUNIST UNION OF YOUTH NIKOLAYEV REGIONAL COMMITTEE OF KOMSOMOL OF UKRAINE	**Group Name**	**Type of Propaganda**
For internal use only	1. Sex Pistols	punk, violence
	2. B-52s	punk, violence
To Secretaries of Gorkoms and Raikoms of Komsomol of Ukraine	3. Madness	punk, violence
	4. Clash	punk, violence
The following is an approximate list of foreign music groups and artists whose repertoires contain ideologically harmful compositions.	5. Stranglers	punk, violence
	6. Kiss	neofascism, punk, violence
	7. Crocus	violence, cult of strong personality
This information is recommended for the purpose of intensifying control over the activities of discotheques.	8. Styx	violence, vandalism
	9. Iron Maiden	violence, religious obscurantism
This information must be also provided to all VIA [vocal instrument ensembles] and youth discotheques in the region.	10. Judas Priest	anticommunism, racism
	11. AC/DC	neofascism, violence
Secretary of the Obkom of Komsomol, P. Grishin	12. Sparks	neofascism, racism

13. Black Sabbath	violence, religious obscurantism	23. Originals	sex
14. Alice Cooper	violence, vandalism	24. Donna Summer	eroticism
15. Nazareth	violence, religious mysticism	25. Tina Turner	sex
		26. Junior English (reggae)	sex
16. Scorpions	violence	27. Canned Heat	homosexuality
17. Gengis Khan	anticommunism, nationalism	28. Munich Machine	eroticism
		29. Ramones	punk
18. UFO	violence	30. Van Halen	anti-Soviet propaganda
19. Pink Floyd (1983)	distortion of Soviet foreign policy ("Soviet aggression in Afghanistan)	31. Julio Iglesias	neofascism
		32. Yazoo	punk, violence
		33. Depeche Mode	punk, violence
		34. Village People	violence
20. Talking Heads	myth of the Soviet military threat	35. Ten CC (10 cc)	neofascism
		36. Stooges	violence
21. Perron	eroticism	37. Boys	punk, violence
22. Bohannon	eroticism	38. Blondie	punk, violence

"APPROVED BY"
Head of the General Department of the Obkom of Komsomol E. Priazhinskaia

FIGURE 6.3. The Approximate List. Author's translation of figure 6.2.

215

made control over the repertoire of the discotheques not only highly in-
effective but also circular. The measures it proposed to curb the spread of
Western music helped to create the conditions that enabled its further
expansion. The very fact that there was a limited list of foreign names implied that only some Western bands were problematic, while others, including dozens of bands that were not listed but whose music circulated
in tape-recorded copies, were not. Furthermore, the fact that the "harmful ideas" associated with Western music were described in very narrow
and precise terms simultaneously suggested to Komsomol activists that
the Western music that did not seem to represent these ideas was ideologically acceptable.

Each band on the list was associated with one or two of the following
harmful ideas: punk, violence, vandalism, eroticism, religious obscuran-
tism, religious mysticism, racism, neofascism, cult of strong personality,
sex, homosexuality, nationalism, anticommunism, anti-Soviet propaganda,
and the myth about the Soviet military threat. The list also makes clear
that specialists in the Central Committee of the Komsomol followed, at
least sporadically, the lyrics of some Western bands. One album (marked
simply "1983") by the British band Pink Floyd was characterized as a "distortion of Soviet foreign policy"—that is, it allegedly misrepresented the
Soviet involvement in Afghanistan as "Soviet aggression in Afghanistan."

Pink Floyd's 1983 album *The Final Cut* indeed contained a song entitled "Get Your Filthy Hands off My Desert" with the following lyrics:

Brezhnev took Afghanistan.
Begin took Beirut.
Galtieri took the Union Jack.
And Maggie, over lunch one day,
Took a cruiser with all hands.
Apparently, to make him give it back.[10]

The album was deemed "ideologically harmful" because of the short reference, "Brezhnev took Afghanistan," that suggested occupation and aggression, and the parallel that the song drew between this and the other
wars, which the Soviet media characterized as "imperialist." This focused criticism of a concrete album and a concrete harmful idea reflects
once again the paradox of cultural policy. First, it implies that Pink
Floyd's other albums were perfectly acceptable (in fact, in 1980 and

---

[10] References are made to the following wars: Soviet war in Afganistan, that started in
1979 under Leonid Brezhnev; Israeli war in Lebanon that started in 1982 under Men-
achem Begin; the Falkland War between Argentina and Britain, which took place in 1982,
after Argentine President Leopoldo Galtieri occupied the Falkland Islands, claimed by
Britain as its sovereign territory, and the British prime minister Margaret Thatcher sent the
British Navy to repel them.

216

1981, the Soviet monthly "music magazine" *Krugozor* published an article about Pink Floyd and released several of their earlier songs[11]). Second, it took the meaning of the song literally, while in practice such texts were not read literally by the majority of Soviet youth, who usually neither recognized nor cared about the exact foreign lyrics.

Komsomol Heteroglossia

Andrei, the Komsomol secretary whom we first encountered in chapter 3, like thousands of his contemporaries, became interested in Anglo-American rock music as a schoolboy in the late 1960s. His early passion for that music is captured well by a picture of his fantasy band, which he drew in 1968 at the age of 15, giving it an English name, "The Boys from a Morgue" (figure 6.4). Andrei became a student at a Leningrad college, studying geology. In college he met more music collectors and musicians from "amateur" bands, began actively exchanging tapes of Western bands, and learned much more about music. He explains: "We had a real music *tusovka* [milieu, subculture]. . . . This was the time of Led Zeppelin. Fantastic stuff!! Deep Purple were just starting. The Animals. Luckily we were there for the real musical beginnings!" At college Andrei also became involved in organizing student "recreational evenings" (*vechera otdykha*) and dances that were conducted under the auspices of the Komsomol committee. The committee was required to fulfill a plan for organizing cultural activities among the youth, and Andrei's musical connections came in handy. According to Andrei, the Komsomol committee "learned that I had a circle of friends that included musicians and music collectors and happily handed over to me the responsibility for the music at these events."[12]

Andrei also met organizers of musical events from other colleges who helped with contacts. He started inviting "amateur" rock bands, such as Argonafty (Argonauts) and Zemlyane (Earthlings),[13] to play at his college events. Through the Komsomol channels he also helped them get

[11] In 1980, *Krugozor* included two "flexi-discs" with the songs "Time," "On the Run," and "Money" (from the album *The Dark Side of the Moon*, 1973). In 1981, it released two songs, "Another Brick in the Wall (Part 1)" and "The Trial" (from the album *The Wall*, 1979). All these songs could be described as perfectly antibourgeois, which made them appropriate for the release. Each issue of *Krugozor* contained texts and interviews about international music of different genres and several tear-off flexi-discs with examples of that music. For a discussion of *Krugozor* see McMichael (2005a; 2005b).

[12] Cf. the relationship between organizers of jazz concerts and the Komsomol committees in the 1950s in chapter 5.

[13] Both bands were among the first popular Leningrad bands. By the early 1970s, many amateur bands had Russian names and sang in Russian.

1968.

FIGURE 6.4. Andrei's drawing of his imaginary rock band, The Boys from a Morgue (1968).

invited to the festival of amateur music in Estonia. The amateur status of these bands allowed them to include in their repertoire the kind of music that professional musicians would not be able to perform at state-run concerts. Furthermore, Andrei's affiliation with the Komsomol committee, and the communist themes of his recreational events—most coincided with the celebrations of such anniversaries as Revolution Day, May Day, Victory Day, and the Day of Soviet Geologists—made it less likely that the repertoire of his concerts would be subjected to intense scrutiny by the Komsomol or by party bosses. Andrei was also actively involved in other aspects of the Komsomol work of the committee. As we saw in chapter 3, he was a devoted Komsomol member and felt passionate about communist ideals.

After graduating from college Andrei took the job of geological scientist at a Leningrad research institute and quickly joined the institute's Komsomol committee. One of the reasons for joining was again his desire to continue organizing rock concerts and youth dances: a leading position in the Komsomol helped with both ideological and material support (from providing the necessary Komsomol context for these events, to giving him access to funds, equipment, concert halls, transportation, etc.). Another reason for joining the committee was Andrei's

desire to participate in various other Komsomol activities, organize social campaigns, solve social problems, and so forth. Clearly, for Andrei it
did not seem contradictory to be passionate about both Lenin and Led
Zeppelin.

As we saw in chapter 3, when the secretary of the institute's Komsomol committee, Sasha, left that position, Andrei was elected to replace
him. In November 1982 Andrei had to deliver his first speech as the new
secretary in front of a large meeting of the rank-and-file members. Parts
of that speech were analyzed in chapter 3; here, I look at another, which
is relevant to our current discussion about the spread of bourgeois
cultural influences among the Soviet youth. Reacting to the party campaigns against the growing influence of bourgeois culture Andrei declared:

> One of the most important directions in the work of the Komsomol is
> political-ideological education of young people. The formation of the
> Marxist-Leninist worldview, an *uncompromising attitude toward bour-*
> *geois ideology and morality*, the education of young men and women in
> the spirit of Soviet patriotism and socialist internationalism—these are
> the primary tasks facing the ideological leadership of our Komsomol
> organization.[14]

The emphasized phrase in this quote is directly linked to the critical texts
that were considered earlier. Compare this phrase, for example, with a
phrase in the 1981 article in the newspaper *Komsomolskaia Pravda*,
quoted above, which attacked Western bourgeois music. That article used
similar authoritative phraseology to argue that contemporary Western
rock stars lacked "an uncompromising attitude [*nepremirimoe otnoshenie*]
toward the vices of the bourgeois world." As we saw, this rhetoric was also
widespread in other texts in the media, party documents, and sociological
studies during the late 1970s and early 1980s, and Andrei was clearly very
familiar with it.[15] In his speech, Andrei declared that achieving the "uncompromising attitude toward bourgeois ideology and morality" must be
one of "the central tasks" of his Komsomol committee—that is, his committee had to fight all manifestations of the "bourgeois ideology and
morality," which, according to the critical discourse in the media, included
the growing influences of Western rock music.

---

[14] "*Odnim iz vazhneishikh napravlenii raboty komsomola iavliaetsia ideino-politicheskoe
vospitanie molodezhi. Formirovanie marksistsko-leninskogo mirovozzreniia*, neprimirimogo
otnosheniia [genitive case] k burzhuaznoi ideologii i morali, *vospitanie iunoshei i devushek v
dukhe sovetskogo patriotizma i sotsialisticheskogo internatsionalizma—vot perveishie
zadachi stoiashchie pered ideologicheskim aktivom nashei komsomol'skoi organizatsii.*" Emphasis added here and in main text.

[15] See other examples with such statements from different sources in chapter 2 (esp.
figure 2.1, paragraph 9).

At the same time, the young people in the audience whom Andrei addressed at the meeting were the same people who attended the "recreational events" and dances that he organized, and to whom he played the recordings of Western rock bands from his collection. Among this audience Andrei had a reputation as a rock music connoisseur. At his recreational evenings he personally announced Western bands and songs in the microphone and often provided detailed information about groups and styles that he learned from foreign music publications circulating among collectors. In 1982, around the time of his speech, Andrei borrowed from a friend an issue of the British magazine *New Musical Express*, which had been brought by a sailor from Western Europe. Andrei painstakingly translated a four-page article from the magazine about the German heavy metal band the Scorpions, typing it up on the Komsomol committee typewriter. In the internal Komsomol documents about "ideologically harmful" groups, such as the one shown in figures 6.2 and 6.3, the Scorpions were blacklisted.[16] Andrei clearly did not share the views that the Scorpions or similar bands were ideologically harmful. At his dances Andrei read excerpts from his translated article, which included the following passage about the problems of the group's guitarist Michael Schenker: "Now Michael's drug addiction became truly 'heavy.' . . . He mixed pills and cocaine with alcohol." Before turning on the recording, Andrei explains, he will end his address by quoting the article's cheerful appeal to the fans: "So, what keeps Michael alive? Of course, the same as you and me—heavy metal!"

As we saw earlier in chapter 3, for many Komsomol secretaries the ethics and aesthetics of the everyday life of socialism were not necessarily reduced to the literal meanings of rules and instructions sent from the higher Komsomol bodies. These secretaries had no problem treating some ideological assignments as "pure formality," knowing that this allowed them to pursue various forms of work "with meaning" with interest and conviction. For Andrei, organizing concerts and dances to rock music, and other aesthetically interesting and creative cultural activities, was part of that work "with meaning."

On the one hand, Andrei seems to fit perfectly the critical portrait of the young as naïve and uncritical, as depicted by the two sociologists mentioned at the beginning of the chapter. Like the young people they described, Andrei did not find it relevant to make a connection between Western music and the politics of anticommunism. On the other hand, however, he was not naïve or apolitical, actively participating in the

---

[16] The list in figures 6.2 and 6.3 was dated 1985, three years after Andrei's translation of the Scorpions article. However, similar campaigns against this and other bands on the list had been ongoing throughout the 1970s and early 1980s.

Komsomol work at school, college, and at the research institute. Nor was he a pure opportunist who, according to the poster described above, wore the mask of a Komsomol activist for instrumentalist and careerist reasons. Andrei decided to become the Komsomol secretary because of his convictions. He later joined the Communist Party and always thought of himself as a good communist. Indeed, a few years later, during perestroika (in the late 1980s), it was very difficult for Andrei to reconcile himself with the new critical discourse that targeted Communist ideals and the authority of Lenin. He describes the gradual loss of ideals of that period as his "personal tragedy."

The discursive formation of late socialism in which the Imaginary West became shaped and circulated, as described in the previous chapter, consisted of diverse statements and pronouncements, many of which were inconsistent with each other and even contradictory. Andrei's discourses also reflected this complex coexistence of messages. His critical speeches as the Komsomol secretary, his excited translations of the articles about Western rock bands, and his announcements at the musical events represented the rich heteroglossia[17] in which Andrei's generation lived in the late 1970s and early 1980s. At the level of the static constative dimension of discourse these diverse messages might seem to contradict each other. However, Andrei treated many of the critical pronouncements about bourgeois culture as purely performative ritualized forms of authoritative discourse whose original constative meaning were irrelevant and whose performative reproduction enabled other important activities, meanings, and experimental aesthetics to emerge.

The authoritative texts in the repertoire of Andrei's pronouncements were written according to the "generative" principles of authoritative discourse. For example, all of the texts contained similar phraseological blocks, such as "uncompromising attitude," "bourgeois morality," "the spirit of Soviet patriotism and socialist internationalism," and "ideologically harmful." The circular rhetorical structure of these texts and the ritualized contexts in which they circulated (Komsomol meetings, Central Committee instructions, propaganda posters, front-page articles in newspapers) made them recognizable to Andrei and his young audiences as unmistakable examples of authoritative discourse, allowing them to interpret these texts not simply as literal statements about reality but as performative acts that enabled new, important, interesting, and experimental meanings, activities, and pursuits. This does not mean that authoritative texts were completely empty of meaning. Rather, this dynamic allowed Andrei and his audiences to accept some critique of bourgeois popular culture as meaningful and accurate (e.g., that capitalism tended to

---

[17] Bakhtin (1994).

commodify art or that the capitalist state led imperialist and neocolonial wars), while reading other critical claims about that culture as "pure formality" (e.g., that the aesthetics of Western rock music was flawed, evil, and anti-Soviet).

This is why Andrei's seemingly contradictory discourses cannot be seen as simply an indication of his duplicity. Indeed, as Andrei himself commented later, both types of texts—his antibourgeois speeches and his translations of the articles about Western bands—were equally important to him in the early 1980s because they represented crucial interests and ideals, and his active, creative, and responsible engagement in the social life of those years. He kept both texts in the same folder marked "1982" among documents and pictures in his private archive.

Moreover, for Andrei and his audiences the music and other information about Western rock bands constituted not a "real" distant foreign world but a world of the Imaginary West that existed locally and that they actively authored themselves. This is why Andrei's fascination with the stories of the drug addictions of Western rock stars did not preclude him from launching vigorous campaigns against the heavy drinking among Komsomol members of his institute. Similarly, despite Andrei's active promotion of the "ideologically harmful" music, the Komsomol raikom of his district recognized him as an outstanding secretary, who initiated interesting and creative Komsomol work, and awarded his committee with the honorary diploma "for active work in the communist education of youth."

Letters from Siberia

We have considered how the symbols and objects of the Imaginary West emerged and circulated among younger generations between the 1950s and the early 1980s. However, it remains to be seen how members of that generation explicitly reflected on and discussed the relation between Western cultural influences and Communist values in their lives. The discussion that follows will show that the culture of late Soviet society, with its ubiquitous references to the communist future, was in fact perfectly compatible with the aesthetic of some forms of rock and jazz music, with its focus on experimental sounds, improvisation, and its readiness to break with all canons. The improvisational, sound-centered and non-verbal character of this music (the lyrics of most Western bands, as mentioned in chapter 5, were neither understood nor important in that context) was particularly well suited for the creative production of meaningful life. This meaningful life could be located in the imaginary worlds and in the worlds of *vnye*, as described in chapters 4 and 5, but it could also be located in the future, including the communist future, as the discussion below demonstrates. In this way, the most non-Soviet sounds of hard rock Western bands of the 1970s became peculiarly compatible, for some Soviet youths, with the ideals of the Communist project. This aesthetic allowed even the most devoted young Soviet communists to articulate a more cosmopolitan and creative interpretation of the communist ideals than those offered by the authoritative rhetoric of the party.

A glimpse into this creative process of reflection and reinterpretation can be found in the conversations among friends of that generation recorded in their personal correspondences. The following are excerpts from the letters written in the mid-1970s by Alexandr (born in 1959), at first from the remote town of Yakutsk in northern Siberia, four and a half thousand miles east of Moscow, and later from Novosibirsk, to his friend Nikolai (born in 1959) who lived in Leningrad. We have met both earlier (in chapter 5). Alexandr and Nikolai had been school friends in Yakutsk for several years until in 1974, at age 15, Nikolai moved with his parents to Leningrad. In 1976, Alexandr finished school and also moved from Yakutsk to Novosibirsk, to study mathematics at Novosibirsk University. Between 1974 and 1978 the friends corresponded regularly. In their letters they discussed a broad variety of topics: Communism, philosophy, art, mathematics, science, poetry, Western rock music, friendship, morality, love, and so on.[18]

Komsomol Secretary

Alexandr's father was a factory mechanic and his mother a medical doctor. He grew up feeling strongly about communist ideals and values and often reflected upon them in his letters. Some of his more passionate pronouncements may sound atypical of his generation, most members of which would feel awkward using such language, especially with friends. Perhaps, growing up in a relatively remote provincial town, Alexandr was less likely to encounter the actively detached attitude to socialist realities sometimes encountered in larger urban centers (as we saw in chapter 4). At the same time, he certainly was not an "activist" who repeated party

---

[18] The letters are quoted with the authors' permission. The discussion below is limited to the letters written by Alexandr and a few prominent themes to which he regularly returned. To stress the continuity of these themes the letters are not always quoted chronologically. This makes it easier to consider them as elements of one coherent discourse, which is particularly important since Alexandr wrote nineteen letters in a relatively short period of time, between 1975 and 1978, and received as many from Nikolai—that is, for three and a half years the friends were writing on average one letter a month.

223

rhetoric without ever doubting it or arguing with it. In fact, Alexandr considered himself a principled and independent-minded person, and he often disagreed with the opinions of party bureaucrats and articles in the Soviet press. In school and at the university Alexandr consistently volunteered for lead positions in the Komsomol and was always active in various political initiatives. During the same years he was also an active fan of Western bands, bought and sold records through unauthorized ("black market") channels, and became a connoisseur of Western rock. What makes Alexandr's example particularly interesting is not only his equally passionate dedication to communism and Western rock, but his explicit contemplation of how to relate them to each other.

Alexandr joined the Komsomol in 1973 in his Yakutsk school and quickly became engaged in its activities. In the ninth grade he was re-elected to the post of the school's Komsomol secretary and proudly wrote to Nikolai on April 25, 1975:

> I have been elected the secretary of the Komsomol committee of the school [number omitted] for the second term. I've now plunged and engrossed myself [v"elsia i vgryzsia] in the Komsomol work. I run around, demand, convince, compile, regulate, reprimand, organize, and so on and so forth. In short, I have sunk up to my head in work.

Komsomol and ideological activities were a recurrent topic in the friends' discussions, and they sometimes disagreed on their importance. When Nikolai responded to Alexandr's letter with a remark that in his school the Komosomol rituals amounted to nothing but a senseless tedium, Alexandr responded, on May 13, 1975: "You write, I'm quoting, 'these [Komsomol] meetings are only a waste of time.' But doesn't the Komsomol life of your school depend on the ordinary members? Go to the committee meeting and tell them that the Komsomol work conducted in your school is not interesting, but tedious and compulsory [obiazalovka]."

Like the Komsomol secretary Andrei, Alexandr was convinced that the Komsomol work, despite all its pro forma and senseless rituals, could also involve important "work with meaning" and that one's active and moral position could overturn the usual tedium of authoritative rituals. This conviction sharply distinguished him from such people as Inna and her friends (from chapter 3), who insisted on living *vnye* and tried to avoid the Komsomol altogether, refusing even to contemplate whether the Komsomol had any meaning. For Alexandr, being a Komsomol member meant being actively engaged in Komsomol activities. Moreover, an honest position, in his opinion, had to be critical. In the same letter he wrote: "As for those Komsomol members who only bear that name [i.e., who are Komsomol members nominally, but in fact are uninvolved in it]—I hate them more than anyone else."

224

The following year the friends returned to discussing the distinction between communist ideals and the practice of ideological routine they encountered in school. On August 15, 1976, Alexandr justified his decision to be active in the Komsomol by stressing his general devotion to the communist idea and to the goal of achieving it in practice, against all odds:

> I believe in communism, and my belief is unshakable. It is so enormous that there would be enough for several more people. But this is not brainless, not blind faith. I do not like very loud words, but will say one thing: the building of communism is the task of my life. However, to be able to build it one must know it, and know not only theory, but how to put theory to life. This is why I joined the Komsomol, this is why I cherish [*dlia menia dorogo*] everything connected with it.

Apart from his activities as the school's Komsomol secretary, Alexandr pursued an extremely diverse array of interests and achieved success in most of these pursuits. He excelled in sciences and humanities; in fact, he was so good in math that he was chosen for the city's highly selective mathematics team to participate in the math Olympics among high school teams from the cities and towns of the Republic of Yakutia. He wrote about his successes on April 5, 1975: "In the math Olympics I took fourth place among both specialized schools of math and physics and regular schools.[19] Our city team won first place in all three Olympics [at the Yakutia Republic level], which had almost never happened before." Apart from math, Alexandr also read a lot of literature, experimented with writing poetry, hoping one day to get published,[20] and spent much time perfecting his English. In the next letter, on April 25, 1975, he wrote: "Recently we had the English language Olympics among city schools. I participated at the tenth-grade level[21] . . . and won first place in two subjects and second place in the third subject. I won first place overall."

In the summer of 1976, Alexandr was admitted to the mathematics department of Novosibirsk University and moved to Novosibirsk. In the meantime, his Leningrad friend Nikolai failed his entrance exams to Leningrad University and was planning to spend the following year

---

[19] Specialized "physics and mathematics" high schools taught a much more advanced curriculum in these sciences than regular high schools. Alexandr studied in a regular school, but he also attended an after-school math club at his school and was clearly good enough to compete against the best students from specialized schools.

[20] A few years later a selection of his poems was published in a popular Novosibirsk literary journal.

[21] Equivalent to high school seniors; at that time Alexandr was in the ninth grade (equivalent to a high school junior).

preparing to take them again the next summer. The friends discussed how best to structure Nikolai's preparations for the exams; on December 4, 1976, Alexandr sent him an outline, suggesting a list of books in linear algebra, differential calculus, physics, literature, and philosophy, and what questions to think about:

> Every day, except Sunday, work for eight hours. Distribute them as follows:
> First, four hours of math [list of books] . . .
> Then two hours of physics [list of books] . . .
> Then two hours of philosophy and literature. Read the following:
>   Lenin "Materialism and Empirio-Criticism"
>   The philosophy of ancient Greeks (Socrates, Diophantos and others)
>   Hegel and Feuerbach
>   Of course, Marx and Engels—anything that interests you.
> Don't be afraid to ask questions that are considered politically problematic. Of course, ask them to yourself [*zadavai ikh naedine*] and try to answer them. For example, try thinking why Marx is right and Western ideologues are wrong. Or is it the other way around?
> By the way, here is a question worth discussing: What is art and what is its purpose?

Alexandr's extensive list in different subjects and his emphasis not only on the philosophical and political economic works of Marx, Engels, and Lenin, but also ancient Greeks and German idealists reflected his affinity to the Soviet ideal of a well-educated and critically thinking person. Furthermore, although he was convinced of the ultimate correctness of the communist idea, in his opinion one had to arrive at this conviction through reading and critical questioning not simple repetition of the party line. At the same time, he warned Nikolai against doing this critical questioning too openly. Alexandr seemed perfectly aware of how Soviet authoritative discourse worked, and, like many of his contemporaries mentioned in the previous chapters, he distinguished between the formulaic authoritative rituals one was expected to repeat and the meaning of the ideals that, he believed, one also had to have. For Alexandr, repeating formulaic structures of authoritative discourse and engaging in critical reflection on the meaning of communist ideas were two distinct activities that were not in contradiction because the former enabled the latter. A moral and thinking person had to be able to do both. This was a departure from the position of a proverbial activist who repeated the party pronouncements verbatim and did not engage in their critical assessment.

The last question in the letter—what is art and what is its purpose?—reflected Alexandr's interest in the relationship between aesthetics, critical thinking, and communist ideals. As we will see, the convergence of these themes was directly linked with how Alexandr and many of his peers interpreted the growing importance of Western rock music in their lives in relation to the values and realities of the Soviet society in which they lived.

Critical Reading of Rock

Alexandr and Nikolai, like many of their friends, started collecting recordings of Western rock bands in middle school in the early 1970s. The friends often discussed rock music in their letters. Alexandr's relationship to that cultural form was complex and full of paradoxes. He was not only a passive listener of rock music, but he was also interested in how it "worked" on aesthetic and psychological levels, how it affected its listeners, and, as a result of that, what its place was in the future society.

As discussed in chapter 5, the paradoxes of Soviet cultural policy translated into an ambivalent relationship of the state to Western music. Different examples of that music were celebrated in the media as examples of internationalism or common people's culture (jazz, blues), but at the same time they were attacked for flawed bourgeois aesthetics, lack of realism, unharmonious and unmelodious sound, violation of "the balance of mental and physiological functions," and for being "music-drug, music-sleeping-pill, music-deceit." In the 1970s a whole series of critical articles in the youth press drew on a similar rhetoric to describe the insidious effects of low frequencies, loud volumes, and distorted sounds of Western rock bands on the human psyche. As we saw in chapter 5, the state rhetoric opposed the "wild sounds, convulsive rhythms, and repulsive moaning" of bourgeois rock and roll to good "genuine light music [that is] joyful, gracious, and melodic [and includes] playing beautiful folk tunes."[22] It was precisely this relationship between the sounds, distortion, convulsive rhythm, moaning, low frequency, and other aural characteristics of new Western rock and their impact on the psychology and physiology that interested Alexandr. Drawing on the language of these critical accounts, however, he completely reinterpreted the meaning of the effects they described. For Alexandr the emotional and psychic effect of rock music on its listeners was not a problem but a potential strength of this musical genre. It opened up possibilities for experimenting with new futurist aesthetics that went beyond the primitive realism of

[22] P. Kantor, "O legkoi muzyke" [On Light Music], daily tear-off calendar, October 30, 1961, quoted in *Ptiuch*, December 1998, 21.

227

pleasing light tunes. On August 13, 1975, he wrote, explicitly drawing on the authoritative discourse of the Soviet media's critique:

> I love rock and roll. Yes, this is a musical drug [*muzykal'nyi narkotik*], and its aftereffects are usually not obvious (although sometimes not so harmless). The thing is that, as you know, modern bands cannot avoid using amplifiers, and often the sounds of the bass guitar cross the limit of the frequency that we are able to hear (the lower limit) producing the so-called infra-sounds, that definitely influence our psyche. The lower the sound, the stronger the effect. Very low frequency sounds subdue us and can even kill, although rock and roll never goes that far.

Soviet authoritative discourse drew heavily on scientific references; in this case, references to physical processes (infrasonic, frequency limit) and psychological effects (influence on the psyche, subduing effect) were meant to be a criticism. Instead of achieving its critical goal, this genre, in fact, gave Alexandr the vocabulary to talk about Western music while combining it with his interest in science, which was perfectly Soviet. Discussing these scientific facts enabled him to "ground" his interest in rock music in the objective scientific laws that authoritative discourse supported but that were outside of it. This external grounding allowed Alexandr to reinterpret his relationship to this Western art in meaningful terms that neither contradicted the communist ideals and aesthetics nor necessarily agreed with the interpretations of these ideals and aesthetics in the authoritative rhetoric. In the rest of the quote he explained that, in fact, it was precisely the psychological effects of rock music that made him like it so much: "When I hear this music I want to dance, dance improvisationally and wildly, spill out all my extra energy and forget myself as much as possible. I don't like quiet songs—I mean not slow, but quiet. If this is rock and roll it must be loud. There are plenty of 'screaming' [*orushchie*] songs that I adore." Alexandr's interest in communism and Western rock meant that he rearticulated them together. By the end of his last year in school, having heard most recordings that circulated among his friends in Yakutsk, Alexandr decided that rock music was no longer innovative enough, and it no longer made sense to devote one's time and energy to such music since it had fallen behind other more pressing tasks. In the letter dated March 11, 1976, he again compared rock music with science, this time arguing that the former was losing urgency:

> It seems to me that rock music today is experiencing a crisis, and, one may even say, it is gradually losing importance and withdrawing into the background. Its peak happened in 1967 and 1968, the years of the so-called protest of the young, various hippies, beatniks, etc. Now

all this is dying out, although there are still quite a few groups. However, I think that it makes no sense to study their work any more or immerse oneself into it too deeply. I may be wrong, but it seems to me that we, the generation of the 1970s, have to face such grand tasks as the synthesis of protein life, controlled thermonuclear reaction, the blossom of cybernetics, and it is a crime to waste time pursuing some fruitless activity, and especially do so with passion. Now every minute must be counted [*na schetu*]. One needs to acquire a huge amount of knowledge, and at least to figure out the main tasks facing our civilization.

Even this critical account shows how seriously Alexandr treated Western rock music from the start. His discussion of that music on a par with scientific tasks facing the civilization is only possible because he did not see it as inherently unimportant, bourgeois, or flawed. He thought about it seriously, making an ethical argument about the loss of its importance and its withdrawal "into the background," rather than arguing against its aesthetic value. It followed that Alexandr could change his mind if he encountered new examples of that music that proved worthy of the future tasks he cared about. This indeed happened during his first year at Novosibirsk University. As before Alexandr became very active in the Komsomol work and in the studies of mathematics, literature, and music. On January 21, 1977, at the beginning of his second semester at the university, he wrote to Nikolai: "I am still between two poles: mathematics and poetry. . . . my poetry takes a lot from mathematics, but the opposite connection, alas, does not exist." At the university he also met serious collectors of Western music among his fellow students and became exposed to the recordings of many more new bands whose music circulated through unauthorized channels. At the beginning of his second year at the university, on August 24, 1977, Alexandr wrote about his diverse new interests:

> Now, a little bit about my passions. I still pursue literature. My music interests have changed somewhat. In addition to "strict" classical music (Bach, Mozart) and rock classics (the Beatles), I have now literally plunged myself into rock. Especially Uriah Heep.[23] I worship this band. Their concert album *Salisbury* [1971] without a doubt is a real masterpiece. . . . In mathematics I seem to have chosen my specialization. It is a part of algebra called ring theory [a two-page discussion of ring theory with graphs and formulas follows].

[23] British 1970s band whose style straddled the line between art rock and hard rock, with its distinctively rich choral and orchestral arrangements and vocals. It became extremely popular in the Soviet Union for a few years in the mid-1970s.

229

In the next letter, on October 7, 1977, Alexandr described the student system of music exchange in which he actively participated and the prices of Western records at the university black market for collectors. (For comparison, a student's monthly stipend was 40 rubles):

> The records at our black market [*barakholka*] are quite expensive. For example, the album *Salisbury* costs about 70 rubles and *Ram* [McCartney, 1971] costs 50 rubles if they are sealed [*zapechatany*—in original cellophane wrap]. But if they have been opened they cost about 40 to 45 rubles, sometimes even 30. What are your prices [in Leningrad]? By the way, here the system of music exchange [*sistema obmena*] is quite well developed. Do you have one too?

Nikolai was a serious Beatles fan, but Alexandr considered their music outdated, compared to the more experimental sound of new British art rock and hard rock bands. In the following letter, dated December 14, 1977, he wrote about the kind of music that he and his fellow students collected at Novosibirsk University:

> Many of our students have personal collections of stereo recordings of the best rock bands. Although I must say that as far as the Beatles are concerned, you hear them only rarely. It is more common here to listen to Deep Purple, Led Zeppelin, Pink Floyd, Yes, Queen, Wings, King Crimson, Alice Cooper, Uriah Heep, and less frequently others. I underlined those that I like the most.

Alexandr explained that he especially liked the bands that played "complicated and unmelodious" music, not simple or pretty music. It was these qualities, he wrote, that attracted him to the music of the British band Uriah Heep: "Some compositions sound to me simply as a wailing of my soul, and I get hysterical." For Alexandr, the experimental, unusual, improvisational aesthetic of such bands made them much more compatible with his vision of future-oriented aesthetics than the realistic, pretty, and unchallenging music of the professional Soviet pop groups authorized by the state.[24] In other words, he not only disagreed that Western rock music was bourgeois and anti-Soviet but in fact considered the avant-garde aesthetics at the root of that music as perfectly compatible with communist ideals.

Alexandr wrote on September 8, 1977, about the new bands he discovered and liked:

> In general, I see in music a tendency to reject any harmony of sounds but to embrace the harmony with the human mind and spirit. Consider

[24] The same creative, improvisational, and future-oriented aesthetic made American jazz important to the previous generation.

a sequence of acoustic signals that somehow affects our hearing—for this sequence to become music it is necessary that it acts either aesthetically (i.e., a person receives aesthetic pleasure) or psycho-aesthetically (i.e., a person receives psycho-aesthetic pleasure beyond his morals or beliefs—in short, beyond his intellect). All or most of classical music produces an aesthetic affect, while the best rock music produces a psycho-aesthetic affect.

The importance of the best music for Alexandr was not in the realistic beauty and literal meanings (what he called the level of the "intellect") but in the enabling of meanings and imaginations beyond realist beauty, intellect, morals, and beliefs at the psycho-aesthetic level. Developing this discussion further, Alexandr explicitly argued in the next letter on November 23, 1977, that the best examples of Western rock music, like any music, must affect the person physiologically, aesthetically, and spiritually, and that such music enables the future and is already located in the future, along with the best aesthetic achievements of humanity:

> Nikolai, I'm surprised that you don't know the band King Crimson and their concert album *Lizard* [1970]. You see, rock music has made a huge step forward. This is no longer pop music [*estrada*]. It is much higher, deeper and more powerful than pop music. For example, the band Yes has one composition on its album *Relayer* [1974] that deserves to be called music that will live forever [*v vekakh*].

Alexandr's understanding of the communist future, with its ultimate aesthetic, scientific, and social liberation of humanity, was both similar to and yet quite different from the future described in the party rhetoric that criticized "bourgeois" Western mass culture without knowing much about it or what it meant to people like Alexandr. For him the ideals of communism and the experimental music of British art rock belonged to the same future.

The Festival of Political Songs

During the academic year 1977–78, Alexandr was actively collecting tape-recordings of albums and learning and thinking more about Western rock. In the same months, he continued to be active in the university Komsomol committee and in that capacity was elected to the organizing committee of an important cultural and ideological event, the Fifth International Festival of Political Song, which was to take place at the university in May 1978. Alexandr spent the academic year preparing for this event. The festival was attended by artistic and political delegations

231

from dozens of socialist and postcolonial countries and by some communist delegations from Western countries. These included Chile, Bolivia, Ecuador, Zimbabwe, Togo, Bangladesh, Palestine, East Germany, Poland, Cuba, Portugal, and Greece. The festival's theme was the international solidarity of the Communist parties and workers' movements around the world against the imperialism of the bourgeois West. The festival promoted the kind of international popular music of protest that was presented in the party discourse as good and progressive; at the same time, it explicitly criticized the music of bourgeois mass culture, including popular Western rock stars. After the festival took place at the beginning of May, Alexandr described with enthusiasm its musical concerts and singing competitions, which were attended by thousands. On May 8, 1978, he wrote about the spontaneous transformation of the concerts at the festival into lively anti-imperialist, antibourgeois political rallies, "when thousands shouted in unison, 'When we are together we are unbeatable!' [*Kogda my ediny, my nepobedimy!*]."He described the final event, the burning of "dozens of effigies of imperialists in a three-story bonfire" to a "loud unison of 'Hurray!' and 'Viva!' "

Alexandr was extremely excited about the festival's anti-imperialist message and the demonstration of international antibourgeois solidarity. Ending his lengthy description of the festival he wrote: "This is impossible to describe, this had to be seen!" However, despite Alexandr's active and enthusiastic involvement in the festival's political message, he did not subscribe to the opposition it made between the progressive international music of anti-imperialist solidarity and the bourgeois music of Western rock. The former was important to him in the context of the communist political event, but he would not record these political songs for his personal collection. It was the latter (Western rock) that he sought out on the black market, exchanged with friends, and constantly listened to at home during all those months that he tirelessly worked as a member of the organizing committee of the festival. For Alexandr these two supposedly different forms of music were not in opposition, nor did he see the practice of buying Western "bourgeois" records on the black market as contradicting his communist convictions and the antibourgeois message of his international festival. Alexandr's letter that described in detail and with excitement the anti-imperialist political festival ended, ironically with one of his occasional requests for help getting jeans:

Now about the *jeans* [in English]. If you manage to find them [*dostat'*], how much would they cost? If the price is appropriate I will send you a money order. *O'Key* [in English]. I gave you my sizes in the past, but in case you lost them—length 5 or 6 (approximately 110–12 centimeters from the hips), size 46 or 48.

In introducing this seemingly paradoxical dimension into his letter about the festival of antibourgeois solidarity, Alexandr introduced not consumerist desires and black market morality but rather a discursive dimension of the Imaginary West, to which jeans, Western rock music, English words, and the slang word *dostat'* (to obtain through black market channels) collectively pointed. This imaginary world was not opposed to the anti-imperialist festival or to Alexandr's communist values— on the contrary, it was perfectly compatible with them. Communist values, Soviet slogans and anticolonialist songs of political solidarity were explicitly, intellectually, and morally part of the communist project. American jeans, Western art rock, black market networks of music lovers, as well as theoretical mathematics and poetry were aesthetically and even "psycho-aesthetically" connected to the same future of humanity.

Echoes of the Future

The communist rhetoric in Alexandr's letters was not a mindless activist's reiteration of every party pronouncement. On the contrary, in Alexandr's view his belief in the communist idea gave him moral grounds to disagree with conservative interpretations of this idea by some party bureaucrats and teachers. Alexandr argued for a more cosmopolitan, agentive, and aesthetically experimental understanding of communism, in which elements of bourgeois culture and Soviet values were perfectly compatible. In the letters he often discussed his vision against the conservative positions of older professors and party bureaucrats. At the university he occasionally confronted them openly. His feeling of entitlement to this moral position was enabled by the fact that, as argued earlier, the Soviet system, despite its formulaic rhetoric and political control, promoted and valued critical judgment, independent thinking, aesthetic experiment, and internationalist identity.

While still in school, Nikolai once wrote to Alexandr that their teachers launched a strict campaign banning certain types of appearance. Boys were not allowed to wear their hair long and girls were reprimanded for wearing bright red nail polish and uniform dresses that teachers considered too short. During a school Komsomol meeting the older teachers harshly criticized these fashions, calling them uncultured (*nekul'turnye*) and products of Western influence that were unworthy of the Soviet youth.[25] Alexandr replied to Nikolai on April 25, 1975, that he mentioned that incident to friends in his Yakutsk school:

[25] I discuss a similar dispute on fashion in a Soviet school in chapter 5.

Just so you know, we feel solidarity with you on the question of dress in case you start a debate about it with your teachers. Incidentally, as the secretary of the Komsomol committee of school [number omitted], I am in complete disagreement with your teachers on the question of dress and hair. I believe they have to be reminded that Chekhov said: "Everything in the person must be wonderful: face, dress, soul, and thoughts,"[26] and that Pushkin said: "One can be a worthy human being, and yet care about the beauty of one's nails."[27] It's a pity that I can't be there—I would have loved to have a real dispute with those morons [*pridurki*].

Two years later, Nikolai wrote about a debate he and his friends had with their professor of aesthetics who criticized Western rock music as trivial, and ridiculed their interest in it as a sign of naïveté, political immaturity, and a lack of aesthetic education. Alexandr responded on January 21, 1977, writing from Novosibirsk University:

Tell your professor of aesthetics that one cannot look at the surrounding world from a prehistoric position, because from that pit our life is almost invisible—what's visible is only our heels and, pardon my language, our asses [*zadnitsy*]. One must be at least a little bit ahead of us to be able to look us in the eyes. This is especially [important] for her—the supervisor of human character and the mentor of human conduct. Because from a higher ground one can clearly see that rock music is a worthy successor of the classics, and that "the Beatles" is an unprecedented phenomenon of our life that in its impact on the human mind is, perhaps, comparable with space flights and nuclear physics. . . . One cannot educate us not knowing what we value [*chem my zhivëm*], over what we suffer, and what and why we love. Tell her that I love Bach, Vivaldi, Tchaikovsky, Rachmaninov, Shchedrin, and yet, with no reservation, I can put next to them Paul McCartney. If she does not understand this she is not a teacher of live, developing aesthetics, but a preacher of dogmatic aesthetics—which is no better than religion.

In these responses Alexandr explicitly linked the symbols and forms of aesthetics that were deemed "bourgeois" and uncultured with the officially celebrated achievements of Soviet socialism (space exploration, nuclear physics) and the canon of Russian and international culture (Tchaikovsky, Rachmaninov, and so on). His support of communist ideals and his use of prescribed ideological formulas to articulate them did not preclude him from disagreeing with the interpretations of these ideals by conservative party bureaucrats and teachers—or from sending

[26] *V cheloveke vsë dolzhno byt' krasivo: i litso, i odezhda, i dusha, i mysli.*
[27] Byt' mozhno del'nym chelovekom, i dumat' o krase nogtei.

these thoughts across the country through the Soviet mail. Comparing a dogmatic conservative version of the communist aesthetics to religious dogma, Alexandr argued for a need to reinterpret communism in nondogmatic, aesthetically innovative, future-oriented terms. While older party bureaucrats saw in Western rock music only corrupting bourgeois values, Alexandr saw in it a kind of orientation toward the future that he also saw in the best classical music, mathematical theories, space exploration, and texts of Marx and Lenin. For him, all the scientific, aesthetic, and ethical concerns represented in these different forms of knowledge were linked to his firm belief that it was meaningful and important to devote one's life to working for the future of humanity.

Indeed, this futuristic ethos emerged as central to Alexandr's discourse, whichever topic he wrote about. In the letter, from September 8, 1977, quoted above, next to a discussion of rock music, Alexandr continued another argument with Nikolai about the importance of ring theory in mathematics, in which he specialized at the university. To Nikolai's remark that ring theory was too abstract and had no immediate practical application, Alexandr responded that the real concerns should be not about current issues but about the future: "Fundamental science does not have to justify its importance by people's immediate needs. . . . The human being is given a mind to engage in abstract thinking. If a human being contemplated each time why he needs to think about this or that, and whether what he invents will be eatable [whether his inventions have immediate practical application—i.e., if they produce food], then it is doubtful that he would ever become a human being. I can give you a 100 percent guarantee that in the next 500 to 1,000 years the investigation conducted by ring theory will become useful . . . and that there will come a day when someone will say: 'They did not work in vain!'" Ring theory, mathematics, and science in general were important because they worked for the future. The same was true about Alexandr's understanding of art and music. In the following letter (November 23, 1977), continuing a dispute with Nikolai about music Alexandr wrote: "[i]f the composition is so deeply thoughtful and so masterly performed that a person falls under the influence of music not only physiologically but also aesthetically and spiritually—only that kind of music has a future. This is why Bach, Beethoven, Stravinsky, and Gershwin have a future. This is why rock music has a future."

In the critique of the professor of aesthetics quoted above, Alexandr accused her of lagging behind his generation, stating immutable dogmas, and sitting in a pit from which the new was not visible. Ultimately, he accused her of speaking in a circular discourse and therefore of not being able to formulate the future. This is why she was a preacher and not a mentor or supervisor. She only repeated somebody else's dogmatic rhetoric,

235

with its frozen constative meanings, without making her own interpretations. Alexandr felt himself to be reclaiming the vision of the future from such bureaucrats, trying to participate in it as its author rather than merely its hero, a shift I analyzed in chapter 4. Thus, although his passionate communist discourse may seem strikingly different from that of the people who claimed to be living *vnye* the Soviet system, as we saw in chapter 4, they in fact share many commonalities. Like them, Alexandr found it important and interesting to engage in the production of new, unanticipated meanings (author) enabled by his performative reproduction of the forms of authoritative discourse (hero).

It was that future-oriented aesthetics of rock music and the ability to make an interpretation of that future in one's own terms that made rock music particularly appealing to Alexandr and to many members of his generation. Not all Western bands captured the imagination of these Soviet adolescents of the 1970s in the same way. The bands whose albums traveled and translated particularly well across political and cultural borders during that period, and then in tape-recorded copies throughout the Soviet Union, tended to share a certain aesthetic. Most of them played a version of art rock or hard rock; their music was neither "light" nor "melodious"; their compositions included multiple parts, with rich instrumental arrangements, complex, passionate, often operatic vocals, improvisational passages, changes in key, heavy guitar riffs, overdrive sounds and distortions, and an overall trancelike quality. Despite differences in styles, these different groups shared a musical aesthetic marked by a break with realism and the predictable, circular, and immutable aesthetic of light "melodious" music. It was precisely that break that made Western rock seem so perfectly appropriate for the work of constructing vibrant imaginary worlds.

The music of these bands in the late Soviet context resonated unusually well with something of which these bands were probably unaware—the futuristic, avant-garde, experimental aesthetics that remained an important part of the ethos of socialism even during the late Soviet period, despite strict party control and immutable authoritative rhetoric. Indeed, Alexandr's comments about the future were directly indebted to these experimental aesthetics of the revolution. The opposition that Alexandr made between "the best examples of rock music" and simple state-approved pop bands that played pleasing, realistic tunes was not the opposition between bourgeois culture and communist culture but between two strands that coexisted within Soviet culture, between dogmatic circular aesthetic forms and future-oriented experimentations and innovations.

The importance of this futurist strand of Soviet culture could also be seen in the Russian "amateur" rock scene that emerged in the 1970s—in the music, lyrics, and names of the first bands. These bands differed profoundly from the "professional," state-authorized Soviet bands with approved repertoires and flat, descriptive names such as Singing Guitars (*Poiushchie gitary*), Merry Boys (*Vesëlye rebiata*), "The Troubadours" (*Pesniary*). By contrast, the amateur bands experimented with sound and drew in their lyrics on the tradition of serious Russian poetry. Most of them tended to invent names for themselves that referred to imaginary worlds, travels through time and space, different species, and so on. Although at first these names were mostly English, from the early 1970s they were increasingly Russian—Argonauts (*Argonafty*), Myths (*Mify*), Earthlings (*Zemliane*), Time Machine (*Mashina Vremeni*), Green Ants (*Zelenye murav'i*), Aquarium (*Akvarium*), Jungles (*Dzhungli*), Zoo (*Zoopark*), Nautilus (*Nautilus Pompilius*), Television (*Televizor*), Cinema (*Kino*), and so on.

The experimental sound of music that came from an imaginary elsewhere and shifted the constative meanings of authoritative discourse was what made it so interesting and exciting to the last Soviet generation. A similar connection to an aesthetic form that transcended authoritative discourse, allowing for creativity and imagination without requiring opposition to the socialist realities that enabled it, made many other aesthetic forms important for this generation. Among them were pre-Soviet poetry, theoretical science, and foreign languages. For many music lovers of that generation this connection translated into creations of the Imaginary West and into caring about "deep truths" and about "timeless" and "universal" problems of life.[28] For people like Alexandr, it translated into caring about the imaginary future worlds that differed from the descriptions provided in Soviet authoritative discourse but were nevertheless invested in communist imaginations and desires to break with fixed canons. Many others of Alexandr's contemporaries reflected on this future-oriented aesthetic of Western rock quite explicitly. Describing his early attraction to Western rock, Nikolai Gusev, a leader of the celebrated amateur bands Strannye Igry (Strange Games) and AVIA, remarked in the 1980s: "I have always been very interested in the avant-garde of the 1920s, which is for me on a par with punk rock of the more serious and fine varieties designed to tear down the walls. The Soviet avant-garde of the 1920s, Constructivism, El Lissitzky, and so on were a huge breakthrough, a heavy blow on a hammer."[29]

[28] Recall the musician's words from chapter 4: "We're interested in universal problems which don't depend on this or that system, or on a particular time. In other words, they were here a thousand years ago, and they still exist—relations between people, the connection between man and nature" (Cushman 1995, 95).

[29] Nikkila (2002). Unusual experimental sounds, images, and texts were often used by avant-garde artists as powerful aesthetic tools for creating the future. See chapter 5 n6. See also Greil Marcus's (1990) fascinating history that traces some avant-garde roots of rock.

237

Chapter 7
Dead Irony:
Necroaesthetics, *"Stiob,"* and the *Anekdot*

Let them read on my gravestone:
He wrestled with the notion of species and freed himself from
its hold.
—Velimir Khlebnikov[1]

Balancing between irony and genuine fascination is what
has always interested me most. I want to avoid the situation,
where my stuff could be interpreted 'straight', unambiguously.
—Nikolai Gusev[2]

Mit'ki

Around 1980 a curious group of artists called Mit'ki (pronounced *meet-KEE*) appeared in Leningrad. Its members turned their daily existence into an aesthetic project, performing the practice of living grotesquely *vnye* (inside/outside) the sociopolitical concerns of the system. According to the group's mythology, a real Mitёk (singular of Mit'ki, pronounced mee-TYOK) did not know any "news" of the Soviet world, did not read newspapers or watch television, and did not even go shopping unless absolutely necessary. In fact, he knew only two local shops, a wine shop and a bread shop. The fact that the Mit'ki made no effort to seek out this knowledge meant that they had more time and energy to spend on collective drinking, painting, and neverending *obshchenie* (interaction), on constantly performing the role of oblivious, friendly, and all-accepting loafers who were unaware of the common concerns for career, success, money, beauty, health, and so forth. The Mit'ki recited oral anecdotes, myths, and epics about their lives, describing themselves, in an early-1980s text, as follows:

[1] From the poem, "Let Them Read on My Gravestone" (1904) in Khlebnikov (1987, 196).

[2] Nikolai Gusev, a leader of the famous Leningrad theatrical rock bands of the 1980s, Strannye Igry (Strange Games) and AVIA. Quoted in Nikkila (2002).

Mitëk, of course, earns not more than seventy rubles a month [the lowest wage] in his boiler room, where he works one twenty-four-hour shift a week doing absolutely nothing, because he is unpretentious: for example, he can sustain himself for months on cheap processed soft cheese [*plavlennyi syrok*], considering this product tasty, good, and economical, to say nothing of the fact that its consumption does not require spending time on cooking (Shinkarev 1990, 18).

The mention of boiler rooms and rare work shifts are, of course, references to real trends in the lives of some young people at that time, (as was seen in chapter 4). One heroic Mitëk allegedly devised a way of preparing food for himself for a month in advance, saving on time and money:

[He] bought three kilos of jellied meat products [*zelets*], thirty kopecks a kilo,[3] four loaves of bread, two packs of margarine for extra nutrition, thoroughly mixed these products in a washing bowl [*taz*], cooked this substance, then preserved it in a ten-liter glass jar and stored it in the fridge. The dish could be consumed cold or warm. In this way, provisions for one month cost only three rubles and also saved tons of time (Shinkarev 1990, 18).

Although the Mit'ki's ironic aesthetic may seem reminiscent of postmodern cynical detachment from everything, their obliviousness, in fact, was a reversal of that position—it was based on a good-natured acceptance of everything. This form of irony, having roots in Russian folklore and in the humor of the absurd in Russian literature and art,[4] also displayed unmistakably late-socialist characteristics. Thus, it has been suggested that the character of the Mitëk is similar to the prototypical "wise fool" character in Russian fairytales, such as Ivan the Fool (*Ivan-durak*), a naïve young peasant man with a golden heart, who always "gets the girl" in the end. In fact, however, the Mitëk character is a late-Soviet inversion of Ivan the fool. For an illustration of this point consider a typical Mit'ki epic:

The captain of an ocean liner yells from the bridge: "Woman overboard!" An American runs on deck. In one spirited motion he tears away his white shorts and a white T-shirt with the slogan "Miami Beach." He wears steel-colored bathing trunks, his body is covered in a bronze tan. Everyone watches breathlessly. The American runs to

---

[3] A very cheap price.

[4] For example, the satirical novels of Gogol, Bulgakov, and Voinovich, and the absurdist stories and poems of Kharms, Khlebnikov, and Kruchenykh. Indeed, Nancy Ries observes that Russian speakers constantly cite or imply "the parallels between their own absurd experiences and the absurd images made famous by [writers] and countless others" (Ries 1997, 51).

the railing, gracefully flies over, and enters the water without a splash. He confidently cuts the waves in international breaststroke toward the woman. But . . . ten meters from his goal he drowns!

The captain yells again: "Woman overboard!" A Frenchman runs on deck. In one sweeping motion he tears away his blue shorts and a blue T-shirt with the motto "L'Amour Toujours," remaining in yellow bathing trunks with parrots on them. Everyone watches breathlessly. The Frenchman soars over the railing like a bird, performing three somersaults before he hits the water without a splash! He elegantly swims in international butterfly strokes to save the woman. But . . . within five meters from his goal he drowns!

The captain roars again: "Woman overboard!" The door to the broom closet opens and a Russian stumbles on deck, blowing his nose and hiccupping. "What broad? Where?" He's wearing a threadbare, torn, greasy quilted jacket. His pants form huge bubbles over his knees. He slowly takes off his jacket, his striped sailors' shirt, and un-buttons the only button on his fly, remaining in baggy, dirty, knee-length underwear.[5] His body is white and bulky. Shivering with cold, he clutches at the railing, awkwardly tumbles overboard, and falls into the water with a lot of noise and splashes. And . . . drowns instantly!

The Russian is, of course, a Mitëk. There is no expected punch line that should come when he approaches the woman—he does not let it happen, drowning before the suspense. In the traditional Russian fairytale, a sophisticated foreigner (a prince from overseas, a supernatural being) loses in the end, and the local unsophisticated hero, like Ivan the Fool, wins. In the Mit'ki story, however, neither of them wins. The unexpectedness of this ending is part of the Mit'ki aesthetics. It creates an effect of being ultimately oblivious of a need to be "cool": not only are the hero's clothes, behavior, and body the opposite of the "cool" American and Frenchman, but so is his unawareness of this fact. He fails to win not because he is not good enough but because the very discourse of winning and losing is alien to him. He does not lose either. He is simply oblivious of the competition, being not quite within the discursive field where the competition is articulated—he is *vnye* that field. Not surprisingly, the Mit'ki's motto was: "The Mit'ki don't want to defeat anyone" (*Mit'ki nikogo ne khotiat pobedit'*).

Such stories were repeated endlessly, often in front of audiences who had heard them many times before. This ritualized recounting was as important

---

[5] Slang that literally means "family underpants."

FIGURE 7.1. Book cover. *Mit'ki: Narrated by Vladimir Schinkarev and Drawn by Alexandr Florenskii* (1990). Drawn in the early 1980s.

in the construction of the Mit'ki universe as other ritualized practices that accompanied them: collective drinking, toasting, hugging, and the use of particular phrases, exclamations, and gestures by the audiences. Even the tone of voice in which the Mit'ki spoke was ritualized, mixing emotional dramatism with grotesque kindness and verging almost on hysteria (Guerman, 1993b). The Mit'ki's speech was full of diminutive forms, real and invented, in nicknames, nouns, adjectives, and even verbs. Addressing friends and strangers they used the diminutive kinship terms *bratishka* (my little brother) and *sestrënka* (my little sister). Even the name of the movement conveyed the kinship metaphor: the Mit'ki as plural of Mitëk (a particularly tender diminutive form of the name Dmitry) meant "little Dmitries." The Dmitry in question was the group's member Dmitry Shagin, whose parents called him Mitëk. Others collectively adopted the name to suggest that they were Dmitry's brothers because he invented this style of living and because they considered his parents, both Leningrad artists,[6] to be their common "spiritual parents" (Guerman 1993b). But there was more to this name—it referred to a certain kinship imagination, such as the kinship metaphors common among various milieus of *svoi*. Recall that members of the Archaeological Circle discussed in chapter 4 claimed that it consisted of "people from your kin (*rodnye*). . . . not simply relatives, but intimate and dear people," "very close people, who are related to you," and whose ties were "closer than family ties."

The Mit'ki's manner of addressing others as "little brothers" and "little sisters" comprised a kind of kinship public of *svoi* that was based neither on family ties nor on pure friendship but on a rejected boundary between them, with brotherly and sisterly feelings and deep involvement in one anothers' lives. There was a gender division in this kinship public— a real Mitëk was a man; women figured in it as little sisters, wives, lovers, friends, comrades, but not the Mit'ki. Men had more time and less social pressures than women, especially married women, to experiment with the requisite practices of aimless *obshchenie*, collective drinking, and the necessary oblivious disposition. At the same time, the Mit'ki rejected the traditional role of masculine men, performing a grotesque lack of masculine heroism and physical sex appeal.

However small and isolated the world of the Mit'ki was, in the early 1980s, the style of everyday living and interacting that they had perfected was a grotesque version of an aesthetic of irony that became particularly widespread during late socialism. This lifestyle was so densely aestheticized that the living itself turned almost into an art project.[7] The very ethos of

[6] Vladimir Shagin and Natalia Zhilina.

[7] This aesthetic is epitomized also in the artistic installations of everyday life under socialism by the artist Ilya Kabakov, whose topics include Soviet communal apartments and Soviet public toilets. See Tupitsyn (1991) and Boym (1999).

aestheticizing one's life in such ironic terms became a common late-socialist phenomenon. As Vail and Genis pointed out, in late Soviet society "[t]he freedom of creative living seemed to be the most real freedom" and "extraordinary behavior (*ekstravagantnoe povedenie*)" in one's daily life became seen as "an artistic act" (Vail' and Genis 1996, 198–99). This is why, although the Mit'ki's lifestyle was not representative of a norm of behavior in late-Soviet society, they were not simply a marginal phenomenon but a symptom of a widespread cultural shift that was taking place in that society, especially among members of the last Soviet generation. This is clearly seen in the spread of a similar aesthetic among broad groups of this generation (see examples below), and in the fact that the Mit'ki became extremely famous for their lifestyle and philosophy during perestroika in the late 1980s and in the post-Soviet years.

This chapter will analyze how the multiple internal displacements and deterritorializations of the Soviet system during late socialism, and the paradoxical cultural, social and psychic effects they produced, also led to the emergence of a peculiar humor of the absurd, like that practiced by the Mit'ki, and of the genres of subtle irony that reacted to the paradoxes of the everyday. A particularly interesting feature of these humorous genres was their refusal to accept any boundary between seriousness and humor, support and opposition, sense and nonsense. These genres had roots in the older Russian tradition of the humor of the absurd; however, during late socialism they took very particular new forms and became a truly ubiquitous element of the everyday. The chapter will focus on several of these humorous genres and lifestyles, some marginal and some widespread, arguing that they all engaged with the same paradoxes and discontinuities of the system, exposing them, reproducing them, changing their meanings, and pushing them further.

Necrorealists

At about the same time as the Mit'ki emerged, in the late 1970s, in Leningrad, another group of young friends began staging what they called provocations [*provokatsiia*]—bizarre events that took place in public places in front of unsuspecting audiences. The group's lifestyle, interests, and practice eventually led to the development of an artistic aesthetic that they termed "necrorealism." Later, in the early 1980s, they began filming these provocations on an 8-mm camera, calling their film genre necrorealism.[8] In the following analysis we will be interested less

---

[8] For a particularly detailed analysis of the necrorealist movement see Mazin (1998), Berry and Miller-Pogacar (1996).

243

in the cinematographic output of necrorealists than in the aesthetic of living and relating to reality that their milieu developed. As with the Mit'ki (the two groups did not know each other), this aesthetic should be seen not as a marginal phenomenon, but as a symptom of the broader cultural shifts that occurred in late Soviet society. Like the Mit'ki, the necrorealists also achieved fame and success during perestroika and in the post-Soviet period.

Collective pranks of the future necrorealists began in the mid-1970s. In the winter of 1976, a group of fifteen-year-old boys, all school friends, walked around a cinema in their neighborhood in Leningrad. The line of people queuing up for the tickets was so long that getting into the movie was out of the question. However, the cinema's administrator spotted the group, and suggested that if they cleared the snow in front of the cinema he would let them see the film for free. The boys readily agreed, were given wooden snow shovels, and set out to work. Hard work soon made them hot and one of them, Evgenii Yufit, suggested, "Let's take off some clothes"; and he took off his winter coat, sweater, and undershirt, looking strangely naked against the snow. The gesture was both rational (he was indeed hot) and absurd. Without any discussion the others followed suit, focusing on the absurd aspect of the event: some undressed above the waist, some undressed below the waist, and one of them undressed completely, remaining only in his winter boots. The situation turned into a provocation, and the original plan to see the movie was forgotten. They then started aimlessly throwing snow in different directions with manic enthusiasm. The second floor of the cinema had large windows looking down onto the street and the public waiting for the film stared in amazement at the scene below; some people smiled embarrassingly, some were outraged. Yufit remembers that a scandal was in the air: "A group of people ran out to the street, someone called the police, everyone was yelling." Just before the situation turned dangerous, the boys dropped their wooden shovels, grabbed their clothes, and ran away in different directions.[9]

The absurd nudity, the aimless hyperactivity, and the fact that the boys did not run away as a group to gleefully discuss the provocation but instead dispersed in different directions point to a particular aesthetic of public spectacle that they were developing. Central to that aesthetic was a refusal of clear-cut boundaries between reality and performance, common sense and absurdity. It was also key to be spontaneous, to be able to suddenly join in and get into the right groove when a provocation was in the air, and to avoid any explicit analysis or explanation of

[9] Author interview with Yufit. See also Mazin (1998, 40).

what went on and for what reason. This aesthetic was becoming a permanent presence in their lives. They referred to it as "dim-witted merriment" (*tupoe vesel'e*) and "energetic idiocy" (*energichnaia tupost'*)[10] and were always ready collectively to participate in spontaneous events in that style.

The friends belonged to the last Soviet generation (their leader, Yevgenii Yufit, was born in 1961). In a few years, the group became bigger and its provocations more frequent and elaborate. By this time they often had a general planned idea; however, it was always open-ended enough to allow for improvisations. A regular kind of provocation was a massive brawl that included dozens of participating men and went on for hours, in various contexts, in front of the unsuspecting public. The brawls were not particularly violent or bloody, had no clear cause or aim, and were always accompanied by energetic running, falling, hopping, arm-swinging and other exaggerated physical movements (Mazin 1998, 58).

One such brawl involving twenty to thirty men took place in the winter of 1984. It began in the forest on the outskirts of Leningrad, moved across a frozen lake, migrated into a suburban train station, and ended finally on a suburban train. Suburban trains jam-packed with people returning to the city from their dachas were a particularly attractive venue to stage the brawls. In such circumstances, explains Yufit, "many passengers would always be dragged into the brawl and eventually would get completely confused, not knowing whom they were fighting, for what reason, and what was going on. Once we got some soldiers involved, a whole platoon, together with their officers. I was fighting side by side with a Soviet army major."[11] They tried to involve "serious people" with a clear sense of honor and morality, especially authoritative figures and subjects of Soviet ideological myths (the army officers combined all these and were therefore perfect), who were ready to get involved if someone needed help. These people were then made to face a situation in which what seemed perfectly clear a minute before suddenly stopped making any sense.

Another notable provocation took place in the winter of 1984 and became mythologized in necrorealists' memories as "the beating of Zurab." Zurab was a full-size rubber mannequin of a man that was stolen from a forensic criminological laboratory. It was given a Georgian name, Zurab, that sounded exotic in the Leningrad context.[12] They dressed Zurab differently depending on the occasion. That evening, during the rush hour in the center of Leningrad, necrorealists staged a regular aimless brawl

[10] Yufit's archive, quoted in Mazin (1998, 58–59n65).

[11] Author interview.

[12] It also had connotations of homoeroticism—Zurab was a typical character of jokes about homosexuals.

among several dozen men. It started on the fifth floor of a building under construction that was missing the front wall, which made the fighting men visible to the pedestrians on the street. Zurab, wearing a winter jacket and a winter hat, was at some point dropped from the fifth floor to the street so that the pedestrians could see him fall. A group of fighting men ran out from the building and proceeded to hit the lying body of Zurab with wooden sticks, shouting that they needed to finish him off.

Yufit remembers: "Pedestrians on the street thought that it was a real person. People ran over, screaming and yelling: 'You murderers! What are you doing?' . . . Everyone was running about, they tried to get a glimpse of the 'human body' lying there." There were "more screams and uproar, the police showed up." However, at the most agitated moment, Zurab's head tore off and the petrified pedestrians saw the spongy plastic innards where his neck was cut, realizing that something was not quite as it seemed. "The crowd was in complete shock, stupefaction. They were like idiots. I remember the glazed-over eyes, all wide open."[13] People started backing off in dismay muttering something unclear to themselves, and the fighting men grabbed Zurab and ran in different directions. Like before, the brawls were mostly spontaneous. Although the idea to have a brawl involving Zurab was planned, the throwing and beating of Zurab were spontaneous acts that started unraveling in a particular direction because the pedestrians had become interested.

Another provocation took place in the mid-1980s, near suburban railroad tracks. Two members of the group were on one side of the tracks, wearing sailors' jackets, with pants pulled down to their ankles and heads swathed in bloody bandages. Several others, also heavily bandaged, hid in the bushes beside the tracks. When a train approached, the first pair started energetically imitating an act of sodomy, and the others jumped out from the bushes simulating a knife fight. The bizzare sight in the middle of a deserted countryside must have left engine drivers bewildered and confused. The trains reacted with long loud hoots, while moving away at a high speed.

The Undead

In 1982, Yufit started clandestinely filming fragments of these provocations on an 8-mm camera. This footage was later incorporated into their first short films.[14] These short films also included peculiar new

---

[13] See Mazin (1998, 26).

[14] Some footage of the abovementioned forest brawl and the "beating of Zurab" were used in the short 1985 film *Lesorub* (Woodcutter); the footage by the rail tracks was used

characters. One moment they looked like recognizable heroes of social-ist realism—soldiers, sailors, scientists, doctors, officials; the next mo-ment they looked like the insane or the "living dead," swathed in bloody bandages and plastered with zombie clay.[15] These characters ran and fought, performed strangely agitated activities and homoerotic acts, or simply wandered around aimlessly. The films made references to the process of transformation from life to death, to various stages of ca-daver transformation and biological decomposition, to multiple at-tempts at suicide that fail, to various wounded, bandaged, crawling, and drowned characters. The topic of the life-death borderline was a central theme in their discussions, pranks, and films. The group's fa-vorite reading at the time included books on criminology, forensic med-icine, and physiological pathology, including Avdeev's textbook, *A Short Guide to Forensic Medicine* (1966), especially chapters, such as "Studies of Cadavers with Putrid Transformations." Images from the books influenced plots and the make up of characters in the films. How-ever, their representations concentrated not on the feelings of horror and dread that death may invoke but on its absurdity and on the fasci-nation with death, not as a state, but as a process. These interests made that genre quite different from Western horror films about zombies and vampires or their comic imitations.[16]

These activities and films point to an important aspect of the necrore-alist aesthetic. Their strange and scandalous provocations and images, from aimlessly fighting men to decomposing corpses, were tools for achieving an effect that was quite different from a constative true or false reading of these scenes. They aimed to create an unexpected feeling of the uncanny within the ordinary, to dislocate the mundane everyday world, and to make the audience suspect that a whole other dimension might exist within that world that until that moment had been invisible or misrecognized.

Various biological and psychological metaphors were particularly suit-able for this project. Teetering on the border between life and death, san-ity and insanity, they focused on a particular biopolitical effect of Soviet authoritative discourse. Like every modern state, the Soviet state drew a

---

in the short 1987 film *Vesna* (Spring) (Mazin 1998, 26, 51). First films also included *Urine-Crazed Body Snatchers* (*Mochebuitsy trupolovy*, 1985) and *Suicide Monsters* (*Vepri suit-sida*, 1988). For discussions of necrorealist films see Mazin (1998); Graham (2001); Alaniz and Graham (2001); Alaniz (2003).

[15] The kind of makeup used in horror films about zombies.

[16] Dobrotvorsky (1993) finds in early necrorealist films elements of "Mack Sennett's slapstick style of the 1910's and the shock aesthetics of the French avant-garde, as well as the unrestrained eccentricity of the Soviet cinema of the 20's" (1993, 7).

line between bare life and political life (Agamben 1998). Agamben argues that to be recognized by the modern state as a full human subject one has to be seen as having both these forms of life—having only bare life, without sociopolitical life, downgrades one to the status of being less than human.[17] The Soviet state drew the distinction between these forms of life differently in different periods, but always with a vengeance—from Stalin's division between "the Soviet people" and "the enemies of the people," to a symbolic denial of life to cultural "deviationists" such as *stilyagi* (e.g., in 1949 *Krokodil* referred to them as a nonhuman species, calling them parrots and canaries, who "aren't alive as we understand the word, but . . . flutter above life's surface, so to speak"[18]), to Brezhnev's division between citizens and those stripped of citizenship and his equation of political dissidents with psychiatric patients.

The necrorealists' reference to the zone between life and death, between sanity and insanity, between healthy citizens and decomposing bodies was a refusal not only of the authoritative discourse's boundary between bare life and political life but of the whole discursive regime in which this boundary was drawn. The Mit'ki's practices achieved the same. They looked like good Soviet citizens who obeyed the law and were content with everything; however, in fact they downgraded themselves to the level of bare life. This association of the citizen (performance of the authoritative form, the appearance of a citizen) with a noncitizen (complete unanchoring or even disintegration of constative meaning) undermined any clear distinction between the two. Many groups and milieus that insisted on having a *vnye* relationship to authoritative discourse of the Soviet state also rejected the very discursive regime in which the boundary between political life and bare life was drawn. For example, Inna and her friends in the Archeological Circle (in chapter 4) claimed to be "organically different" from a common Soviet person, suggesting that the distinction between person and nonperson simply could not apply to them.

The border zones between life and death are often explored in popular culture—for example, in the figures of the "living dead" or the "undead." Slavoj Žižek explains the ontology of these figures by drawing on Kant's distinction between positive, negative, and indefinite judgment. In positive

---

[17] The displacement of this boundary allowed the Nazi German state to treat the mentally ill as having bare life only, and therefore as half-dead already, making possible state programs of methodical extermination through euthanasia. What distinguishes the contemporary state is that the line between political and bare life "no longer appears as a stable border dividing two clearly distinct zones. This line is now in motion and gradually moving into areas other than that of political life—[involving] the doctor, the scientist, the expert, and the priest" (Agamben 1998, 122).

[18] See my discussion of the *stilyagi* in chapter 5.

judgment the logical subject is ascribed a predicate (e.g., "the soul is mortal"), in negative judgment the subject is denied a predicate (e.g., "the soul is not mortal"), and in indefinite judgment the subject cannot be assigned either positive or negative predicate and is instead assigned a nonpredicate (e.g., "the soul is non-mortal") (Žižek 1994b, 26; Kant 1998). The difference between the undead and ordinary humans from the world of the living and the dead is the same as that between indefinite judgment and negative judgment: "a dead person loses the predicates of a living being, yet he or she remains the same person; an undead, on the contrary, retains all the predicates of a living being without being one," without being a person (Žižek 1994b, 29).[19]

The characters, images, and metaphors created by necrorealists invoked precisely this zone between the living and the dead. In some of their early films these characters were "the undead"; in others they were various psychotic figures running or crawling about. They looked and walked almost like people though clearly lacking personhood; they existed *vnye* (inside/outside) the domain of speech, producing only grunts, moans, and shrieks. The Mit'ki's characters shared this in-betweenness but manifested it differently. Their oblivious disposition, grotesque friendliness, and exaggeratedly diminutive stylized speech appeared slightly demented or psychotic. The characters of both these groups lived in the zone between the inside and outside of the boundaries drawn by Soviet authoritative discourse, in a zone that refused the boundary between bare and political life and constituted the world of *vnye*. The Mit'ki rejected the *sociopolitical* effect of this boundary, refusing to fit either of the two subject positions that it created, the pro-system "activist" and the anti-system "dissident." Necrorealists refused the *biopolitical* effect of the boundary, and therefore did not fit either of the two subject positions it created, "the living" and "the dead." The Mit'ki invented a new person; necrorealists invented a new species.

Stiob

We will use the slang term *stiob*[20] to refer to the ironic aesthetic practiced by groups such as the Mit'ki and necrorealists. *Stiob* was a peculiar

[19] See also Žižek (1993a) for a more extensive discussion of this argument.

[20] See Yurchak (1999; 2005) for discussions of *stiob* and its post-Soviet transformations. The way *stiob* is used here in fact reflects the sense it originally had in the late 1970s and early 1980s, which was only one of several contemporary meanings of this term. There were also other terms that referred to similar "absurdist" forms of irony such as *telega*, *shiza*, *prikol*. See Diana Blank's discussion of *prikol* and other forms of humor and cynicism in post-Soviet Ukraine (2004; 2005).

form of irony that differed from sarcasm, cynicism, derision, or any of the more familiar genres of absurd humor. It required such a degree of *overidentification* with the object, person, or idea at which this *stiob* was directed that it was often impossible to tell whether it was a form of sincere support, subtle ridicule, or a peculiar mixture of the two. The practitioners of *stiob* themselves refused to draw a line between these sentiments, producing an incredible combination of seriousness and irony, with no suggestive signs of whether it should be interpreted as the former or the latter, refusing the very dichotomy between the two.

This type of irony shared some elements with Bakhtin's notion of carnivalesque parody: it cannot be understood simply as a form of resistance to authoritative symbols because it also involves a feeling of affinity and warmth toward them. Bakhtin emphasized that "men who composed the most unbridled parodies of sacred texts . . . often sincerely accepted and served religion" (1984, 95). However, unlike Bakhtin's parody, Soviet *stiob* was not limited to temporally and spatially bounded and publicly sanctioned "carnivals." Rather, it functioned in a much broader array of contexts, literally as an everyday aesthetic of living. In extreme cases, as with the Mit'ki and the necrorealists, life as a whole transformed into neverending *stiob*, with no "ordinary" location left outside of it. The main artistic creations of these groups were not paintings, films, or staged provocations but a "total art of living" with its own *stiob* philosophy, language, forms of behavior, ethical norms, styles of interaction, drinking habits, unhealthy diet, and so forth. Furthermore, unlike Bakhtin's parody, the *stiob* practiced by these groups performed a displacement of the symbolic order, creating in it zones that were in-between, without ever acknowledging this fact explicitly. In other words, *stiob* was another strategy that neither supported nor opposed the discursive field that it engaged but rather deterritorialized it from within.

This is why the aesthetic of *stiob* differed from the irony of *sots-art* (a term for unauthorized "socialist art" coined in ironic imitation of Anglo-American "pop art") practiced by the older generation of artists critical of the Soviet system.[21] Their work tended to ridicule the system's political slogans and socialist realist images by mixing ideological symbols with symbols of popular culture. The aesthetic of *stiob* among the last Soviet generation, on the contrary, avoided any political or social concerns or straightforward affiliation with support or opposition of anything. Like the groups and milieus discussed in chapter 4, those who practiced it also

[21] This generation included artists such as Vitaly Komar and Alexander Melamid, Ilya Kabakov, and Eric Bulatov. See Kabakov (1995); Hillings (1999); Kabakov, Tupitsyn, and Tupitsyn (1999); Epstein (2000; 1995); Boym (2001; 1999); Erjavec (2004); Groys (2004); Buck-Morss (2000).

considered any political positions "uninteresting." Later, during the reforms of perestroika, Yufit was asked how his artistic work intervened in the realm of politics. His response demonstrated a typical refusal to engage with this problematic altogether, to the point of never explicitly acknowledging this refusal:

Well, there are such injuries, including those resulting from airplane crashes that may have an effect on various political figures. In this sense, politics certainly does enter the sphere of my interests. However, such injuries make it very difficult to identify who is who. The remnants of the bodies get scattered around an area of up to three square kilometers. An extremely complex injury. . . . But a cadaver is a cadaver. . . . I am interested in its metamorphoses . . . in the transformations of form and color. In a kind of necroaesthetics. During the first and second months shocking changes occur. The cadaver becomes spotty as a jaguar and puffy as a behemoth. And this happens only under certain conditions. Which is particularly interesting. But as for politics . . . well, I don't really know (quoted in Mazin 1998, 42).

Yufit's response was based neither on outright sarcasm directed at political concerns nor on straightforward engagement with them, but on an aesthetic of ambivalence that positioned itself *vnye* the authoritative discursive field, and therefore was unable to articulate the "political." By refusing to identify with a political position, and also refusing to claim that this nonidentification was itself a conscious political position, Yufit refused to be placed into the discursive field where the political boundary between being "for" and being "against" the system was drawn. Instead, his response was articulated in a different discursive dimension altogether—one that was located both *inside* and *outside* Soviet authoritative discourse and both *within* the Soviet spatial universe but *not within* its discursive parameters.

However, while Yufit refused to provide any metacommentary that would explain how to interpret his discourse, he was still not innocent or unaware of its own absurd irony. For this type of discourse it was important to remain within a general style that was open to improvisations, refused any well-defined agendas or messages, and was always ready to push the absurdity further, without ever acknowledging it. The question asked of Yufit was about politics, and he began his response by referring to "political figures." They experienced "an extremely complex injury," their bodies were separated into fragments, scattered around a huge area, and could not be identified. They were reduced to nonpersons, neither political nor human ("a cadaver is a cadaver"), remaining in the zone between life and death, metamorphosing, transforming in form and color, becoming "spotty as a jaguar and puffy as a behemoth."

Such short instances of spontaneous *stiob* discourse contained the whole philosophy of necrorealism. From the language used to the spontaneous absurdity of the narrative and the descriptions of various bizarre figures, events, creatures, entities, and transformations, they refused every possible binary distinction, always balancing in multiple zones in-between.

This kind of *stiob* aesthetic developed in the context of late socialism, when the authoritative representations of reality became immutable, ubiquitous, and hypernormalized, and when their straightforward support or criticism smacked of idiocy, narcissism, and bad taste. Instead of such activist and dissident dispositions, the aesthetic of *stiob* was based on a grotesque "overidentification"[22] with the *form* of an authoritative symbol, to the point that it was impossible to tell whether the person supported that symbol or subverted it in a subtle ridicule. In the best examples of *stiob* these two positions were merged into one, and the authors themselves did not draw a clear line between them. In addition to the act of *overidentification* with the symbol, the *stiob* procedure involved a second act: the *decontextualization*[23] of that symbol.

Overidentification is the precise and slightly grotesque reproduction of the authoritative form (e.g., the text of a slogan, the script of a ritual, the speech from a podium, the gesture of voting in favor, a visual image of propaganda art or simply mundane formulaic elements of the Soviet everyday). Decontextualization is the act of placing this form in a context that is unintended and unexpected for it. By being overly devoted to replicating the precise form of authoritative texts, rituals, and images the *stiob* procedures unanchored the constative meanings associated with them, thus making meaning unclear, indeterminate, or even irrelevant. In other words, *stiob* served as a model of the "performative shift." As a result, the symbol could suddenly appear baffling or absurd.[24]

What the Mit'ki and the necrorealists overidentified with, as shown above, were the representations of the Soviet person and the Soviet everyday in authoritative discourse—party speeches and slogans, mundane practices of Soviet life, the art of socialist realism.[25] Decontextualizing these overidentified representations shifted their associated meanings in unexpected and absurd directions. The Mit'ki turned their whole lifestyle

[22] See Žižek (1993b).

[23] See Urban (1996) and Urban and Silverstein (1996) for a general discussion of decontextualization.

[24] This feeling of the absurd is based on a sudden recognition of the arbitrariness of the signifier-signified link in the linguistic sign (e.g., any word that is repeated a certain number of times starts sounding "absurd").

[25] Dittmer described this aesthetic in China as "hypercoherence" with an ideologically designated ideal of behavior (Dittmer 1981, 146–47). See also Anagnost (1997, 191).

into a grotesque socialist-realist representation of Soviet life, associating its optimism, energy, and confidence in the bright tomorrow with a complete lack of problems, concerns, aspirations, and goals. Necrorealists pushed this project further, emulating the raw biological vitality and energetic activism of the socialist-realist hero but dissociating it from meaning, speech, and personhood.

By the early 1980s, *stiob* became an aesthetic common to many artistic groups in the Soviet Union and socialist countries of Eastern Europe. This aesthetic was employed, for example, in the theatrical performances of the Slovene rock group Laibach and the Russian rock group AVIA. Laibach performed overidentification with the serious, heroic, and slightly terrifying part of the communist symbolism and in the process of decontextualization mixed linguistic, visual, and aesthetic symbols of communism with those of Nazi "Blut und Boden"[26] ideology, without making the origin of these symbols too explicit (Žižek 1994c, 72; Yurchak 1999). Their stage design was beautiful, excessive, awe-inspiring, and never too clear, with symbols that could fit any number of ideologies (leather uniforms, red flags, slogans yelled in German, Russian, English and Slovene, the deafening sound of trumpets, relentless drumming, dead animals, flaming torches). It was impossible to know for sure how to read it. AVIA overidentified with the agitprop enthusiasm of various periods of Soviet ideology, and in the process of decontextualization mixed the avant-garde aesthetics of the optimistic 1920s and the frozen ideological form of the stagnant 1970s with elements of punk and slightly erotic cabaret. In AVIA performances up to twenty actors in workers' overalls fervently marched in columns, shouted slogans and "hurray," and built human pyramids. In the role of "young builders of communism" they looked so cheerfully zealous that sometimes it all verged on insanity (Yurchak 1999; 2004). In the late 1980s, I was AVIA's manager and witnessed the audience reaction. Many audience members at the performances of Laibach and AVIA, especially older people and foreigners, were uncertain how to interpret these happenings and often came up with diametrically opposite interpretations. After one AVIA concert in Kiev, in 1987, a couple of older communists came backstage to thank the group for the atmosphere of a real communist celebration saying that it had become so rare to encounter young people genuinely devoted to communist ideals. After another concert, a different elderly couple thanked the group for the devastating satire of totalitarianism; that couple had spent years in Stalinist

---

[26] The Nazi ideology "blood and soil" claimed that people of German descent (blood) were naturally rooted in German soil, as opposed to "rootless" Jews and Roma who had no soil (Etlin 2002, 9).

camps. The reactions to Laibach's performances were similarly ambiguous: after a concert in a New York club, in the 1980s, the audience divided into those who applauded Laibach's devastating antifascism and those who shouted that these "fascists" should be kicked out of America.[27]

Scary Little Poems

My analysis so far has focused on relatively exceptional cases and groups not to argue that they represented some norm of behavior during late socialism but rather to treat them as a symptom of a cultural shift that was taking place in late Soviet society. In the late 1970s and early 1980s, the aesthetics of *stiob*, including its necrorealist variety, became widespread, albeit usually in a less extreme form, among groups of "ordinary" Soviet citizens, especially members of the last Soviet generation. This chapter considers how these aesthetics of irony operated among such "ordinary" citizens in various "ordinary" contexts and discourses.

One example of a common discourse of this type was a folkloric genre known as "scary little poems" (*stishki-strashilki*)—two- and four-liners that, in gruesome detail, described little children as agents or objects of extreme violence. Violent folklore of this type can be found in different cultural and historical contexts; however, the Soviet Union experienced a true explosion of this genre in the period from the 1960s to the early 1980s (Mazin 1998, 42; Belousov 1998). Hundreds of new scary little poems emerged and one frequently heard them in various contexts, narrated by friends and acquaintances, with listeners invariably reacting in a combination of laughter and recoil. Typical scary little poems went like this (translations mine):

Alësha was cooking meat stew with no sound,
His daddy was legless and crawling around.

A little girl found a grenade in the field.
"What is this, uncle?" with trust she appealed.
"Pull on the ring," he said, "you will find out."
For a while her bow will be flying about.

A little boy Vitya played with a gun,
Taking it apart was tricky but fun.

[27] Author interviews with Laibach in Ljubljana in 1995. For more on Laibach see Monroe (2005); Žižek (1993b); Gržinić (2000; 2003); Erjavec (2003). Other examples of *stiob* aesthetics included Soviet "parallel cinema" (Matizen 1993) and Sergei Kuryokhin's musical group Popular Mechanics (Yurchak 1999).

His finger by accident pulled on the trigger,
His brain sprayed the ceiling with splatter and vigor.[28]

The explosion of this folkloric genre points to the same shift in late Soviet society that brought about the emergence of the Mit'ki, the necro-realists, and the aesthetics of *stiob*. All these genres were united by their reliance on producing the feeling of the uncanny, which is important for understanding the conditions and effects of this cultural shift. One meaning of "uncanny" (in its original German form, *unheimlich*), according to Freud, is something familiar, intimate, connected to home (1919, 245). This meaning is crucial for the understanding of the un-canny as a psychological phenomenon. The feeling of the uncanny is linked to the disgust or horror experienced when the coherent appear-ance of the familiar and intimate world is suddenly disrupted by evi-dence of its unnatural, constructed quality. Among the usual objects that invoke this feeling are "death and dead bodies . . . the return of the dead . . . spirits and ghosts," inexplicable forms of behavior, epileptic seizures, and manifestations of insanity (241). What unites these different experiences, argues Freud, is the fact that they are invoked not by something unknown, but, on the contrary, by "something which is fa-miliar and old-established in the mind and which has become alienated from it only through the process of repression" (241). When one recog-nizes inexplicable behavior as "the working of forces hitherto unsus-pected in his fellow-men" one gets a feeling that one has been always "dimly aware of them in remote corners of his own being" (243). This feeling is the uncanny.

Scary little poems, like necrorealist images and Mit'ki practices, pro-duced this feeling at the level of the everyday. They staged little para-doxes and incongruities within the most mundane and familiar aspects of Soviet reality, making their audiences "dimly aware" that they them-selves were intimately involved and enmeshed in these paradoxes and in-congruities. As with the earlier example, scary little poems were narrated in the mundane contexts of schools, homes, conversations with friends.

---

[28] *Mal'chik Alesha varil kholodets,*
po polu polzal beznogii otets.

Devochka v pole granatu nashla.
"Chot eto, diadia?" sprosila ona.
"Derni kolechko", diadia skazal.
Dolgo nad polem bantik letal.

Malen'kii Vitya s ruzh'ishkom igral.
On s liubopytstvom ego razbiral.
Pal'tsem nelovko nazhal na kurok -
Prysnuli druzhno mozgi v potolok

They were also an example of *stiob* that imitated the performative shift of everyday symbols and representations of authoritative discourse. The opening part of such poems (one or two lines) described an innocent child, suggesting a commonsense interpretation; the closing part made any interpretation absurd or impossible by introducing an inexplicably violent event into the mundane context. The poems presented their listeners with the impossibility of having a direct, literal reading of reality, focusing on a shift between form and meaning within that reality, of which the witnesses were "dimly aware," and in which they participated usually without contemplating.

Gerontocracy

The emergence of such necroaesthetics, as one element of *stiob*, was boosted in the late 1970s and early 1980s by a curious development in Soviet authoritative discourse. For over two decades the lineup of the politburo of the Communist Party, the state's supreme leadership, remained practically unchanged. Like other signifiers of authoritative discourse, the portraits and names of the politburo members were constantly invoked in the media, on political billboards, and in speeches, usually in the form of a list. This list was well known to everyone, but the constative meaning of its names was relatively unimportant. Beyond a few leading figures most people were uncertain what name corresponded to what face. The politburo was experienced as one multifaced and multinamed entity that remained fixed in its form for years as a perfect example of hypernormalized authoritative discourse.

Similarly, the televised speeches of its members were read primarily as performative rituals of authoritative discourse and not as constative statements that could be interpreted literally. This is why even the speeches that were enunciated relatively unclearly (at that time Brezhnev's aging speech was becoming increasingly slurred) functioned almost as well as those that were enunciated clearly. The shift of authoritative discourse (fixed immutable form, coupled with unfixed, indeterminate, sliding meaning) played itself out in the context of the politburo with dead irony. As political bodies the human beings that constituted the politburo remained fixed and immortal (fixed form), but as biological bodies they were now quickly aging and becoming frail (unfixed, sliding meaning). The average age of the politburo members increased from fifty-five in 1966 to seventy in the early 1980s, with the leading group close to eighty. (In retrospect this period has been called "the period of gerontocracy.") The uncoupling of form and meaning in this case was that while these figures were on the verge of dying as biological beings, they functioned as immortal authoritative forms. As a result, the news of Brezhnev's death in 1982, while not surprising, still caught most people completely off guard. That moment, remembers Andrei Makarevich, made him suddenly realize that until then he had perceived Brezhnev not as a human being but as a "biblical figure that would live eight hundred years" (Makarevich 2002, 14).

A high-ranking death at the level of the party-state leadership became a regular occurrence. Between 1982 and 1985, the following members of and candidates to the politburo died: Suslov (January 1982, age 80), Brezhnev (November 1982, age 72), Kiselev (January 1983, age 66), Pel'she (May 1983, age 85), Andropov (February 1984, age 70), Ustinov (December 1984, age 76), Chernenko (March 1985, age 74).[29] In the early 1980s, on average one figure from the politburo was dying every six months. Bare life literally exploded into the immutable universe of political life—in the form of death. This did not mean, however, that authoritative discourse experienced a rupture. Quite the contrary, in accordance with its principles, the representation of high-ranking deaths quickly became normalized and ritualized. The now frequent deaths became represented by identical obituaries in the newspapers, identical phrases and idioms, identical announcements on the television, televised funeral proceedings from Red Square, identical mourning symbols, flags, and portraits on the streets, somber music on the radio, and so on. As a result of this normalizing process, the focus in high-ranking funerals shifted from the biological rupture of death to the political stability and continuity of the discourse that represented it. It became more important to keep the language in which funerals were described unchanged at the expense of the precision with which it depicted these events (recall the discussion in chapter 2 of a cliché formula from the Red Square funerals that referred to the *bodies* that were "buried on Red Square *by* the Kremlin Wall," even when in fact the *ashes* were buried *inside* the wall). A Soviet *anekdot* (joke) reacted to the frequency of high-ranking deaths and to the shift of focus in the ritual of the funeral from rupture and discontinuity to regularity and continuity. A man is approaching Red Square where the funeral of another politburo member is taking place. Since attendance at these funerals was restricted to important party members with invitation passes, the man is stopped by a policeman: "Do you have a pass?" He replies: "I have a season ticket."

However, this shift between the immutable authoritative form of leading symbols and their sudden biological death introduced new temporal, spatial, and *biopolitical* discontinuities between the form and meaning of authoritative discourse. It was in that context that such aesthetics of irony

---

[29] Six of them were politburo members and one a candidate to the members.

as necrorealism, the Mit'ki, and scary little poems developed and came to prominence. These genres played with temporal, spatial, and biopolitical discontinuities of late Soviet reality, and the context of the period provided them with the right metaphors for this work—metaphors centered on being between death and life, sanity and insanity, health and sickness, innocence and monstrosity, and so on. Indeed, death rituals and cemeteries are particularly evocative of temporal, spatial, and biological discontinuities because, as argued for the "undead" above, they are located both inside and outside the life of the community, blurring the boundary between life and death.[30] As Foucault pointed out: "[H]eterotopia [spatial discontinuity] begins to function fully when men are in a kind of absolute break with their traditional time; thus, the cemetery is indeed a highly heterotopian place, seeing that the cemetery begins with that strange heterochronia [temporal discontinuity] that loss of life constitutes for an individual, and that quasi-eternity in which he perpetually dissolves and fades away" (Foucault 1998c, 182).

In the case of the necrorealists, by staging their provocations in the most mundane contexts of Soviet life they made it apparent that even in these contexts spatial, temporal, and biopolitical discontinuities were lurking. Their absurd events materialized suddenly and rushed by quickly, giving their witnesses no time to understand what had just happened. Naked men ran away in different directions, massive brawls had no obvious goal and ended as unexpectedly as they emerged, trains passed bandaged fornicating sailors at high speeds, a person beaten by violent men with sticks turned out to be a dummy—and then they all abruptly disappeared. What went on defied social taboos and rational understandings, leaving the witnesses wondering whether they had observed a group of lunatics and drunkards, or were themselves going insane, or if perhaps there was something "bigger" going on. The open-endedness and indeterminacy of meaning was central to these provocations. They operated as models of the performative shift par excellence. The form of these events was always recognizable and suggested a certain interpretation, only to suddenly lose any possibility of being interpreted. The Mit'ki's lifestyle, as well as the mundane narration of scary little poems, performed the same work. All these genres illustrated a profound displacement of late Soviet reality—the ubiquitous, immutable, and fixed authoritative form that framed and enabled everyday life in the midst of the shifting and unpredictable meaning for which this form stood. Overidentifying with the performative dimension of authoritative discourse, these genres exploded its constative dimension and left one

---

[30] Joseph Roach points out that cemeteries remind the living of "the constructedness, the permeability, and not infrequently the violence" of the community's boundaries (1995, 55).

with an uncanny feeling that one routinely inhabited and reproduced this process in oneself.

The Directive

As argued above, the aesthetics of *stiob*, including its necroaesthetic variety, were not limited to esoteric artistic groups. On the contrary, they became truly widespread during late socialism, especially among members of the last Soviet generation. They were practiced even by conscientious young communists, local Komsomol leaders, and members of the Komsomol committees. The following example considers how this creative form of irony was practiced in the Komsomol committee and what effects it produced. As chapter 3 showed, the work of many Komsomol committees involved writing speeches and compiling reports in the genre of authoritative discourse, while simultaneously subjecting them to the performative shift. This resulted in the production of multiple temporal and spatial discontinuities and deterritorializations in the Komsomol life, such as the distinction between "pure formality" and "work with meaning," the production of the publics of *svoi*, the worlds of *vnye*, various forms of "free" time, the Imaginary West, and so on.

Members of the Komsomol committees reacted to the discontinuities that they themselves introduced through these activities by making comments in the genre of *stiob*. One of the most common examples was to produce an imitation document, similar to actual documents, in the regular authoritative style. For instance, in August 1983, Andrei, the Komsomol secretary in chapters 3 and 5, and his friends in the Komsomol committee celebrated his thirtieth birthday. After work they drank to his health in the committee room and presented him with a congratulatory document, the Directive (*Ukazanie*) (figures 7.2 and 7.3). The text was an insider joke among the members of the committee. It was typed on official letterhead with a registration number and date, in the very locus of the ideological production, the committee room, by the very people who conducted the Komsomol work and composed Komsomol reports. All these markers created an expectation of authoritative discourse.

Having been written at the time when the high-ranking deaths became frequent (the early 1980s), this document drew on the style of the obituaries written in authoritative discourse and published on these occasions. The text usually opened with two phrases: The first announced that some group "has suffered a great loss" (*poterpel bol'shuiu utratu*). Depending on the deceased, that group was "Soviet music culture," "Soviet armed forces," "Soviet science," "all Soviet people," and so on. The next phrase announced the death with the formula "from this life departed"

СССР
Министерство цветной металлургии

СОЮЗАЛЮМИНИЙ

Всесоюзный научно-исследовательский и проектный институт

[NAME OF INSTITUTE]

УКАЗАНИЕ

12 августа ___ 197 83 г.   № ___001___

ЛЕНИНГРАД

13 августа 1953 года цветная металлургия СССР потерпела большую утрату. Пришел в жизнь вдохновитель и мистификатор, бессменный руководитель засолочного пункта и директор Василеостровской канатной дороги, отчим эстонского попса, герой монгольского эпоса [ANDREI'S NAME]

Эта дата розовыми буквами вписана в биографию [INSTITUTE]

В ознаменование этого выдающегося события УКАЗЫВАЮ рабочим коллективам и отдельным гражданам на соблюдение производственной дисциплины и соблюдение тишины после 23 часов. Приступить к поздравлению в виде подношений, объятий, приподаний, похлопываний, поцелуев и перетягивания каната.

Вр.И.о.секретаря
всего комитета   [NAME]

FIGURE 7.2. Directive produced by Andrei's Komsomol committee for his thirtieth birthday (1983).

USSR

Ministry of Non-Ferrous Metallurgy

• • •

SOYUZ-ALUMINUM

• • •

The All-Soviet Scientific Research and Design Institute

DIRECTIVE

August 12, 1983   N 001

LENINGRAD

On August 13, 1953 the non-ferrous metallurgical industry of the USSR suffered a great loss. To this life came an inspirational leader and master of mystery, unwavering manager of a pickling station, and the director of the Vasilievskii Island ski lift, the father-in-law of Estonian pop, and the hero of Mongolian epics, Andriushen'ka [Last Name].

This date is inscribed in rosy letters into the biography of the [Name] Institute!

In commemoration of this outstanding event I COMMAND to the working collectives and private citizens the observation of the industrial discipline and silence after 23:00 hours. Proceed to congratulate him by way of gift-offering, embracing, self-prostrating, back-patting, kissing, and engaging in a tug of war.

Temporary replacement Secretary   [Last Name]
of the Committee   [Signature]

FIGURE 7.3. Directive. Author's translation of figure 7.2.

(*ushël iz zhizni*), followed by a formulaic list of titles and achievements and, at the end, the name of the deceased. On November 12, 1982, *Pravda* announced Brezhnev's death with the text: "The Communist Party of the Soviet Union and all Soviet people have suffered a great loss. From this life departed a devoted successor of the great Lenin's work, ardent patriot, outstanding revolutionary, and combatant for peace and communism, a great political and state figure of contemporary times, Leonid Il'ich Brezhnev."[31]

The "directive" produced by the members of the Komsomol committee started in this style but quickly mixed it with another genre, pointing to a shift and multiplicity of meanings associated with Andrei's authoritative posts, occupations, and discourses—he is the organizer of the Komsomol work, conscientious secretary who cared for the well-being of young employees, ingenious inventor of strategies for avoiding senseless formalities and meaningless work, creator of a friendly community of *svoi* among the committee and rank-and-file members, connoisseur of Western rock music, organizer of musical concerts of "amateur" bands and dances, and so on. The first sentence starts in the authoritative style of an obituary: "On August 13, 1953 the non-ferrous metallurgical industry[32] of the USSR suffered a great loss." The following sentence inverts the formula's meaning: the great loss was suffered because of Andrei's birth, not death. The nonstandard phrase "to this life came" (*prishël v zhizn'*) is fashioned as a humorous parallel to the authoritative formula, "from this life departed." By mixing the styles of an obituary and a birthday announcement, the document blurs the boundary between death and life, introducing an ironic zone in-between, a temporal discontinuity in the style that was similar to necroaesthetics. In the list of Andrei's titles, authoritative formulas are again mixed with other genres. Andrei is described in an authoritative formula as an "inspirational leader" (*vdokhnovitel'*) and in an imitation ironic formula as a "master of mystery" (*mistifikator*), hinting that his work as the Komsomol secretary amounted not only to fulfilling the tasks that he saw as meaningful but also avoiding the work that he considered meaningless, even if reporting it in documents. In another authoritative formula he is described as an "unwavering manager" (*bessmennyi rukovoditel'*), but what he is manager of is not the Komsomol committee

---

[31] "*Kommunisticheskaia partiia Sovetskogo Soiuza, ves' sovetskii narod ponesli tiazhëluiu utratu. Iz zhizni ushël vernyi prodolzhatel' velikogo dela Lenina, plamennyi patriot, vydaiushchiisia revoliutsioner i borets za mir, za kommunizm, krupneishii politicheskii i gosudarstvennyi deiatel' sovremennosti Leonid Il'ich Brezhnev*" ("Obrashchenie," *Pravda*, November 12, 1982, 1).

[32] A reference to the research conducted in the institute.

262

but a "pickling station" (*zasolochnyi punkt*), a reference to the committee as friends involved in frequent drinking celebrations that Andrei organized (in Russia pickles are often eaten after a shot of vodka).

The phrase "the director of Vasilievskii Island ski-lift" mixes references to intensify the effect of the discontinuity: Vasilievskii Island, a district in Leningrad where the institute was located, is a low, flat island that lies at the mouth of the Gulf of Finland and that was frequently flooded in those years. A reference to a "ski-lift" in that context is a funny incongruity. "The father-in-law of Estonian pop" (*otchim estonskogo popsa*) and "the hero of Mongolian epics" (*geroi mongol'skogo eposa*) parallel each other: the former refers to a Westernized Soviet republic, the latter to a "traditional" non-Western Soviet satellite. This again invokes the shift and discontinuity at the core of Andrei's activities: his work on organizing rock concerts of "amateur" bands and his skillful work in composing long texts in the impressive but unclear authoritative style, to which the "Mongolian epics" refers. Following the style of the obituaries, this list of characteristics ends with Andrei's name. However, instead of the authoritative formula that included name (Andrei), patronymic (Nikolaevich), and last name, it referred to him in a diminutive form "Andriushen'ka,"[33] underscoring the changed meaning of the figure of the Komsomol secretary (he was not a "boss" but one of *svoi*).

The third sentence describes the date of Andrei's birthday using an authoritative formula of referring to important ideological dates as being "inscribed in red letters" (*krasnymi bukvami*) in the Soviet calendar. For example, the leading articles in *Pravda* every year announced May Day anniversaries by the phrase: "this date is inscribed in red letters in our calendar."[34] However, the directive changes it to "inscribed in rosy letters" (*rozovymi bukvami*), reinterpreting the meaning that the date of Andrei's birthday had—it was important, but not exactly for the ideological reasons suggested in the authoritative genre. The last two sentences again juxtapose authoritative and parodic genres. "In commemoration of this outstanding event I command to the working collectives and private citizens . . . after 23:00 hours . . ." is modeled on the Minister of Defense's order, published in newspapers on anniversary occasions, to conduct fireworks in major cities. For example, on May 9, 1983, *Pravda* wrote: "In commemoration of the thirty-eighth anniversary of the victory of the Soviet people in the Great Patriotic War, I command today, at 22:00 hours local time to carry out celebratory artillery fireworks in

---

[33] On mixing of genres, see Bakhtin (1986), Hanks (2000, 127).

[34] *Eta data vpisana krasnymi bukvami v nashem kalendare.*

[list of cities]." The directive's parodic order ends with a list of friendly and absurd congratulatory gestures.

This document focused on multiple discontinuities—temporal, spatial, semantic—in the discourse and activities of Andrei and his Komsomol committee. As an example of *stiob* it did not simply ridicule authoritative discourse, but rather imitated its performative shift, associating authoritative forms with unanticipated meanings, and suggesting that these reinterpretations were creative, ingenious, agentive, and not unethical. It suggested that Andrei neither subscribed to all constative meanings of authoritative discourse nor rejected them all, but engaged in their creative interpretation and shift. This is why he could see himself and be seen by others as simultaneously a "master of mystery," who knew both how to avoid senseless aspects of ideological work and instead organize rock concerts, and as a conscientious Komsomol secretary, who conducted important work, believed in communism, and was proud of his honorary diplomas that recognized that fact.

Personal Profile

Consider another humorous document that demonstrates particularly well the temporal, spatial, and biopolitical discontinuities at the level of late Soviet authoritative discourse. This document was produced in 1983, again by Andrei and his Komsomol committee members, on an official form entitled "Personal Profile for Human Resources" (*Lichnyi listok po uchëtu kadrov*). Such forms were filled out when a person was hired for a new job. They contained information about one's social origin, ethnicity, education, professional and other occupations, awards, reprimands, membership in the party and other associations, and so forth. The length and depth of the information in this document makes it a particularly interesting example of *stiob*. The document again juxtaposes forms of authoritative discourse with other discourses and makes references to diverse historical periods and events, social, ethnic, sexual, and biological identities, forms of collective entertainment, the Imaginary West, and so on. For reasons of space—it is five pages long— we will consider only some questions and answers from the form.

The entry for Andrei's place of birth is an imaginary place with an obscene name, "Lower Up-Your-Mother-Ville" (*Nizhnie Matiugi*) and his social origin is identified by an ideologically problematic prerevolutionary and nonproletarian background: "from landed gentry" (*iz posadskikh*). The status of his party membership is marked as "member" (*chlen*), instead of "party member" (*chlen partii*), making an explicit sexual joke,[35] the date of his entry into the party is marked an absurd "32.13.01" (day 32 of month 13), and the number of his party card is similarly absurd "0.75"—a reference to a common slang expression for a large bottle of vodka (which held 0.75 liters). All these entries introduced temporal and spatial discontinuities in Andrei's social, biological, and political life.

The box for "scientific works and inventions" is filled out with three decidedly absurd scientific research projects that Andrei had supposedly conducted: "Further inquiries into the question of the influence of the paranoiac gonococcus on the phase structure of the optimal sound of Eric Burdon,"[36] "Growing facial hair in extreme conditions,"[37] and "The secret of longevity."[38] The reference to "paranoiac gonococcus" (a form of dementia caused by long-term exposure to gonorrhea) and other biological references in this list mixed the topics of sexuality, disease, insanity, life, and death in the style reminiscent of necroaesthetics. The reference to Eric Burdon, a member of the British rock group The Animals, refers to Andrei's extraordinary interest in and knowledge about Western rock music. The "secret of longevity" makes a reference to absurd temporalities and the realities of gerontocracy.

The question in the document about previous occupations is a long sentence that instructs one to list: "Work performed from the beginning of professional activities (including studies in higher and specialized middle educational institutions, military service, participation in partisan units and secondary employment)." The document also asks one to mention "these institutions, organizations, and enterprises by the names they had at the time" and to list previous "military service with the mention of the rank held." This question, on forms issued in the early 1980s, itself suggests a complex and absurd mix of temporalities. It asks about multiple facts and events of a distant past, even about one's possible participation in the partisan units during World War II that had ended forty years earlier. Such questions were ubiquitous in Soviet personal profile forms. They represented a typical example of a frozen authoritative formula that remained intact for decades, illustrating the profound temporal discontinuity in authoritative discourse.[39] It is precisely on this discontinuity between frozen form and constative meaning that Andrei and his

---

[35] *Chlen,* like English "member," was slang for penis. Another common slang joke that played on the double meaning of the expression "member" was to call limousines for the members of the Central Committee "member-mobiles" (*chlenovoz*)—limousines for penises.

[36] *Eshchë raz k voprosu vliianiia paranoicheskogo genokokka na frazovuiu strukturu optimal'nogo zvuchaniia Erika Bërdona.*

[37] *Vyrashchivanie volosianogo pokrova na litse v ekstremal'nykh uslaviiakh.*

[38] *Sekret dolgoletiia.*

[39] On the persistence of this type of historical questioning as part of Soviet identity politics see Ssorin-Chaikov (2003, 106).

friends focus when answering this question. They push this temporal discontinuity further, adding references to multiple stories, political affiliations, life, death, biology, and drinking. In this *stiob* description Andrei's professional occupations include: "Participation in the battle of Borodino" (the decisive battle of Russian troops against Napoleon's army in 1812), "Liberation of the Far East from the White Guard" (during the Civil War in 1924), "The taking of Berlin" (by the Soviet Army in 1945), his own birth in "Ward 6 of maternity hospital," and the years he spent at the university mentioned simply as "blurred" (a reference to his frequent drinking with friends).

Answering the question about one's "government awards" the friends again chose to focus on temporal and biopolitical discontinuities: although Andrei never received any medals, his list includes: "The Cross of St. George" (a medal from the prerevolutionary tsarist Russian empire), "The Order of People's Friendship"[40] (a Soviet medal awarded for contributions to internationalist work), and imaginary medals with such names as, "Medal of the Fourth Exhibition of Service Dogs in Berdishchi"[41] and "Medal to tomcat Tikhon from loving female cats."[42] The answers in this humorous form present Andrei's life at the intersection of multiple temporalities (old, new, Soviet, prerevolutionary, imaginary), political affiliations (Soviet, tsarist Russian, Western), and biologies and sexualities (human, animal).

Prigov's Obituaries

Similar humorous documents that engaged the discontinuities of authoritative discourse circulated at the time not only in most Komsomol committees but also among most members of the last Soviet generation in various venues and contexts. For example, strikingly similar texts were produced at that time by an "amateur" Moscow poet Dmitrii Prigov, a sculptor by occupation whose literary work was unrecognized and unpublished by the state until after the Soviet Union collapsed.[43] In the early 1980s, when Prigov wrote the texts analyzed below, he was unknown to the majority of Soviet people,[44] and Andrei and his friends

[40] *Orden druzhby narodov.*

[41] *Medal' chetvertoi vystavki sluzhebnogo sobakovodstva v Berdshchakh.*

[42] *Medal' kotu Tikhonu ot liubiashchikh koshek.*

[43] In post-Soviet 1990s, Prigov achieved extraordinary fame as a "postmodern" poet, writer, and performer.

[44] At that time Prigov's texts existed in a small samizdat circulation among Moscow intellectuals. Prigov began his literary experiments after the Soviet state confiscated his art studio and he could no longer practice sculpting.

could not have heard of him or his writings. The striking parallel in their *stiob* engagements with authoritative discourse constitutes an important ethnographic fact about the discursive shifts of the late Soviet period.

In the early 1980s, Prigov wrote a series of short vignettes entitled "Obituaries" (*Nekrologi*) that were published many years later in the collection *Soviet Texts* (1997). In the authoritative style of Soviet obituaries, Prigov's texts "announced" the deaths of the nineteenth-century classical authors of Russian literature, most of whom had been dead for over a century. The texts overidentified with the form of authoritative obituary and decontextualized it by mixing it with historical temporalities and references. True to the genre of *stiob* the text never acknowledged its irony.

The obituaries treated the classics of Russian literature as bureaucrats of the party and the Soviet state, calling them "comrades" and providing lists of their heroic achievements. Pushkin's obituary reads: "The Central Committee of the CPSU, Supreme Soviet of the USSR, and Soviet government with the deepest sorrow" announce the death of "the great Russian poet Alexandr Sergeevich Pushkin," on February 10, 1837, "as a result of a tragic duel." After describing the poet's high moral character, the obituary ends with the declaration: "Comrade Pushkin will forever remain in the hearts of his friends and people who knew him closely as a playboy, boozer, womanizer, and mischief-maker (*guliaka, balagur, babnik i okhal'nik*)." Prigov wrote similar obituaries for "Comrade Lermontov," "Comrade Dostoyevsky," and "Comrade Tolstoy." The final "obituary" Prigov wrote for himself: "The Central Committee of the CPSU, Supreme Soviet of the USSR, and Soviet government with deepest sorrow announce that on June 30, 1980, on the fortieth year of his life, Prigov Dmitrii Aleksandrovich, is living in Moscow."

Everything in these texts, including Prigov's obituary for himself that announces his life rather than death, is strikingly similar to the two abovementioned humorous documents written in Andrei's Komsomol committee. Prigov's texts mixed histories, life, death, sexuality, and literary canons within the frame of authoritative discourse, creating temporal, spatial, biopolitical, and semantic discontinuities. Prigov's literary style has some roots in the Russian tradition of the literature of the absurd,[45]— but his texts were undeniably a cultural product of late socialism. His style has been called "quasi-poetry" (Borukhov 1989)—a kind of poetry that is supposed to function neither as real poetry nor its parody, but as something that refuses the boundary between the two, much like the central principle in the aesthetics of *stiob* and in the whole ethos of the last Soviet generation.

[45] In the 1920s, Daniil Kharms also wrote short stories about famous poets and writers canonized by Soviet Russian culture.

Civil Defense

In her diary, Lena (born in 1963), a student in the Department of Journalism at Leningrad University, employed the genre of *stiob* to describe the class called "Civil Defense" (*Grazhdanskaia oborona*) that was mandatory and universally considered boring and meaningless. The class discussed how to practice civil defense in case of war. The textbook for the class provided graphic illustrations of nuclear explosions and biological disasters, with notoriously bad drawings by amateur army artists and dry descriptions of various types of injuries, effects of radiation, and first aid measures. These texts and images were perfect objects of *stiob*. On January 16, 1983, Lena wrote:

> Civil defense is a great subject. My textbook has wonderful illustrations of how citizens behave in the case of a nuclear war. For example, tidy, attractive citizens, who unanimously follow the codex of the builder of communism,[46] peacefully enter a fallout shelter. A phlegmatic young man, with blood gushing from his body like a fountain, stands next to a confident and skillful nurse. And there are other realistic pictures in which no one shows any signs of panic.

Formulaic images of confident nurses and calm, bleeding citizens, with no signs of pain or panic, were reminiscent in style, color, and schematic primitivism of the socialist realist images of Soviet citizens, workers, and scientists on propaganda billboards and posters. Lena refers to these images when she quotes the authoritative formula, "citizens who unanimously follow the codex of the builder of communism." The formulaic, frozen representation in these visuals and texts depicted Soviet citizens as political symbols who neither looked nor reacted in a human way. Lena's *stiob* focused on this version of discontinuity between authoritative form and meaning, producing a similar effect to that of necroaesthetics.

Two Letters to Inna

The aesthetics of *stiob* engaged with authoritative discourse in other contexts too. It is easily found in the correspondence and diaries of the 1970s and early 1980s. The following two excerpts are from letters written to Inna (first encountered in chapter 4), a student in the history department of Leningrad University, by her university friend. The first

---

[46] *Opriatnye, privlekatel'nye grazhdane, kotorye edinodushno sleduiut kodeksu stroitelia kommunizma.*

letter was written on July 25, 1981, when Inna's friend was working at the Leningrad Museum of Ethnography:

> Hello-hello, my dear Inchik![47]
> Today at the museum I played a prank. We have there a plaque . . . that reads: "Lenin is greeting someone or other," I can't remember whom. That sign was in the archaeology hall, in a certain sense it was uselessly lying around [*valialsia*]. . . . The hall also contains some works of Gerasimov[48]—the reconstructed sculptural portraits of various Neanderthals and Australopithecuses, and the gallery is headed by a chimp, which is right to the point. . . . In short, I combined them.

Inna's friend subjected an authoritative formula to *stiob* procedure. She took a sign with an authoritative phrase that was supposed to accompany a photo of Lenin, and, without doing anything to the sign itself, decontextualized it, moving it from the front hall in the museum, where photos of the revolution were displayed, to another hall that held a display of human evolution placing it next to a stuffed chimp. The prank introduced multiple discontinuities into authoritative discourse—semantic (from authoritative symbol to museum artifact), temporal (from Soviet history to the evolution of species), biological (from Lenin to chimp)—making the meaning of this phrase slide in hilarious ways. The ambiguity of the message (Inna's friend did not state anything explicitly, only moved a perfectly official symbol around) allows Inna's friend to produce it openly. The second letter Inna's friend sent the next year, in July 1982, from a collective farm (*kolkhoz*) where she worked with her fellow students during the summer:

> Dear Inchik!
>
> *What will I do here all alone*
> *Without a man*
> *—from a folk song*
>
> It's always like this! This is how tender youthful maidens turn into spinsters, frightening in their self-reliance, whom common folks call emancipated, and who are known in the high party and government spheres as "the new image of the Soviet woman, liberated from centuries of slavery."

Here, as in the previous letter, quotation marks appear in the original, signifying direct quotations from authoritative discourse. The meaning of this

[47] Diminuitive for Inna.
[48] Mikhail Gerasimov—Soviet physical anthropologist who invented a method for reconstructing facial features from the skull structure.

FIGURE 7.4. The envelope of the letter sent to Inna by her friend in July 1982. Handwriting on the left reads: "Let us strike kitsch with PRAVDA!"

authoritative formula is again reinterpreted: the new liberated Soviet women suffers from hard physical labor and a lack of male sexual attention. Even the envelope of the letter (see figure 7.4), which is exposed to public view, contains a *stiob* remark that quotes an authoritative formula but displaces its meaning. The large stamp, which Inna's friend put on the envelope, says: "Seventy years of *Pravda*. Organ of the Central Committee of the CPSU. The newspaper was founded on May 5, 1912, by V. I. Lenin." Underneath the stamp on the envelope, Inna's friend writes in the style of an authoritative slogan: "Let us strike kitsch with PRAVDA!"[49] The meaning of this phrase is based on the ambiguity of the word *pravda*—it is both a noun that means "truth" and the name of a newspaper. The author draws on the meaning of *Pravda* as newspaper. She spells that word in capital letters, as it was spelled when used as the newspaper title—she overidentifies with this authoritative form. However, she simultaneously decontextualizes it too. The verb "strike with" suggests that *pravda* is also used as a regular word, "truth," which in turn suggests

[49] *Vdarim PRAVDOI po poshlostiam!*

270

that the kitsch that needed to be struck was the ideological stamp itself. The authoritative symbol (the text and image on the stamp) is subjected to *stiob* procedure. Again it is the phrase's ambiguity that allows the author to write it openly on the envelope.

Two Postcards from an Engineer

In the early 1980s, a young engineer from the town of Savelovo, outside Kalinin, wrote two postcards to his friend Maria, a biologist in Leningrad. These were typical short anniversary postcards that, like millions of other postcards, were sent to friends and relatives on the occasion of Revolution Day, May Day, Victory Day, and other holidays all over the country. Traditionally they contained congratulations, personal news, and questions about the addressee's well-being. Sometimes they also contained occasional remarks that reproduced authoritative forms, subjecting their meanings to the kinds of displacements discussed above. The first postcard (November 10, 1981) refers to the end of tedious work on a collective farm, where engineers and students from the cities were sent in the early Fall to assist with harvesting vegetables:

> Dear Marusia!
> All of us here warmly congratulate you with the holiday and wish you health, well-being and creativity. We have finally entered a more or less regular mode: there is no need to run to the ranch,[50] no need to shake the apple trees, break your nails weeding, or load bags with potatoes. . . . The harvest has been collected, and now we are waiting to know what will happen with it. For, *as the party teaches us, the main task is not only to collect, but also to preserve*[51] (emphasis added).

The italicized phrase is a precise quote from authoritative discourse, which the letter does not subvert but decontextualizes: the Soviet collective farm is referred to by an American word "ranch," suggesting the alienating work of seasonal laborers. A direct quote of the party's teaching about the need to preserve the harvest and the ironic phrase "now we are waiting to know what will happen with it" refer to Soviet agriculture's traditional loss of much of the harvest in storage and transportation. The implication of these comments is that although engineers helped to collect the harvest, the collective farms would lose much of it;

---

[50] *Ne nado bezhat' na rancho*—a slang reference to agricultural fields.
[51] *Kak partiia uchit, glavnoe ne tol'ko sobrat', no i sokhranit'*.

the authoritative formula (in italics) is quoted verbatim, but its meaning is displaced.

The second postcard, written a year later (November 10, 1982), again quotes two formulas of authoritative discourse. In this case they were placed in quotation marks in the original:

Dear Marusia! Congratulations!
After a series of unpleasant events such as my hospitalization, a period of relative peace and quiet has begun. I am well, and as the cosmonauts say, "am ready to fulfill any task for the Motherland."[52] And the Motherland calls us to participate in the *subbotnik*[53] on the occasion of the fortieth anniversary of the victory of Moscow. Yet another silly whim [*ocherednaia blazh'*]. So tomorrow we are going to a meeting to "support the initiative of Muscovites."[54]

The meaning of both authoritative formulas is inverted in the phrase "yet another silly whim." Of all examples, this is the most straightforward suggestion of the meaninglessness of authoritative claims. The implication is that the author had no choice but to participate in the initiatives that were presented as voluntary but which were in fact mandatory and, in his opinion, senseless.

The letters and postcards quoted above explicitly referred not only to formulas of authoritative discourse but also to their enunciators. In the letters of Inna's friend, these enunciators were "a plaque that reads" and "the high party and government spheres." The engineer's letters referred to these enunciators thus: "as the party teaches us," "as the cosmonauts say" and "the Motherland calls us." These references act as quotations of authoritative formulas. Recall the raikom secretary Sasha, from chapter 3, who helped his friends write Komsomol speeches. Before dictating phrases in authoritative discourse, he would at first joke, then clear his throat and say in the well-trained voice of a spokesperson: "OK, let's start." These markers do not only introduce the genre of authoritative discourse, they also provide a link to the performative power that is "delegated" to such "authorized spokespersons" of this discourse (Bourdieu 1991, 106). This link, and the fact that authoritative forms are cited with perfect accuracy, allowed for a performative shift that made the meaning of the remarks open-ended and unanchored. This openness of meaning was an important part of the aesthetic that refused to choose between the positions in the pro-/anti-dichotomy. At the same time this ambiguity allowed one to make such comments relatively openly, even writing

---

[52] *Gotov vypolnit' liuboe zadanie Rodiny.*
[53] *Subbotnik*—the so-called voluntary unpaid Saturday work day.
[54] *Podderzhivat' initsiativu moskvichei.*

them on regular mail envelopes without feeling that this act was too dangerous.

Although these letters seem strikingly different from the passionate letters written by Alexandr from Yakutsk and Novosibirsk in chapter 6, they, in fact, share with them one crucial characteristic: using different techniques and achieving different results, they were engaged in the same process of reproducing authoritative forms that enabled them to introduce new meanings neither limited to nor determined by the constative meanings of authoritative discourse. How various people of this generation envisioned meaningful life was different, but the processes and aesthetics of this production were similar.

Reeling Out *Anekdoty*

Another popular genre of irony that became ubiquitous during late socialism was the famous *anekdot,* a short, formulaic joke that can be repeated by different people in different contexts. Unlike the previous examples of humor, except for scary little poems, the *anekdot* was a genre of folklore without an author. In Russia this genre neither started nor ended with late socialism. However, during the late-socialist period, it acquired particular characteristics that it did not have before or after. In different historical, political, and social contexts such genres as *anekdoty* may focus on different topics, have different functions and meanings, conditions of circulation, and rituals of narration, and the number and frequency with which *anekdoty* are encountered in everyday life may also change.[55]

Although *anekdoty* existed in earlier periods of Soviet history (Thurston 1991; Graham 2003b), between the late 1960s and the early 1980s, Russian folklorists and philologists noted a significant rise in the number of the *anekdoty* that were in regular circulation and in the frequency with which they were encountered. They also observed the rise to prominence of a collective ritual of narrating endless rounds of *anekdoty*. The ritual was referred to as "reeling out" (*travit' anekdoty*), as if they were mounted on a spool of rope. In those years, it was almost impossible to go through a single day without hearing and telling *anekdoty*. Folklorist Alexandr Belousov argues that, in the 1960s, a shift occurred in the nature of *anekdoty*. In the early 1960s one occasionally heard and told *anekdoty*, but not daily and usually as an isolated incident. However, from the mid 1960s, he observed that the number of *anekdoty* started increasing; they

[55] In the Soviet Union many *anekdoty* circulated even in Stalin's times (Thurston 1991). See discussion of the *anekdoty* and their historical change during and after late socialism in Yurchak (1997a).

273

became a ubiquitous part of daily conversations; and it became "a custom to tell *anekdoty* during all cigarette breaks at the university." When in the late 1960s, Belousov moved from Leningrad to Tartu University (Estonia), he discovered a similar situation there. *Anekdoty* were ubiquitous and people were always hungry for new ones: "Every time I went back to Leningrad or Moscow my colleagues asked me to bring fresh anekdoty."[56]

In the late 1960s, whole new series of *anekdoty* appeared. Andrei Siniavskii observed that the huge and popular series of *anekdoty* about the civil war hero commander Chapaev (*anekdoty pro Chapaeva*) emerged and grew in number and popularity in the context of the fiftieth anniversary of the October (Bolshevik) Revolution in 1967 (Terz 1981, 175). Another series about Lenin (*leniniana*) emerged during preparations for Lenin's one hundredth anniversary in 1970.[57] In his description of the late Soviet period, folklorist Miron Petrovskii called it "anekdotcentrist" (1990, 47) and Siniavskii called it, alluding to *anekdoty*, "the era of popular oral art, of prosperity of a huge folkloric genre" (Terz 1981, 167).[58] Others have described the period as "the golden age of the Soviet anecdote" (Zand 1982) and even suggested that *anekdoty* became "perhaps the most significant new art form" to emerge during that time (Fagner and Cohen 1988, 170).

At the same time, the collective ritual of "reeling out" endless rounds of *anekdoty* in a group became a ubiquitous part of daily *obshchenie* practiced in various contexts and groups, among friends, acquaintances, and total strangers. Although it was inappropriate to engage in it during various formal interactions, professional or party meetings, outside of these contexts *anekdoty* were told relatively openly. A boss could "reel out" with his or her employees, and a Komsomol secretary could "reel out" with the rank and file. Siniavskii points out that this ritual became common in all Soviet republics and socialist countries of Eastern Europe during this period:[59]

> As soon as two Russians or three Jews get together, or citizens of any other nationality of Soviet, or Czech, or Polish, i.e., socialist, upbringing—they start "reeling out" *anekdoty* interrupting each other. . . . It is pleasant to ask the question: "Do you remember an *anekdot*, in which Chapaev . . . ?" And to hear back—"Of course! But let me tell you another one." We are so used to telling *anekdoty* like the latest news . . . or at least to finding out who remembers which ones. (Terz 1981, 167)

[56] Author interview.
[57] Belousov, personal communication.
[58] See also Kurganov (1997) and Graham (2003b) for discussions of *anekdoty*.
[59] See also Banc (1990).

An American journalist in the Soviet Union described the ritual of reeling out, in the early 1980s, as follows:

> In company, the first jokes emerge after several rounds of drinking, like little secrets. By the time tea is served [at the end of a meal], the jokes start to flow, and flow, and flow. During one drunken evening, I remember our Armenian host had guided us through several broad categories of jokes: Stalin jokes, Brezhnev jokes, emigration jokes and jokes about Georgians (a local treat). At three in the morning, he rose, swaying, to announce a new round of *anekdoty:* "And now . . . jokes about camels!" (Zand 1982).

Importantly, in the ritual of reeling out, all sorts of jokes—"political" and otherwise (sexual, ethnic, etc.)—were narrated together in one long session. Moreover, in that mix there were invariably many old jokes, which usually did not seem problematic. Although telling and hearing new jokes was important for the listeners and prestigious for the teller, in the ritual of reeling out it was also important to repeat the jokes others might have heard previously, even many times. Most *anekdoty* were heard by a person more than once; people took part in the reeling out not only to hear new jokes, or any particular "type" of jokes, but to participate in this enjoyable collective ritual itself that contributed to producing groups *svoi*.[60] The importance of collective repetition and enjoyment of old jokes was described in a 1960s "meta-joke":

> To be able to "reel out" more *anekdoty* per evening, a group of friends had them numbered. When in the evening members of the group got together, one started with "number 15," and everyone laughed. Another person added "number 74" and everyone laughed again. But when the third one said "number 108" there was a long silent pause, and then one man said in embarrassment: "How could you tell that one in front of the ladies?"

The End of the Ritual

With the changes of perestroika in the late 1980s, folklorists observed that the number of new *anekdoty* told on a daily basis very sharply diminished, and the ritual of reeling out virtually disappeared from daily life (Petrovskii 1990, 49). This fact was also widely discussed in the media and personal conversations, with many people complaining: "There are no *anekdoty* any more!" It seemed no longer relevant to tell

---

[60] Compare with the importance of ritualized repetition of the same narratives and stories by the Mit'ki above.

anekdoty about the recent Soviet past, and there were very few new anekdoty about the present. The disappearance of the *anekdoty* was also observed in East European countries.[61] At the same time, publishers started compiling series and collections of *anekdoty*, most of which turned into historical accounts of the bygone era, with such titles as: *The History of the USSR in Jokes* (Duborskii 1991). In 1995 the popular weekly *Ogonëk* wrote with regret about the disappearance of the once vibrant and creative oral genre and its replacement with printed collections of old jokes: "When in the past [*anekdoty*] were spread by word of mouth, they were cherished and savored during conversations like dessert. But today, multiplied in lousy booklets and fat tomes, they have totally disappeared from everyday life" (Erokhin 1995, 43).

According to Belousov, who has been collecting and writing about *anekdoty* for years, in the late Soviet period there were many about Brezhnev, in the beginning of perestroika there were some about Gorbachev, but in the post-Soviet 1990s there were practically none about Yeltsin.[62] A bibliographer in the department of Russian literature at the St. Petersburg Public Library mentioned that among the published collections the library acquired between the late 1980s and 1995, most *anekdoty* were from the Soviet period, with only a few about the post-Soviet life. Among these, some addressed new post-Soviet phenomena—advertisements, Western products (Tampax, Snickers), but there were practically no *anekdoty* about political life: "Even the October [1993] events in Moscow[63] were not reflected in *anekdoty*. In the past, an event of such scale was bound to produce thousands of them!" Since the early and mid-1990s, when these observations were made, the situation has changed somewhat, with more new anekdoty emerging today.[64] However, most of them still focus on the phenomena mentioned by the bibliographer, and political discourse remains underrepresented, at least by old standards. Moreover, the number of *anekdoty* in daily circulation remains considerably lower than in Soviet times, and, what is particularly important, the ritual of reeling out has not reclaimed its dominant position as a ubiquitous form of daily interaction. Telling *anekdoty* became a more sporadic occurrence, limited to certain contexts and groups of friends.[65]

[61] Verdery describes the same phenomenon in Romania (1996, 96).

[62] Author interview.

[63] A standoff between Yeltsin's government and the Russian Parliament, that ended in an armed fighting on the streets of Moscow.

[64] Notable among them in the mid-1990s were *anekdoty* about New Russians (the new rich) and the mafia. See Graham (2003a; 2003b).

[65] See Yurchak (1997a); Pesmen (2000); and Graham (2003b). In the recent years the number of *anekdoty* and other humorous genres seems to be growing again. See Blank (2005) on the discussion of such genres in contemporary Ukraine.

Humor That Has Ceased to Struggle

Understanding the reasons for the sudden explosion of *anekdoty* into the everyday during late socialism, and then their near disappearance from it during and after perestroika, is key to understanding the role that this genre of humor played in the late Soviet context. The meaning of *anekdoty*, especially political *anekdoty*, has often been associated with "resistance" to the system, ironic subversion of its dogmas or a clandestine statement of "truth," of what one "really thinks" (Dundes 1987). However, the role of *anekdoty* in the context of late socialism was different and more complex. Like *stiob*, the genre reacted to and was enabled by certain shifts in authoritative discourse that took place during this period. It is no coincidence that the dominance of reeling out coincided with the hypernormalization of authoritative discourse in the 1960s, or that it nearly disappeared from everyday life in the late 1980s, when authoritative discourse collapsed.

Late Soviet *anekdot* can be compared to political humor of other genres. Peter Sloterdijk makes a distinction between two types of political humor. The first is "kynicism"—the cheeky side of cynicism, the attitude of the fool or the clown to the ruler. Kynics "take the liberty of confronting prevailing lies" which provokes "a climate of satirical loosening up in which the powerful, together with their ideologists of domination, let go affectively—precisely under the onslaught of the critical affront by kynics." In ancient Greece the kynic "farts, shits, pisses, masturbates on the street, before the eyes of the Athenian market," consciously ridiculing the norms of social morality and exposing them as arbitrary (1993, 103).

Sloterdijk contrasts kynicism with another type of humor that he calls "humor that has ceased to struggle" (1993, 305).[66] This type of humor differs from both jaded cynicism and explicit acts of kynic ridicule and subversion of dominant norms, and refuses to be charged with the moral pathos of exposing "lies" and stating "truths." It pokes fun at the kind of things that may make us outraged or disempowered, but still, for various reasons, remain important, meaningful, and even dear because we identify with them, support them, believe in them, at least to an extent, or simply recognize them as immutable and therefore not worth struggling with.

The humor of *anekdoty* balanced in the zone that traversed boundaries between support and opposition, sanity and insanity, social responsibility and cynicism, rationality and absurdity, life and death. It is striking, for example, that not only Brezhnev could be the negative protagonists of political *anekdoty* at that time but also the dissidents. The following two

[66] Sloterdijk (1993) also contrasts it with "cynical reason." See also Žižek (1991a), Yurchak (1997a), Navaro-Yashin (2002).

anekdoty illustrate this refusal to be associated with the moral position of a dissident who wants to expose lies, showing the difference between the discourse of *anekdoty* and the discourse of dissent (compare with the discourse about dissidents in chapter 3):

> A dissident walks out of his house. It is starting to rain. He looks up and says with indignation: "They [the party] always do just what they want!" The next day when he walks out, the sun is shining brightly. He looks up and says with indignation: "Of course! For this they find the money!"

> A big crowd of people is quietly standing in a lake of sewage coming up to their chins. Suddenly a dissident falls in it and starts shouting and waving his hands in disgust: "Yuk! I cannot stand this! How can you people accept these horrible conditions?!" To which the people reply with a quiet indignation: "Shut up! You are making waves!"

In the first joke, the dissident is portrayed as a "psychotic" who is over-fixated on the constative dimension of discourse, attempting to read meaningful messages into the events of the natural world and interpreting literally the representations of reality that, according to "normal" people, were not supposed to be read as such. Lacan's illustration of the psychotic's unanchored relation to the symbolic order is strikingly similar to this joke: "Everything has become a sign for him. . . . If he encounters a red car in the street—a car is not a natural object—it's not for nothing, he will say, that it went past at that very moment" (Lacan 1993, 9).[67] In the second joke, the dissident's moral claim is reinterpreted as a banal and moralistic observation and a disregard for others, but the joke also made fun of all of "us," who are in fact standing up to our necks in sewage and recognize this fact.

This humor did not target some abstract "them" (the system, the dissidents) but looked inside—at those who told the jokes, at their own personal and collective involvement in the paradoxes of socialism. As Sloterdijk points out: "Only when the joke goes inward and one's own consciousness, admittedly from on high but not too ungraciously, inspects itself, does there arise a serenity that reveals not a kynic laughter, nor a cynical smile, but a humor that has ceased to struggle" (1993, 305).

As earlier argued, *stiob* also belonged to this variety of humor. The practitioners of *stiob* refused to articulate clearly the target of their irony and tried to avoid situations where their acts would be read straightforwardly

---

[67] Compare with the story in chapter 3, about a person who, after having been caught with literature protesting the war in Afghanistan, was also suspected by his colleagues of distributing pornography.

and unambiguously, considering this trivial, uninteresting, and silly. *Stiob* also refused the moral language of resistance or support. Recall the Mit'ki's slogan above: "The Mit'ki don't want to defeat anyone." *Stiob* and *anekdoty* differed from both the kynic's explicit subversion of the symbols and norms of power and the more hidden forms of cynical ridicule.[68]

Participating in the ritual of reeling out *anekdoty* as one long, collective narrative that was frequently repeated was a way of collectively making metaphoric references to the paradoxes and discontinuities in which everyone participated daily. Repeatedly, but momentarily, exposing these paradoxes and discontinuities at the collective and personal levels was funny and important because it showed to everyone that everyone one else was also involved in the reproduction of these paradoxes. The rituals provided a model of involvement in performative shift and of the personal and collective discontinuities this created. As demonstrated earlier, the parodic Komsomol documents did the same.

To operate in this way, *anekdoty*, like *stiob*, tended to be structured as a particular class of humor—humor that achieves what Michel Pecheux calls "the 'Munchhausen effect,' in memory of the immortal baron who lifted himself into the air by pulling on his own hair" (Pecheux 1994, 150). This humor is centered on the displacements and discontinuities of the person: a pupil "telephoned his headmaster to excuse himself from school, and when asked 'Who am I speaking to?' replied 'It's my father!' "; or, "There are no cannibals left in our area, we ate the last one last week" (Pecheux 1994, 151). Žižek describes a similar effect in the absurdist jokes of Groucho Marx: "Say, you remind me of Emmanuel Ravelli."—"But I am Emmannuel Ravelli."—"Then, no wonder you look like him!" (Žižek 1994b, 32).

However, unlike these examples, the *anekdoty* did not expose personal discontinuities but only hinted at them, which allowed one to keep the paradox outside of critical scrutiny and analysis. The rigid narrative structure of the *anekdot*—to remain funny *anekdot* had to be repeated without even minor changes—allowed participants to avoid facing the paradox explicitly. Instead, the paradox was coded on the level of the *anekdot*'s structure. In many anekdoty, one part quoted an authoritative formula or described an authoritative claim or presupposition (the phrases in quotes), and the other part introduced a discontinuity or inversion:

What is the most constant element of the Soviet system?
"Temporary problems."

[68] Clandestine ridicule is discussed, for example, in Mbembe (1992; 2001) in the post-colonial context.

In what aspects is socialism better than other systems?
In that "it successfully overcomes difficulties" that do not exist in other systems.

What is the difference between capitalism and socialism?
"In capitalism man exploits man," but in socialism it's the other way around.

What does the phrase "capitalism is at the edge of an abyss" mean?
It means that capitalism is standing at the edge looking down, trying to see what we are doing there.

A letter to *Pravda* from a small town of Riazan' says: Dear Comrades, you often write that "In capitalist countries people don't have enough to eat [*nedoedaiut*]." Perhaps, *that stuff*, of which they don't have enough to eat, could be sent to us in Riazan'?

In the next examples, the authoritative claims that are articulated in form but displaced in meaning are: Soviet people look to the future with optimism; communism will be a society of plenty; life in communism will be happy and unproblematic.[69]

What is the difference between a Soviet pessimist and a Soviet optimist?
A Soviet pessimist thinks that things can't possibly get any worse, but a Soviet optimist thinks that they will.

How will the problem of lines in shops be solved in communism?
There'll be nothing left to line up for.

What would happen if they started building communism in the Sahara Desert?
There would soon be shortages of sand.

What will life in communism be like?
Everyone will have a personal television set and a personal helicopter. For example, if you hear on the television that milk is sold in Sverdlovsk, you will jump in your helicopter and fly to Sverdlovsk to get milk.

This narrative structure of the *anekdot*, like in the case of *stiob*, performed a displacement of discourse, creating a feeling of the incongruous that is central in the perception of most types of humor (Curco

---

[69] Seriot (1992) describes similar political aphorisms published in Yugoslav newspapers during the reforms of the 1980s, when the first half of this statement quoted a party formula, and the second inverted its meaning—e.g., "Our way is really unique: no one would have the idea to follow it!"

1995, 37). But the *anekdot* also worked at the larger social level, engaging with discontinuities of the whole discursive regime and with one's participation in them. This level was amplified by the repetition of many jokes together, in one reeling out session, and of the repetition of such sessions day after day. *Anekdoty* functioned on that level not as isolated jokes or comments but as a discourse that constantly, on a daily basis, engaged with discontinuities of the social and the personal.

It was that broader discursive level that made the ritual of reeling out so intensely enjoyable, pleasurable, and addictive, especially in those years. Its pleasure was akin to the pleasure produced by Freud's "tendentious jokes" (jokes that cannot be openly told in public contexts, such as racist, sexist, sexual, and political jokes). Freud argued that such jokes, apart from producing the pleasure of laughter, also "produce new pleasure by lifting suppressions and repressions" (1960, 137), allowing for the social situations, which produced these repressions, to continue. However, Freud's psychological metaphor of "repression" in the description of this joke-work is problematic—it reduces the function of this humorous engagement to the level of personal psyche. In the context discussed here, this reduction parallels the familiar binary models of split subjects and repressive regimes. It is paramount to recognize that *anekdoty* did not function as isolated jokes in relation to isolated psyches, but constituted a complex discourse based on collective reeling-out sessions that were constantly repeated in different contexts and with different participants. This highly ritualized social discourse indeed produced "new pleasure" but one that was not purely psychological. It was linked to engaging, releasing, exposing, and enabling a complex set of discontinuities at personal, discursive, social, temporal, and other levels (as the earlier discussion of *stiob* demonstrated). This discourse indeed worked as Sloterdijk's "humor that has ceased to struggle." Its reeling-out rituals worked "like a drainage system—regulating, balancing, equilibrating—as a universally accepted regulative mini-amoralism" (Sloterjik 1993, 305). By engaging with the paradoxes, absurdities, and discontinuities of late-socialist life at the level of metaphor, this humor did not allow for them to be misrecognized completely; at the same time, by refusing to engage these paradoxes explicitly, the jokes allowed them to continue. Both these effects of the *anekdot* discourse were crucial. They enabled one to have a meaningful, creative, ethical life in the spaces and zones that traversed the boundaries between support and opposition, and therefore they became yet another technique in the ongoing deterritorialization of Soviet reality.

This book began with a paradox: the spectacular collapse of the Soviet Union was completely unexpected by most Soviet people and yet, as soon as people realized that something unexpected was taking place, most of them also immediately realized that they had actually been prepared for that unexpected change. Millions became quickly engrossed, making the collapse simultaneously unexpected, unsurprising, and amazingly fast. This complex succession of the unexpected and the unsurprising revealed a peculiar paradox at the core of the Soviet system. For years that system managed to inhabit incommensurable positions: it was everlasting and steadily declining, full of vigor and bleakness, dedicated to high ideals and devoid of them. None of these positions was a mask. They were each real and, as I have tried to show, mutually constitutive. Understanding this peculiar dynamic is crucial for the understanding of the nature of state socialism.

This book set out to explore this paradox of the Soviet system by closely examining the internal shifts, at the level of everyday life, in the discourse, language, ideology, ethics, social relations, time, and space on which this paradox was predicated. It also focused on the new unanticipated meanings, communities, relations, identities, interests, and pursuits that this paradox enabled. To address these issues the book explored the period of late socialism through the eyes of the last Soviet generation.

From the outset I argued that the various binary models of state socialism that remain widespread cannot adequately address these issues. Dichotomies such as oppression and resistance, truth and lies, official culture and unofficial culture, the state and the people, public self and private self overlook the complex meanings, values, ideals, and realities that constituted the Soviet system and, defying clear-cut divisions, existed both in harmony with the state's announced goals and in spite of them. For great numbers of Soviet citizens, many of the fundamental values, ideals, and realities of socialism were of genuine importance, despite the fact that many of their everyday practices routinely reinterpreted the announced norms and rules of the socialist state.

Let us formulate a preliminary conclusion: the paradox of late socialism stemmed from the fact that the more the immutable forms of the system's authoritative discourse were reproduced everywhere, the more the system was experiencing a profound internal displacement. This displacement of the system was in turn predicated on mass participation in the reproduction of the system's authoritative forms and representations, enabling the emergence of various forms of meaningful, creative life that were relatively uncontrolled, indeterminate, and "normal" (i.e., not perceived as out of the ordinary or alternative). Having this normal life was in turn predicated on participating in the performative reproduction of the system's authoritative forms and representations. Reproducing the system and participating in its continuous internal displacement were mutually constitutive processes.

When the changes of perestroika made it no longer important or possible to reproduce the experience of the system's immutability, the paradoxical processes of late socialism could no longer continue. At the same time, the early changes of perestroika revealed and articulated something that was already part of everyone's life but remained unarticulated in a broad discourse—namely, that by unanimously participating in the system's institutions, rituals, discourses, and lifestyles everyone was involved in the system's continuous displacement. This realization was unexpected, since the system's hegemony of form made it appear monolithic and immortal, and yet this revelation was also completely unsurprising, since it articulated the processes of displacement that the majority had implicitly known and in which it had long been involved. What exactly was that moment of rupture that occurred in the Soviet discursive regime during the early perestroika? How was the unexpected and yet unsurprising revelation introduced into the system, and how did it lead to the spectacular unraveling of late socialism? Before we answer these questions, let us revisit some of the central points in the book.

As we saw, the paradox at the core of late socialism went back to the early Soviet period. In fact, it was rooted in what Claude Lefort identified

283

as the general paradox of modern ideology, which in the Soviet context translated into the goals of total liberation by means of total control. Under the conditions of this paradox, the disappearance of the external metadiscourse on ideology in the late 1950s, against which ideological discourse could be calibrated, drove that discourse to hypernormalization. This normalizing shift can be observed especially clearly at the level of language. In the absence of a shared external linguistic "norm," any new party text could be potentially seen as a deviation. In multiple individual and collective attempts to avoid this ambiguity, the production of political discourse among the leadership, and following them, on all other levels, became increasingly organized through collective writing and personal imitation, leading to a hypernormalization of that language on all levels of linguistic, narrative, and textual structure that made it increasingly more fixed, predictable, citational, and cumbersome. The same process took place on all other levels of ideological discourse, from visual propaganda and the structure of ideological rituals, to the organization of routine practices of everyday life.

This normalizing process followed the general principle of presenting all knowledge as knowledge that was already established. As a result, the temporality of authoritative discourse shifted into the past, conveying new facts in terms of preexisting facts. The author's voice converted into the voice of a mediator of preexisting discourse rather than the creator of new discourse. In the case of ideological language these shifts became apparent in all structural layers—lexicon, morphology, syntax, semantics, pragmatics, narrative structure, rhetorical organization, intertextuality and so on (chapter 2).

This new circular model of language represented the immutability and predictability of knowledge and was closed to unexpected ruptures and shifts. To stress that this ideological discourse started playing a new role, I used Bakhtin's term, referring to it as "authoritative discourse"—a kind of discourse that employs a special script to demarcate itself from all other discourses with which it coexists; it cannot be changed by them but they must refer to it as a condition of their existence. The period of late socialism was marked by very special conditions of the production and circulation of this authoritative discourse in its linguistic and nonlinguistic varieties. The ubiquitous reproduction of the forms of authoritative discourse in various contexts where they circulated became more meaningful and constitutive of everyday reality than the constative (referential) meanings these forms might have had. Most Soviet people actively participated in the acts and rituals that reproduced these fixed forms of authoritative discourse whether in elections, meetings, speeches, examinations, texts, parades, or reports—but they also learned that the constative meanings of that discourse were, in most cases, unanchored

284

from the form, made relatively unpredictable and open to new creative interpretations.

To understand the logic and implications of such reproduction and circulation of discourse, I have drawn on John Austin's discussion of the performative and its critical reading by other theorists, and I proposed a method for analyzing discourse that goes beyond these readings. Following Austin, I differentiated between the "constative" (Austin's term for referential) meaning in discourse (using words or other signs to state facts and describe reality) and its "performative" meaning (using words to achieve actions in the world). Constative acts describe reality and can be true or false; performative acts do not describe anything and cannot be true or false. They can only be successful or unsuccessful in achieving something. The ability of certain acts of speech to perform things in the world is predicated not on the intention of the speaker who utters them but on the conventions of their use. If one makes an oath under appropriate conditions, while internally intending not to keep it, the oath is not made any less powerful in the eyes of those who accepted it as such.

Austin's further elaboration, later emphasized by Derrida (1977), was that utterances of a living language cannot be simply divided into clear-cut groups as constative and performative. In fact, all utterances to some degree play both these roles, although these roles remain irreducible to each other and are not in a binary either-or relationship. Their relationship is dynamic and can change historically in different ways.

Starting with Austin's distinction, I have drawn on what I called two coexisting *dimensions* of discourse—the constative dimension and the performative dimension. I argued that an utterance that describes reality (i.e., operates on the level of the constative dimension), when used in a particular way, may experience an increase in the role of its performative dimension. Which dimension is central to an utterance or another discursive act depends on the context and may change. As a result of the historical development of discourse, its constative role of describing reality may become less anchored and predictable, while its performative role of introducing particular effects in the world may grow in importance. The performative dimension is important not only in language but also in nonlinguistic acts. Various physical, spatial, legal, and other ritualized acts, for example, those in wedding ceremonies, acts of voting, parades, and examinations, do not just refer to preexisting persons, groups, institutions, states, citizenships, but also produce them as such.

In the late Soviet context, when authoritative discourse became hypernormalized, its performative dimension grew in importance and its constative dimension became unanchored from concrete core meanings and increasingly open to new interpretations. Authoritative discourse experienced what I have termed performative shift. In most contexts where that discourse circulated and was dominant it became less important to interpret its texts and rituals literally, as constative descriptions of reality, and more important to reproduce them with great precision. This does not mean that the constative dimension of this discourse simply disappeared or that the discourse transformed into empty rituals. On the contrary, its constative dimension became profoundly important, having opened the realm of creative innovation, unpredictable meaning, and reinterpretation of socialist life. The performative acts of reproducing authoritative forms were neither necessarily about the intention of the speaker nor about the description of reality. Acts of speaking in authoritative language, practicing ideological rituals, or voting in favor of resolutions at the party meetings in most cases were not about stating one's opinion about constative meanings of these discursive forms but about successfully carrying out ritualized acts that inaugurated the production and reproduction of the institutions, laws, hierarchies, and subject positions, with all the possibilities and limitations that came with them, including enabling one to have a meaningful life, pursue interests, education, careers, ethical values, ideals and hopes for the future, have friendships, belong to a community, and even reject some bureaucratic interpretation of the constative meaning of such acts.

The reproduction of the forms of authoritative discourse became powerfully constitutive of Soviet reality but no longer necessarily described that reality; it created the possibilities and constraints for being a Soviet person but no longer described what a Soviet person was. As a result, through its ritualized reproduction and circulation, authoritative discourse enabled many new ways of life, meanings, interests, relations, pursuits, and communities to spring up everywhere within late socialism, without being able to fully describe or determine them. The production of such internal discontinuities within Soviet life as a result of the performative shift became a central principle of all practices of late socialism.[1]

This production of the new was also an agentive and creative process, which was neither necessarily supportive of nor necessarily opposed to the values and ethics of socialism. This is why that creative process should not be reduced to resistance against dominant norms and rules. In fact, as we saw in the previous chapters, it allowed for a whole multiplicity of positions, including the possibility of continuing to subscribe to socialist ethics and communist ideals, sometimes, paradoxically, in spite of the state. Members of the last Soviet generation, who were born

---

[1] For example, this principle became increasingly central in the operations of the Soviet "economy of shortage" that have been profoundly analyzed. See Nove (1977), Kornai (1980), Verdery (1996), Ledeneva (1998), Yurchak (1999).

and came of age during the period of late socialism became particularly skilled in the performative reproduction of the hypernormalized forms of authoritative discourse and became particularly actively engaged in creating new meanings, pursuits, identities, and forms of living that were enabled by that reproduction. One of the common contexts in which members of that generation became routinely exposed to authoritative discourse was through the local Komsomol organizations to which the overwhelming majority of them nominally belonged.

As described in chapter 3, the Komsomol work was organized, supervised, and reported by local Komsomol leaders of different levels in the organizational hierarchy. Although many of those in the higher positions received special training for this work, the majority of local leaders and rank-and-file Komsomol members learned the skills of this performative process on the job. They learned to differentiate between the kinds of work they called "pure formality" and "work with meaning" and learned that performing the former enabled conducting, creating, and interpreting the latter. They also learned the importance of reproducing precise formulas of authoritative discourse in texts, reports, rituals, institutional practices, and so on. For example, they learned to practice special arrangements and styles of interaction with the higher Komsomol bodies and common Komsomol members, engaging in these complex activities as an indivisible and constitutive part of the process of the Komsomol work but without reporting them as such. The result of this complex relationship to authoritative discourse, for millions of those involved in it in local organizations, was the creation of an unanticipated cultural "surplus" of meanings and realities that did not necessarily oppose the state's communist goals but did not necessarily follow them either.

One unintended effect of this cultural production in Komsomol activities was the emergence of the publics of *svoi* or "normal people," as chapter 3 examined. While *svoi* is an old concept in Russia, in the context of late socialism it acquired characteristics of a sociality of "normal" Soviet people that was defined by its relationship to authoritative discourse. As a public that was brought about by the performative shift of that discourse, *svoi* became a kind of deterritorialized public. Although most Soviet people unanimously participated in public practices and activities conducted in authoritative discourse (meetings, votes, parades, speeches), which made the public of *svoi* people seem identical to what authoritative discourse described as "the Soviet people," in fact, the meanings of these activities substantially shifted. Being one of *svoi* meant understanding that it was important to participate in these ideological rituals, paying special attention to their performative dimension, because such participation enabled creative productions of "normal life" that went beyond, though not necessarily in opposition to, those that

287

these rituals and texts described. This relationship to authoritative discourse distinguished the *svoi* from the *activists*, associated with excessive ideological activism, and the *dissidents*, associated with excessive critique of the system—both of whom tended to read ideological descriptions at the level of constative meanings, interpreting them as true or false.

As I argued in the subsequent chapters late socialism became marked by the emergence of lifestyles and communities that, like the publics of *svoi*, had a particular relation to authoritative discourse defined as "being *vnye*"—that is, occupying a position that was simultaneously inside and outside of the rhetorical field of that discourse, neither simply in support nor simply in opposition of it. This relation actively defied boundaries and binary divisions, becoming a dynamic site where new meanings were produced. Being *vnye* authoritative discourse became a dominant mode of living during late socialism that, in some extreme cases translated into having little involvement with the system's constative concerns, and even being ignorant of them. This relation also enabled many people to introduce new meanings and concerns into the life dominated by authoritative discourse, and even enabled many to preserve socialist ideals and to continue subscribing to future-oriented ethics of socialism.

Both the publics of *svoi* and the relationship of being *vnye* were constitutive and indivisible elements of the Soviet system, not its opposites. They were enabled by Lefort's paradox of Soviet ideology and the effects of the paradoxes of the Soviet state's cultural policy that, along with the propaganda of the leading role of the party, also advocated the values of critical thinking, personal creativity, inquisitiveness, and education and explicitly and implicitly sponsored these pursuits in financial, temporal, and other terms. As chapter 4 demonstrated, this paradox became mapped on the spheres of education, art, cultural production, and scientific research. It enabled the emergence of milieus, lifestyles, and interests that were completely congruous with those described in authoritative discourse and yet profoundly different from them. Many of these milieus, lifestyles, and interests were focused on the forms of knowledge, codes, and meanings that were not articulated in authoritative discourse, but instead came from various imaginary "elsewheres"—such as, theoretical science, ancient languages, nineteenth-century poetry, religion, Western rock music, and so on. The meaning of these milieus and their occupations cannot be reduced to the opposition to the system. Rather they were in a deterritorialized relationship toward it, locating themselves simultaneously inside and outside cultural practices, ethics, and ideals.

The same internal paradox also shaped the Soviet state's cultural policy toward international influences. The state's simultaneous attempts to promote good cultural internationalism and to contain bad influences of the bourgeois culture enabled the emergence, in the 1950s and 1960s, of various imaginary worlds as part of the Soviet everyday. One of the most significant among them for the last Soviet generation was the Imaginary West, which I explored in chapter 5. The cultural products and forms of knowledge that constituted this imaginary world were again partly produced or enabled by the state itself. Furthermore, the state's focus on such extreme examples as naïve deviationists and immoral loafers who fell under bourgeois cultural influences only contributed to normalizing the interests in Western culture among masses of "normal" Soviet youth who were educated, hard-working, and, as good Soviet citizens, did not identify with the objects of this critique.

The state's policy toward technology involved in cultural production contained the same paradox. The promotion of shortwave radio, the increasing production of inexpensive shortwave sets, and the inconsistencies of state policies of jamming foreign stations also helped to normalize listening to foreign stations among the majority of Soviet citizens. Similarly, the state's production of millions of tape-recorders and inconsistent attitudes of state bureaucrats and media to Western rock music and jazz contributed to the normalization and growth of interest in that music among millions of Soviet fans. As a result, neither music nor radio, nor other cultural products, were necessarily associated with an anti-system identity. Indeed, as we saw in the case of some devoted young communists, their interest in Western rock often produced ingenious attempts to combine communist ideals with bourgeois aesthetics (chapter 6). Their beliefs in communism gave them moral grounds from which to disagree with the conservative interpretations of Western cultural influences by party bureaucrats. In a fascinating twist, the innovative, unusual, and experimental sound of Western rock bands became for them much more compatible with the future-oriented ethos of communist imaginations than the predictable realism of "light music" performed by state-authorized Soviet orchestras and pop groups.

These multiple internal displacements and reinterpretations of the system—drawing on the ubiquitous shift between the performative and the constative dimensions that took place in all spheres of authoritative discourse—resulted in the development of a particular aesthetic of absurd irony among members of the last Soviet generation, known in slang as *stiob*. That form of irony engaged with the paradoxical discursive, social, and psychic effects produced by these multiple displacements. By refusing the boundary between reality and performance, seriousness and humor, support and opposition, sense and nonsense, bare life and political life, life and death, this humor imitated the performative shift of authoritative discourse and all the concomitant paradoxes and discontinuities that

289

resulted from it in the everyday. When mundane symbols and situations were subjected to this humorous treatment, their constative meanings were suddenly unanchored and made open-ended, unpredictable, absurd, or simply irrelevant. This not only exposed the internal displacements of mundane Soviet life but also made visible that these displacements were not deviations from that life, but its constitutive and indivisible elements—its everyday norm that was routinely practiced by most people. This genre of absurd irony took various forms, from spontaneous comments in letters and conversations to ritualized jocular narratives, artistic performances, practical jokes, and the *anekdoty*. It was practiced by artists, Komsomol committees, "amateur" writers, and most ordinary citizens, and became turned into a spectacular form of folkloric creativity that dominated the everyday life of late socialism. This genre of absurd irony became itself involved in the reproduction and exacerbation of the internal paradoxes of the system, allowing them to remain relatively unarticulated in any more explicit critical analysis and therefore contributing to their role as constitutive yet displacing principles of late socialism.

This paradoxical relationship toward the system was intensely creative and agentive. In the course of this relationship the system's authoritative representations of itself were everywhere unanimously reproduced, but the meanings of Soviet life were reinterpreted and displaced from within. The last Soviet generation that practiced this style of living engaged with the authoritative discursive field of the Soviet system as Bakhtin's author-hero engages with the literary text. They were the system's heroes, who lived according to the script of reality provided by authoritative discourse, and, at the same time, the system's authors, who created their own new, unanticipated interpretations of reality within the parameters afforded by performative reproductions of the form of that authoritative script.

On the level of fixed authoritative form, the system remained immutable—rituals were reproduced, reports were filed, plans were fulfilled, and parades were attended. This performative reproduction of form enabled Soviet people to introduce new, unpredictable, creative meanings into their lives, producing "normal life" that was neither determined by nor limited to the announced goals and norms described in the constative pronouncements of discourse. In the course of its own functioning the Soviet system was undergoing internal mutation and deterritorialization—*not* necessarily as a form of an opposition to communist ideals and goals and often precisely in the name of these ideals and goals. These practices can be seen as a move toward greater freedom from some of the fixed, unavoidable meanings and controls of the system but one that was not coded in the emancipatory rhetoric of grand narratives, such as the discourse of the dissidents or the calls for "living in truth."

The Unexpected

A sudden rupture of this discursive regime began in 1985. When Mikhail Gorbachev became the new general secretary of the Communist Party and introduced his reforms, he unwittingly broke with the circular structure of authoritative discourse—unwittingly, because he did not realize, and no one else did, that he indeed effected a major break of authoritative structure and that this break would create such far-reaching and irreversible consequences. The break, as demonstrated in Michael Urban's analysis, could be observed already in the very first speeches that Gorbachev gave in his new post. At first, Gorbachev's speeches, like those of the previous general secretaries, followed the familiar circular narrative structure described in chapter 2. They started by naming a "lack"—in Gorbachev's case, some economic difficulties and a general disinterestedness in society that, he claimed, needed to be overcome.

However, the next step was different from the long-standing circular scheme. In accordance with the usual circularity, Gorbachev would need to explain that, in order to overcome this lack, it was necessary to apply more intensely certain measures that had been applied and failed earlier, or that everyone needed to develop more individual spontaneity and inventiveness but be sure to subsume them completely under party control. Gorbachev did not necessarily argue against these propositions or this kind of narrative, but, in his early speeches he inserted another question: "How do we correct the present situation and what are the reasons current remedies are not showing results?" Even more importantly, he suggested that he and the party lacked sufficient knowledge to answer that question. He introduced a completely new theme that broke with the circular narrative structure—namely, that this question should be addressed to "economic administrators," "various specialists" and "ordinary citizens" (Urban 1986, 154) and not to the party leadership—that is, it had to be articulated in a discourse other than authoritative discourse.

By organizing his speeches in this way, Gorbachev reintroduced into the narrative structure of authoritative discourse the voice of an external commentator or editor of ideology who could provide expert metadiscourse grounded in "objective scientific knowledge" located outside the field of authoritative discourse. This voice and, even more importantly, the ontological possibility of inhabiting it opened up spaces for public discussion *about* authoritative discourse in genres other than that discourse,

291

creating a possibility of eventually questioning the whole discursive structure of socialism. Even though this critical discussion was conducted with the idea of preserving and improving socialism, returning to its fundamental ideals, and reproducing the leading role of the party, it in fact ruptured the discursive regime and undermined the very basis of late socialist discursive formation and of the party's leading role.

In its first three or four years, perestroika was not much more than a deconstruction of Soviet authoritative discourse. It achieved its first irreversible results at the level of discourse by questioning the discursive regime: the ideological signifiers that until then had been rarely read as constative utterances became suddenly interrogated *precisely* at the constative dimension of discourse, their supposed "literal" meanings scrutinized in a growing number of publications and televised debates. This was a reversal of the earlier performative shift of Soviet ideology.

As we saw in the previous chapters, during late socialism but before perestroika, the hypernormalized visual representations in authoritative discourse (e.g., political slogans and billboards on the streets, visual propaganda and parades), had been "transparent" and "invisible" to pedestrians. They had not been read solely as constative descriptions and statements but tended to transform into a formulaic landscape that functioned as a set of visual performative acts that enabled reality without describing it in any predictable way. Exposing this fact alone would be nothing new. However, by publicly acknowledging that ideological texts and visuals were not read literally by their audiences, the discourse of perestroika achieved something much more important than merely describing some "truth." It reintroduced a public metacommentary about authoritative discourse, providing a venue for discussing the principles according to which this discourse functioned in everyday life. This type of metadiscourse, which had not existed since the 1950s, became a ubiquitous presence in all publications and broadcasts of perestroika by 1987, undermining the performative model of authoritative discursive field. An example is provided in the following 1987 article published in a magazine of visual arts. Writing about visual propaganda on the city streets, the article declared not that propaganda was wrong but that the conditions of its functioning as a discourse had shifted, leading to a change of its meaning. What mattered most was the metadiscursive voice of such publications, which explicitly and publicly, on the pages of the mass publications, described the performative shift of ideology:

Today, with increasing frequency we encounter the . . . most elementary replication of content in visual form. As a result, on posters, placards, and huge billboards the same "mannequins" perform roles of men and women. They simply change clothes to become builders of

BAM,[2] soldiers, drivers of combine harvesters, cosmonauts, and so on. . . . Questionnaires conducted by our specialists on the central streets of large cities have convincingly demonstrated that the majority of pedestrians are unable to recollect what is depicted on the closest propaganda billboard. Therefore, elements of visual propaganda have grown invisible: they are present in the urban space materially, but they do not penetrate people's consciousness (Chebotarev 1987, 21, 23).

By describing that performative model of authoritative discourse, this metacommentary inadvertently forced the audience to treat authoritative discourse at the level of its *constative* dimension that described—or rather failed to describe—reality literally. This introduction of a metadiscourse affected how authoritative texts and reports were written and interpreted on all levels. According to the komsorgs and secretaries whom we encountered in chapter 3 and elsewhere, in 1986, after the Nineteenth Party Conference, they received instructions to stop using formulaic linguistic constructions in their speeches and start using new "fresh" (*svezhie*) terms. The speeches were now supposed to be shorter and their circular structure was to be broken. It was demanded that every speech should now provide "real self-criticism" (*real'naia samokritika*), should admit "real problems" (*real'nye problemy*), and should propose a new, unfamiliar, creative approach (*tvorcheskii podkhod*) to solving them.

The metadiscourse on ideology also became quickly introduced into all other levels of the authoritiative discursive field—in the media, in the party and Komsomol speeches; during rallies, meetings, and discussions where performing the acts of voting without paying attention to constative meanings was no longer relevant, interesting, or desirable. In those early years, between 1985 and 1988, this metadiscourse undermined not so much the Soviet state, concrete institutions of power, or concrete laws but the principle of the performative shift according to which late socialism operated. This was a "discursive deconstruction" of the late Soviet system, and in that process lay the beauty, excitement, and initial hope of perestroika. The form of living that had been based on displacing reality and creating unanticipated and unaccounted meanings and forms of life within it was no longer possible or relevant. Authoritative discourse was imploding and with it the system itself, and the process was irreversible. For many people this experience was both exhilarating and traumatic (remember Tonya's description at the beginning of the book).

[2] Baikal-Amur Railroad (*Baikalo-Amurskaia Magistral'*)—a "heroic" contruction project of the 1970s.

As we saw above, Gorbachev's innovation also undermined one of the master signifiers of authoritative discourse—the leading role of the party (see chapter 2). This rupture happened in the name of the ideas represented by other master signifiers—in order to return to "the pure word of Lenin" and to a revitalized socialism. A famous political poster during perestroika depicted Lenin sitting on the stairs beside a lectern with the Soviet national emblem and writing notes on his notepad. The message on the poster read: "Let Lenin speak!" (*Slovo Leninu!*), suggesting that after the system came under criticism, the last resort and the last unchallenged wisdom was the original word of Lenin. However, the tight narrative structure of authoritative discourse meant that with the undermining of one master signifier (the party), the whole system was undermined, and quite soon the discursive field began crumbling. By 1988 or 1989, the party had lost its prestige and millions started leaving its ranks—an act that would have been simply unthinkable a year or two previously. After that, the figure of Lenin came under fire as well in a whole array of publications and documentary films.[3]

Mikhail, one of the school and then university komsorgs whom we encountered in chapter 3, experienced that rupture of discourse as a profoundly personal transformation. In the context of public critical discourse in the media, Mikhail, in his own words, "reconsidered my understanding of the meaning of life" and experienced a profound "break of consciousness" (*perelom soznaniia*).[4] Andrei, another secretary, at first welcomed the crisis of the *apparat* (middle-level party bureaucracy), which he had always considered rotten and immoral. However, he suffered greatly when eventually the party as a whole began collapsing. Between 1989 and 1991 he gradually came to a new conviction that it was not just the party bureaucracy that was wrong, but the party itself, its very idea—"that the party would not exist without the *apparat*, that the apparat was the corollary (*sledstvie*) of the party, its core (*sterzhen'*). That they were one and the same."

The party's eventual loss of the status as a master signifier of authoritative discourse in the eyes of millions of its members—following the introduction of the initial idea that the party did not know the answer to all problems—further exacerbated the crisis of authoritative discourse as a whole, eventually and inevitably leading to the collapse of the external anchoring point of that discourse and its central master signifier—Lenin. That symbol was the last one to fall, after which the system could no longer sustain itself. Andrei remembers that moment in the late 1980s:

The idea that Lenin knew all the answers was changing for me drop by drop. At first I read something, then there was something on the

---

[3] See Yurchak (1999) and (2005) for discussions of the unravelling of the figure of Lenin.

[4] Mikhail used the same term as Tonya, quoted at the beginning of chapter 1.

television, then on the radio. One detail after the other, a new image started appearing (*vyrisovyvat'sia*)—that it was all the same, that we should thank God that Lenin had not lived longer than he had. That he was the actual initiator, generator of everything, and that Stalin was only his logical extension. . . . For me to reach this realization was a difficult process that took a while. Lenin was the last symbol in which I became disillusioned.

The paradox of late socialism turned out to be this: the more meticulously and unanimously the system's authoritative forms were reproduced in language, rituals, and other acts, the more its constative meanings became disconnected from form and thus allowed to shift in diverse and increasingly unanticipated directions. This shift enabled the introduction of new forms of life, publics, persons, lifestyles, temporalities, spatialities, imaginary worlds, and visions of the future. This is why the more the system was represented, with the help of all its citizens, as monolithic and immutable, the more it mutated and became internally deterritorialized and increasingly unknown, and vice versa: the continual internal displacement of the system insured the continual performative reproduction of its ritualized forms, institutions, rhetoric, and rules, making it seem all the more immutable and predictable. The very feeling of Soviet life's fixed, eternal, and immutable nature was necessary and constitutive of the system's continuous internal shift and deterritorialization. The more the system seemed immutable, the more it was different from what it claimed it was.

This was not a static, self-perpetuating machine of a type familiar from structural-functionalist accounts, but a dynamic and agentive process of internal reorganization. However, it would be wrong to equate this process simply with progressive stagnation or decay. In fact, the Soviet system could probably have continued in this way for much longer than it did. Indeed, the feeling of its immutability was not entirely misconstrued, not least because Soviet youth so profoundly reinterpreted socialism that it was experienced not simply as a hegemonic rhetoric of the state but as "normal" life, full of creative worlds, imaginary spaces, and meaningful forms of sociality. The collapse of that world was unexpected *also* because these meaningful worlds made life so complex, full, creative, and "normal," and because they depended for their very existence on the performative reproduction of immutable authoritative forms. When the changes of perestroika began, however, they completely overtook everyone because they articulated in a metadiscourse something that had already happened and had been lived by everyone—the mutation and internal shift of the system's discursive parameters. Soviet late socialism provides a stunning example of how a dynamic and powerful social system can abruptly and unexpectedly unravel when the discursive conditions of its existence are changed.

Afterword: Post-Soviet Entrepreneurial Governmentality

Understanding the nature of Soviet late socialism, the concern of this book, has important implications for our understanding of the processes of postsocialist transformation since the collapse of the Soviet state. One important observation can be made about the postsocialist system in Russia in light of the previous discussions: the principle of the performative shift that shaped the relations between Soviet people and authoritative discourse during late Soviet years did not disappear in the post-Soviet period. On the contrary, in the new context this principle continued to play a central role in shaping the decisions and activities of many members of the last Soviet generation. To understand the continuing importance of this principle in the new postsocialist context we may consider, for example, how the sphere of private business activity emerged in the early 1990s.

According to a classical understanding of entrepreneurship, Soviet citizens were not supposed to be good at inventing and running private businesses because for generations they grew up and lived in a society in which private business was practically nonexistent. The mere adoption in the Soviet Union of the laws on individual private activity (1986) and on cooperatives (1988) could not teach anyone overnight how to be a businessperson. And yet, in the late 1980s, great numbers of Soviet people, especially members of the last Soviet generation, quickly started creating new private businesses and turned out to be exceptionally good at it. These people had acquired particular forms of entrepreneurial knowledge and skills during the period of late socialism, in contexts where no private business activity existed, by having to operate within the Soviet system itself. How did this happen?

In the narrow sense, entrepreneurship refers to the industrious, systematic economic activity of organizing and operating a profit-making business venture and assuming the risks of possible failure. However, this activity can also be understood in a wider sense as belonging to a family of governing activities that are not restricted to the sphere of economics, markets, and profits. In Foucault's definition, governing activities aim to shape or affect people's conduct and can involve different types of relations: "the relation between self and self, private interpersonal relations involving some form of control or guidance, relations within social institutions and communities and, finally, relations concerned with the exercise of political sovereignty" (Gordon 1991, 2–3). The kind of knowledge, skills, and rationality necessary for devising and conducting such governing activities Foucault called governmental rationality or *governmentality* (1979; 1991).

The concepts of governmentality may allow us to collect under one analytical lens diverse governing activities from the Soviet and post-Soviet contexts. Thus, we may speak of an *entrepreneurial governmentality* (Yurchak 2001a) as a way of knowing what may constitute entrepreneurial activity, who can act entrepreneurially, and what or who can be acted upon in an entrepreneurial way. This entrepreneurial governmentality comprises particular knowledge, skills, and ways of thinking about the practice of governing that were developed in the sphere of ideological work during late socialism and later became crucial for devising, shaping, and conducting activities in the sphere of private business in the post-Soviet context. For example, to be a Komsomol secretary during late Soviet period, as we saw in chapter 3, was to fulfill projects and achieve results by creatively distinguishing between those assignments that were "pure formality" and those that were "work with meaning," conducting some of them only at the level of form (in speeches, rituals, reports) and others in practice, endowing them with new meanings, guiding one's own conduct and that of the rank-and-file members accordingly, compiling reports of selected activities for superior institutions, and so on. All these were elements of late-socialist entrepreneurial governmentality that shared one unique feature—they were organized around the procedures of subjecting authoritative rules, texts, and assignments to the performative shift, whereby the form of these rules, texts, and assignments was meticulously reproduced but the meanings associated with them were shifted and open to new interpretations. The Komsomol secretaries' involvement in this shift did not necessarily mean that they were simply cynical opportunists who did not believe any communist goals and values. On the contrary, as we have seen, this shift allowed many of them to continue subscribing to socialist goals and values and be serious about participating in the work directed at achieving the social good.

In the late 1980s, when the reforms of perestroika reached the sphere of economics and the Komsomol was allowed to experiment with private business activity, the knowledge, skills, and forms of rationality that constituted the late-socialist entrepreneurial governmentality proved to be of crucial importance in this experimentation. At that time many active Komsomol secretaries started thinking of themselves as private entrepreneurs and businessmen, originally without necessarily giving up their identities as Komsomol secretaries. Eventually their work in "youth centers" and "cooperatives" under the auspices of the Komsomol organization turned many Komsomol committees into private firms and banks.[5] They managed to conduct this transformation not simply because of their privileged position, organizing skills, and access to resources, but, most importantly, because the form of entrepreneurial governmentality that they had learned earlier enabled them to devise, conduct, organize, guide, and represent complex activities of various people in the new context of quickly changing state ideologies, laws, rules, taxes, uncertainties, and forms of risk (for a discussion of this process see Yurchak 2001a).[6]

Today many members of this group of entrepreneurs continue shaping their worlds in the terms that they found socially and personally meaningful, often turning to the familiar logic of the performative shift in this process. They still avoid relating to the Russian state and its institutions and laws, at the level of constative meaning only, turning to the principle of the performative shift to render many of their activities invisible to, or misrecognized by, the state. However problematic this persistent relationship with the Russian state is, the hopes of Russia's future may lie precisely in these people's continuing deterritorialization of all state attempts to control authoritative rule and meaning.

[5] Most of the early private entrepreneurs were members of the last Soviet generation and came to post-Soviet business from two main backgrounds: 40 percent came from the Komsomol activism and another 40 percent from industry and science (Kryshtanovskaia 1996; Medvedev 1998). See also Solnick (1998, 118).

[6] Since the late 1980s, some characters in this book have been involved in creating private firms in the spheres of entertainment, travel, telecommunications, engineering, and publishing, while others have pursued their interests in education, art and family.

Bibliography

Abu-Lughod, Lila. 1986. *Veiled Sentiments: Honor and Poetry in a Bedouin Society*. Berkeley: University of California Press.

Agamben, Giorgio. 1998. *Homo Sacer: Sovereign Power and Bare Life*. Trans. Daniel Heller-Roazen. Stanford: Stanford University Press.

Aksyonov, Vassily. 1987. *In Search of Melancholy Baby*. New York: Random House.

Alaniz, José. 2003. Necrotopia: Discourses of Death and Dying in Late/Post-Soviet Russian Culture. PhD diss., University of California, Berkeley.

Alaniz, José, and Seth Graham. 2001. Early Necrocinema in Context. In *Necrorealism: Contexts, History, Interpretations*, ed. Seth Graham, 5–27. Pittsburgh: Russian Film Symposium.

Aliev, A. 1968. *Narodnye traditsii, obychai i ikh rol' v formirovanii novogo cheloveka* [People's Traditions and Customs, and Their Role in the Formation of the New Man]. Makhachkala: [no publisher].

Alpatov, V. M. 1991. Istoriia odnogo mifa. Marr i marrizm [The History of One Myth: Marr and Marrism]. Moscow: Nauka.

Althusser, Louis. 1971. Ideology and Ideological State Apparatuses. In *Lenin and Philosophy and Other Essays*, trans. and ed. Ben Brewster, 127–86. London: Monthly Review Press.

Anagnost, Ann. 1997. *National Past-Times: Narrative, Representation, and Power in Modern China*. Durham: Duke University Press.

Anderson, Benedict. 1983. *Imagined Communities: Reflections on the Origin and Spread of Nationalism*. London: Verso.

Andreyev, A., et al. 1980. *The Komsomol: Questions and Answers*. Moscow: Progress Publishers.

Apollonio, Umbro, ed. 1973. *Futurist Manifestos*. London: Thames and Hudson.

Appadurai, Arjun. 1990. Disjuncture and Difference in the Global Cultural Economy. *Public Culture* 2 (2): 1–24.

Arnol'dov, A. I., et al. 1984. *Marksistsko-leninskaia teoriia kul'tury* (Marxist-Leninist Theory of Culture). Moscow: Politizdat.

Austin, John. 1999. *How to Do Things with Words*. Oxford: Clarendon Press.

Avdeev, M. I. 1966. *Kratkoe rukovodstvo po sudebnoi meditsine* [A Short Guide to Forensic Medicine]. Moscow: Meditsina.

Bach, Jonathan. 2002. The Taste Remains: Consumption, (N)ostalgia, and the Production of East Germany. *Public Culture* 14 (3): 545–56.

Bakhtin, Mikhail. 1984. *Problems of Dostoevsky's Poetics*. Ed. and trans. Wayne C. Booth. Minneapolis: University of Minnesota Press.

———. 1986. *Speech Genres and Other Late Essays*. Eds. Vern W. McGee, C. Emerson, and M. Holquist. Austin: University of Texas Press.

———. 1990. Author and Hero in Aesthetic Activity. In *Art and Answerability: Early Philosophical Essays by M. M. Bakhtin*, eds. Michael Holquist and Vadim Liapunov, 4–256. Austin: University of Texas Press.

———. 1994. *The Dialogical Imagination: Four Essays by Mikhail Bakhtin*, ed. Michael Holquist. Austin: University of Texas Press.

———. 2000. *Avtor i geroi: k filosofskim osnovam gumanitarnykh nauk* [Author and Hero: Toward Philosophical Bases of Humanitarian Sciences]. St. Petersburg: Azbuka.

Bakhtin, Mikhail, and P. N. Medvedev. 1991. *The Formal Method in Literary Scholarship: A Critical Introduction to Sociological Poetics*. Trans. Albert J. Wehrle. Baltimore, MD: Johns Hopkins University Press.

Balina, Marina, Nancy Condee, and Evgeny Dobrenko, eds. 2000. *Endnote: Sots-Art Literature and Soviet Grand Style*. Evanston, IL: Northwestern University Press.

Banc, C. 1990. *You Call This Living?: A Collection of East European Political Jokes*. Athens: University of Georgia Press.

Barnett, Robert. 2002. The Secret *Secret*: Cinema, Ethnicity, and Seventeenth-Century Tibetan-Mongolian Relations. *Inner Asia* 4: 277–346.

Baudrillard, Jean. 1988. Simulacra and Simulations. In *Jean Baudrillard: Selected Writings*, ed. Mark Poster, 166–84. Stanford, CA: Stanford University Press.

———. 1994. *Symbolic Exchange and Death*. London: Sage.

Beissinger, Mark R., and Crawford Young, eds. 2002. *Beyond State Crisis? Postcolonial Africa and Post-Soviet Eurasia Compared*. Baltimore, MD: Johns Hopkins University Press.

Bell, Catherine. 1992. *Ritual Theory, Ritual Practice*. New York: Oxford University Press.

Belousov, A. F., ed. 1998. *Russkii shkol'nyi fol'klor: ot 'vyzyvanii' Pikovoi damy do semeinykh rasskazov* [Russian School Folklore: From Summoning the Queen of Spades to Family Stories]. Moscow: Ladomir.

Benjamin, Walter. 1969a. The Task of the Translator. In *Illuminations: Essays and Reflections*. Ed. Hannah Arendt, (69–82). New York: Schocken.

———. 1969b. The Work of Art in the Age of Mechanical Reproduction. In *Illuminations: Essays and Reflections*, ed. Hannah Arendt, (217–52). New York: Schocken.

Berdhal, Daphne. 1999. "(N)Ostalgie for the Present: Memory, Longing, and East German Things." *Ethnos* 64 (2): 192–211.

300

Bergan, Ronald. 1997. *Eisenstein: A Life in Conflict*. New York: Overlook Press.

Berry, Ellen E., and Anessa Miller-Pogacar. 1996. A Shock Therapy for the Social Consciousness: The Nature and Cultural Function of Russian Necrorealism. *Cultural Critique* (Fall): 185–203.

Bhabha, Homi. 1984. Of Mimicry and Man: The Ambivalence of Colonial Discourse. *October* 28 (Spring): 125–33.

———, ed. 1990. *Nation and Narration*. London: Routledge.

———. 1997. *The Location of Culture*. London: Routledge.

Blank, Diana. 2004. Fairytale Cynicism in the Kingdom of Plastic Bags: Powerlessness of Place in a Ukrainian Border Town. *Ethnography* (Fall): 349–78.

———. 2005. *Voices from Elsewhere: An Ethnography in Place in Chelnochovsk-na-Dniestre, Ukraine*. PhD diss., University of California, Berkeley.

Blinov, I. Ya. 1948. *Iazyk agitatora* [The Language of the Agitator]. Moscow: Ogiz-gospolitizdat.

Bonnell, Victoria. 1997. *Iconography of Power: Soviet Political Posters under Lenin and Stalin*. Berkeley: University of California Press.

Bordo, Susan. 1990. Reading the Slender Body. In *Body/Politics: Women and the Discourses of Science*, eds. Jacobus, M., Keller, E. F., and Shuttleworth, S., 83–112. New York: Routledge.

Borneman, John. 1998. *Subversions of International Order: Studies in the Political Anthropology of Culture*. Albany: State University of New York Press.

Borodin, E. I. 1962. *500 slov. Kratkii slovar' politicheskikh, ekonomicheskikh i tekhnicheskikh terminov* [500 Words: A Short Dictionary of Political, Economic, and Technical Terms]. Moscow: Molodaia Gvardiia [Young Guard].

Borukhov, Boris. 1989. Vertikal'nye normy stilia [Vertical Norms of Style]. *Mitin zhurnal* 25.

Bourdieu, Pierre. 1977. *Outline of a Theory of Practice*. Cambridge: Cambridge University Press.

———. 1991. *Language and Symbolic Power*. Cambridge, MA: Harvard University Press.

Boym, Svetlana. 1994. *Common Places: Mythologies of Everyday Life in Russia*. Cambridge, MA: Harvard University Press.

———. 1999. Ilya Kabakov: The Soviet Toilet and the Palace of Utopias. *Artmargins: Contemporary Central and Eastern European Visual Culture*. http://www.artmargins.com/content/feature/boym2.html.

———. 2001. *The Future of Nostalgia*. New York: Basic Books.

Brennan, Timothy. 2001. The Cults of Language: The East/West of North/South. *Public Culture* 13 (1): 39–63.

Brodsky, Joseph, and Vaclav Havel. 1994. The Post-Communist Nightmare: An Exchange. *New York Review of Books* 41 (4): 28–30.

Brovkin, Vladimir. 1998. Komsomol and Youth. In *Russia after Lenin: Politics, Culture and Society*, 108–25. London: Routledge.

Brown, Wendy. 2003. Neo-Liberalism and the End of Liberal Democracy. *Theory and Event* 7 (1). http://muse.jhu.edu/journals/theory_and_event/v007/7.1brown.html.

Buck-Morss, Susan. 2000. *Dreamworld and Catastrophe: The Passing of Mass Utopia in East and West*. Cambridge, MA: MIT Press.

301

Bulgakowa, Oksana. 1994. Povelitel' kartin—Stalin i kino, Stalin v kino [Rule of Motion Picture—Stalin and the Pictures, Stalin at the Pictures]. In *Agitatsiia za schast'e. Sovetskoe iskusstvo stalinskoi epokhi* [Agitation for Happiness: Soviet Art of Stalin's Epoch], 65–70. St. Petersburg: State Russian Museum.

———, ed. 1995. *Die ungewöhnlichen Abenteuer des Dr Mabuse im Lande der Bolschewiki: Das Buch zur Filmreihe 'Moskau-Berlin'*. Berlin: Fieunde der Deutschen Kinemathek.

Burlatskii, Fyodor. 1988. Posle Stalina. Zametki o politicheskoi ottepeli [After Stalin: Notes on the Political Thaw]. *Novyi Mir* 10: 153–97.

———. 1990. *Vozhdi i sovetniki. O Khrushcheve, Andropove i ne tol'ko o nikh . . .* [Leaders and Advisors: About Khrushchev, Andropov and not only them . . .]. Moscow: Izdatel'stvo politicheskoi literatury [Political Literature Press].

———. 1997. *Glotok svobody. Kniga pervaia* [A Gulp of Freedom: First Book]. Moscow: RIK Kul'tura.

Butler, Judith. 1990. *Gender Trouble: Feminism and the Subversion of Identity*. New York: Routledge.

———. 1993. *Bodies That Matter: On the Discursive Limits of Sex*. New York: Routledge.

———. 1997a. *The Psychic Life of Power: Theories in Subjection*. Stanford, CA: Stanford University Press.

———. 1997b. *Excitable Speech: A Politics of the Performative*. New York: Routledge.

Calhoun, Craig. 2002. Imagining Solidarity: Cosmopolitanism, Constitutional Patriotism, and the Public Sphere. *Public Culture* 14 (1): 147–71.

Casey, E. S. 1996. How to Get from Space to Place in a Fairly Short Stretch of Time: Phenomenological Prolegomena. In *Senses of Place*, eds. S. Feld and K. Basso, 13–52. Santa Fe, NM: School of American Research Press.

Cavell, Stanley. 1995. What Did Derrida Want of Austin? In *Philosophical Passages: Wittgenstein, Emerson, Austin, Derrida*. Bucknell Lectures in Literary Theory, No. 12, Cambridge, MA: Blackwell: 42–65.

Chakrabarty, Dipesh. 2000. *Provincializing Europe: Postcolonial Thought and Historical Difference*. Princeton, NJ: Princeton University Press.

Cheah, Pheng. 1998. Given Culture: Rethinking Cosmopolitical Freedom in Transnationalism. In *Cosmopolitics: Thinking and Feeling beyond the Nation*, eds. Pheng Cheah and Bruce Robbins, 290–328. Minneapolis: University of Minnesota Press.

Chebotarev, A. N., ed. 1987. *Nagliadnaia agitatsiia. Opyt, problemy, metodika* [Visual Propaganda: Experience, Problems, Methodology]. Moscow: Plakat.

Cherednichenko, Tatyana. 1994. *Tipologiia sovetskoi massovoi kul'tury. Mezhdu Brezhnevym i Pugachevoi* [Typology of Soviet Mass Culture: Between Brezhnev and Pugacheva]. Moscow: RIK Kul'tura.

Chernov, Sergei. 1997a. Istoriia istinnogo dzhaza [The History of Real Jazz]. *Pchela* 11: 31–35.

———. 1997b. Klub "Kvadrat": dzhaz-shmaz i normal'nye liudi. ["Kvadrat" Club: Jazz-shmaz and Normal People]. *Pchela* 11: 36–42.

———. 1997c. Piterskie kluby. Blesk i nishcheta [Petersburg Clubs: Glamour and Poverty]. *Pchela* 10: 12–17.

Chin, Gabriel J., and Saira Rao. 2003. Pledging Allegiance to the Constitution: The first Amendment and Loyalty Oaths for Faculty at Private Universities. *University of Pittsburgh Law Review* (Spring): 431–82.

Chomsky, Noam. 1986. *Knowledge of Language: Its Nature, Origins, and Use.* New York: Praeger.

Clark, Katerina. 1995. *St. Petersburg: Crucible of Cultural Revolution.* Cambridge, MA: Harvard University Press.

Clark, Katerina, and Michael Holquist. 1984. *Mikhail Bakhtin.* Cambridge, MA: Harvard University Press.

Comaroff, Jean, and John Comaroff. 1991. *Of Revelation and Revolution: Vol. 1.* Chicago: University of Chicago Press.

Coombe, Rosemary J. 1998. *The Cultural Life of Intellectual Properties: Authorship, Appropriation, and the Law.* Durham, NC: Duke University Press.

Culler, Jonathan. 1981. Convention and Meaning: Derrida and Austin. *New Literary History* 13: 15–30.

Curco, C. 1995. Some Observations on the Pragmatics of Humorous Interpretations: A Relevance Theoretic Approach. *Working Papers in Linguistics: Pragmatics.* University College London 7: 27–47.

Cushman, Thomas. 1995. *Notes From Underground: Rock Music Counterculture in Russia.* Albany: State University of New York Press.

de Certeau, Michel. 1975. *Une Politique de la Langue: La Revolution Française et les Patois: L'Enquete de Gregoire.* Paris: Gallimard.

———. 1988. *The Practice of Everyday Life.* Berkeley: University of California Press.

Deleuze, Gilles and Felix Guattari. 2002. *A Thousand Plateaus: Capitalism and Schizophrenia.* London: Continuum.

DeMartini, J. R. 1985. Change Agents and Generational Relationships: A Reevaluation of Mannheim's Problem of Generations. *Social Forces* 64: 1–16.

Derrida, Jacques. 1977. Signature Event Context. *Glyph* 1: 172–97.

Dittmer, Lowell. 1981. Radical Ideology and Chinese Political Culture: An Analysis of the Revolutionary *Yangbangxi.* In *Moral Behavior in Chinese Society,* eds. Richard W. Wilson, Sidney L. Greenblatt, and Amy Auerbacher Wilson, 126–51. New York: Praeger.

Djurić, Dubravka, and Miško Šuvaković, eds. 2003. *Impossible Histories: Historic Avant-Gardes, Neo-Avant-Gardes, and Post-Avant-Gardes in Yugoslavia, 1918–1991.* Cambridge, MA: MIT Press.

Dobrotvorsky, S. 1993. A Tired Death. In *Russian Necrorealism: Shock Therapy for New Culture,* ed. Miller-Pogacar, Anessa, 7–8. Exhibition Catalog. Bowling Green, OH: Bowling Green State University.

Dovlatov, Sergei. 1993. *Remeslo: Selected Prose in Three volumes.* Vol. 2. St. Petersburg: Limbus Press.

Dreyfus, Hubert, and Paul Rabinow, eds. 1983. *Michel Foucault: Beyond Structuralism and Hermeneutics.* 2nd ed. Chicago, IL: University of Chicago Press.

Dubovskii, M. 1991. *Istoriia SSSR v anekdotakh* (The History of the USSR in Jokes). Minsk: Everest.

Dunayeva, E. 1950. Cosmopolitanism in the Service of Imperialist Reaction. *Current Digest of the Soviet Press* 2 (16).

Dundes, Alan. 1987. *Cracking Jokes: Studies of Sick Humor Cycles and Stereo-types*. Berkeley, CA: Ten Speed Press.

Dunham, Vera. 1976. *In Stalin's Time: Middle-Class Values in Soviet Fiction*. Cambridge: Cambridge University Press.

Duranti, Alessandro. 1993. Intentions, Self, and Responsibility: An Essay in Samoan Ethnopragmatics. In *Responsibility and Evidence in Oral Discourse*, eds. Jane Hill and Judith Irvine, 24–47. Cambridge: Cambridge University Press.

———. 1997. *Linguistic Anthropology*. Cambridge: Cambridge University Press.

Edele, Mark. 2003. Strange Young Men in Stalin's Moscow: The Birth and Life of the Stiliagi, 1945–1953. *Jahrbücher für Geschichte Osteuropas* 50: 37–61.

Egbert, Donald D. 1967. The Idea of "Avant-garde" in Art and Politics. *The American Historical Review* 53 (2): 339–66.

Ellis, Frank. 1998. The Media as Social Engineer. In *Russian Cultural Studies: An Introduction*, eds. Catriona Kelly and David Shepherd, 274–96. Oxford: Oxford University Press.

Epstein, Mikhail. 2000. Postmodernism, Communism, and Sots-Art. In *Endquote: Sots-Art Literature and Soviet Grand Style*, eds. Marina Balina, Nancy Condee, and Evgeny Dobrenko, 3–29. Evanston, IL: Northwestern University Press.

Erastov, N. P. 1979. *Psikhologiia obshcheniia* [Psychology of Communication]. Yaroslavl': [no publisher].

Erjavec, Aleš, ed. 2003. *Postmodernism and the Postsocialist Condition: Politicized Art under Late Socialism*. Berkeley: University of California Press.

Erokhin, A. 1995. Iumor v Rossii [Humor in Russia]. *Ogonek* 14 (April): 40–43.

Etlin, Richard, ed. 2002. Art, Culture, and Media under the Third Reich. Chicago, IL: University of Chicago Press.

Ewing, Katherine. 1997. *Hegemony, Consciousness, and the Postcolonial Subject*. Durham, NC: Duke University Press.

Fabian, Johannes. 2001. *Anthropology with an Attitude: Critical Essays*. Stanford, CA: Stanford University Press.

Fagner, D., and G. Cohen. 1988. Abram Terz: Dissidence, Diffidence, and Russian Literary Tradition. In *Soviet Society and Culture: Essays in Honor of Vera Dunham*, eds. Terry L. Thompson and Richard Sheldon, 162–77. Boulder, CO: Westview Press.

Fain, A., and V. L. Lur'e. 1991. *Vse v kaif!* [Everything Super!]. Leningrad: Lena Productions.

Fairclough, Norman. 1989. *Language and Power.* London: Longman.

———. 1992. *Discourse and Social Change.* Cambridge: Polity Press.

Faraday, George. 2000. *Revolt of the Filmmakers: The Struggle for Artistic Autonomy and the Fall of the Soviet Film Industry*. College Station, PA: Penn State University Press.

Fauchereau, Serge. 1992. *Malevich.* New York: Rizzoli.

Fedotov, Vladimir. 2001. Tot kto proizvodil "rok na kostiakh" [The One Who Produced "Rock on Bones"]. *Argumenty i fakty*, February 14.

Feiertag, Vladimir. 1997. Istoriia istinogo dzhaza [The History of Real Jazz]. *Pchela* 11. http://www.pchela.ru/podshiv/11/jazz.htm.

———. 1999. *Dzhaz ot Leningrada do Peterburga* [Jazz from Leningrad to Petersburg]. St. Petersburg: Kul't Inform Press.

Foucault, Michel. 1972. *The Archeology of Knowledge and the Discourse of Language.* New York: Pantheon Books.

———. 1979. Governmentality. *Ideology and Consciousness* (Autumn): 5–21.

———. 1983. Subject and Power. In *Michel Foucault: Beyond Structuralism and Hermeneutics,* 2nd ed., eds. Hubert Dreyfus and Paul Rabinow, 208–26. Chicago: University of Chicago Press.

———. 1991. Questions of Method. In *The Foucault Effect: Studies in Governmentality,* eds. Graham Burchell, Colin Gordon, and Peter Miller. Chicago: University of Chicago Press.

———. 1998a. What Is an Author? In *Aesthetics, Method, and Epistemology.* ed. James Faubion, 205–22. New York: The New Press.

———. 1998b. On the Archeology of the Sciences: Response to the Epistemology Circle. In *Aesthetics, Method, and Epistemology,* ed. James Faubion, 297–333. New York: The New Press.

———. 1998c. Different Spaces. In *Aesthetics, Method, and Epistemology,* ed. James Faubion, 175–85. New York: The New Press.

Fraser, Nancy. 1992. Rethinking the Public Sphere: A Contribution to the Critique of Actually Existing Democracy. In *Habermas and the Public Sphere,* ed. Craig Calhoun, 109–43. Cambridge, MA: MIT Press.

———. 1995. Pragmatism, Feminism, and the Linguistic Turn. In *Feminist Contentions: A Philosophical Exchange,* eds. Seyla Benhabib, Judith Butler, Drucilla Cornell, and Nancy Fraser, 157–72. New York: Routledge.

Freud, Sigmund. 1919. The "Uncanny." In *Standard Edition of the Complete Psychological Works of Sigmund Freud,* ed. James Strachey, 17: 219–52. London: Hogarth Press and the Institute of Psycho-Analysis.

———. 1960. *Jokes and Their Relation to the Unconscious.* James Strachey, ed. New York: Norton.

Frey, M. 1925. *Les transformations du vocabulaire française?: L'epoque de la revolution (1789–1800).* Paris: Les Presses Universitaires de France.

Friedrich, C. J., and Z. K. Brzezinski. 1965. *Totalitarian Dictatorship and Autocracy.* Cambridge, MA: Harvard University Press.

Gal, Susan. 1995. Language and the "Arts of Resistance." *Cultural Anthropology* 10 (3): 407–24.

Gal, Susan, and Gail Kligman. 2000. *The Politics of Gender after Socialism: A Comparative-Historical Essay.* Princeton, NJ: Princeton University Press.

Gardiner, Michael. 1992. *The Dialogics of Critique: M. M. Bakhtin and the Theory of Ideology.* London: Routledge.

Gessen, Masha. 1997. *Dead Again.* London: Verso.

Gilroy, Paul. 1984. Leisure Industries and New Technology. In *World View 1985,* eds. Ayrton, P., and V. Ware. London: Pluto Press.

———. 1991. *There Ain't No Black in the Union Jack: The Cultural Politics of Race and Nation.* Chicago, IL: University of Chicago Press.

Gladarev, Boris. 2000. Formirovanie i funktsionirovanie milieu na primere archeologicheskogo kruzhka LDP-DTYu, 1970–2000 [Formation and Functioning of a Milieu on the Example of the Archeological Circle of LDP-DTYu].

St. Petersburg: Center for Independent Sociological Research. http://www. indepsocres.spb.ru/boriss.htm.

Glebkin, Vladimir. 1998. *Ritual v Sovetskoi kul'ture* [Ritual in Soviet Culture]. Moscow: Yanus-K.

Gordon, Colin. 1991. "Governmental Rationality: An Introduction." In *The Foucault Effect: Studies in Governmentality with Two Lectures by and an Interview with Michel Foucault*, eds. Graham Burchell, Colin Gordon, and Peter Miller. Chicago, IL: University of Chicago Press.

Gorham, Michael. 2000. Mastering the Perverse: State Building and Language "Purification" in Early Soviet Russia. *Slavic Review* 58 (1): 133–53.

Gorky, M., V. Molotov, K. Voroshilov, S. Kirov, A. Zhdanov, and J. Stalin. 1937. *History of the Civil War in the U.S.S.R. (From the Beginning of the War to the Beginning of October 1917). Volume I: The Prelude of the Great Proletarian Revolution.* New York: International Publishers.

Graffy, Julian. 1998. Cinema. In *Russian Cultural Studies: An Introduction*, eds. Catriona Kelly and David Shepherd, 165–91. Oxford: Oxford University Press.

Graham, Seth, ed. 2001. *Necrorealism: Contexts, History, Interpretations.* Pittsburg: Russian Film Symposium.

———. 2003a. The Wages of Syncretism: Folkloric New Russians and Post-Soviet Popular Culture. *Russian Review* 62, 1 (January): 37–53.

———. 2003b. A Cultural Analysis of the Russo-Soviet Anekdot. PhD diss., University of Pittsburgh.

Gray, Piers. 1993. Totalitarian Logic: Stalin on Linguistics. *Critical Quarterly* 35 (1): 16–36.

Grebenshchikov, Boris. 1996. Saigon. *Pchela* 6. http://www.pchela.ru/podshiv/6/ saigon.htm.

Grebnev, A. 1967. *Kak delaetsia gazeta. Teoriia i praktika sovetskoi partiinoi pressy. Kafedra zhurnalistiki i literatury Vysshei Partiinoi Shkoly pri TsK KPSS. Kurs lektsii. Pervyi krug* [How the Newspaper Is Made: Theory and Practice of the Soviet Party Press]. Moscow: Department of Journalism and Literature of the Higher Party School of the Central Committee of the Communist Party of the Soviet Union.

Greenhouse, C. J. 1996. *A Moment's Notice: Time Politics across Cultures.* Ithaca, NY: Cornell University Press.

Grigor'ev, V. P. 1986. *Slovotvorchestvo i smezhnye problemy iazyka poeta* [Word Creation and Related Problems in Poetic Language]. Moscow: Nauka.

Grossberg, Lawrence. 2000. (Re)con-Figuring Space: Defining a Project. *Space and Culture* 4 (5): 13–22.

Groys, Boris. 1992. *The Total Art of Stalinism: Avant-Garde, Aesthetic Dictatorship, and Beyond.* Trans. Charles Routlege. Princeton, NJ: Princeton University Press.

———. 2003. "The Other Gaze: Russian Unofficial Art's View of the Soviet World." In *Postmodernism and the Postsocialist Condition: Politicized Art under Late Socialism*, ed. Aleš Erjavec, 55–89. Berkeley: University of California Press.

Gržinić, Marina. 2000. Synthesis: Retro-Avant-Garde, or, Mapping Post-Socialism in Ex-Yugoslavia. In *Artmargins: Contemporary Central and Eastern European*

Visual Culture, http://www.artmargins.com/content/feature/grzinic.html, September 26.

————. 2003. Neue Slowenische Kunst. In *Impossible Histories: Historic Avant-Gardes, Neo-Avant-Gardes, and Post-Avant-Gardes in Yugoslavia, 1918–1991*, eds. Dubravka Djurić and Miško Šuvaković, 246–69. Cambridge, MA: MIT Press.

Guattari, Felix. 1995. *Chaosmosis: An Ethico-Aesthetic Paradigm*. Trans. Paul Bains and Julian Pefanis. Bloomington: Indiana University Press.

Gudkov, Lev, and Boris Dubin. 1994. Ideologiia besstrukturnosti. Intelligentsiia i konets sovetskoi epokhi [Ideology of Unstructuredness: Intelligentsia and the End of the Soviet Epoch]. *Znamia* 11: 166–79.

Guerman, Mikhail. 1993a. Mitki [sic]: Paintings, Destiny Mythology. In *Mitki [sic]: The Retrospective Exhibition 10 Years of the Movement*. St. Petersburg: State Russian Museum, http://www.kulichki.com/mitki/museum/zhivo.html.

————. 1993b. New Trends in the Mitki [*sic*] Speech Culture. In *Mitki [sic]: The Retrospective Exhibition 10 Years of the Movement*. St. Petersburg: State Russian Museum, http://www.kulichki.com/mitki/themitki/newtrends/html.

Guilhaumou, J. 1989. *La Langue Politique et la Revolution Française: de l'Evenement la Raison Linguistique*. Paris: Meridiens Klincksieck.

Guk, Olesia. 1997. Valentin Tikhonenko: tarzan v svoem otechestve [Valentin Tikhonenko: Tarzan in His Fatherland]. *Pchela* 11: 21–28.

Gupta, Akhil. 1995. Blurred Boundaries: The Discourse of Corruption, the Culture of Politics, and the Imagined State. *American Ethnologist* 22 (2): 375–76.

Habermas, Jürgen. 1991. The Structural Transformation of the Public Sphere: An Inquiry into a Category of Bourgeois Society. Cambridge, MA: MIT Press.

Hall, Stuart. 1988. The Toad in the Garden: Thatcherism among the Theorists. In *Marxism and the Interpretation of Culture*, eds. C. Nelson and L. Grossberg, 35–57. Urbana: University of Illinois Press.

Hanks, William F. 2000. *Intertexts: Writings on Language, Utterance, and Context*. Lanham, MD: Rowman and Littlefield.

Han-Pira, E. N. 1991. Iazyk vlasti i vlast' iazyka [The Language of Power and the Power of Language]. *Vestnik Akademii Nauk SSSR* [Herald of the Academy of Sciences of the USSR], 4: 12–24.

Hanson, Stephen. 1997. *Time and Revolution: Marxism and the Design of Soviet Institutions*. Chapel Hill: University of North Carolina Press.

Haraway, Donna. 1991. *Simians, Cyborgs, and Women: The Reinvention of Nature*. New York: Routledge.

Havel, Václav. 1986. The Power of the Powerless. In *Living in Truth*. London: Faber and Faber.

————. 1993. The Post-Communist Nightmare. *New York Review of Books* 40 (10): 8–10.

Hebdige, Dick. 1988. *Subculture: The Meaning of Style*. London: Routledge.

Hill, Jane, and Bruce Mannheim. 1992. Language and World View. *Annual Review of Anthropology* 21: 381–406.

Hillings, Valerie, L. 1999. Komar and Melamid's Dialogue with (Art) History. *Art Journal* 58, no. 4 (Winter): 48–61.

Hirschkop, Ken. 1997. Bakhtin, Philosopher and Sociologist, In *Face to Face: Bakhtin in Russia and the West*, ed. Carol Adlam, 54–67. Sheffield: Academic Press.

Hollywood, Amy. 2002. Performativity, Citationality, Ritualization. *History of Religions* 42 (2): 93–115.

Holquist, Michael. 1990. *Dialogism: Bakhtin and his World*. London: Routledge.

Hough, Jerry F. 1979. *How the Soviet Union Is Governed*. Cambridge, MA: Harvard University Press.

Humphrey, Caroline. 1983. *Karl Marx Collective: Economy, Society, and Religion in a Siberian Collective Farm*. Cambridge: Cambridge University Press.

———. 1989. "Janus-Faced Signs"—the Political Language of a Soviet Minority Before *Glasnost'*. In *Social Anthropology and the Politics of Language*, ed. Ralph Grillo, 145–75. New York: Routledge.

———. 1994. Remembering an "Enemy": The Bogd Khann in Twentieth-Century Mongolia. In *Memory, History and Opposition under State Socialism*, ed. R. Watson, 21–44. Santa Fe, NM: School of American Research Press.

———. 1995. Creating a Culture of Disillusionment. *Worlds Apart: Modernity through the Prism of the Local*, ed. Daniel Miller, 43–68. New York: Routledge.

———. 2001. *Marx Went Away But Karl Stayed Behind*. Updated edition of *Karl Marx Collective: Economy, Society and Religion in a Siberian Collective Farm*. Ann Arbor: University of Michigan Press.

———. 2002a. Cosmopolitanism and *Kosmopolitizm*. Paper presented at the Annual Meeting of the American Anthropological Association, New Orleans, November.

———. 2002b. *The Unmaking of Soviet Life: Everyday Economies after Socialism*. Ithaca, NY: Cornell University Press.

Hunter, Isobel. 1999. *Zaum* and Sun: The "First Futurist Opera" Revisited. *Central Europe Review* 1, no. 3 (July).

Iampolsky, Mikhail. 1995. Death in Cinema. In *Re-Entering the Sign: Articulating New Russian Culture*. Ellen E. Berry and Anessa Miller-Pogacar, eds. Ann Arbor: University of Michigan Press: 270–88.

Ikonnikova, S. N. and Lisovskii, V. T. 1969. *Molodezh' o sebe, o svoikh sverstnikakh* [Youth about Itself and its Peers]. Leningrad: Lenizdat.

———. 1982. *Na poroge grazhdanskoi zrelosti* [On the Eve of Civic Maturity]. Leningrad: Lenizdat.

Jakobson, Roman. 1960. Closing Statement: Linguistics and Poetics. In *Style in Language*, ed. T. A. Sebeok, 350–77. New York: Wiley.

Jameson, Fredric. 1992. *Postmodernism or the Cultural Logic of Late Capitalism*. Durham, NC: Duke University Press.

Joravsky, David. 1970. *The Lysenko Affair*. Cambridge, MA: Harvard University Press.

Jowitt, Kenneth. 1993. *New World Disorder: The Leninist Extinction*. Berkeley: University of California Press.

Kabakov, Ilya. 1995. Ilya Kabakov. Uber die "Totale" Installation/On the "Total" Installation. Stuttgart: Cantz.

Kabakov, Ilya, Margarita Tupitsyn, and Victor Tupitsyn. 1999. About Installation. *Art Journal* 58, no. 4 (Winter): 62–73.

Kalinin, Mikhail I. 1935. *Stat'i i rechi. Ot VI do VII s'ezda sovetov SSSR* [Essays and Speeches: From the 6th to the 7th Congress of the Soviets of the USSR.] Moscow: Partizdat.

Kant, Immanuel. 1998. *Critique of Pure Reason.* Trans. ed. Paul Guyer and Allen W. Wood. Cambridge: Cambridge University Press.

Kaplan, Fanni. 1997a. Letiat muzykal'nye volny s zakata [Musical Waves of the Sunset Are Flying]. *Pchela* 11: 46–48.

———. 1997b. Soprotivlenie na Nevskom prospekte [Resistance on Nevskii Prospect]. *Pchela* 11: 29–30.

Kharkhordin, Oleg. 1999. *The Collective and the Individual in Russia: A Study of Practices.* Berkeley: University of California Press.

Khlebnikov, Velimir. 1987. *Letters and Theoretical Writings,* vol. 1 of *Collected Works of Velimir Khlebnikov,* eds. Ronald Vroon and Charlotte Douglas. Cambridge, MA: Harvard University Press.

Kniazeva, Marina. 1990. *Deti zastoia* [Children of the Stagnation]. *Literaturnaia gazeta* June 13.

Kondakov, N. I., ed. 1941. *Iazyk gazety. Prakticheskoe posobie i spravochnik dlia gasetnykh rabotnikov. Tsentral'nyi kabinet redaktorov pri otdele propagandy i agitatsii TsK VKPb* [Language of the Newspaper: Practical Manual and Reference Book for Newspaper Employees. Central Cabinet of Editors at the Department of Propaganda and Agitation of CC VKPb]. Moscow-Leningrad: Legprom.

Kornai, Janos. 1980. *Economics of Shortage.* Amsterdam: North-Holland Publishing.

Kostomarov, B. G. 1994. *Iazykovoi vkus epokhi. Iz nabliudenii nad rechevoi praktikoi mass-media* [Language Taste of the Epoch: From Observations of the Speech Practices of Mass Media]. Moscow: Pedagogika-Press.

Kotkin, Stephen. 1995. *Magnetic Mountain: Stalinism as a Civilization.* Berkeley: University of California Press.

Kravchenko, Aleksei. 1969. *Spravochnik sekretaria pervichnoi partiinoi organizatsii* [Reference Book for the Secretary of a Primary Party Organization]. Moscow: Izd-vo politicheskoi literatury [Political Literature Press].

Kristeva, Julia. 1986. Word, Dialogue and Novel. In *The Kristeva Reader,* ed. Toril Moi, Oxford: Basil Blackwell.

Kriuchkova, T. B. 1982. K voprosu o mnogoznachnosti 'ideologicheski-sviazannoi leksiki [On the Question of Polysemy of 'Ideologically Bound' Lexicon]. *Voprosy Iazykoznaniia* [Issues of Linguistics] 1: 28–36.

Krivulin, Viktor. 1996. *Nevskii do i posle Velikoi Kofeinoi Revoliutsii. Interview with Viktor Krivulin* [Nevsky before and after the Great Coffee Revolution: Interview with Viktor Krivulin] *Pchela* 6: 4–9.

Krotov, Iakov. 1992. Sovetskii zhitel' kak religioznyi tip [Soviet Inhabitant as a Religious Type]. *Novyi mir* (May): 245–50.

Kruchenykh, Alexei. 1988a. New Ways of the Word. In *Russian Futurism through its manifestoes 1912–1928,* eds. A. Lawton and H. Eagle. Ithaca, NY: Cornell University Press.

————. 1988b. Declaration of Transrational Language. In *Russian Futurism through its Manifestoes 1912–1928*, eds. A. Lawton and H. Eagle. Ithaca, NY: Cornell University Press.

Kryshtanovskaia, Olga. 1996. Finansovaia oligarkhiia v Rossii [Financial Oligarchy in Russia]. *Izvesttiia* January 10.

Kupina, N. A. 1999. *Iazykovoe soprotivlenie v kontekste totalitarnoi kul'tury* [Language Resistance in the Context of Totalitarian Culture]. Ekaterinburg: Izdatel'stvo Ural'skogo universiteta.

Kurganov, E. 1997. *Anekdot kak zhanr* [Anecdote as a Genre]. St. Petersburg: Akademicheskii Proekt.

Lacan, Jacques. 1988. The Seminar of Jacques Lacan. In *Book 3. The Psychoses, 1955–1956*, ed. Jacques-Alain Miller, New York: Norton.

Lahusen, Thomas, and Gene Kuperman, eds. 1993. *Late Soviet Culture: From Perestroika to Novostroika*. Durham, NC: Duke University Press.

Laibach. 1983. Ten Items of the Covenant. *Nova Revija (Slovene Review for Cultural and Political Issues)* No. 13/14.

Lampland, Martha. 1995. *The Object of Labor: Commodification in Socialist Hungary*. Chicago: University of Chicago Press.

Lane, Cristel. 1981. *The Rites of Rulers: Ritual in Industrial Society: The Soviet Case*. Cambridge: Cambridge University Press.

Ledeneva, Alena. 1998. *Blat: Russian Economy of Favours*. Cambridge: Cambridge University Press.

Lee, Andrea. 1981. *Russian Journal*. New York: Random House.

Lefort, Claude. 1986. *The Political Forms of Modern Society: Bureaucracy, Democracy, Totalitarianism*. Cambridge, MA: MIT Press.

Lemon, Alaina. 1998. "Your Eyes are Green Like Dollars": Counterfeit Cash, National Substance, and Currency Apartheid in 1990s Russia. *Cultural Anthropology* 13 (1): 22–55.

Lemon, Lee, and Marion Reis, eds. 1965. *Russian Formalist Criticism: Four Essays*. Lincoln: University of Nebraska Press.

Leont'ev, A. A. 1975. "Psikhologia obshcheniia v professional'noi deiatel'nosti lektora" [Psychology of Communication in the Professional Activity of a Lecturer]. In *Voprosy lektsionnoi propagandy. Teoriia i praktika.* [Issues of Lecture Propaganda: Theory and Practice], vol. 2, 54–61. Moscow: Znanie.

Levinson, Stephen. 1983. *Pragmatics*. New York: Cambridge University Press.

Lisovskii, V. T. et al., eds. 1978. *Aktual'nye problemy teorii i praktiki nravstvennogo vospitaniia studentov* [Contemporary Problems in the Theory and Practice of the Moral Education of Students]. Leningrad: Izdatel'stvo LGU.

Losev, A. 1978. Pis'ma [Letters]. *Kontinent. Literaturnyi, obshchestvenno-politicheskii i religioznyi zhurnal* [Continent: Literary, Socio-Political and Religious Journal], 16.

Lukashanets, A. A., et al. 1988. *Obshchestvo—iazyk—politika* [Society—Language—Politics]. Minsk: Vysheishaia Shkola.

Lur'e, Lev. 1997. Pokolenie vyshedshee iz kholoda [A Generation that Came out of the Cold]. *Pchela* 11: 17–19.

———. 1998. Semidesiatye kak predmet istorii russkoi kul'tury. Materialy diskussii [The Seventies as an Object in the History of Russian Culture: Notes of a Discussion]. In *Rossiia/Russia* 1 (9).

———. 2003. *Zanimatel'naia istoriia Peterburga* [Popular History of St. Petersburg], a series of programs on Radio Ekho Peterburga. August 7.

Mahmood, Saba. 2001. Feminist Theory, Embodiment, and the Docile Agent: Some Reflections on the Egyptian Islamic Revival. *Cultural Anthropology* 16 (2): 202–36.

Makarevich, Andrei. 1994. Interview on weekly program *Vzgliad*, Ostankino Channel, June 24.

———. 2002. *Sam ovtsa. Avtobiograficheskaia proza* [A sheep yourself: Autobiographical Prose]. Moscow: Zakharov.

Makarevich, E. 1987. V ozhidanii tret'ei volny [Awaiting the Third Wave]. *Molodoi Kommunist* [Young Communist] 1.

Mann, Thomas. 1980. *The Magic Mountain*. Trans. H. T. Lowe-Porter. New York: Vintage.

Mannheim, Karl. 1952. *Essays on the Sociology of Knowledge*. London: Routledge.

Marcus, Greil. 1990. *Lipstick Traces: A Secret History of the Twentieth Century*. Cambridge, MA: Harvard University Press.

Marr, N. Ia. 1977. *Iazyk i myshlenie* [Language and Cognition]. Letchworth, England: Herts.

Marshak, Samuil. 1937. Vystuplenie na torzhestvennom otkrytie dvortsa pionerov. [Address at the Opening Ceremony of the Palace of Pioneers]. Sankt-Peterburgskii gorodskoi dvorets tvorchestva iunykh. Letopis' dvortsa [St. Petersburg City Palace of Youth Creativity: History of the Palace], http://www .anichkov.ru/Histori_child.

Matizen, Viktor. 1993. Stiob kak fenomen kul'tury [*Stiob* as a Phenomenon of Culture]. *Iskusstvo Kino* 3: 59–62.

Mazin, Viktor. 1998. *Kabinet Nekrorealizma: Yufit i* [The Cabinet of Necrorealism: Yufit and.] St. Petersburg: Ima Press.

Mbembe, Achille. 1992. The Banality of Power and the Aesthetic of Vulgarity in the Postcolony. *Public Culture* 4, no. 2 (Spring): 1–30.

———. 2001. *On the Postcolony*. Berkeley: University of California Press.

McMichael, Polly. 2005a. "After All, You're a Rock and Roll Star (At Least That's What They Say)": *Roksi* and the Creation of the Soviet Rock Musician. *Slavonic and East European Review* 83 (4).

———. 2005b. The Making of a Soviet Rock Star, Leningrad, 1972–1987. PhD diss., University of Cambridge. Forthcoming.

Medvedev, Roi. 1997. Stalin i iazykoznanie. Kak bylo razrusheno gospodstvo ucheniia Marra [Stalin and Linguistics: How the dominance of Marr's teaching was destroyed]. *Nezavisimaia gazeta* April 4.

———. 1998. *Kapitalizm v Rossii?* [Capitalism in Russia?] Moscow: Prava cheloveka.

Mertz, Elizabeth. 1996. Recontextualization as Socialization: Text and Pragmatics in the Law School Classroom. In *Natural Histories of Discourse*, eds., Michael Silverstein and Greg Urban, 229–49. Chicago: University of Chicago Press.

311

Mikeshina, L. A. 1999. Znachenie idei Bakhtina dlia sovremennoi epistemologii [The Significance of Bakhtin's Ideas for Contemporary Epistemology]. *Filosofiia nauki* [Philosophy of Science] 5.

Mitchell, Timothy. 1990. Everyday Metaphors of Power. *Theory and Society* 19: 545–77.

Monroe, Alex. 2005. *Interrogation Machine: Laibach and NSK.* Cambridge, MA: MIT Press.

Morris, Rosalind. 1995. All Made Up: Performance Theory and the New Anthropology of Sex and Gender. *Annual Review of Anthropology* 24: 567–92.

Munting, R. 1984. Lend-Lease and the Soviet War Effort. *Journal of Contemporary History* 19: 495–510.

Nadkarni, Maya, and Olga Shevchenko. 2004. The Politics of Nostalgia: A Case for Comparative Analysis of Postsocialist Practices. *Ab-Imperio.*

Nafus, Dawn. 2003a. Time, Sociability, and Postsocialism. PhD diss., Sidney Sussex College, Cambridge University.

Nafus, Dawn. 2003b. The Aesthetics of the Internet in St. Petersburg: Why Metaphor Matters. *The Communication Review* 6: 185–212.

Navaro-Yashin, Yael. *Faces of the State: Secularism and Public Life in Turkey.* Princeton, NJ: Princeton University Press.

Nikkila, Anton. 2002. Russian Industrial Noise: Pioneers, Youth League and Party Members. *The Wire Magazine,* November 1.

Nove, Alec. 1977. *The Soviet Economic System.* London: Allen and Unwin.

NSK. 1991. *Neue Slowenische Kunst.* Los Angeles: AMOK Books.

Nyíri, Pal, and Joana Breidenbach. 2002. Living in Truth: Physics as a Way of Life. *Anthropology of East Europe Review* 20, no. 2 (Autumn): 43–54.

Nyomarkey, Joseph. 1965. Factionalism in the National Socialist German Workers' Party, 1925–1926. *Political Science Quarterly* 80, no. 1 (March): 22–47.

Oushakine, Sergei. 2001. The Terrifying Mimicry of Samizdat. *Public Culture* 13 (2): 191–214.

Paperno, Irina. 2002. Personal Accounts of the Soviet Experience. *Kritika: Explorations in Russian and Eurasian History* 3 (4): 577–610.

Pecheux, Michel. 1994. The Mechanism of Ideological (Mis)recognition. In *Mapping Ideology,* ed. Slavoj Žižek, 141–51. London: Verso.

Pechkin, I., and M. Cherniakhovskii. 1988. Torzhestvo plakata ostrogo i dinamichnogo [Triumph of a Sharp and Dynamic Poster]. *Nagliadnaia agitatsiia* 4: 4–12.

Pelevin, Victor. 1999. *Generation P.* Moscow: Vagrius.

———. 2002. *Homo Zapiens.* Trans. Andrew Bromfield. New York: Viking.

Pesmen, Dale. 2000. *Russia and Soul: An Exploration.* Ithaca: Cornell University Press.

Petrovskii, Miron. 1990. Novyi anekdot znaesh'? [Do You Know a New Anecdote?] *Filosofskaia i sotsial'naia mysl'* 5: 46–51.

Pocheptsov, G. 1997. Processes of Political Communication in the USSR. In *Political Discourse in Transition in Europe 1989–1991,* eds. P. Chilton, M. Ilyin, and J. Mey, 51–68. Amsterdam: John Benjamins Publishing Company.

312

Popov, Valerii. 1996. Krysha: interv'iu s Valeriem Popovym [Roof: An Interview with Valerii Popov]. *Pchela* http://www.pchela.ru/podshiv/6/krisha.htm.

Prigov, D. A. 1997. *Sovetskie teksty* [Soviet Texts]. Moscow: Izdatel'stvo Ivana Limbakha.

Pudovkina, Elena. 2000. *Klub "Derzanie"* [Club "Dare"]. *Pchela* http://www.pchela.ru/podshiv/26_27/club.htm.

Rabinow, Paul. 1989. *French Modern: Norms and Forms of the Social Environment.* Cambridge, MA: MIT Press.

Rancière, Jacques. 2002. The Aesthetic Revolution and Its Outcomes. *New Left Review* 14: 133–51.

Richmond, Yale. 2003. *Cultural Exchange and the Cold War: Raising of the Iron Curtain.* University Park: Pennsylvania State University Press.

Ries, Nancy. 1997. *Russian Talk.* Ithaca, NY: Cornell University Press.

Riordan, Jim, ed. 1989. *Soviet Youth Culture.* Houndmills: Macmillan Press.

Roach, Joseph. 1995. Culture and Performance in the Circum-Atlantic World. In *Performativity and Performance*, eds. Andrew Parker and Eve Kosofsky Sedgwick, 45–63. London and New York: Routledge.

Rofel, Lisa. 1999. *Other Modernities: Gendered Yearnings in China after Socialism.* Berkeley: University of California Press.

Rogov, K. Iu. 1998. 'O proekte "Rossiia/Russia"—1970-e gody.' [About the project "Rossiia/Russia"—the 1970s]. *Rossiia/Russia* 1 (9): 7–11.

Rosaldo, Michelle. 1982. The Things We Do with Words: Ilongot Speech Acts and Speech Act Theory in Philosophy. *Language in Society* 2: 203–37.

Rossianov, K. 1993. Stalin as Lysenko's Editor: Reshaping Political Discourse in Soviet Science. *Configurations* 1 (3): 439–56.

Roxburgh, A. 1987. *Pravda: Inside the Soviet News Machine.* New York: George Braziller.

Rudy, Stephen. 1997. *Introduction.* In *Roman Jacobson: My Futurist Years*, ix–xvi. New York: Marsilio Publishers.

Ryazanova-Clarke, Larissa, and Terrence Wade. 1999. *The Russian Language Today.* London: Routledge.

Saint-Simon, Henri de. 1825. *Opinions littéraires, philosophiques et industrielles.* Paris: Bossange.

Savchuk, Valerii. 1995. *Konets prekrasnoi epokhi. Monolog filosofa* [The End of a Belle Epoque: Monologue of a Philosopher]. In *Konets prekrasnoi epokhi. Fotopostskriptum* [The End of a Belle Epoque: Photo-Postscriptum], eds. Dmitrii Pilikin and Dmitrii Vilenskii. Exhibition catalog. St. Petersburg: Fond Svobodnaia Kul'tura.

Schein, Louisa. 1998. Importing Miao Brethren to Hmong America: A Not So Stateless Transnationalism. In *Cosmopolitics: Thinking and Feeling Beyond the Nation*, eds. Pheng Cheah and Bruce Robbins, 163–91. Minneapolis: University of Minnesota Press.

Schmitt, Carl. 1985. *Political Theology: Four Chapters on the Concept of Sovereignty.* Trans. George Schwab. Cambridge, MA: MIT Press.

Schoenhals, M. 1992. *Doing Things with Words in Chinese Politics: Five Studies.* Berkeley: Institute of East Asian Studies, University of California.

313

Scott, James. 1990. *Domination and the Arts of Resistance: Hidden Transcripts.* New Haven, CT: Yale University Press.

Selishchev, Afanasii. 1928. *Iazyk revoliutsionnoi epokhi: iz nabliudenii nad russkim iazykom, 1917–1926* [The Language of the Revolutionary Epoch: From Some Observations on the Russian Language, 1917–1926]. Moscow: Rabotnik Prosveshcheniia.

Searle, John. 1977. Reiterating the differences: A Reply to Derrida. In *Glyph* 1: 198–208.

———. 1983. The Word Turned Upside Down. *New York Review of Books*, October 27.

Seriot, Patrick. 1985. *Analyse Du Discours Politique Sovietique.* Paris: Institut D'Etudes Slaves.

———. 1986. How to Do Sentences with Nouns. In *Russian Linguistics* 10: 33–52.

———. 1992. Officialese and Straight Talk in Socialist Europe. In *Ideology and System Change in the USSR and East Europe*, ed. Michael Urban, 202–14. New York: St. Martin's Press.

Shinkarev, V. 1990. *Mit'ki, opisannye Vladimirom Shinkarevym i narisovannye Aleksandrom Florenskim* [Mit'ki. Narrated by Vladimir Shinkarev and Drawn by Aleksandr Florenskii]. Leningrad: SP Smart.

Shlapentokh, Vladimir. 1989. *Public and Private Life of the Soviet People: Changing Values in Post-Soviet Russia.* New York: Oxford University Press.

Silverstein, Michael. 1979 Language Structure and Linguistic Ideology. In *The Elements: A Parasession on Linguistic Units and Levels*, eds. P. Clyne et al., 193–247. Chicago, IL: Chicago Linguistic Society.

———. 1993. Metapragmatic Discourse and Metapragmatic Function. In *Reflexive Language: Reported Speech and Metapragmatics*, ed. John A. Lucy, 33–58. Cambridge: Cambridge University Press.

Skvortsov, L. I. 1964. Ob otsenkakh iazyka molodezhi (zhargon i iazykovaia politika). [About the Evaluations of the Language of Youth (Slang and Language Policy)]. *Voprosy Kul'tury* 5.

Slezkine, Yuri. 1996. N. Ia. Marr and the National Origins of Soviet Ethnogenetics. *Slavic Review* 55, (4): 826–62.

Sloterdijk, Peter. 1993. *Critique of Cynical Reason.* University of Minnesota Press.

Smith, Hedrick. 1976. *The Russians.* Revised Edition. New York Ballantine Books.

Smith, Michael G. 1998. *Language and Power in the Creation of the USSR, 1917–1953.* Berlin: Mouton de Greyter.

Solnick, Steven. 1998. *Stealing the State: Control and Collapse in Soviet Institutions.* Cambridge, MA: Harvard University Press.

Solzhenitsyn, Alexander. 1974. *The Gulag Archipelago, 1918–1956: An Experiment in Literary Investigation.* New York: Harper and Row.

Sosin, Gene. 1999. *Sparks of Liberty: An Insider's Memoir of Radio Liberty.* University Park: Pennsylvania State University Press.

Spravochnik sekretaria pervichnoi partiinoi organizatsii. 1969. [Reference Book for the Secretary of a Primary Party Organization]. Moscow: Izdatel'stvo Politicheskoi Literatury [Political Literature Press].

Ssorin-Chaikov, N. 2003. *The Social Life of the State in Subarctic Siberia*. Stanford, CA: Stanford University Press.

Stalin, I. V. 1950a. Otnositel'no marksizma v iazykoznanii [On Marxism in Linguistics]. *Pravda*, June 20.

———. 1950b. K nekotorym voprosam iazykoznaniia. Otvet tovarishchu E. Krasheninnikovoi [On Some Issues in Linguistics: Response to Comrade E. Krasheninnikova]. *Pravda*, July 4.

———. 1950c. Tovarishcham D. Belkinu i S. Fureru [Response to Comrades D. Belkin and S. Furer]. *Pravda*, August 2.

———. 1950d. *Marksizm i voprosy iazykoznaniia* [Marxism and Questions of Linguistics]. Moscow: Gosudarstvennoe izdatel'stvo politicheskoi literatury [State Political Literature Press].

Stark, David, and Laszlo Bruszt. 1998. *Postsocialist Pathways: Transforming Politics and Property in East Central Europe*. Cambridge: Cambridge University Press.

Starr, Frederick. 1994. *Red and Hot: The Fate of Jazz in the Soviet Union 1917–1991*. New York: Limelight Editions.

Stites, Richard. 1989. *Revolutionary Dreams: Utopian Vision and Experimental Life in the Russian Revolution*. Oxford: Oxford University Press.

———. 1993. *Russian Popular Culture: Entertainment and Society Since 1990*. Cambridge: Cambridge University Press.

Stites, R., and J. von Geldern, eds. 1995. *Mass Culture in Soviet Russia: Tales, Poems, Songs, Movies, Plays, and Folklore, 1917–1953*. Bloomington: Indiana University Press.

Strada, Vittorio. 1998. O proekte "Rossiia/Russia" [About the project "Rossiia/Russia"]. *Rossiia/Russia* 1 (9): 11–13.

Strathern, Marilyn. 2002. On Space and Depth. In *Complexities: Social Studies of Knowledge Practices*, eds. John Law and Annemarie Mol, 88–115. Durham, NC: Duke University Press.

Strathern, Marilyn. 1988. *The Gender of the Gift*. Berkeley: University of California Press.

Strauss, Claudia. 1997. Partly Fragmented, Partly Integrated: An Anthropological Examination of "Postmodern Fragmented subjects." *Cultural Anthropology* 12: 362–404.

Strugatsky, Arkady, and Boris Strugatsky. 1979. *Roadside Picnic*. Trans. Antonina W. Bouis. Harmondsworth: Penguin.

Stump, Jordan. 1998. *Naming and Unnaming: On Raymond Queneau*. Lincoln: University of Nebraska Press.

Tassi, Aldo. 1993. Person as the Mask of Being. *Philosophy Today* 37: 201–10.

Taussig, Michael. 1992. *The Nervous System*. New York: Routledge.

———. 1993. *Mimesis and Alterity: A Particular History of the Senses*. New York: Routledge.

Terz, A. [Siniavskii, Andrei]. 1981. "Anekdot v anekdote." [An Anecdote in an Anecdote]. In *Odna ili dve russkikh literatury* [One or Two Russian Literatures], ed. Niva, Georges, 167–79. Lausanne: L'Age d'Homme.

Thom, Françoise. 1989. *Newspeak: The Language of Soviet Communism*. London: Claridge Press.

315

Thurston, R. 1991. Socialist Dimensions of Stalinist Rule: Humor and Terror in the USSR, 1935–1941. *Journal or Social History* 24 (3): 541–62.

Todorov, Tzvetan. 1998. Mikhail Bakhtin: The Dialogic Principle. Trans. Wlad Godzich. Minneapolis: University of Minnesota Press.

Toporov, Viktor. 1996. My vypivali kazhdyi den' [We Drank Every Day]. *Pchela* http://www.pchela.ru/podshiv/6/krishna.htm.

Troitsky, Artemy. 1988. *Back in the USSR: The True Story of Rock in Russia.* Boston: Faber and Faber.

Tupitsyn, Victor. 1991. The Communal Kitchen: A Conversation with Ilya Kabakov. *Art Magazine* (October): 48–55.

Turovskaya, Maiia. 1993a. Lectures on the Totalitarian Film of Stalin and Hitler. Unpublished manuscript. Duke University. Department of Slavic Languages and Literatures.

———. 1993b. The Tastes of Soviet Moviegoers during the 1930's. In *Late Soviet Culture: From Perestroika to Novostroika.* Thomas Lahusen and Gene Kuperman, eds. Durham, NC: Duke University Press.

Urban, Greg. 1996. Entextualization, Replication, and Power. In *Natural Histories of Discourse*, eds. Michael Silverstein and Greg Urban, 21–44. Chicago: University of Chicago Press.

Urban, Michael. 1986. From Chernenko to Gorbachev: A Repoliticization of Official Soviet Discourse? *Soviet Union/Union Sovietique* 13 (2): 131–61.

Uvarova, I. and K. Rogov. 1998. Semidesiatye: khronika kul'turnoi zhizni [The Seventies: A Chronicle of the Cultural Life]. *Rossiia/Russia* 1 (9): 29–74.

Vail', Petr, and Alexandr Genis. 1988. *60-e. Mir sovetskogo cheloveka* [The 60s: The World of the Soviet Person]. Ann Arbor: Ardis.

———. 1991. Strana slov [The Country of Words]. *Novyi Mir* 4:239–51.

Veller, Mikhail. 2002. Khochu v Parizh [I Want to Go to Paris]. In *Khochu byt' dvornikom* [I Want to Be a Street Sweeper], 263–91. St. Petersburg: Folio.

Verdery, Katherine. 1996. *What Was Socialism, and What Comes Next?* Princeton, NJ: Princeton University Press.

Vilenskii, Dmitrii. 1995. Svideteli epokhi. Monolog fotografa [Witnesses to an Epoch: Monologue of a Photographer]. In *Konets prekrasnoi epokhi. Fotopostskriptum* [The End of a Belle Epoque: Photo-Postscriptum], eds. Dmitrii Pilikin and Dmitrii Vilenskii. Exhibition Catalog. St. Petersburg: Fond Svobodnaia Kul'tura.

Vite, Oleg. 1996. Izbirateli—vragi naroda? (Razmyshleniia ob adekvatnosti elektoral'nogo povedeniia i faktorakh, na ee uroven' vliiaiushchikh) [Are the Electorate Enemies of the People? Contemplations about the Adequacy of the Electorate Behavior and the Factors That Affect its Level]. *Etika Uspekha* 9: 58–71.

Volkov, Solomon. 1995. *St. Petersburg: A Cultural History.* New York: Free Press.

Voloshinov, V. N. 1986. *Marxism and the Philosophy of Language: Main Problems of the Sociological Method in the Science of Language.* Trans. Ladislav Matejka and I. R. Titunik. Cambridge, MA: Harvard University Press.

Voronkov, Valerii and Chikadze, E. 1997. Leningradskie evrie: etnichost' i kontekst [Leningrad Jews: Ethnicity and Context]. In *Biograficheskii metod v izuchenii postsotsialisticheskikh obshchestv* [Biographical Method in the Study of Postsocialist Societies], 74–78. St. Petersburg: Center for Independent Sociological Research.

Wanner, Catherine. 1998. *Burden of Dreams: History and Identity in Post-Soviet Ukraine*. University Park: Pennsylvania State University Press.

Warner, Michael. 2002a. Publics and Counterpublics. *Public Culture* 14 (1): 49–90.

———. 2002b. *Publics and Counterpublics*. New York: Zone Books.

Wedeen, Lisa. 2000. *Ambiguities of Domination*. Chicago: University of Chicago Press.

Wierzbicka, Anna. 1990. Antitotalitarian Language in Poland: Some Mechanisms of Linguistic Self-Defence. *Language and Society* 19: 1–59.

Wilde, Oscar. 1930. The Decay of Lying. In *Intentions*. New York: A. & C. Boni.

Willis, P. 1990. *Common Culture: Symbolic Work at Play in the Everyday Cultures of the Young*. Boulder: Westview Press.

Young, John. 1991. *Totalitarian Language: Orwell's Newspeak and Its Nazi and Communist Antecedents*. Charlottesville: University of Virginia Press.

Yurchak, Alexei. 1997a. The Cynical Reason of Late Socialism: Power, Pretense, and the Anekdot. *Public Culture* 9, no. 2 (Winter): 161–88.

———. 1997b. Mif o nastoiashchem muzhchine i nastoiashchei zhenshchine v rossiiksoi telereklame [Myth of a Real Man and a Real Woman in Russian TV Advertising]. In *Sem'ia, Gender, Kul'tura*, [Family, Gender, Culture] ed. V. Tishkov, Moscow: Institut etnologii i antropologii rossiiskoi akademii nauk [Institute of Ethnology and Anthropology of the Russian Academy of Sciences].

———. 1999. Gagarin and the Rave Kids: Transforming Power, Identity, and Aesthetics in the Post-Soviet Night Life. In *Consuming Russia: Popular Culture, Sex, and Society Since Gorbachev*, ed. Adele Barker, 76–109. Durham, NC: Duke University Press.

———. 2000. Privatize Your Name: Symbolic Work in a Post-Soviet Linguistic Market. *Journal of Sociolinguistics* 4 (3): 406–34.

———. 2001a. Entrepreneurial Governmentality in Post-Socialist Russia: A Cultural Investigation of Business Practices. In *The New Entrepreneurs of Europe and Asia*, eds. Victoria Bonell and Thomas Gold, 278–324. Armonk, NY: M. E. Sharpe.

———. 2001b. Muzhskaia ekonomika. Ne do glupostei kogda kar'eru kuesh'! [Male Economy: There Is No Time for Trivialities When You Are Forging Your Career]. *Neprikosnovennyi zapas* 19, no. 5.

———. 2002a. Muzhskaia ekonomika. Ne do glupostei kogda kar'eru kuesh'! [Male Economy: There Is No Time for Trivialities When You Are Forging Your Career]. *O Muzhe(n)stvennosti* [On (Fe)maleness], ed. Sergei Oushakine, Moscow: New Literary Review.

———. 2002b. Imaginary West: I Want to Go to Paris Again. Paper presented at the annual meeting of American Anthropological Association, New Orleans.

———. 2003a. Russian Neoliberal: Entrepreneurial Ethic and the Spirit Of "True Careerism." *Russian Review* 62 (January): 27–90.

———. 2003b. Soviet Hegemony of Form: Everything Was Forever, Until It Was No More. *Comparative Studies in Society and History* 45, no. 3 (July): 480–510.

————. 2005. Nochnye tansty s angelom istorii: kriticheskie kul'tural'nye issledyvaniia post-sotsializma [Night Dances with the Angel of History: Critical Cultural Studies of Postsocialism]. In *Rossiiskie Kul'tural'nye Issledovaniia* [Russian Cultural Studies], ed. Alexandr Etkind. Forthcoming. St. Petersburg: Letniisad.

Zaitsev, Genadii. 1996. Rok klub [Rock Club]. *Pchela* 6. http://www.pchela.ru/podshiv/6/rokclub.htm.

Zand, Arie. 1982. *Political Jokes of Leningrad*. Austin, TX: Silvergirl.

Zaslavsky, V. and Fabris, M. 1982. Leksika neravenstva—k probleme razvitiia russkogo iazyka v sovetskii period. [Lexicon of Inequality: On the Problem of the Development of the Russian Language during the Soviet Period]. *Revue des Etudes Slaves* 3: 387–401.

Zdravomyslova, Elena. 1996. Kafe Saigon kak obshchestvennoe mesto [Café Saigon as a Public Place]. In *Materials of the International Seminar Civil Society in the European North*. St. Petersburg: Centre for Independent Social Research.

Zemskaia, E. A. 1996. Klishe novoiaza i tsitatsiia v iazyke postsovetskogo obshchestva [Clichés of Newspeak and Citations in the Language of Post-Soviet Society]. *Voprosy Iazykoznaniia* 3: 23–31.

Zemtsov, I. 1984. *Manipulation of a Language: Lexicon of Soviet Political Terms*. Fairfax: Hero Books.

Zhdanov, A. A. 1950. On Music: Concluding Speech at a Conference of Soviet Music Workers, 1948. In *On Literature, Music and Philosophy*, 52–75. London: Lawrence and Wishart Ltd.

Žižek, Slavoj. 1982. The Principles of Stalinism. A Short Course. In *Dometi* 1, 2. Zagreb: Rijeka.

————. 1991a. *The Sublime Object of Ideology*. London: Verso.

————. 1991b. *For They Know Not What They Do*. London: Verso.

————. 1993a. *Tarrying with the Negative*. Durham, NC: Duke University Press.

————. 1993b. Why Are Laibach and NSK Not Fascists? *M'ARS* 3/4: 3–4.

————, ed. 1994a. *Mapping Ideology*. London: Verso.

————. 1994b. Kant as a Theoretician of Vampirism. *Lacanian Ink* 8 (Spring): 19–33.

————. 1994c. *The Metastases of Enjoyment*. London: Verso.

————. 1999. The Thing from Inner Space. *Artmargins: Contemporary Central and Eastern European Visual Culture*. http://www.artmargins.com/content/feature/zizek1.html, April 1.

status, 132; spaces of, 156, 161n. See also *vnyenakhodimost'*; *svoi*

vnyenakhodimost' (inside/outside-ness), 133–34

voice: of author (*see* authorial voice); author-hero of memoirs and diaries, 6, 29; dialogized, 18, 19, 133; of enunciator (of discourse), 47, 67–69, 272; external, of discourse (*see* external voice); of mediator (of knowledge/discourse), 59–61, 67–76; of originator (of knowledge/discourse), 59–61, 67–76

Voice of America, 178, 178n36. *See also* radio (Western broadcasts)

Voinovich, Vladimir, 4, 239n4

Voloshinov, V. N., 18. *See also* Bakhtin

voting, 114, 117, 129: elections, 15, 23–25, 129; at Komsomol meetings, 102; performative dimension of, 15, 23, 24, 25, 75, 76, 293; ritual of, 15, 76; and standardization of Soviet life, 37

Vysotskii, Vladimir, 123–24, 129, 129n6, 137, 140, 141. *See also* "author's song"

Warner, Michael, 116–17

Wedeen, Lisa, 17

Wolf Hunt (*Okhota na volkov*, song), 124. *See also* Vysotskii

work with meaning, 93–98, 118, 224, 259, 287, 297. *See also* "pure pro forma"

World War II, 3n9, 94, 166, 181n43, 265; "second front" of, 166

x-ray plates. *See* "rock on bones"

Yeltsin, Boris, 276, 276n63

Yosif Vainshtein Orchestra, 166, 181. *See also* jazz, Soviet

Young, John, 5

Young Technician (*Iunyi Tekhnik*), 177. *See also* radio

Yufit, Evgenii, 244–46, 251. *See also* necrorealists

Zdravomyslova, Elena, 145, 147

Zhdanov, Andrei, 46, 163–64

Žižek, Slavoj, 17, 73, 161n, 248, 249, 253, 278

Zone, the (*zona*), 158, 160–62. See also *Stalker* (film); Tarkovsky, Piotr

Zurab, 245–46, 246n14. *See also* necrorealists

INFORMATION Series